Truth of God

The Truth of God

By

True Islam

ALL IN ALL PUBLISHING

ATLANTA

The Truth of God

First Printing: Second Edition
April 2007

Published by

ALL IN ALL PUBLISHNG
a division of
ALL IN ALL PRODUCTIONS

To order additional copies or to reach True for speaking engagements, please contact the Publisher.

This book is dedicated to Louis Farrakhan and all of the Muslim Followers of the Honorable Elijah Muhammad who continue to believe as he taught.

Table of Contents

List of Illustrations

Acknowledgements

My sincerest thanks to all those who have helped in some small or great way in the completion and publication of this project: my mother, Self Justice Allah, Sister Katera X, Understanding and Soledad Allah, Wakeel Allah, Lord King Savior Allah, Sister Kia Muhammad, Ashahed Muhammad, Sister Nakeesha X, Barnar Cushmeer Muhammad, Sister Nicole Angelic Muhammad, Dr. Tisa Muhammad, Reginald Muhammad, and Ricardo Vuarez, and anyone else whom I might have failed to mention; my sincerest apologies.

Preface

The Truth of God is the latest fruit of my seventeen-year academic study of the teachings of the Honorable Elijah Muhammad. These years of study have convinced me that the objective, empirical evidence absolutely supports and even confirms the basic contours of this teaching. My objective with this work is to share some of that empirical evidence with two communities: the community of religious scholars and the 'lay' or non-scholarly community of interested readers. These two communities speak two different languages. Trying to communicate to both communities in one writing has proved terribly difficult. On the one hand, I am speaking to historians of religion, i.e. those intimately familiar with the various texts engaged here (Bible, Qur"§n, Vedas, hieroglyphic texts, etc.) and the multitude of issues confronting readers of these texts. I am therefore obligated to present the material in a scholarly fashion, providing full citations, discursive footnotes, original scripts (Hebrew, Greek, Arabic), etc. I am also required, where necessary, to lay out my arguments fully and this often involves discussion of Hebrew, Greek or Arabic grammar. Such linguistic digressions are, at best, difficult for the lay reader to follower and, at worst, down-right tortuous. I have tried to simplify the discussion as much as possible without sacrificing the necessarily detail. Still, most readers will find some of this discussion difficult to follow. But that is OK. Not everything in this work is for everyone who will read it. Hopefully, however, most of it will be digestible to most, if not all readers.

In order to help achieve this admittedly optimistic goal, I have placed at the beginning of each chapter a non-technical introductory summary summarizing the chapters for the benefit of lay-readers. This should make the intellectual passage through each chapter easier. Chapter Seven, which involves significant discussion of linguistic matters, also includes a thorough summary at the end. I have also included at the end of this work a glossary. All technical terms used in this writing will be marked by an asterisk (*) and defined in the glossary. There is also a list of abbreviations used in order to help readers 'decode' the sources cited in the footnotes.

Introduction

12. WE BELIEVE that Allah (God) appeared in the Person of Master W. Fard Muhammad, July, 1930; the long-awaited "Messiah" of the Christians and the "Mahdi" of the Muslims.

Point Number 12, What the Muslims Believe

On March 7, 1998 the Board of Ulema of the Italian Muslim Association issued a fatwa (legal opinion) against the Nation of Islam and its leader, Louis Farrakhan. The official text was issued in Arabic and Italian by the President, Shayk 'Ali Moallim Hussen, and the English translation was provided by Prof. Abdul Hadi Palazzi, Secretary-General of the Italian Muslim Association and Director of the Cultural Institute of the Italian Islamic Association. The IMA raised the question, "Can Mr. Farrakhan and his followers be accepted as 'Muslim' in the sense that this word is defined by the Shari'a (Divine Law of Islam)?" What followed was a forceful condemnation:

> Regarding the "Nation of Islam", their official doctrine is that Allah appeared in the form of a human being named Fareed [sic] Muhammad, and that this "incarnation* of God" chose another man, called Elijah Muhammad, as his Prophet. This is a clear contradiction of the Monotheistic* faith (Tawhîd), and of the Koranic teaching according to which Mohammad (blessings and peace upon him) is the Seal of the Prophets. That is enough to say that everyone who belongs to the "Nation of Islam" is not, ipso facto, a Muslim, but an unbeliever.
>
> Muslims must declare this truth, and each one of them who keeps silent while listening to Mr. Farrakhan being called "a Muslim leader" is sinning. Since the matter concerns "faith and unbelief," it is not permitted to avoid a judgment due to political or diplomatic considerations. Every marriage between

* All terms marked by asterisk appear in Selected Glossary.

a Muslim and a member of the "Nation of Islam" is null and void, and whoever, after becoming a member of this organization, wants to return to Islam, must repent and be re-converted. In case he was married, he must re-celebrate his wedding; in case he performed the Pilgrimage, he must perform it again.

We pray to Allah to make all this clear to our brothers in Islam, and to help them never to deviate from the doctrine that was revealed in the Holy Qur'an and that is presently accepted by the Islamic Community. And we call upon Allah as a Witness of what we say.

Though such a proclamation carries no real dogmatic authority - such as, for example, pontifical edicts of the Roman Catholic Church - it is nevertheless significant for its perspective and the force of its polemic.* Members of the Nation of Islam (NOI) are here declared "unbelievers" and marriage to them unrecognized. Muslims who refuse to openly criticize Louis Farrakhan are themselves guilty of sinning. The message is clear: while the perceived slackness in observance of the practical Shari'a does not preclude the NOI's membership in the 'Islamic Community', its aberrant doctrine - the incarnation of God and prophethood of Elijah Muhammad - most certainly does.

The relationship between the NOI and the larger Islamic community has been precarious since the inception of the former in the 1930's. In the March 1958 edition of the Islamic Review, published out of the Islamic Center in Washington, D.C., the NOI was denounced as a "caricature of Islam." The following year, however, Elijah Muhammad made hajj (he actually made 'umra, the lesser pilgrimage) during which he was accorded all the respect of a Muslim dignitary from the West.

The fundamental point of contention between the NOI and the larger Muslim world is unquestionably the Honorable Elijah Muhammad's doctrine of the Godhead. It is Muhammad's bold claim that "God is a man, and we just can't make Him other than a man"[1] - a Black Man, to be precise - which is most disconcerting to traditional Muslims.[2] Zafar Ishaq Ansari, in his study of Black Muslim theology, noted in 1981:

---

[1] Elijah Muhammad, Message to the Black Man (Newport News: United Brothers Communications Systems, 1965), 6.

[2] Cf. Mustafa El-Amin, The Religion of Islam and the Nation of Islam: What is the Difference? (Newark: El-Amin Productions, 1991), 3ff.

> Th(is) concept (of God)...is quite distinct, and indeed unique. Despite Islamic trappings, it is far too foreign for ordinary Muslims even to understand, let alone accept...The distinguishing characteristic of this concept of God is its unmistakable anthropomorphism* (i.e. God in the form of a man).[3]

No less condemning have been Christian polemics*. Pastor Gino Jennings of the Church of Our Lord Jesus Christ in Philadelphia, Pennsylvania, in a televised 'debate' with mainly NOI sympathizers and one-time-members, declared that Elijah Muhammad's teaching on God is a 'lie' that contradicts scripture:

> We do not believe God is a man. We do not believe God is flesh or blood...God is a spirit and not a man...If any messenger says a revelation came to him about God, that messenger's message must accord with scripture...If I teach something about God that is not true and it contradicts the scripture, you are justified in saying I am a lie.[4]

Rev. Frederick Price, pastor of the Crenshaw Christian Center in California, mockingly argues in his book, Race, Religion, and Racism[5]:

> Elijah Muhammad says that 'the Father is also a man.' Look closely at what (he) says: "Allah is God. The coming of the Son of Man-the Infidels are Angry: Who is His father if God in not His father? God is His father, but the father is also a man..." Note that (Eliajh Muhammad) did not say that Allah manifested himself in the 'form of a man.' Elijah Muhammad said, "...the Father is also a man..." That's different than saying someone manifested himself in the form of a man.
> What does the Bible say? In Numbers 23:19, it is written: "God is not a man, that He should lie, nor a son of man, that He should repent. Has He said, and will He not do? Or has He spoken, and will He not make it good?"

---

[3] Zafar I. Ansari, "Aspects of Black Muslim Theology," Studia Islamica 53 (1981), 142. I will throughout this work use the term "anthropomorphism" in its strict sense of God in the form of a man.

[4] See the debate at http://www.truthofgod.com/site/pages/media_telecasts_4.asp.

[5] Volume 3: Jesus, Christianity and Islam (Los Angeles: Faith One Publishing, 2002).

> Just the first part of the verse is the key part: 'God is not a man, that He should lie..." Yet, we have Elijah Muhammad, who came after the Bible, saying 'the father is also a man...' The Bible says, 'God is not a man...'[6]
> If Allah gave Mr. Muhammad this, and Allah is the same as Jehova God, and Jehova God is the author of the Bible, then Jehova and Allah are both confused.[7]

Whether outright condemning or attempting to make mockery the message from these polemics is the same: Elijah Muhammad's teaching on God contradicts the scripture (Bible and Qur"§n). Elijah Muhammad, for his part, was equally condemning in his retort.

> The ignorant belief of the Orthodox Muslims that Allah (God) is some formless something and yet He has an Interest in our affairs, can be condemned in no limit of time. I would not give two cents for that kind of God in which they believe.[8]

This teaching of the Hon. Elijah Muhammad proved a great trial to members of the NOI. Minister Louis Farrakhan, in Study Guide 19: The Knowledge of God, affirmed that

> This critical point of belief of the Honorable Elijah Muhammad (and those of us who believes as He believes) was the cardinal point around which the Nation of Islam had its demise (1997, 5).

While there are many polemical works juxtaposing NOI doctrines with those of "Orthodox Islam" and/or Christian theology, as well as a growing number of academic histories of the Nation[9], there are few academic studies of Elijah Muhammad's doctrine by Biblical scholars, Islamicists or scholars of religion. This lacuna in Western scholarship was pointed out by Herbert Berg in his provocative article, "Elijah Muhammad: An African American Muslim Mufassir?"[10] Charges of 'heresy*' routinely issued by Sunni and Shiite Muslims alike consistently

---

[6] Race, Religion, and Racism, 7.
[7] Race, Religion, and Racism, 12.
[8] Muhammad Speaks, November 24, 1972; cited by Ansari, op. cited, 147.
[9] The most promising is Mattias Gardell, In the Name of Elijah Muhammad: Louis Farrakhan and the Nation of Islam (Durham [N.C.]: Duke University Press, 1996).
[10] Herbert Berg, "Elijah Muhammad: An African American Muslim Mufassir?" Arabica 45 (1998) 321.

fail to consider the question of Elijah Muhammad's place within the pale of Islam from a historical perspective. One of the best examples of Sunni dogmatism passing as an academic refutation of the Nation of Islam's theology is Mustafa El-Amin's The Religion Of Islam and the Nation Of Islam: What is the Difference? The book is little more than a juxtaposition of NOI doctrine with current Sunni dogma. While select Qur'anic verses are scattered throughout the text, the history of interpretation of these verse is not elucidated, nor is there any discussion of the so-called "anthropomorphic verses" or the overwhelmingly anthropomorphic presentation of God in the Sunnah. El-Amin fails to examine the question from the context of the history of Islamic thought, which has gone through many changes since the death of Prophet MuÈammad of Arabia (PBUH). In the end, readers of this work are no more informed than they were previously about Elijah Muhammad's place within or without the pale of Islam as determined by the Arabic sources.

In this work, I hope to explore the question, "Did the Hon. Elijah Muhammad teach true Islam," from a History-of-Religions perspective. In Part One, The Bible, The Qur'§n, and Point Number 12, I demonstrate that the Hebrew and Arabic Scriptures clearly attest to an anthropomorphic deity; that is to say the God of the Prophets, from Abraham to MuÈammad b. ‡Abd Allah, as revealed in the Scriptures in their original Hebrew and Arabic, was a man, a divine, transcendent man; indeed, a Black Man. It is imperative that the question be examined from the point of view of the scriptures in their original languages, for it was for good reason that King James commissioned the Bible to be "translated out of the original tongues, diligently compared and revised." All current English translations of the Bible and Qur'§n are inadequate for this discussion, because they all make interpretive decisions informed by theological considerations that were foreign to the original authors of these texts. Part Two, The Bible, The Qur'§n, and The Secret of the Black God, will demonstrate that the God of these scriptures according to Biblical and Islamic tradition is indeed a Black deity, with a black body, which he created from primordial dark matter, exactly as claimed by Elijah Muhammad.

Figure 1

The Honorable Elijah Muhammad

Part One

The Bible, the Qur"ān, and Point Number 12

Chapter I:

The God of the Bible

1. Introductory Summary

It is popularly assumed and even explicitly affirmed by Jewish and Christian theologians that God is an immaterial and formless spirit. Muslim theologians generally refrain from calling God a 'spirit,' but nonetheless also affirm that He is immaterial and formless, possessing "neither body nor substance." Such an understanding of God derives from neither the Bible nor the Qur"§n and Sunna, but instead derives from later interpretations of these texts. These later interpretations were influenced by Greek philosophy, particularly the ideas of the Greek philosophers Plato and Aristotle who are largely responsible for the development of the idea of an immaterial and formless deity. The God of the Books (Bible and Qur"§n) in their original languages – Hebrew and Greek for the Bible and Arabic for the Qur"§n and Sunna – is neither immaterial nor formless. Like the gods of the Ancient Near East* generally, the God of the Books is anthropomorphic,* that is to say he has a form (morphe) like that of a man (anthropos).

Biblical passages such as Isa. 31:3 ("The Egyptians are human and not divine, and their horses are flesh and not spirit") and John 4:24 ("God is spirit, and those that worship him must worship him in spirit and in truth") are usually understood to confirm God as an immaterial and formless spirit. However, an analysis of these passages in their original Hebrew and Greek contexts demonstrates that this is not the case. The Hebrew term *rû*[a]È and Greek term pneuma, used in these passages to characterize God as spiritual, both imply a luminous,* material substance. Divine spirituality in the Bible implies both materiality (though of a much more refined nature than gross matter) and anthropomorphism.* Thus, the spirit seen by the medium of En-Dor (I Sam 28:8-19) and the spirit (*rû*[a]È) encountered by Eliphaz (Job 4:12-21) are anthropomorphic. God too is understood in Biblical tradition to possess a human form, but one composed of this spiritual substance rather than flesh. Mortal flesh (*bāśār*) characterizes fallen man as it resulted from Adam's transgression and expulsion from Eden. At his creation, however, even Adam lacked this mortal flesh, though he clearly had a human form made of the substance *ădāmāh* (earth). In other words, by characterizing God as spiritual does not, in Biblical tradition, mean he is immaterial and formless; just the opposite is true.

The very concept of an immaterial and formless deity was developed by the Greek philosophers who were repulsed by the anthropomorphic gods of the older Greek pantheon (circle of gods). The Ionian philosopher Xenophanes (570-475 BC) was one of the earliest to reject the anthropomorphism of the gods and argue that God should be characterized as non-anthropomorphic. Plato (428 – 348 BC) is pretty much the author of the very notion of 'immateriality'; before him it was recognized that all things, including spirit, was in some since material, even if that materiality was so subtle you could not see it. It was Plato's famous student, Aristotle (384-322 BC) who first explicitly applied this new concept of immateriality to God, his so-called "Unmoved Mover."

1.1. Anthropomorphism and the God of the Israel

The God of normative Jewish, Christian and Islamic tradition is wholly spiritual,[11] commonly described as "a perfect, pure spirit,"[12] "a nonembodied mind"[13]. According to this tradition, God's spirituality, affirmed in Isaiah 31:3 and John 4:24, necessarily implies that he is immaterial[14] and formless[15]. But as is well-known now, such an

---

[11] See Joshua Hoffman and Gary S. Rosenkrantz, The Divine Attributes (Oxford: Blackwell Publishing, 2002) 12: "Judaism, Christianity, and Islam have traditionally maintained that God is a spiritual thing that exists outside the realm of divinely created physical things. Thus, these three religions are forms of psychotheism, the belief in a wholly spiritual God or gods."

[12] P. Heinisch, Theologie des Alten Testaments (1940), 29; H.H. Rowley, The Faith of Israel (Philadelphia: Westminster Press, 1957), 75f.

[13] See C.Glenn Kenadjian, "Is the Doctrine That God is Spirit an Incoherent Concept?" Journal for the Evangelical Theological Society (hereafter JETS) 31 (1988): 191: "According to Scriptures and to traditional Christian theology, God is conceived of as thinking and acting spirit, completely lacking any material components whatever. In essence this means that God is a nonembodied mind."

[14] See for example Louis Berkhof, Systematic Theology (Grand Rapids: Wm. B. Eerdmans Publishing Co., 1941) 66: "The idea of spirituality of necessity excludes the ascription of anything like corporeity to God...By ascribing spirituality to God, we also affirm that He has none of the properties belonging to matter, and that He cannot be discerned by bodily senses." See also Sam Whittemore Fowler, "The Visual Anthropomorphic Revelation of God," PhD. Dissertation. Dallas Theological Seminary, 1978, 53: "The very essence of spirit is immateriality and invisibility." Richard Swinburne, The Coherence of Theism (Oxford: Claredon Press, 1977) 99, describing God as an 'Omnipresent Spirit,' notes: "That God is a person, yet one without a body, seems the most elementary claim of theism."

[15] Raphael Patai, Hebrew Goddess (New York: Ktav, 1967) 21 notes that the God of the Jews, "being pure spirit...is without body, he possesses no physical attributes and hence no sexual traits. To say that God is either male or female is therefore completely

understanding of spirituality and of the divine is thoroughly Hellenistic*; that is to say, it is Greek philosophic tradition that gave to the world, and to the monotheistic* religions in particular, this divine, immaterial and formless spirit.[16] The very notion of immateriality is the brainchild of the Greek Philosopher Plato.[17] Semitic* tradition, however, even Semitic revelatory tradition (i.e. the "Religions of the Book" – Judaism, Christianity and Islam) possessed no such understanding prior to contact with Hellens or carriers of Hellenistic culture.[18] The ancient Near Eastern (ANE)* and Semitic 'God of

---

impossible from the viewpoint of traditional Judaism." The concept of God as a spirit is not universal in Islam because for many råÈ (spirit) is created. Thus, as D.B. Macdonald ("The Development of the Idea of Spirit in Islam," ActOr 11 [1931]: 328) remarks concerning "the belief of the great majority of Muslims down to the present time": "...All§hu råÈ, which for us means 'God is a spirit,' and which seems to us the simplest and most intelligible statement about God, is for them a most horrible blasphemy." Macdonald is here specifically referring to the views of Wahh§bÊ Islam, and points out that it is possible for some Persian Muslims to refer to God as al-råÈ al-aÐíam, "The Great Spirit" and råÈ kullÊ, the "Universal Spirit." See also idem, "From the Arabian Nights to Spirit," Muslim World (hereafter MW) 9 (1919): 336-348. Henri Masse (Islam [Beirut: Khayat Books and Publishing, 1966] 206) observes also that "the Mutazelites considered Allah to be Pure Spirit." Whether one was willing to characterize God as "spirit" or not, there is agreement between Jews, Chrsitians and Muslims that he is "immutable without figure, form, colour or parts. He is not a body composed of substances or elements. He is not an accident inherent in a body nor does He dwell in any particular place." Muhammad Ibrahim H.I. Surty, "The Concept of God in Muslim Tradition," ***Islamic Quarterly*** 37 (1993): 127f. On the idea of spirit in Islam v. also Louis Massignon, "The Idea of Spirit in Islam," in The Mystic Vision. Papers from the Eranos Yearbook (Princeton: Princeton University Press, 1968) 319-323.

[16]R. Renehan, "On the Greek Origins of the Concepts Incorporeality and Immateriality," in Greek, Roman, and Byzantine Studies 21 (190): 105-138. On the Greek origin of the divine spirit see also below.

[17] Ibid. and see below.

[18] A. Dudley, "Old Testament Anthropomorphism," Milla wa-Milla 13 (1973): 15-19; F.E. Peters, "Hellenism and the Near East," Biblical Archaeologist Winter (1983): 33-39. Daniel Boyarin, "The Eye in the Torah: Ocular Desire in Midrashic Hermeneutic," Critical Inquiry 16 (1990): 553 argues that "only under Hellenic influence do Jewish cultures exhibit any anxiety about the corporeality or visibility of God; the biblical and Rabbinic religions were quite free of such influences and anxieties (emphasis original)." See also Gedaliahu Stroumsa, "The Incorporeality of God: Context and Implication of Origen's Position," Religion 13 (1983): 345-358; Harry A. Wolfson, "Maimonides of the Unity and Incorporeality of God," Jewish Quarterly Review (hereafter JQR) 56 (1965): 112-136. On Christian Hellenism see below. On Islam see Morris S. Seal, Muslim Theology: A Study of Origins with Reference to the Church Fathers (London: Luzac and Company Limited, 1964); R.M. Frank, "The Neoplantonism of >ahm Ibn 'afwân," Museon 78 (1965): 395-424; idem, "The Divine Attributes According to the Teachings of Abu L-Hudhayl Al-'Allaf," Museon 82 (1969): 451-506; Daud Rahbar, "Relation of Muslim Theology to the Qur"an," MW 51 (1961): 44-49 and below. On the early Islamic orthodox rejection of Greek scientific works thought to be "contaminated" by theological error see Ignaz Goldziher, "The Attitude of Orthodox

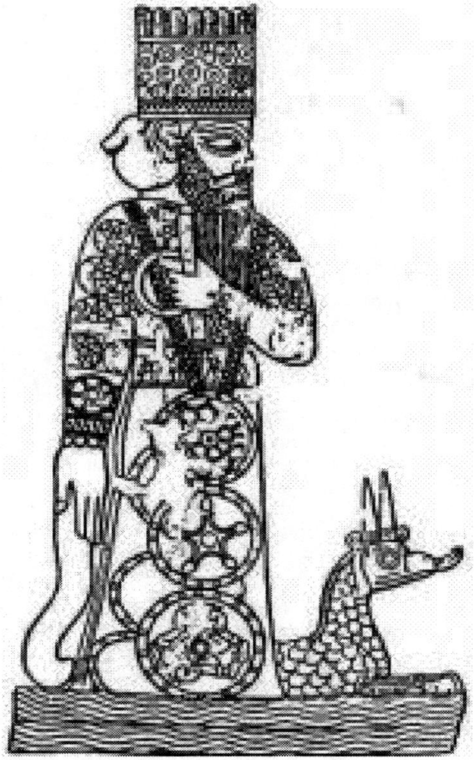

Figure 2

The Babylonian 'King of the Gods' Marduk (from J. Black & A. Green, *Gods, demons and symbols of ancient Mesopotamia*,1992)

Islam Toward the 'Ancient Sciences," in Merlin L. Swartz (ed.), Studies on Islam (New York and Oxford: Oxford University Press, 1981) 185-215.

Religion' was always anthropomorphic (Greek, anthropos='man', morph¿= 'form'): that is to say he/they possessed human form (Figure 2).[19] While representation of the divine in animal form (theriomorohism,* Greek therion, 'animal' and morph¿ 'form') is met with in all periods of religious history in the ANE, it is not the case that belief in anthropomorphism succeeded an earlier belief in theriomorphism.[20] The gods of the ANE were transcendently* anthropomorphic: they possessed bodies human in form, but supreme in holiness, substance, and sublimity.[21] In the ancient literatures the theriomorphs or animal

---

[19] On the anthropomorphic deities of the ANE see now Esther J. Hamori, "'When Gods Were Men': Biblical Theophany and Anthropomorphic Realism," Ph.D. dissertation. New York University, 2004, 191-235 and further: Mark S. Smith, ***The Origins of Biblical Monotheism: Israel's Polytheistic Background and the Ugaritic Texts*** (Oxford: Oxford University Press, 2001) 27-35; Karen Armstrong, A History of God: the 4000-Year Quest of Judaism, Christianity, and Islam (New York: A.A. Knopf, 1993) 3-39; Georges Roux, Ancient Iraq, Third Edition (London and New York: Penguin Books, 1992) 85-98; .G. Lambert, "Ancient Mesopotamian Gods: Superstition, Philosophy, Theology," ***RHR*** 204 (1990): 115-30; Maryo Christina Annette Korpel, A Rift in the Clouds: Ugaritic and Hebrew Descriptions of the Divine (Münster: Ugarit-Verlag, 1990), but on Korpel's forced attempt to impute metaphoric intentions to the Canaanites see the review by Marvin H. Pope in Ugarit-Forschungen (hereafter UF) 22 (1990):497-502; Marvin H. Pope and Jeffrey H. Tigay, "A Description of Baal," UF 3 (1971): 117-129; James B. Pritchard, "The Gods and their Symbols," in idem, The Ancient Near East in Pictures, Relating to the Old Testament (Princeton: Princeton university Press, 1954), 160-85. Edwin M. Yamauchi, in his article "Anthropomorphism in Ancient Religions," ***Bibliotheca Sacra*** 125 (1968): 29-44, adequately understanding neither ancient Near Eastern nor Israelite anthropomorphism, overstated the differences between the two. See also his "Anthropomorphism in Hellenism and in Judaism," ***Bibliotheca Sacra*** 127 (1970): 212-22.

[20]Already in 1939 Johannes Hemple ("Die Grenzen des Anthropomorphismus Jahwes im Alten Testament," Zeitschrift für die alttestamentliche Wissenschaft (hereafter ZAW) 16 [1939] 75) was able to dismiss this 'naiven entwicklungsgeschichtlichen Auffassung..., daß etwa regelmäßig der Theriomorphismus dem Anthropomorphismus habe vorausgehen müssen" ("naïve evolutionary view...that for instance theriomorphism must have preceded anthropomorphism." In fact, "keine Aufeinanderfolge des Therio- und Anthropomorphismus klar nachweisbar ist" ("no 'following-of-each-other' of theriomophism and anthropomorphism is clearly demonstrable"). Henri Frankfort has pointed out that such a theory of "Stufenfolge" ('sequence of stages') "ignores the fact that the earliest divine statutes which have been preserved represent the god Min in human shape. Conversely, we find to the very end of Egypt's independence that gods were believed to be manifest in animals." Ancient Egyptian Religion: an interpretation (1948; New York: Harper & Row, 1961) 11. For a balanced statement of the situation in Pre-dynastic Egypt, see Françoise Dunand and Christiane Zivie-Coche (edd.), Gods and Men in Egypt: 3,000 BCE to 395 CE (trans. from the French by David Lorton; Ithaca: Cornell University Press, 2004) 16-22; David P. Silverman, "Divinity and Deities in Ancient Egypt," in Byron E. Shafer (ed.), Religion in Ancient Egypt: Gods, Myths, and Personal Practice (Ithaca : Cornell University Press, 1991) 7-87, esp. 9-30.

[21] On transcendent anthropomorphism in ANE and Classical (Greek) tradition see Ronald S. Hendel, "Aniconism and Anthropomorphism in Ancient Israel," in Karel van der Toorn (ed.), The Image and the Book. Iconic Cults, Aniconism, and the

forms were so-called 'attribute animals', meaning they represented particular characteristics or 'attributes' of the otherwise anthropomorphic deities.[22]

This is true as well of the God of the scriptures, Bible and Qur"§n. Israel stood in linguistic, cultural and religious continuity with her neighbors in the Levant.[23] And as Morton Smith pointed out in a classic article, Israel participated in "the common theology of the ancient Near East."[24] This means that the God of Israel and the gods of the ANE actually differed less than has been supposed.[25] Like the gods of the ANE, the God of Israel and biblical tradition was anthropomorphic* (Figure 3).[26] The single

---

Rise of Book Religion in Israel and the Ancient Near East (CBET 21; Leuven: Uitgewerig Peeters, 1997) 206-228; Jean-Pierre Vernant, "Dim Body, Dazzling Body," in Michel Feher, Ramona Naddaff and Nadia Tazi (edd.), Fragments for a History of the Human Body: Part One (New York: Zone, 1989) 19-47.

[22] On the attribute animal in Egyptian religion see especially Erik Hornung, Conceptions of God in Ancient Egypt: the One and the Many (Ithaca: Cornell University Press, 1982)109-25.

[23] Mark S. Smith, The Early History of God: Yahweh and the Other Deities in Ancient Israel, 2nd Edition (Grand Rapids, Mich.: William B. Eerdmans Pub. Co., 2002) 19-31; Michael David Coogan, "Canaanite Origins and Lineage: Reflections on the Religion of Ancient Israel," in Patrick D. Miller, Jr., Paul D. Hanson, and S. Dean McBride (edd.), Ancient Israelite religion: essays in honor of Frank Moore Cross (Philadelphia : Fortress Press, 1987) 115-124; John Day, "Ugarit and the Bible: Do They Presuppose the Same Canaanite Mythology and Religion?" in George J. Brooke, Adrian H.W. Curtis and John F. Healey (edd.), Ugarit and the Bible: proceedings of the International Symposium on Ugarit and the Bible, Manchester, September 1992 (Münster: Ugarit-Verlag, 1994) 35-52.

[24] "The Common Theology of the Ancient Near East," Journal of Biblical Literature 71 (1952): 135-147.

[25] Bernhard Lang, The Hebrew God: Portrait of an Ancient Deity (New Haven; London: Yale University Press, 2002); Nicholas Wyatt, "Degrees of Divinity: Some mythical and ritual aspects of West Semitic kingship," UF 31 (1999): 853-87; Edward L Greenstein, "The God of Israel and the Gods of Canaan: How Different were they?" Proceedings of the Twelfth World Congress of Jewish Studies, Jerusalem, July 29-August 5, 1997, Division A (Jerusalem: World Union of Jewish Studies, 1999) 47-58; J. J. M. Roberts, "Divine Freedom and Cultic Manipulation in Israel and Mesopotamia," in idem, The Bible and the Ancient Near East: Collected Essays (Winona Lake, Indiana: Eisenbrauns, 2002) 72-85.

[26] On biblical anthropomorphism and an anthropomorphic deity see Kempel, "Grenzen des Anthropomorphismus Jahwes"; Frank Michaeli, Dieu a l'Image de l'Homme. Etude de la notion anthropomorphique de Dieu dans l'Ancien Testament (Neuchâtel-Paris: Delachaux & Niestlé, 1950); James Barr, "Theophany and Anthropomorphism in the Old Testament," Vetus Testamentum Supplemental Volume (hereafter VTSup) 7 (1959): 31-38; E.LaB. Cherbonnier, "The Logic of Biblical Anthropomorphism," HTR 55 (1962): 187-208; idem, "In Defense of Anthropomorphism," in Reflections on Mormonism: Judaeo-Christian Parrallels. Papers delivered at the Religious Studies Center Symposium, Brigham Young University, March 10-11, 1978, 155-173; Benjamin Uffenheimer, "Myth and Reality in Ancient Israel," in S.N. Eisenstadt (ed.), The Origins and

Figure 3

Inscribed Hebrew seal from the southern kingdom of Judah dated to the 7th cent. B.C. The seal bears the name Elishama son of Gedalyahu ("Yahweh is Great") and shows an image of Yahweh as a bearded deity enthroned between two burning incense stands on a boat (from Othmar Keel and Christoph Uehlinger, ***Gods, Goddesses, and Images of God in Ancient Israel*** [Augsburg Fortress Publishers, 1998])

Diversity of Axial Age Civilations (Albany: State University of New York Press, 1986) (="Biblical Theology and Monotheistic Myth," Immanuel 14 [1982] 7-25); Meir Bar-Ilan, "The Hand of God: A Chapter in Rabbinic Anthropomorphism," in Rashi, 1040-1990. Hommage à Ephraïm E. Urbach, ed. Gabrielle Sed-Rajna (Paris: Patrimoines, 1993) 321-335; Jacob Neusner, "Conversation in Nauvoo about the Corporeality of God," BYU Studies 36 (1996-97): 7-30; Stephen Moore, "Gigantic God: Yahweh's Body," Journal for the study of the Testament (hereafter JSOT) 70 (1996): 87-115; idem, God's Gym: Divine Male Bodies of the Bible (New York: Routledge, 1996); Hendel, "Aniconism and Anthropomorphism," 205-228; Rimmon Kasher, "Anthropomorphism, Holiness and the Cult: A New look at Ezekiel 40-48," ZAW 110 (1998): 192-208; Karel van der Toorn, "God (1) אלהים," in Karel van der Toorn, Bob Becking, Pieter W. van der Horst (edd.), Dictionary of Deities and Demons in the Bible (2nd ed.; Leiden; Boston: Brill; Grand Rapids, Mich.: Eerdmans, 1999; hereafter DDD) 361-365; J. Andrew Dearman, "Theophany, Anthropomorphism, and the Imago Dei: Some Observations about the Incarnation in the Light of the Old Testament," in Stephen T. Davis, Daniel Kendall, Gerald O'Collins (edd.), The Incarnation: An Interdisciplinary Symposium on the Incarnation of the Son of God (Oxford; New York: Oxford University Press, 2002) 31-46; James L. Kugel, The God of Old: Inside the Lost World of the Bible (New York: Free Press, 2003) 5-107; Hamori, " 'When Gods Were Men.' On early Christian and Islamic anthropomorphism see below.

most important effect of the Jewish, Christian and Muslim intercourse in Late Antiquity with Greek philosophic tradition was the total eclipsing in these religions of the anthropomorphic God of Religion by the formless God of Philosophy. In all three religions, the God of Abraham, Moses, Jesus, and Muhammad was supplanted by the God of Xenophanes, Plato, Aristotle and Cleanthes.

1.2. Is the Biblical God a Formless, Immaterial Spirit?

Rev. Fred Price argued:

> Mr. Muhammad goes on to state...: 'Did God say that He was a Mystery God, or did someone say it of Him? If He were a spirit and not a man, we would all be spirits and not human beings!' **It appears Mr. Muhammad has not accurately read the Bible** (emphasis mine-TI), which clearly states that God is a Spirit, and so is man...In John 4:24 (KJV), it records the fact that Jesus, speaking to the woman at the well in Samaria, referred to God as follows: '...God is a Spirit...' (emphasis original) John also says, in Chapter 1, Verse 1, 'In the Beginning was the Word (Jesus) and the word was with God...' If the word, Jesus, was 'with God,' the Word should know who, or what, God was or wasn't. In John 4:24...Jesus Himself said, '...God is a Spirit...' But Mr. Muhammad says, 'God is a man and not a spirit'...Somebody is confused here.[27]

Agreed, someone is confused, but it is surely Rev. Price. In fairness to the Reverend, the average reader of John 4:24 also assumes that, as a spirit, God is here described as formless and immaterial. Again, spirituality is commonly thought to necessitate incorporeality* (lacking a body). They also assume that, since God is spirit, he can't be a man. But, as we shall demonstrate, these assumptions betray unfamiliarity on the part of these readers with the scriptures in their original Hebrew and Greek contexts.

1.3. Not 'A' Spirit

The God of biblical tradition is spiritual, but he is not a formless spirit. The very concept of 'formless spirit' is completely foreign to the Semitic and biblical Weltanschauung (world view). "Hebraic antiquity always imagined Yahweh (God) as humanlike. The notion of the deity

---

[27] Race, Religion, and Racism, 24.

as a fully spiritual being, without body, would have been totally incomprehensible to the ancient Hebrew."[28] Herman Gunkel, the great biblical scholar of the last century, rightly pointed out further: "The notion of God's incorporeality*...was first attained by the Greek philosophers."[29] R. Renehan has demonstrated that the very notion of 'immateriality' is the brainchild of Plato.[30] This is not because the ancient Hebrews and pre-Hellenic Near East were incapable of thinking abstractly about God.[31] On the contrary, they thought holistically, integrating the spiritual, material, and ethical into a unified whole.[32] This is true of their view of man as well as God.

Isa. 31:3 contrasts mortal flesh and divine spirituality: "The Egyptians are human ("*ādām*) and not divine ("*Àl*); and their horses are flesh (*bāśār*), and not spirit (*rû*ªÈ)." Here the two contrasting sets, human ("*ādām*) vs. divine ("Àl) and flesh (*bāśār*) vs. spirit (*rû*ªÈ) are parallel and therefore "*ādām* (human) is synonymous with *bāśār* (flesh) and "Àl (divine) with r*û*ªÈ (spirit).[33] These terms are used adjectivally[34] to contrast the corruptible, mortal sphere with the eternal, powerful, and creative divine sphere.[35] But they do not describe God as a spirit:

> The Spirit is not identical with God but is the agency of his historical activity in the world...(T)he doctrine of the (exclusive) spirituality of God has no place in the (Old Testament). The apparent exception is Isa. 31:3...Even here, however, the issue is not the spirituality of God in opposition to anything material, but that of his vitality as opposed to the creaturely weakness upon which an alliance with Egypt rests (cf. vs. 1). Yahweh is not pure spirit, for his Spirit, like his Word, is the agency of his activity."[36]

---

[28] Hermann Gunkel, "Influence of Babylonian Mythology Upon the Creation Story," in Bernhard W. Anderson (ed.), ***Creation in the Old Testament*** (Issues in Religion and Theology 6; Philadelphia: Fortress Press and London: SPCK, 1984) 29, translated by Charles A. Muenchow from ***Schöpfung und Chaos in Urzeit und Endzeit*** (1895).
[29] Gunkel, "Influence," 113.
[30] See below.
[31] See Hendel, "Aniconism and Anthropomorphism."
[32] H. Wheeler Robinson, 'Hebrew Psychology,' in The People and the Book, ed. Arthur S. Peake (Oxford: Clarendon Press, 1935).
[33] Theological Dictionary of the Old Testament (hereafter TDOT; Grand Rapids, Mich., W. B. Eerdmans Pub. Co., [1974-) 1:330 s.v. "בשר *bāśār*" by N.P. Bratsiotis.
[34] K. Van Der Toorn, "God (1)" in DDD, 361.
[35] Betz, "'To Worship God,'" 71, n. 13; Theological Dictionary of the New Testament (hereafter TDNT; Grand Rapids, Mich., Erdmans 1964-) 6:365 s.v. "πνευμα," by Baumgärtel.
[36] Anderson, "God, OT view of," The Interpreter's Dictionary of the Bible, 4 vols. (hereafter IDB; New York : Abingdon Press, [1962]) 3:422f.

Shailer Mathews notes also:

> Even among the prophets Jahweh was described with such vivid anthropomorphism as to enable persons to form a mental picture of his appearance. Not only was he portrayed as an old man with white hair, but he had passions and policies like those of the rulers of his time...The conception of God as spirit did not appear in the Old Testament. To the theologizing historians who in the eighth century (B.C.) unified and expanded the literary data of their religion, God was not a spirit but possessed a spirit (emphasis mine-TI).[37]

John 4:24, which has Isa. 31:3 as its background,[38] is no exception. The Greek reads: πνευμα ό θεός (pneuma ho theos; Latin spiritus est deus). This is best translated "God is spirit" rather than "God is a Spirit." The absence of the indefinite article here is grammatically small but theologically significant as it indicates that John 4:24 is not attempting an ontological definition of God, i.e. God is a spirit as opposed, for instance, to a man.[39] This is confirmed by 1 John 1:5, "God is Light" (not a light) and 1 John 4:8, "God is Love," where the same constructions are used. God is spiritual, but not a spirit.

1.4. Biblical 'Spirit' Not Immaterial and Formless

The contrast in Isa. 31:3 between divine spirit and mortal flesh, and the denial to God of the latter, is significant. The broader context of John 4:24 implies the same contrast.[40] We will look further at this opposition between spirit and flesh below. But for now it is important to point out that the contrast does not mean spirit is immaterial. "(S)pirit in the biblical tradition is not simply an abstraction, but a fairly concrete image."[41] Both the Hebrew רוח, *rû^a*È and Greek πνευμα, pneuma literally

---

37 The Growth of The Idea of God (New York: Macmillan Company, 1931), 71-2

38 On Isa. 31:3 as background to John 4:24 see A. M. Hunter, The Gospel According to John. Commentary (Cambridge [Eng.] University Press, c1965) 160; Otto Betz, "'To Worship God in spirit and in Truth': Reflections on John 4, 20-26," in A. Finkel and R. Frizzel (edd.), Standing Before God: Studies on Prayer in Scripture and in Tradition with Essays in Honor of John M. Oesterreicher (New York: Ktav Publishing House, 1981) 59.

39 Raymond E. Brown, The Gospel According to John. Introd., translation, and notes. The Anchor Bible, no. 29-29A (Garden City, N.Y., Doubleday, 1966-), 172: "This is not an essential definition of god, but a description of God's dealing with men."

40 TDNT 6:439 s.v. "πνευμα"; Betz, "'To Worship God,'" 59;

41 Marcus J. Borg, "The God Who is Spirit," in Karen Armstrong and Frederick W. Schmidt (edd.), The Changing Face of God (Harrisburg, PA: Morehouse Publishing, 2000) 47.

mean "wind, breath, air in motion" and thus contain a definite, if subtle and rarified materiality. "The constitutive factor of πνευμα (pneuma=spirit) in the Greek world is always its subtle and powerful corporeality* (emphasis added-TI)."[42] Herman Gunkel, in his groundbreaking religio-historical study on the Holy Spirit,[43] noted that the Hebrew *rû*ªÈ in Jewish tradition, even when applied to God, was materially conceived, a kind of Lichtstoff (light-particles).[44] Thus we see that Louis Berkhof's statement, "The idea of spirituality of necessity excludes the ascription of anything like corporeity to God,"[45] is simply unbiblical. [46]

Nor is the biblical 'Spirit' necessarily formless. In fact, it is, at least in some case, clearly anthropomorphic. Thus, in Job 4:12-21 Eliphaz[47] describes seeing a spirit (*rû*ªÈ) pass by so terrifying that the hair on Eliphaz's body bristled (v.15).[48] Eliphaz could see the form (תמונה *temunah*) of the *rû*ªÈ stand before his eyes and could hear its voice (v16). Though he could not exactly make out its appearance (מראה), "The description clearly suggests some type of anthropomorphic appearance."[49] It is quite possible that this anthropomorphic *rû*ªÈ or spirit is one of the "*ĕlōhîm* (gods) of the divine assembly which surrounded God.[50] Likewise, in Ezekiel 8:2, the prophet sees the divine

---

[42] TDNT 6:239 s.v. "πνευμα," 357.

[43] Die Wirkungen des heiligen Geisten, nach der populaeren Anschauug der apostolischen Zeit und nach der Lehre des Apostels Paulus ('The Effect of the Holy Spirit according to the popular view during the Apostolic Era and according to the Doctrine of the Apostle Paul") (Goettingen: Vandenhoeck and Ruprecht, 1888) 47f.

[44] Paul Volz, Der Geist Gottes und die verwandten Erscheinungen im Alten Testament und im anschliessenden Judentum ("The Spirit of God and Related Phenomena in the Old Testament and in Later Judaism") (1910) used a similar term: ruach-Stoff, "spirit matter" (23). The Qumran documents (Dead Sea Scrolls) likewise attest to a corporeal pneumatology: 'spirits' *rûÈôt* are material substances. See Devorah Dimant, "Dualism at Qumran: New Perspectives," in J. H. Charlesworth (ed.), Caves of Enlightenment: Proceedings of the American Schools of Oriental Research Dead Sea Scrolls Jubilee Symposium (1947-1997) (North Richland Hills, TX: BIBAL Press, 1998) 55-72.

[45] Systematic Theology 66.

[46] See further below.

[47] On the possibility that Eliphaz is only recounting another's experience see Gary V. Smith, "Job IV: 12-21 Is it Eliphaz's Vision?" Vetus Testamentum (hereafter VT) 4 (1990): 453-63.

[48] See Shalom M. Paul, "Job 4:15 – A Hair Raising Encounter," ZAW 95 (1983): 118-121.

[49] Hamori, " 'When Gods Were Men'," 178-9.

[50] See especially James E. Harding, "A Spirit of Deception in Job 4:15? Indeterminacy and Eliphaz's Vision," Biblical Interpretation 13 (2005): 137-66. On the Divine Council in Hebrew Literature see Michael S. Heiser, "The Divine Council in Late Canonical and Non-Canonical Second Temple Jewish Literature," Ph.D. diss., unpublished, University of Wisconsin-Madison, 2004; Lowell K. Handy, Among the

Kabôd (Glory of God) like a man (איש[51] דמות כמראה lit.: 'the likeness of the appreance of a man') which he identifies as the Spirit (רוח *rûaḥ*; v. 3). In I Sam 28:8-19 when the medium of En-Dor raised for Saul the spirit of Samuel it had the form (תאר *to'ar*) of an old man (איש זקן, *'îš zaqin*; v. 13). This anthropomorphic spirit is explicitly identified as an אלהים, *'ĕlōhîm* "divinity."[52] The first century historian Josephus provides evidence that this anthropomorphic 'spirit' or spiritual man represented what God himself was thought to be like, at least in some circles. In his rendering of this story (Ant., 6.332f), the medium of En-Dor describes Samuel's appearance as "God-like (θεοπρεπη)" and, upon Saul's question, answered that she saw "someone in form like God."[53] John R. Levison has demonstrated that Isaiah 63:7-14 and Haggai 2:5 presuppose a tradition in which the Spirit of Yahweh, the Angel of the Presence (מלאך פנין), and the anthropomorphic *mal'āk YHWH*[54] (Angel of the Lord) who delivered Israel from Egypt to Canaan were identified.[55] This all demonstrates that divine spirituality in the Hebrew Bible (hereafter HB) is anthropomorphic, not "invisible and intangible...without form and substance."[56]

Flesh (בשר *bāśār*/σαρξ, sarx), in both the HB and New Testament (NT), was characterized by weakness, corruption, and mortality, all that is antithetical to God, who therefore had no relation to it.[57] But this does not mean that he is incorporeal* (body-less), as H. Wheeler Robinson points out:

> to speak of God as 'spirit' (Isa. 31:3) does not mean that Yahweh is formless...The majestic figure seen by Isaiah in the

---

Host of Heaven: The Syro-Palestinian Pantheon as Bureaucracy (Winona Lake, Indiana: Eisenbrauns, 1994); Patrick D. Miller, "Cosmology and World Order in the Old Testament: The Divine Council as Cosmic Political Symbol," in idem, Israelite Religion and Biblical Theology: Collected Essays (JSOTSupp 267; Sheffield: JSOT Press, 2000) 422-444; E. Theodore Mullen Jr. The Assembly of the Gods (Harvard Semitic Monographs 24; Chico, California: Scholars Press, 1980).

51 Following the LXX's implied איש rather than the MT's אש.

52 On the various significances of *'ĕlōhîm* in the Hebrew Bible see now Dmitri Slivniak, "Our God(s) is One: Biblical אלהים and the Indeterminacy of Meaning," Scandinavian Journal of the Old Testament 19 (2005) 5-23.

53 Antiquities, 6.332f.

54 On the anthropomorphic *mal'āk* YHWH see now Kugle, God of Old, 5-36; Charles A. Gieschen, Angelomorphic Christology: Antecedents and Early Evidence (Leiden; Boston : Brill, 1998), Chap. Three; Hannah, Michael and Christ, Chap. 1; DDD, s.v. "Angel of Yahweh," by S. A. Meier, 53-58.

55 "The Angelic Spirit in Early Judaism," Society of Biblical Literature Seminar Papers 34 (1995): 464-493.

56 G.H. Dix, "The Seven Archangels and the Seven Spirits," Journal of Theological Studies (hereafter JTS) 28 (1926-27): 245, 248, 250.

57 See Bratsiotis, "בשר *bāśār*." 317-332; TDNT VII:100ff. s,v, σαρξ.

temple is in human form, though endowed with superhuman qualities. If we ask for further definition, we shall find that the 'glory' of Yahweh, His full visible manifestation, is conceived in terms of dazzling and unbearable light. Yahweh's body is shaped like man's, but its substance is not flesh but 'spirit,' and spirit seen as a blaze of light…a form wrought out of *rūach*-substance."[58]

Even pre-lapsarian Adam (i.e. Adam before his 'lapse' or fall), who was clearly anthropomorphic, lacked flesh, at least according to the Apostle Paul. His body was material, made from the 'dust from the ground (עפר מן־האדמה *ʿāpār min-hāʾădāmāh*, Gen. 2.7), but he did not acquire his כתנות עור, 'coats of skin', i.e. fleshy body, until after his fall (Gen. 3:21).[59] Paul thus distinguished man's σωμα ψυχικον *soma psychikos* or 'physical body' of Gen. 2:7 from his σωμα της σαρκος soma tes sarkos 'fleshy body' (Rom. 6:6; 7;24; Col. 2:11) of Gen. 3.21 acquired after the fall.[60] Paul also affirms the anthropomorphic nature of spirit. He can refer to the resurrected Christ as a "life-giving spirit (1 Cor. 14:15)" and could even declare that "the Lord is the Spirit (ό δε κυριος το πνευμα εστιν; 2 Cor. 3:17)." While the identification of the κυριος kyrios ("Lord") here has been the source of great disagreement, Mehrdad Fatehi has, it seems to me, put the question beyond dispute:

---

[58] Robinson, 'Hebrew Psychology,' 367.

[59] There is a long tradition of interpreting כתנות עור as Adam's fleshy body. See Philo Deus 56; QG 1, 53; Stephen D. Ricks, "The Garment of Adam in Jewish, Muslim, and Christian Tradition," in Benjamin H. Hary, John L. Hayes and Fred Astren (edd.), Judaism and Islam: Boundaries, Communications and Interactions, (Leiden: Brill, 2000) 203-225; M.E. Vogelzang and W.J. van Bekkum, "Meaning and Symbolism of Clothing in Ancient Near Eastern Texts," in Scripta signa vocis: studies about scripts. Scriptures, scribes, and languages in the Near East, presented to J.H. Hospers by his pupils, colleagues, and friends (Groningen: E. Forsten, 1986) 272ff; Gary Anderson, Genesis of Perfection: Adam and Eve in Jewish and Christian Imagination (Louisville: Westminster John Knox Press, 2001) 117-134; idem, "The Garments of Skin in Apocryphal Narrative and Biblical Commentary," in James L. Kugel (ed.), Studies in Ancient Midrash (Cambridge: Harvard University Center for Jewish Studies, 2001) 110-125; Stephen N. Lambden, "From Fig Leaves to Fingernails: Some Notes on the Garments of Adam and Eve in the Hebrew Bible and Select Early Postbiblical Jewish Writings," in Paul Morris and Deborah Sawyer (edd.), A Walk in the Garden: Biblical, Iconographical and Literary Images of Eden (Sheffeild: JSOT Press, 1992) 79-82.

[60] See especially discussion in Nils Alstrup Dahl and David Hellholm, "Garment-Metaphors: the Old and the New Human Being," Adela Yarbro Collins and Margaret M. Mitchell (edd.), Antiquity and Humanity. Essays on Ancient Religion and Philosophy Presented to Hans Dieter Betz on His 70th Birthday (Tübingen: Mohr Siebeck, 2001) 147-150.

the Lord here is the exalted Christ[61] who is 'the Spirit' in spite of the fact that he is a man. Regarding Paul's description of Christ as a πνευμα ζωοποιουν, "life-giving spirit" (1 Cor. 14:15), James Dunn pointed out that it presupposes Christ's possession of what Paul calls a σωμα πνευματικον, soma pneumatikos "spiritual body."[62] This was a substantive body, but one lacking flesh, σαρξ, sarx.

> (Paul) affirms also that pneumatic (from pneuma 'spirit') existence is a form of existence neither physical/fleshy nor incorporeal. There are many kinds of σωματα somata (bodies), heavenly as well as earthy, non-fleshy as well as fleshy (15:40).[63]

And Paul affirms, in agreement with the Hebrew Scriptures and Jewish tradition, that God has a luminous and spiritual, yet anthropomorphic body. Christ's luminous soma pneumatikos or spiritual body, also called 'Body of Glory (σωμα της δοξης, soma tes doxes)' is the image (εικων, eikÙn) of God's own form (μορφη θεου, morph¿ theos; Col. 1:15; II Cor 4:4;Phil. 2:6). As a number of scholars have demonstrated, Paul's use of μορφη θεου, morph¿ theos 'Form of God' in Phil. 2:6 is rooted in the Jewish tradition of God's luminous, anthropomorphic form, the כבוד kā<u>b</u>ôd/Glory, after which Adam was created.[64] Christ's 'Body of Glory'

---

[61] The Spirit's Relation to the Risen Lord in Paul. An Examination of Its Christological Implications (Tübingen: Mohr Siebeck, 2000). See also the brief but poignant comments in TDNT 6:439 s.v. "πνευμα"418-19.

[62] "1 Corinthians 15:45 – last Adam, life-giving spirit," in Barnabas Lindars, Stephen S. Smalley (edd.), Christ and Spirit in the New Testament (Cambridge: University Press, 1973) 138.

[63] Dunn, "1 Corinthians 15:45," 129. See also idem, "The 'Body' in Colossians," in Thomas E. Schmidt and Moisés Silva (edd.), To Tell the Mystery: Essays on New Testament Eschatology in Honor of Robert H. Gundry (Sheffeild: Sheffeild Press, 1994) 162-81; Dale B. Martin, The Corinthian Body (New Haven/London: Yale, 1995) 6; W.D. Davis, Paul and Rabbinic Judaism: Some Rabbinic Elements in Pauline Theology (3rd Edition; London: SPCK, 1970) 177ff; Joachim Jeremias, " 'Flesh and Blood Cannot Inherit The Kingdom of God' (1 Cor. XV.50)," NTS 2 (1955-6): 151-159.

[64] Gilles Quispel, "Ezekiel 1:26 in Jewish Mysticism," Vigiliae Christianae (hereafter VC) 34 (1980): 1-13; Jarl Fossum, "Jewish-Christian Christology and Jewish Mysticism," VC 37 (1983): 26-287; idem, "The Image of the Invisible God: Colossians 1.15-18a in the Light of Jewish Mysticism and Gnosticism," in idem, The Image of the Invisible God: Essays on the Influence of Jewish Mysticism on Early Christianity (Universitätsverlag Freiburg Schweiz, 1995) 13-39; Seyoon Kim, The Origin of Paul's Gospel (Tübingen: J.C.B. Mohr (Paul Siebeck), 1981) 137-267; Gedaliahu G. Stroumsa, "Form(s) of God: Some Notes on Meãaãron and Christ," HTR 76 (1987): 269-288; Alan F. Segal, "Paul and the Beginning of Jewish Mysticism," in John J. Collins and Michael Fishbane (edd.) Death, Ecstasy, and Other Worldly Journeys (New York: State University of New York Press, 1995) 95-122; idem, Paul the Convert. The Apostolate

is a likeness (εικων, eikōn) of this form: "He who has seen me has seen the Father (Jhn. 14:9)," for he looks just like God.

1.5. The Greek Philosophic Origins of Divine Incorporeality

Hebrew as well as NT Greek spirituality, even divine spirituality, was therefore corporeal*; that is to say it was characterized by a luminous, subtle materiality. It is in Greek philosophic tradition that such ideas as divine incorporeality* begin: in fact, it is to this tradition that we owe the very concept of "immateriality." As R. Renehan notes in his important study, "On the Greek Origins of the Concepts Incorporeality and Immateriality"[65]:

> Few concepts have been more influential, for better or worse, in the history of Western philosophy and theology than those of incorporeal beings and immaterial essences. Their importance for the particular directions which European thought long took pondering such problems as the nature of deity, soul, intellect, in short, of ultimate reality, is not easily exaggerated...Such concepts are the creation of Greek philosophy. Prior to that even 'spirit' was material, in Egypt, Greece, and elsewhere.[66]

---

and Apostasy of Saul the Pharisee (New Haven/London: Yale University Press, 1990) 35-71; idem, "The Risen Christ and the Angelic Mediator Figures in Light of Qumran," in James H. Charlesworth (ed.), Jesus and the Dead Sea Scrolls (New York: Doubleday, 1992) 302-328; Markus Bockmuehl, "'The Form of God' (Phil. 2:6): Variation on a Theme of Jewish Mysticism," JTS 48 (1997) 1-23; Morna D. Hooker, "Adam Redivivus: Philippians 2 Once More," in Steve Moyise (ed.), The Old Testament in the New Testament (Sheffield: JSOT Press, 2000) 220-234. On morphῄ in Phil. 2:6 as the "visible aspect or physical appearance of God" see also Dave Steenburg, "The Case Against the Synonymity of *Morphῄ* and *Eikōn*," Journal for the Study of the New Testament (hereafter JSNT) 34 (1988): 77-86. See also Behm, TDNT 4:751 s.v. "μορφη" who notes that: "The μορφη θεου (Form of God) in which the pre-existent Christ was is simply the divine δοζα (doxa/Glory)." On the relation of the Greek doxa, Hebrew Kavod, and the form of God see also L.H. Brockington, "The Septuagintal Background to the New Testament use of ΔΟΣΑ," in D.E. Nineham, Studies in the Gospels. Essays in Memory of R.H. Lightfoot (Oxford: Basil Blackwell, 1955) 1-8; R.P. Martin, "μορφη in Philippians ii.6," Expository Times 70 (1958-59): 183-84. On God's anthropomorphic Kavod in Biblical tradition see further Moshe Weinfeld, Deuteronomy and the Deuteronomic School (Oxford: The Clarendon Press, 1972) 191-209, esp. 200-206; idem, TDOT 7:31-33 s.v. כבוד; Tryggve N.D. Mettinger, The Dethronement of Sabaoth: Studies in the Shem and Kavod Theologies (CWK Gleerup, 1982) Chapters Three and Four; J. E. Fossum, "Glory," DDD 348-52.

[65] Renehan, "On the Greek Origins."

[66] Renehan, "On the Greek Origins," 105.

Figure 4

Plato

A number of Presocratics (i.e. Greek philosophers before the time of Socrates) laid 'stepping stones' leading to a fully explicit notion of incorporeality/immateriality. The Ionian philosopher of Colophon Xenophanes (570-475 BC), in rejecting the anthropomorphic gods of the Greeks and the surrounding Near East, posited an abstract and non-anthropomorphic deity* that would be highly influential to the development of the Christian doctrine of divine transcendence* with its characteristic notion of divine incorporeality/immateriality.[67] But for all its abstraction Xenophanes' deity was still corporeal in a sense.[68] "When all is said and done, it must be recognized that one man was responsible for the creation of an ontology which culminates in incorporeal Being as the truest and highest reality. That man was Plato."[69] Renehan suggests that it was Plato (Figure 4) who coined the term ασωματος, asomatos (incorporeal).[70] Plato's incorporeal Form (ειδος/ιδεα) of the Good, however, was not God.[71] It seems to have been his student Aristotle (384-322 BC) who, understanding the full implications of the term ασωματος asomatos, first used it of the deity, his Unmoved Mover (Cael. 279a17ff, Metaph. 1073a5ff).[72] This novel Platonic/Aristotelian notion of divine incorporeality/immateriality will be taken up and elaborated in Hellenistic Judaism, Patristic Christianity, and heterodox Islam.[73]

---

[67] On Xenophanes' deity v. Werner Jaeger, The Theology of the Early Greek Philosophers. The Gifford Lectures, 1936 (Oxford: The Clarendon Press, 1947) 43ff. On Xenophanes' influence on Christian thought v. Eric Osborn, "Iranaeus on God-Argument and Parody," StPtr 36 (2001): 270-281; William R. Schoedel, "Enclosing, Not Enclosed: The Early Christian Doctrine of God," in W.R. Schoedel and R.L. Wilcken (edd.), Early Christian Literature and the Classical Tradition. In Honerem R.M. Grant (Théologie historique 54; Paris: Éditions Beauchesne, 1979) 75-86.

[68] See discussion in Vernant, "Dim Body, Dazzling Body," 21; Jaeger, Theology of the Early Greek, 43.

[69] Renehan, "On the Greek Origins," 138.

[70] Renehan, "On the Greek Origins," 127-130.

[71] J.B. Skemp, "Plato's Concept of Deity," in Zetesis. Album amicorum door vrienden en collega's aangeboden aan Prof. Dr. E. de Strycker ter gelegenheid van zijn 65e verjaardag (Antwerpen, De Nederlandsche Boekhandel, 1973) 115-121.

[72] Renehan, "On the Greek Origins,"134-5.

[73] Schoedel, "Enclosing, Not Enclosed," notes:

> the antithesis, 'enclosing, not enclosed', first gains currency in Philo as a description of God and seems to owe its striking formulation to an impulse to go beyond the Greek tradition in emphasizing the divine transcendence.
>
> To say that God encloses all things and is not enclosed means for Philo (a) that God is immaterial and not in a place, (b) that he is unknowable in his essence, and (c) that he is creator of all things (Migr. Abr. 183; cf. Leg.. alleg. 3:51…) Such themes presuppose a God who transcends the cosmos and is not simply (as in Greek philosophy) a factor in the totality of things. To be sure, the

Chapter II:

The Man-God of Biblical Tradition

2. Introductory Summary

The God of the Bible is 10 times explicitly called a man (*'îš*, *gibbôr*; Gen. 18; 32:24-30; Ex. 15:3; 33:11; Hos 2:18; Ps. 24:7-10; Isa. 42:13; Zeph. 1:14, 3:17; Jer. 20:11.). The fact that these are literal* characterizations of the God of Israel and not mere metaphors* is confirmed by the Biblical 'theophany* narratives.' 'Theophany' (theos "God" and phainein "to appear") narratives are non-poetic (and therefore non-metaphorical) biblical descriptions of God appearing in human form to a person or group. The biblical authors recorded these encounters using the same literary structures in which they recorded historical encounters between mortals, confirming that these 'theophanies' were understood by the biblical authors to be actual historical, i.e. literal, events.

In these theophany narratives God is presented as a real human being, though divine (e.g. Gen. 18). This presentation is not contradicted by the three passages (Num. 23:19, I Sam. 15:29, Hos. 11:9) which seem to clearly affirm that "God is not a man." Again,

---

emphasis on God's immateriality reflects, as an isolated theme, Plato more than the Bible (emph. mine-TI). But it points here in a new direction. For ultimately, it was to provide a context within which the infinite 'could be detached from the concept of the corporeal, with which it had been essentially united in Greek thought'. An indication of the novelty of Philo's thought in this connection is the emphasis, perhaps for the first time, on the idea that the essence of God is unknowable.

See also John M. Dillon, "The Transcendence of God in Philo: Some Possible Sources," Protocol of the Colloquy of the Center for Hermeneutical Studies in Hellenism and Modern Culture 16 (1975): 1-22; Harry A. Wolfson, "Maimonides of the Unity and Incorporeality of God," JQR 56 (1965): 112-136. On Patristic Christianity see Wiles, Christian Fathers 13, 17, and above. See also Schoedel, "Enclosing, Not Enclosed"; Robert P. Casey, "Clement of Alexandria and the Beginnings of Christian Platonism," HTR 18 (1925): 39-101; Gedaliahu Stroumsa, "The Incorporeality of God: Context and Implication of Origen's Position," Rel 13 (1983): 345-358; Frances M. Young, "The God of the Greeks and the Nature of Religious Language," in William R. Schoedel and Robert L. Wilekn (eds.), Early Christian literature and the classical intellectual tradition. In Honorem Robert M. Grant (Theologie historique 53; Paris: Editions Beauchesne, 1979) 45-74; G. Jantzen, God's World, God's Body (Philadelphia: Westminster Press, 1984), 23-35. On Islam see above and below.

when read in their original Hebrew contexts these passages declare only that God is not a man who lies, repents, or succumbs to jealous wrath, not that he is categorically not a man. God is presented in biblical tradition as a divine man unlike mortal men, the latter prone to weaknesses that God is not. God is therefore not simply anthropomorphic; he is 'transcendently anthropomorphic.' That is to say, God's anthropomorphism is characterized by a holiness which distinguishes him from mortal men.

How is this 'transcendent anthropomorphism'* presented in the Bible? By distinguishing God's thinking and actions from those of mortal men (e.g. men lie, God does not) and by affirming God's immunity from and transcendence above the human fallibilities that characterize man's possession of this mortal body. Because God's body is composed of 'spirit', that is to say a pure, luminous substance, rather than mortal flesh, God is not prone to those weaknesses inherent in the corruptible flesh that resulted from Adam's Fall. God's spiritual body is a brilliantly luminous body that radiates with such great light it puts any mortal unlucky enough to view it in great peril.

2.1. 'Yahweh is a Man'

This incorporeal,* non-anthropomorphic deity of the Greek philosophers is in stark contrast to the God of biblical tradition. The God of the Hebrew Bible (HB) is without question a man. He is anthropomorphic: he has a human form. He is anthropopathic*: he has human feelings. And, importantly, he is called a man repeatedly in the HB, a fact lost in the various English translations. Hebrew has five words (plus their derivatives) for man: איש "îâ, גבר geber, אדם, *'ādhām*, אנוש, *'ᵉnôš* and מת, mt. The last three terms connote human frailty and weakness and as such are never applied to God.[74] It is a different story, however, with איש "îâ and גבר geber. These two terms connote strength, kingship, and spirituality[75] and the HB declares that God is this sort of

[74] TDOT 1:75-87 s.v. אדם *'ādhām* by Maass; 1:345-348 s.v. אנוש, *'ᵉnôsh* by Maass; 9:98-102 s.v. מת, mt; IDB 3:242-46 sv. "Man, Nature of, in the OT."

[75] ***TDOT*** I:222-235s.v. "איש îâ; "îààh§h," by N.P. Bratsiotis; Michael Chernick, "איש As Man and Adult in the Halakic Midrashim," The Jewish Quarterly 73:3 (January, 1983): 254-280; A.F.L. Beeston, "An Alternative Meaning for איש in the old Testament," VT 24 (1974): 110ff; TDOT, 2:367-382 s.v. גבר *gābhar* by Hans Kosmala; ibid, "The Term Geber in the Old Testament and in the Scrolls," Congress Volume, Rome 1968 (VTSup 17; Leiden: E.J. Brill, 1969) 158-69; Geza Vermes, Scripture and Tradition in Judaism. Haggadic Studies (Leiden: E.J. Brill, 1983) 56-66; A. Shafaat, "Geber of the Qumran Scrolls and the Spirit-Paraclete of the Gospel of John," New Testament Studies 27 (1981): 263-69.

man[76]: Yahweh is an איש "*iš* and גבר geber, or rather גבור, *gibbôr*, mighty man.[77] The Book of Exodus states emphatically יהוה איש מלחמה *YHWH* "*iš milḫāmāh*, "Yahweh is a man of war (15:3)."[78] This is not a metaphor*, but a divine title[79] and, according to a tradition of the Jewish rabbis, a description of how Yahweh physically appeared to the Hebrews at the Red Sea. Thus, we read in the rabbinic text Mekhilta de-Rabbi Shimʾon bar YoĖai: "Another interpretation: 'YHWH is a man of war, YHWH is His name (Exod. 15:3).' Because when the Holy One, blessed be He, was revealed at the sea He appeared as a young man making war. 'YHWH is His name.'[80]

---

[76] Gen. 18; 32:24-30; Ex. 15:3; 33:11; Isa 54:4; Hos 2:18; Ps. 24:7-10; Isa. 42:13; Zeph. 1:14, 3:17; Jer. 20:11. Artur Marmerslein The Old Rabbinic Doctrine of God: Essays in Anthropomorphism (New York: Ktav, 1937), 7ff, 65ff; J. Massingberd Ford, "The Epithet 'Man' for God," The Irish Theological Quarterly 38 (1971): 72-76.

[77] Ps. 24:7-10; Isa. 42:13; Zeph. 1:14, 3:17.

[78] Or maybe "Yahweh-that man of war Whose name is Yahweh." See David N. Freedman, "Strophe and Meter in Exodus 15," in Howard N. Bream, Ralph D. Heim, Carey A. Moore (edd.), A Light unto My Path, Old Testament Studies in Honor of Jacob M. Myers (Philadelphia: Temple University Press, 1974), 171. The Samaritan and Aramaic translation have for the most part retained the designations or its sense. Thus, the Samaritan Pentateuch has *gibbôr* in place of "*iš*. The Palestinian Targums (N., Ps. Jon, FT) has *gîbr*" (גיברא) "man." (See Michael L. Klein, The Fragment-Targums of the Pentateuch According to their Extant Sources 2 vols. [Rome: Biblical Institute Press, 1980], 1: 78). Targum Neofiti, "Yahweh is a man (*gîbr*") making wars." Targum Pseudo-Jonathan, "Yahweh is a man (*gîbr*") who makes wars in every generation." Some Jewish exegetes apparently felt embarrassed by this "bold anthropomorphism" however. Onqelos, for example, has "Yahweh is master (*mrî*) of victory in battle." See Israel Drazin's comments in his Targum Onkelos to Exodus (Denver: Ktav Publishing House, Inc and Center For Judaic Studies, 1990), 153 n. 15. The Jerusalem Fragment (Frg. Trg.V) has "The Lord is a man: The Lord, through/with His *yᵉqar šᵉkinta* (the glory of His Shekinah) conducts your victorious battles for you". See Klein, The Fragment-Targums, 1:171, 2:129.

[79] For "*iš milḫāmâ* as a divine title see William H.C. Propp, Exodus 1-18 (New York: Double Day), 515; also Sa-Moon Kang, Divine War in the Old Testament and in the Ancient Near East (Berlin, New York: Walter de Gruyter, 1989), 202-204.

[80] See Arthur Green, "The Children in Egypt and the Theophany at the Sea," Judaism 24 (1975): 446-456; Alan F. Segal, Two Powers in Heaven (Leiden: E.J. Brill, 1977), 35; Elliot R. Wolfson, Through a Speculum that Shines (Princeton, New Jersey: Princeton University Press, 1994), 33ff. This verse was cited by the Sages of the Babylonia Talmud as proof that God appeared in the Bible as an actual man. See Balvi Sanhedrin 1:1, XLII[93A]:

And said R. Yohanan, "What is the meaning of the verse of Scripture, 'I saw by night, and behold a man riding upon a red horse, and he stood among the myrtle trees that were in the bottom' (Zech. 1:8)?"

What is the meaning of, 'I saw by night'?
The Holy One, blessed be he, sought to turn the entire world into night.

Ex. 15:3 is not the only time Yahweh is referred to as an איש "îà.[81] God speaks to Moses face to face, "as a man ("îà) speaketh to his friend (Ex. 33:11)." He appears to Abraham as one of three men, "ānāàîm (plural of "îà).[82] Jacob wrestles with a man ("îà) at Penuel whom he would later identify as Elohim/God (Gen. 32:31).[83] In Hosea (2:18) God even uses the term as a self-designation.[84] God is also a גבור, *gibbôr* "mighty man,"[85] which is the intensive form of גבר *geber*.[86] He is called a *gibbôr milÈāmāh*, "mighty man of war" (Ps. 24:7-10; also Isa. 42:13). In the Dead Sea Scrolls God is called a "mighty man of war (*gibbôr hamilhamah*)" and "man of glory" ("*îà k§bôd*) (1QM, xii, 9-10; 1QM, xix, 2). Thus, even Marjo Korpel, in her extensive study A Rift in the Clouds, Ugaritic and Hebrew Descriptions of the Divine, concedes that "in the Bible God appears as a man ["*yà*]."[87] Walter Eichrodt, in his Old Testament Theology, notes also that

---

'And behold a man riding'-'man' refers only to the Holy One, blessed be he, as it is said, 'The Lord is a man of war, the Lord is his name' (Ex. 15:3)
'On a red horse'-the Holy One, blessed be he, sought to turn the entire world to blood.
When, however, he saw Hananiah, Mishael, and Azariah, he cooled off, as it is said, 'And he stood among the myrtle trees that were in the deep.'

On this passages see Jacob Neusner, The Incarnation of God: The Character of Divinity in Formative Judaism (Philadelphia: Fortress Press, 1988), 169.

[81] Pace. Ford, "The Epithet 'Man'," 72.

[82] On this passage see below.

[83] On Jacobs struggle with God in Gen. 32 see Hamori, " 'When Gods Were Men'," Chap. 3; David F. Pennant, "Genesis 32: Lighten our Darkness, Lord, we Pray," in Richard S. Hess, Gordon J. Wenham and Philip E. Satterthwaite (edd.) He Swore an Oath: Biblical Themes from Genesis 12-50 (2nd Ed.: Carlisle, UK and Grand Rapids, MI: Paternoster Press and Baker Book House, 1994) 175-183; Davidson, Genesis 12-50, 184; Johannes Lindblom, "Theophanies in Holy Places in Hebrew Religion," Hebrew Union College Annual (hereafter HUCA) 32 (1961): 99 notes: "the chief interest of the present narrator was to say that the man who wrestled with Jacob was Yawheh, who blessed the patriarch and gave him a new name, indicating the unique relationship of the chosen people to its God. Yahweh appeared to the patriarch in bodily shape; this occurred in the holy place of Peniel." See also Stephen A. Geller, Sacred Enigmas: Literary Religion in the Hebrew Bible (London and New York: Routledge, 1996), Chap. One; idem, "The Struggle at the Jabbok: the Uses of enigma in a biblical Narrative," Journal of the Ancient Near Eastern Society 14 (1982): 37-61; Tzemah Yoreh, "Jacob's Struggle," ZAW 117 (2004): 95-97; Steve McKenzie, " 'You Have Prevailed,'" The Function of Jacob's Encounter at Peniel in the Jacob Cycle," Restoration Quarterly 23 (1980): 225-231.

[84] On these verses v. Bratsiotis, TDOT, I:230f.

[85] Ps. 24:7-10; Isa. 42:13; Zeph. 1:14, 3:17.

[86] On *gibbôr* v. TDOT, 2:367-382.

[87] Korpel, Rift in the Clouds, 131. On God as an "îà see also Ford, "The Epithet 'Man' and Marmersteinm, Old Rabinnic Doctrine of God.

"God is, without doubt, thought of also in human form, more specifically as a man."[88]

2.2. Anthropomorphic Theophany

These identifications of God as a man are not metaphorical.* The proof of this statement is in the theophany (θεος **theos** "God" and φαίνειν **phainein** "to appear") narratives.[89] In these, God appears to and is seen by the patriarchs and the prophets of Israel. When the patriarchs and prophets encountered God visually, they encountered a divine man, with a wholly - though holy - human form.[90] It is this

---

88 Walter Eichrodt, Old Testament Theology (Philadelphia: Westminster Press, 1967), I: 230.

89 J. Maxwell Miller ("In the 'Image' and 'Likeness' of God," Journal of Biblical Literature (hereafter JBL) 91 [1972]: 292) correctly pointed out: "the theophanic tradition is perhaps the clearest evidence that this view (anthropomorphism) existed among the people of Israel. The biblical writers were extremely cautious, of course, when describing God's theophanies, usually giving more attention to the surroundings of his appearance than to God himself. It is altogether clear from their descriptions, however, that God's bodily form was understood to be essentially like that of a man. "

90 On seeing God in biblical and extra-biblical Jewish and Christian tradition see TDOT 11: 208-242 s.v. ראה *rā'â* by Fuhs; Elliot Wolfson, Through a Speculum that Shines, 13-51; Howard Eilberg-Schwartz, "The Averted Gaze" in idem, God's Phallus and Other Problems for Men and Monotheism (Boston: Beacon Press, 1994) 59-80; Sven Tengström, "Les visions prophétigues du trône de Dieu et leur arrière-plan dans l'Ancien Testament," in Marc Philonenko (ed.), Le Trône de Dieu (Tübingen: J.C.B. Mohr [Paul Siebeck], 1993) 28-99; Mark S. Smith, " 'Seeing God' in the Psalms: The Background to the Beatific Vision in the Hebrew Bible," Catholic Biblical Quarterly (hereafter CBQ) 50 (1988): 171-183; Guy Couturier, "La Vision du Conseil Divin: étude d'une forme commune au prophétisme et à l'apocalyptique," Science et Esprit 36 (1984): 5-43; Christopher Rowland, "The Visions of God in Apocalyptic Literature," Journal for the Study of Judaism (hereafter JSJ) 10 (1979): 137-154; W.W. Graf Baudissin, " 'Gott schauen' in der attestamentlichen Religion," ARW 18 (1915): 173-239. Extra-bilical Jewish: Gary Anderson, "Towards a Theology of the Tabernacle and its Furniture," paper presented to the Orion Center for the Study of the Dead Sea Scrolls and Associated Literature, 2004 available at http://orion.mscc.huji.ac.il/symposiums/9th/papers/AndersonPaper.pdf; Maria E. Subtelny, "Tale of the Four Sages who Entered the Pardes: A Talmudic Enigma from a Persian Perspective," Jewish Studies Quarterly 11 (2004): 3-58; Boyarin, Daniel. "The Eye in the Torah: Ocular Desire in Midrashic Hermeneutic," Critical Inquiry 16 (Spring 1990): 532-550; Boyarin, Daniel. "The Eye in the Torah: Ocular Desire in Midrashic Hermeneutic," Critical Inquiry 16 (Spring 1990): 532-550. Daniel Boyarin, "The Eye in the Torah: Ocular Desire in Midrashic Hermeneutic," Critical Inquiry 16 (Spring 1990): 532-550; Ira Chernus, "Visions of God in Merkabah Mysticism," JSJ 13 (1982): 123-146. Christian: Stephen D. Moore, "The Beatific Vision as a Posing Exhibition: Revelation's Hypermasculine Deity," JSNT 60 (1995): 27-55; Marianne Meye Thompson, " 'God's Voice You have never Heard, God's Form you have never Seen': The Characteristic of God in the Gospel of John," Semeia 63 (1993): 177-204; April D. De Conick, Seek to See Him: Ascent and Vision Mysticism in the Gospel of Thomas (Leiden: E.J. Brill, 1996); idem, "Blessed are Those Who Have Not Seen (Jn 20:29): Johannine Dramatization of an Early

anthropomorphic deity* whom John the Revelator saw enthroned amidst 24 Elders (Chap. 4 and 5), themselves divine men – gods - constituting God's Divine Council.[91] Now, the theophany narratives are not to be compared with so-called 'figurative anthropomorphisms' of the Bible which are indeed often metaphors. The need for this distinction was expressed most eloquently by James Barr in his foundational article in 1959, "Theophany and Anthropomorphism in the OT"[92]:

> The theophanies in which the deity has appeared in human form have often, in treatments of the subject, been taken as merely one among many anthropomorphic statements or ways of speech, or at the most a particular class among them. Thus studies of anthropomorphism commonly begin with those often mentioned references to God's hands, feet, ears, nose, his speaking, smelling, walking in gardens, shutting doors, laughing, wrestling, treading the winepress, rising early in the morning, rejoicing, being disgusted, changing his mind, being jealous, and so on; and the appearances of God in human form are lumped in with all of these as further examples of the same phenomenon. It seems desirable however to make some distinction between them. These frequent expressions about God's ears or nose, his smelling or whistling, are not seriously anthropomorphisms in the sense of trying to come to grips with the form, the **morphe**, of God. The real reason for their prominence has been their offensiveness to rationalistic

---

Christian Discourse," in John D. Turner and Anne McGuire (edd.), The Nag Hammadi Library After Fifty Years: Proceedings of the 1995 Society of Biblical Literature Commemoration (Leiden and New York: Brill, 1997) 381-397; Alexander Golitzin, " 'The Demons Suggest an Illusion of God's Glory in a Form': Controversy Over the divine Body and Vision of Glory in Some Late Fourth, Early fifth Century Monastic Literature," Studia Monastica 44 (2002): 13-43; idem, "The Vision of God and the Form of Glory: More Reflections on the Anthropomorphite Controversy of AD 399," in John Behr, Andrew Louth, Dimitri Conomos (edd.), Abba: The Tradition of Orthodoxy in the West: Festschrift for Bishop Kallistos (Ware) of Diokleia (Crestwood, N.Y. : St. Vladimir's Seminary Press, 2003) 273-297.

[91] On the gods of the Divine Council see further DDD 734-800 s.v. "Sons of (the) Gods," by S.B. Parker; John J. Collins, "Powers in Heaven: God, Gods, and Angels in the Dead Sea Scrolls," in John J. Collins and Robert A. Kugler (edd.), Religion in the Dead Sea Scrolls (Grand Rapids, Michigan/Cambridge, U.K.: William B. Eerdmans Publishing Company, 2000) 9-28. On the Twenty Four Elders of Revelation 4-5 and the Divine Council see R. Dean Davis, The Heavenly Court Judgment of Revelation 4-5 (New York and London: Lanham, 1992); Joseph M. Baumgarten, "The Duodecimal Courts of Qumran, Revelation, and the Sanhedrin," Journal of Biblical Literature 95 (1976): 59-78.

[92] VTSup 7 (1960): 31-38.

thought; and this has led scholars, no doubt quite properly, to point out their value in asserting the personality and activity of the God of Israel. But what is important for the modern justification of the Old Testament may be more trivial for the Old Testament times themselves. These expressions provide a rich vocabulary for the diversity of the divine activity; but for the more precise and particular question which the word "anthropomorphism" should suggest, the question of in what form, if any, God may be known, there is the danger of exaggerating their importance, just as, I submit, it is exaggerating of the importance of Hosea 5:14 or Amos 1:2 to call it a "theriomorphism" when Yahweh is like a lion to Ephraim or roars from Mt. Zion. In contrast with all of this, it is in theophanies where God lets himself be seen that there is a real attempt to grapple with the form of his appearance. Indeed, for Hebrew thought 'form' and 'appearance' may be taken as correlative, and where there is no 'appearance' a passage is of only secondary importance for the idea of form."[93]

Similarly important is the observation of Howard Eilberg-Schwartz:

> To say the body is simply a metaphor like 'God is a lion' or 'God the rock' is to fail to take seriously the distinctive context in which images of the body are used...The ancient Judaic sources after all have special significance. They depict the exceptional cases of religious leaders who were privileged to see God...
> The point is that when they described seeing God, they evoked a human form. The image of the human body is thus of a different order than other metaphors that are used to refer to God. The comparison of God to a lion does not conjure up the image of a lion because this image is not used in contexts that describe God sightings. But when Moses is said to have seen the divine back, and Isaiah the divine robes, and Ezekiel the divine figure, the sources evoke a human image. The human body, then, is the privileged image for imagining what it might be like to gaze on the deity...In the texts of ancient Israel, then, we are dealing with at least two kinds of God images: (I) visual descriptions of what is seen when a character looks upon God and (2) conceptual representations

---

[93] Barr, "Theophany and Anthropomorphism," 31.

> that describe God in contexts in which seeing does not take place.[94]

These observations are given sound confirmation by Jeffrey J. Niehaus who demonstrates through form-critical analysis that the theophany narratives partake of the same Gattung (literary-form) of the historical accounts of interviews between humans.

> This parallel indicates the historical verisimilitude of the theophanies...And if, for instance, such an interview did take place between David and Mephibosheth (2 Sam. 9:6-11) in the manner described, we may say that a historical event gave rise to the Gattung in that case...Theophanies from the Old Testament and from the ancient Near East are, therefore actually cast in a mode of historical reportage.[95]

It is therefore in the theophany narrative that we find the surest source for understanding the nature of divine morphism, that is to say the nature of God's morphē, 'form.' Space however, will only permit the detailed examination of one such narrative.

2.3. Anthropomorphic Realism

> The God of the world's great religions-all-powerful, all-knowing, invisible, and omnipresent-has been a staple of Western thought for some time. Yet...this God is not the same as the God of most of the Bible, the God who appeared to Abraham, Moses, and other biblical heroes (emphasis mine-TI). That God, the 'God of Old,' was actually perceived in a very different way...
>
> The God of Old was not invisible or abstract. He appeared to people-usually unexpectedly; He was not sought out. He was not even recognized. Many biblical stories thus center on a 'moment of confusion,' in which an encounter with God is first mistaken for an ordinary, human meeting. In the biblical world...the spiritual and the material overlapped: everyday perception was in constant danger of sliding into something else, stark but

---

[94] God's Phallus, 116.

[95] God at Sinai: Covenant & Theophany in the Bible and Ancient Near East (Grand Rapids, Michigan: Zondervan Publishing House. 1995) 43-4.

> oddly familiar. God was always standing just behind the curtain of ordinary reality.[96]

This is how James Kugel's most recent, and most fascinating work, the God of Old: Inside the Lost World of the Bible, is introduced. Kugel has as his objective uncovering, through an attentive examination of certain ancient (pre-exilic) texts of the HB, the ancient Israelite conception of God. As he clearly demonstrates, this conception, and that of the HB in general, differs vastly from our own today. The remote, invisible, incorporeal deity* of normative Judaism, Christianity and Islam stands in marked contrast to the anthropomorphic God of ancient Israel who appeared before men and women and was seen. Some of these visual encounters with God begin as encounters with an ordinary, indistinct man whom at least the reader only later discovers is God. This type of theophany is characterized by what Esther J. Hamori has called anthropomorphic realism, i.e. God appears as a realistic or mortal human being.[97] One such episode that Kugel lists in this category and which is treated in detail by Hamori is particularly important and will be examined here: Gen. 18.

2.3.1. Genesis 18

> And Yahweh appeared unto him (Abraham) in the plains of Mamre: and he sat in the tent door in the heat of the day; And he lifted up his eyes and looked, and lo, three men stood by him; and when he saw them, he ran to meet them from the tent door, and bowed himself toward the ground, and said, My Lord, if now I have found favor in thy sight, pass not away, I pray thee, from thy servant. Let a little water, I pray you be fetched, and wash your feet, and rest yourselves under the tree. And I will fetch a morsel of bread, and comfort your hearts; after that ye shall pass on...And they said, 'So do as thou hast said.' And Abraham hastened into the tent unto Sarah, and said, 'Make ready three measures of fine meal...and make cakes upon the hearth.' And Abraham ran unto the herd, and fetched a calf tender and good, and gave it to the servant, who hastened to prepare it. And he took butter, and milk and the calf that he had dressed, And he set it before them; and he stood with them under the tree and they did eat...

[96] Kugel, the God of Old, front jacket flap.
[97] " 'When Gods Were Men'."

> And the men rose up from thence, and looked toward Sodom: and Abraham went with them to bring them on the way. And Yahweh said, 'Shall I hide from Abraham that thing which I do?'...And Yahweh said, Because the cry of Sodom and Gomorra is great, and because their sin is very grievous; I will go down now, and see whether they have done according to the cry of it...
>
> And the men turned their faces from thence, and went toward Sodom: But Abraham stood yet before Yahweh...And Yahweh went his way...

This is truly an astonishing narrative. Robert Davidson, in his commentary, calls it a "profoundly mysterious story."[98] Here, three men ("§n§àîm, Sing. "îâ, איש) suddenly appear to Abraham, one of whom was, at least according to the narrator,[99] Yahweh himself. Abraham entertains the three men with human food, which they did eat, and also invites them to "rest" under a tree, offering to wash their feet. Without a doubt we are dealing with a very bold theophany narrative. Such a presentation of the divine, as a man who eats, rests, and gets his feet washed, certainly does violence to all of our basic assumptions about God. It is not surprising therefore that some have attempted to extricate Yahweh from the epiphany, distinguishing him from the men.[100] But this reading is demonstrably untenable.[101] Likewise, attempts to discern in these men an early appearance of the Christian Trinity have been "universally abandoned by recent exegesis."[102]

The discussion over Yahweh's relationship to the men often hinges on how one should translate אדני at the beginning of v3. The Hebrew consonants are ambiguous and may be read three ways depending on how they are vowled: "ªd̲Ùnay, (reg. pl. "my lords/sirs); "ªd̲Ùnî (my lord/sir) or "ªd̲Ùn§y ("Lord/my Lord"). If we see in these three men regular human beings, or even angels, we would vowle the consonants to read "my lords" or "sirs."[103] However, it is certain that the word is singular because the verbs are singular.[104] Thus it is certain that the

[98] Robert Davidson, Genesis 12-50 (Cambridge: Cambridge University Press, 1979) 63.
[99] Thus the chapter head, "Now Yahweh appeared to him in the plains of Mamre."
[100] E.g. William T. Miller, Mysterious Encounters at Mamre and Jabbok (Chico, California: Scholars Press, 1984) 38.
[101] Victor P. Hamilton, The Book of Genesis, Chapters 18-50 (Grand Rapids, Michigan: William E. Eerdmass Publishing Company, 1995), 3-8.
[102] Gerhard Von Radd, Genesis, A Commentary (Philadelphia: Westminster Press, 1972), 206.
[103] Davidson, Genesis 12-50, 62.
[104] Claus Westermann, Genesis 12-36, trans. John J. Scullion (Minneapolis: Ausburg Publishing, 1981), 278.

addressee is singular.[105] Abraham's invitation is directed at one of the three men. Is this one an angel, maybe of a higher rank than the other men, in which case we should vowle the word as "my lord" ("adÙnî)? Or is it Yahweh Himself who appears with the two other men/angels and is here addressed as "my Lord" ("adÙn§y)? The Masoretic Text (MT), that is to say the standard Hebrew text behind the various English translations, and all the Versions[106] except the Samaritan and its Targum (Aramaic translation/paraphrase) vowle the word as "adÙn§y, Lord. This is justified by v. 13 where Yahweh is clearly the subject; he is here the speaker and Abraham the addressee.

> ...Abraham never called himself servant when speaking to men; likewise he never approached any human being calling him 'My Lord'-neither Pharaoh (ch. 12) nor Avimelech (cf. 20-21) nor when negotiating with Ephron the Hittite prince (ch. 23-here the other call him: Sir!); therefore it is very unlikely that he should have called one of the anonymous strangers 'My Lord!' On the other hand verses 27, 30, 31, 32 give sufficient proof that אדני is in the whole chapter the appellative of God. Therefore we should accept in this case the interpretation of the Massorah, namely, Lord![107]

Many modern commentators, whether inclined to see this as a theophany (appearance of God) or an angelophany (appearance of an angel), disregard the ancient versions and read "adÙnî (my lord/sir).[108] This reading is largely based on the assumption that, even if Yahweh was somehow related to the three men, Abraham could not have known so at this stage in the narrative.[109] The singular mention of the name Yahweh late in the narrative (v. 13) is cited as evidence of a gradual awareness on the part of Abraham of the divine nature of his

---

[105] The Samaritan reading "adÙnay is therefore unacceptable. Westermann, Genesis 12-36, 278.

[106] The Versions include the Greek translation of the Hebrew Bible called the Septuagint (LXX), the Aramaic translations called Targums (Targum Onqelos, Targum Ps.-Jonathan, Targum Neofiti), the Samaritan translation (Sam), and the Latin translation called the Vulgate. See Miller, Mysterious Encounters, 9.

[107] Benjamin Uffenheimer, "Genesis 18-19, A New Approach," in Mélanges André Neher (Paris: Librairie D'Amérique et D'Orient Andrien-Maisonneuve, 1975) 150.

[108] E.g. Westermann, Genesis 12-36, 273; Hamilton, Book of Genesis, 3; Robert Alter, Genesis, Translation and Commentary (New York: W. W. Norton and Company, 1996), 77; E.A. Speiser, Genesis (Garden City, New York: Doubleday & Company, Inc, 1964), 129. Even Hamori, " 'When Gods Were Men'," 9, 11.

[109] Speiser, Genesis, 129; Hamilton, Book of Genesis, 11; Von Radd, Genesis, A Commentary, 206; Davidson, Genesis 12-50, 63;

visitors whom he initially took to be normal wayfarers.[110] But the Masoretic reading, "My Lord," at the beginning of the narrative, implies that Abraham knew he had been visited by God.[111] As Jean-Paul Klein noted, Abraham had experienced a theophanic encounter with God previously at Shechem (Gen. 12:1-4a, 6-8).[112] There Yahweh "showed Himself (*wayyērā'* וירא)" to Abraham. Abraham then built an alter to God, who had "appeared to him (*hannir'e*[*h*] הנראה)."[113] God would appear to Abraham again at Mamre/Hebron (Gen. 17:1-22). Thus, Abraham knew what Yahweh "looked like" and was well capable of recognizing him. The claim that Abraham 'could not' have known it was Yahweh before him is therefore not supported by the narrative.

The internal evidence, read without theological presupposition, establishes that Yahweh is one of the men. The chapter heading, "And Yahweh appeared to him in the plains of Mamre," indicates that the later editor of this narrative clearly took it as a tale of a theophany. In v. 2 Abraham "bowed himself to the ground" before the men and said "If I have found favor in thy sight, pass not away." וישתחו *Wayyištaȇû*, "and he bowed," is the Hithpa'l¿l[114] of שׁחה sh§È§h, "to bow down." This prostration can simply imply deference or homage (Abraham to the Hittites, Gen 23, 7.12) or worship (Isaac Gen 24, 26.48.52). The addition here, however, of "§rß§h "to the earth" "lends an elemental resonance to the obeisance,"[115] as in Ex 34, 8 (Moses to Yahweh). J. van Seters notes, "As if to strengthen this identity, he (the narrator) has Abraham do obeisance to the visitors in a manner befitting only a king or deity. This is certainly more than a show of politeness."[116]

This is further demonstrated by what follows: "If I have found favor in your eyes m§ß§"t*î* È¿n b^e‡*ê*k§." È¿n, "graciousness, favor,"

---

[110] Thus Davidson (Genesis 12-50, 63) argues that, "Part of the charm of the story, however, is that at the outset Abraham did not, and could not, know." See also von Rad, Genesis, 206; Alter, Genesis, Translation and Commentary, 78; Speiser, Genesis. 129; Aalders, Genesis, II: 3; Westermann, Genesis 12-36, 276f; Hamilton, Book of Genesis, 3; J. Kenneth Kuntz, The Self Revelation of God (Philadelphia: Westminster Press, 1967)121. Robert Ignatius Letellier, Day in Mamre, Night in Sodom (Leiden: E.J. Brill, 1995), 83. But v. Masashi Takahashi, "An Oriental's Approach to the Problems of Angelology," ZAW 78 (1966), who says that "immediately their identity is recognized by Abraham (346)."

[111] Hamilton, The Book of Genesis, 3.

[112] "Que se passé-t-il en Genèse 18?" Le point théologique 24 (1977): 76.

[113] See Lindblom, "Theophanies in Holy Places," 95; Kuntz, Self Revelation of God, 116.

[114] Form of Hebrew verb.

[115] Letellier, Day in Mamre, 82.

[116] J. van Seters, Abraham in History and Tradition (New Haven/London, 1975), 212.

"connotes God's spirit of helpfulness."[117] As Robert Ignatius Letellier notes: "The appearance of È¿n in the context of 18,3 is an indicator of divine power at work. Why should Abraham use so weighted a word in welcoming an apparently ordinary visitor?...The verb #br 'to pass by' is frequently used in connection with the appearance of YHWH and a special manifestation of grace, either by his presence or through the agency of his prophet".[118] Letellier thus sees this verb as a nexus linking Gen 18, Ex 33:19 and 2 Kings 4. "The analogy with Gen 18 is strong: YHWH is passing but is prevailed upon by his servant Abraham to accept hospitality and later blesses him with the promise of a son...The verb #br is an alert signal to YHWH's transforming presence."[119]

In v 22, after Yahweh informs Abraham of his intensions for Sodom and Gomorrah, we read, "And the men turned from there and went on toward Sodom while Abraham was still standing before the Lord." Chapter 19 then begins: "The two angels came to Sodom in the evening." This is important in that it establishes that only two of the men, now identified as angels, proceeded to Sodom and Gomorrah, the third man, Yahweh, remaining behind with Abraham. Thus, as Hamilton observes, "Ch. 19 suggests that the trio is really Yahweh and two of His messengers."[120] Gerhard Von Radd notes also: "The most obvious answer (to the identity of the men) seems to be that Yahweh is one of the three men. This assumption would become certainty when in chs. 18:22 and 19:1, after Yahweh's departure, the 'two messengers' come to Sodom."[121] It is clear that the three men here are Yahweh and two of his angles.[122] Hamilton, in his Commentary to the Book of Genesis, argues, "This is the one theophany in the Abraham cycle in which Yahweh appears to Abraham with others at his side."[123]

---

[117] P. Heinisch, Theology of the Old Testament (St Paul, 1955), 92.

[118] Letellier, Day in Mamre, 84f.

[119] Letellier, Day in Mamre, 85.

[120] Hamilton, The Book of Genesis, 7.

[121] Von Radd, Genesis, A Commentary, 204. Von Radd cautions us against 'mixing' "the section in ch. 19.1f f., which derives from a different tradition, with this." This is unnecessary however; the final redactor of this narrative complex, which "begins with ch.18 and does not end until ch.19.38" clearly understood the beginning of ch. 19 as a continuation of chapter 18's conclusion. On the literary relation between chap. 18 and 19 see Hamori, " 'When Gods Were Men'," 14-33; Brian Doyle, 'Knock, Knock, Knockin' on Sodom's Door': The Function of חתפ/תלד in Genesis 18-19," JSOT 28 (2004): 431-448; Thomas M. Bolin, "The Role of Exchange in Ancient Mediterranean Religion and Its Implications for Reading Genesis 18-19," JSOT 29 (2004): 37-56; Alter, Genesis, Translation and Commentary, 77, 80; Speiser, Genesis, 131, 134, 138;

[122] See also Alter, Genesis, Translation and Commentary 77; G. Ch. Aalders, Bible Student's Commentary, 3.

[123] Hamilton, The Book of Genesis, 8.

We thus have in Genesis 18 a very bold theophany narrative in which God himself is presented as a man who eats and rests. Letellier concludes:

> YHWH appears here as a man...This is not to be confused with mere (metaphorical) anthropomorphism. While God is seen as a man and speaks and eats like one, there is no attempt to depict the form of God or to describe his external appearance...It is the human appearance in the theophany that is essential, and there is consistency and cohesion in the OT in presenting these stories systematically. God wills to appear and does so in human shape.[124]

Hamori concludes, "There is no indication in the text...that it is intended metaphorically...In Gensesis 18:1-15, Yahweh is presented in entirely realistic human form, but free from human flaws."[125] Even G. Ch. Aalders, in his Bible Student's Commentary reluctantly admits:

> Undoubtedly we are presented with facts here that are beyond our comprehension. It is totally beyond our understanding that God Himself should appear with two of His holy angels in such realistic human form that they actually ate human food. But this is precisely what God tells us in His word...[126]

2.4. 'God is Not A Man'?

The God of the Hebrew prophets was therefore a man, a mighty man.[127] At least ten times in the HB and two further times in the Dead Sea Scrolls he is referred to as such. These numbers alone would seem to make the case definitive. Yet as any statistician knows, numbers don't tell the whole story. There are three verses in the whole of the biblical canon that, on the surface at least, appear as explicit in their denial of god's divine humanity as the above verses appear as explicit in their affirmation of the same: Num. 23:19; I Sam 15:29; Hos. 11:9. It is one or all of these three verses that are routinely relied on as the Bible's definitive statement about God, despite the fact that they are dwarfed by the others in terms of numbers and narrative elaboration. But the use of these verses individually or collectively to demonstrate that the

---

[124] Letellier, Day in Mamre, 39.
[125] " 'When Gods Were Men'," 43, 72.
[126] Aalders, Bible Student's Commentary, 5.
[127] See Appendix A.

biblical deity is non-anthropomorphic is clearly a parade example of non-contextual exegesis* and even gross negligence. A close reading of these Hebrew passages do not support the use that has been made of them; the passages do not contradict the more numerous affirmations that God is a man. The two critical issues in understanding these verses is the Hebrew syntax and the narrative context.

Num. 23:19 a לא איש אל ויכזב
ו בן־אדם ויתנחם b

The King James Version (KJV) of this verse reads, "God is not a man that He should lie, nor a son of man that he should repent." Fidelity to the Hebrew syntax requires a different translation, however. Both versets (a and b) are better translated as relative clauses. The wâw (ו) followed by a verb reflected for number and gender (יכזב, יתנחם) can have the sense of a relative particle "that/who."[128] The better translation is therefore, "God is not a man who lies, nor a son of man who repents." This small syntactical clarification produces a significant change in meaning. Num. 23:19 is not an absolute denial that God is a man; it only denies that God is a man who lies or repents. Similar is the statement, "I, True Islam, am not a man who smokes." I am denying in this statement not my manhood or humanity, but that I smoke.

The larger context confirms this reading. As commentators have pointed out, the context of this verse is defined by the second half of verset b, the denial of divine repentance. On the surface this seems absolute: the God of Israel does not repent. However, as R.W.L. Moberly has pointed out,[129] divine repentance is a theological axiom of the Hebrew Bible, affirmed 27 times.[130] God does niÈam, repent, in response to humans turning from evil. This willingness on God's part to "change his mind" on behalf of human repentance is a central principle of his relationship with man in general and Israel in particular. It implies that this relationship is genuine and responsive, in which what people do and how they relate to God matters to God.[131] Now God's repenting, niÈam, is different from man's repenting, *šûb*. Human *šûb* involves *kizzēb*, deception, and *šeqer*, "speaking falsely," implying that

---

[128] Seow, A Grammar, 285.
[129] " 'God is Not a Human That He Should Repent' (Numbers 23:19 and 1 Samuel 15:29)," in Tod Linafelt and Timothy K. Beal (edd.), God in the Fray: A Tribute to Walter Brueggemann (Minneapolis: Fortress Press, 1998) 112-123.
[130] 1 Sam 15:11, 35; 2 Sam 24:16; Jer 18:8, 10; 26:3, 13, 19; 42:10; Jon 3:9, 10; 4:2.
[131] Moberly, "God is Not a Human," 112-115.

people do not live up to their promises.[132] In contrast, God does not disappoint. But God reserves the freedom to hold to a decree of his own issuance, or reverse that decree according to man's response. Thus, 1 Sam 15:29, "He is not a man who repents" is sandwiched between 1 Sam 15:11 and 35, both of which declare that Yahweh does repent. The particular context of Num. 23:19 is God's resolve to bless Israel despite the efforts of Balak to extract a curse on Israel from the seer-prophet Balaam; the particular context of 1 Sam 15:29 is God's resolve to give the kingdom of Israel to David and his descendents unconditionally, even when they disobey him.[133]

> The unchangeability of God assures human beings that they are not in the hands of caprice or irresponsible power which often characterizes the conduct of humankind. It is reflected in Yahweh's faithfulness to Israel. At the same time, the changeability of God reveals God in vital relationships with his people. Israel was not in the hands of iron fate or a predetermined order. God should not be equated with "The Absolute" of philosophical theology, if this describes God as existing in isolation from human beings and as in no way effected by mankind's experiences.[134]

Thus, as Moberly rightly notes, "It is against this background of the consistent depiction of Yahweh as 'repenting' that one must set those passages which deny that Yahweh 'repents'."[135] If the seemingly categorical denial in the second half of the versets in Num 23:19 that God repents is to be qualified by the repeated affirmations that God does repent, the statement in the first half of the verset that "God is not a man..." must also be qualified by the repeated affirmations that God is a man.

> The second qualification is that God "is not a human being (*lō' 'îš/ben-'ādām*, Num 23:19a; *lō' 'ādām*, 1 Sam 15:29). In neither passage is this some kind of principle in its own right, but each time it introduces the notion of repenting as

---

[132] Moberly, "God is Not a Human," 116-117.
[133] See Terence E. Fretheim, "Divine Knowledge, Divine Constancy, and the Rejection of Saul's Kingship," CBQ 47 (1985): 595-602.
[134] John T.Willis, "The 'Repentance' of God in the Books of Samuel, Jeremiah, and Jonah," Horizons in Biblical Theology 16 (1994): 156-175 (162).
[135] Moberly, "God is Not a Human,"115.

something characteristic of humanity, and it is from this that God is distanced...[136]

The third passage, Hos. 11:9, further confirms that God's divine humanity is not here denied categorically.

I will not execute My wrath
I will not again destroy Ephraim,
for I am God and not man (כי אל אנכי ולא־איש),
the Holy One in your midst,
and I will not come in wrath.

Here God's 'otherness' is His ability to rise above the emotion of his own hurt and not destroy Ephraim, as a jealous husband would have done having repeatedly caught his wife (Israel) in infidelity.[137] As E. Lab. Cherbonnier well pointed out in his classic article, "The Logic of Biblical Anthropomorphism":

> It is sometimes held that this biblical anthropomorphism is only a manner of speaking, a mere symbol for the hidden, 'wholly other' God who defies all attempts to describe him. A few standard passages are regularly adduced as evidence that the Bible 'at its best' abandons anthropomorphism. Modern scholarship, however, by restoring these passages to their context and so restoring their original meaning, reverses such an interpretation...Hosea 11:9: 'For I am God and not man, the Holy One in your midst.' Here apparently, God is contrasted with man; anthropomorphism is repudiated. The context, however, establishes the contrary. Indeed, Hosea is one of the most daringly anthropomorphic authors of the Bible. He attributes to God Himself the feelings and emotions of the husband whose wife has 'played the harlot.' The contrast between God and man concerns their respective ways of dealing with the situation. Instead of destroying Israel for her faithlessness, as might be expected of man, God is not vindictive. He has resources of mercy and forgiveness for the softening of Israel's heart. This difference between God and

---

[136] Moberly, "God is Not a Human," 117.

[137] Gary Alan Long, "Dead or Alive: Literality and God-Metaphors in the Hebrew Bible," Journal of the Academy of Religion62 (1994):521.

man is not a difference 'in principle.' It is merely 'de facto'-a difference which God intends to overcome.[138]

See also Ulrich Mauser, who poignantly notes:

> The words "I am God and not man" in (Hos. 11:9) have been adduced frequently to justify the contention that, in spite of all their anthropomorphic language, the Old Testament prophets are fully aware of the spiritual nature of God. But nothing could be further from the truth...the godness of God is not denial of his anthropomorphous nature, but the qualitative superiority of God over man which consists in God's will not to fall victim to his wrath but to forgive even in a situation in which man would have lost all sympathy and patience.[139]

We know in fact that this is the correct reading of Hosea, because it is in Hosea that God instructs Israel to no longer call Him Baal (Lord/husband), but call Him My Man ("îâî; 2:18).

The point in these three passages is clearly not that God is not a man, but that God is not like men. As Job recognized, "For He is not a man like me that I might answer Him כי־לא־איש כמני אעננו" (9:32). That a man could deny being a man due to certain qualities that he lacks or possesses in abundance is proved by Prov. 30:1-2, where 'the man הגבר, haggeber' named Agur declares in a moment of self-depreciation, "I am a beast, not a man כי בער אכני מאיש". In Hosea God is thus contrasted with man in that He is full of compassion. In Num 23 and I Sam 15 on the other hand, God "is not a man" in the specific sense that He does not lie (v19) or break His promises as man is prone to do. "Has He promised and will He not do it? Has He spoken, and will He not fulfill it?" Isaiah 46:5,9 contrasts God with the pagan's idols. "To whom will you liken me and make me equal, and compare Me, that we may be alike?...For I am God, and there is no other; I am God, and there is none like me." Cherbonnier again notes:

> Logically, He (God of the Bible) has more in common with these Olympian deities (of Greece) than with Plato's 'Being' or Aristotle's 'Unmoved Mover.' The difference between Yahweh and Zeus is not logical or formal, but factual and 'existential.' The prophets do not charge the pagan deities

---

[138] E.L. Cherbonnier, "The Logic of Biblical Anthropomorphism," ***Harvard Theological Review***, 55 (1962): 187-8.
[139] "Image of God and Incarnation," Interpretation 24 (1970): 348.

> with being anthropomorphic, but with being insufficiently anthropomorphic. At their best, they are counterfeit persons. At their worst, they are frankly impersonal.
> ...(Is 46:5) contrasts the mighty acts of Yahweh with the impotence of every false god: "They lift it upon their shoulders, they carry it;...it cannot move from its place, ...it does not answer" (v. 7). The true God, however, does move and speak; he announces his purpose and brings it to pass (v. 11).
> The intent of such passages is to distinguish Yahweh from idols by precisely these anthropomorphic activities: "They have mouths, but don't speak; eyes, but don't see; they have ears, but do not hear; nose, but do not smell" (Ps. 115:5,6). Pagan gods are contemptible because of their impotence. They cannot even do the things man can do, whereas Yahweh does these things 'par excellence.'[140]

In Hosea, Numbers and I Samuel God exalts Himself above man by contrasting His 'activity' from that of man. God's actions are predicated upon higher principles than those on which man's are predicated-jealousy, for example. On the other hand, God exalts Himself over the idols by contrasting His ability to perform characteristically human acts- seeing with eyes, hearing with ears, etc-to the idols who, though possessing a human shape, can not perform those human deeds. God does them par excellence. This is the Divine Paradox, the Mystery of God; an anthropomorphic deity who is nonetheless utterly different from man-not substantially but qualitatively.

> The particular paradox of belief in an anthropomorphic deity who is nevertheless utterly different from man is related to other paradoxes, and especially to the familiar one which declares that God is both transcendent and immanent, a paradox of which Israel was fully aware. She knew...that God was both like man, and yet entirely different from him.[141]

K. Van Der Toorn in the Dictionary of Deities and Demons of the Bible (2001) observes as well:

> The Israelite concept of God shares many traits with the beliefs of its neighbors. The most fundamental

[140] Cherbonnier, "Logic," 192.
[141] Robert Dentan, ***The Knowledge of God in Ancient Israel*** (New York: The Seabury Press, 1968) 152.

> correspondence concerns the anthropomorphic nature ascribed to God. God's anthropomorphism is external...as well as internal...Over against the anthropomorphism of God found in the Hebrew Bible, there are those texts that stress the difference between God's divinity and man's humanity (Num. 23:19, Hos. 11:9)... A closer look at these examples shows that the opposition does not invalidate the idea of divine anthropomorphism. God's qualities are human qualities, yet purified from imperfection and amplified to superhuman dimensions. Sincerity and reliability are human virtues-even if only God is wholly sincere and reliable. Strength, too, is not the exclusive prerogative of God; he is merely incomparably stronger than humans or animals.
>
> In view of the passages dwelling upon the contrast between God and man, the thesis of God's anthropomorphism should be modified in this sense that God is more than human. Though man has been created in the image of God...there is a huge difference of degree-yet not of nature.[142]

Poray Casimier, Sr., in his polemic against the Nation of Islam entitled, Islamic Imposters: Exposing the Beliefs of Black Muslims, claims that "Three verses from the Bible...sufficiently disprove the NOI's position (that God is a man, not a spirit) – John 4:24, Hosea 11:9, and Numbers 23:19."[143] We can now see the gross error on the part of Mr. Casimier. These verses, when read in the original language and context, in no way contradict the Hon. Elijah Muhammad's claim that "God is a man, and we just can't make him other than a man."

2.5. The Transcendent Body of God

Herman Gunkel said simply: "God (in the Old Testament) was envisioned...like a person, although much more powerful and frightening."[144] The power, terror, and transcendence associated with this 'Man-God' of the Bible are rooted in his **body**. The gods of the ancient Near East and the God of Israel were transcendently anthropomorphic; that is to say, he/they possessed bodies so sublime it/they bordered on the non-body.[145] As Hendel pointed out:

---

[142] K. Van Der Toorn, "God (1)," in DDD, 361ff.
[143] (Chicago: Xulon Press, 2004) 157.
[144] 113.
[145] On transcendent anthropomorphism in the ancient Near East, ancient Israel and Classical (Greek) tradition see above. This is not to deny that the concept of 'mundane anthropomorphism,' or what Esther J. Hamori called 'anthropomorphic realism,' existed

> Yahweh has a body, clearly anthropomorphic, but too holy for human eyes...Yahweh's body was believed to be incommensurate with mundane human existence: it has a different degree of being than human bodies... It is a transcendent anthropomorphism not in form but in its effect, approachable only by the most holy, and absent in material form in the cult...The body of God was defined in Israelite culture as both like and unlike that of humans. [146]

One of the distinguishing characteristics of the body divine is its dangerously luminous and fiery nature.

> The body of the gods shines with such an intense brilliance that no human eye can bear it. Its splendor is blinding. Its radiance robs it of visibility through an excess of light the way darkness causes invisibility through a lack of light...if the god chooses to be seen in all his majesty, only the tiniest bit of the splendor of the god's size, stature, beauty and radiance can be allowed to filter through, and this already enough to strike the spectator with thambos, stupefaction, to plunge him into a state of reverential fear.[147] But to show themselves openly, as they truly are – enargeis – is a terrible favor the gods accord no one...[148]

The gods have "A body invisible in its radiation, a face that cannot be seen directly."[149] To catch a glimpse of a deity could mean death for a human onlooker, because the mortal constitution is unable to bear

---

in ancient Israel (Gen 18; 32: Hamori, "'When Gods Were Men': Biblical Theophany and Anthropomorphic Realism," Ph.D. dissertation. New York University, 2004). On anthropomorphism in ancient Israel see further: Mark S. Smith, The Origins of Biblical Monotheism: Israel's Polytheistic Background and the Ugaritic Texts (Oxford: Oxford University Press, 2001) 86-93; idem, Early History of God, 140-47; Erhard S. Gestenberger, Theologies of the Old Testament (Minneapolis: Fortress Press, 2002) 56.

[146] Hendel, "Aniconism and Anthropomorphism," 223, 225 and above.

[147] See also Mahābhārata 3.40.49: "Mahādeva (Śiva) attacked the afflicted [Arjuna] with martial splendor and brilliance, stunning him out of his wits." Trans. James W. Laine, ***Visions of God: Narrative of Theophany in the Mahābhārata*** (Vienna, 1989), 71; M. Streck, ***Assurbanipal und die letzen assyrischen Könige*** (Leipzig: Hinrichs, 1916) 2, 8-10:84-88: "the radiance of Aššur and Ištar overwhelmed him (Luli, king of Sidon) and he went crazy."

[148] Vernant, "Dim Body," 37.

[149] Vernant, "Dim Body," 37.

it.[150] In order to be seen when such is desired or necessary, or in order to intervene directly in human affairs, the gods must conceal their divine forms.[151] Concealment is achieved either by enveloping the divine body in a mist, fog or cloud to become invisible,[152] or by some sort of divine metamorphosis.[153] This latter is usually done by reducing the divine size and splendor and taking on the appearance of a mortal human (as, for example Master Fard Muhammad, 'the King of Kings,' appearing in Detroit as a mortal silk peddler or a 'prophet').[154]

The best example of transcendent anthropomorphism in the Bible is the inaugural vision of Ezekiel (Ezekiel chapter I). The priest-prophet sees God seated on a glorious throne:

> and seated above the likeness of a throne was something that seemed like a human form. Upward from what appeared like the loins I saw something like gleaming amber, something that looked like fire enclosed all around; and downward from what looked like the loins I saw something that looked like fire, and there was splendor all around. Like a bow in a cloud on a rainy day, such was the appearance of the splendor all around. This was the appearance of the likeness of the glory of Yahweh (1:26-27, the New Oxford Annotated Bible translation).

Ezekiel here sees Yahweh as an enthroned, transcendent anthropos (Ezek. 1:1-28). As Gerhard von Rad pointed out:

---

[150] So the well-known story of Semele who wanted to see her lover Zeus in his glory, but when he appeared in his lightning-like splendor, she could not bear it and was struck dead by a thunderbolt: Apollodorus, *Libr.* 3, 4, 3; Ovid, *Met* 3, 253-315. See Robin Lane Fox, "Seeing the Gods" in idem, ***Pagans and Christians*** (New York: Alfred A. Knopf, Inc., 1987) 102-67 (106-10); Gerard Mussies, "Identification and Self-Identification of Gods in Classical and Hellenistic Times," in R. Van den Broek, T. Baarda and J. Mannsfeld (edd.), ***Knowledge of God in the Graeco-Roman World*** (Leiden: E.J. Brill, 1988) 1-18 (3).

[151] Vernant, "Dim Body," 37: "The paradox of the divine body is that in order to appear to mortals, it must cease to be itself; it must clothe itself in a mist, disguise itself as a mortal, take the form of a bird, a star, a rainbow."

[152] Vernant, "Dim Body," 35; Renehan, "On the Greek Origins," 108-9; Pease, "Some Aspects," 8-11.

[153] On the nature of this metamorphosis see Vernant, "Dim Body," 31-2; Jenny Clay, "Demas and Aude: The Nature of Divine Transformation in Homer," ***Hermes*** 102 (1974): 129-36;

[154]Vernant, "Dim Body," 36; Mussies, "Identification and Self-Identification"; Clay, "Demas and Aude"; H.S. Versnel, "What Did Ancient Man See when He saw a God? Some Reflections on Greco-Roman Epiphany," in Dirk van der Plas (ed.), ***Effigies Dei: Essays on the History of Religions*** Leiden: E.J. Brill, 1987) 43-55 (45-6; H.J. Rose, "Divine Disguises," ***HTR*** 49 (1956): 62-72.

> The light-phenomenon of the 'glory of God' (in Ezekiel 1) clearly displays human contours...nevertheless at the same time an infinite difference and distance is tacitly recognized-first in the matter of mere stature, for Israel conceived Jahweh as gigantic (Mic. I. 3ff.; Is. LXIII. Iff; Ps. XXIV. 9), but also different and distant as regards quality, for the (kabôd) which man has cannot, of course, be remotely compared with the fiery, intensely radiant light which is the nature of Jahweh.[155]

Ezekiel's vision of the deity is at once the most transcendent and the most anthropomorphic of the entire Bible. As Rimmon Kasher observes: "there is perhaps no other biblical prophet whose God is so corporeal as Ezekiel. Anthropomorphism did not, of course, originate with Ezekiel; the Bible offers many anthropomorphic descriptions of the Deity...The prophet Ezekiel belongs to this general biblical tradition and in fact amplifies it."[156] On the other hand Daniel I. Block notes that Ezekiel's vision of God is height of divine transcendence as well:

> Two features of the image are especially significant. First, Ezekiel recognizes the form to be that of a human being (ʾādām). Second, this was no ordinary man. What appeared to be his upper body radiated with the brilliamce of amber (Ḥašmal); his lower body seemed enveloped in a dazzling fiery glow as well...With respect to force and awesomeness, no theophany in the entire OT matches Ezekiel's inaugural vision...the vision proclaims the transcendent glory of God. Everything about the apparition proclaims his glory: the dazzling brilliance of the entire image, the gleam of the creatures' bronze legs, the jewels on the wheels, the crystalline platform, the lapis lazuli throne, the amberous and fiery form of the 'man.' Everything about the vision cries 'Glory!' (cf. Ps. 29:9), even the prophet's frustrating search for adequate forms of expression... Everything about the vision is in the superlative mode. God is alone above the platform, removed from all creatures, and stunning in his radiance.[157]

[155] von Rad, ***Old Testament Theology***, 1:146:

[156] "Anthropomorphism, Holiness and Cult: A New Look at Ezekiel 40-48," ***ZAW*** 110 (1998): 192

[157] ***The Book of Ezekiel*** (Grand Rapids, Michigan: William B. Eerdmans Publishing Company), 106-8

Chapter III:

God the Father in Early Christian Tradition

3. *Introductory Summary*

The God of ancient Israel and the Bible was a divine man. Such was the belief of Jesus of Nazareth also. Jesus was a Hebrew and he believed in the God of the Hebrews. In John 8:16-18 Jesus specifically refers to God as a man (*anthropos*). Jesus was therefore the source of the early Christian tradition according to which God is anthropomorphic. Even though the hallmark of Christian tradition today is the insistence that God is a formless spirit, the early Christians accepted that God was anthropomorphic. It was the Church Fathers, Clement of Alexandria (d. c. AD 216), Origen (AD 185-253) and St. Augustine (AD 354-430) who successfully brought the god of the Greek philosophers – that immaterial and formless God – into the Church. The writings of St. Augustine demonstrate that the indigenous Christians of North Africa, much to his dismay, rejected the immaterial god of Greek philosophy and instead affirmed the anthropomorphic God of the Bible. The Church today therefore owes it god to Plato and Aristotle, not to Jesus.

3.1. *Jesus, Prophet of the Man-God*

Jesus was a Jew and believed in the God of Israel. As Arthur McGiffert in ***The God of the Early Christians*** says,

> Jesus was a devout and loyal Jew, and the God whom he worshipped was the God of his people Israel-the God of Abraham, Isaac, and Jacob. He was not a theologian or a philosopher, and he indulged in no speculations touching the nature of God. So far as we can judge from the Synoptic Gospels and from his attitude reflected there, he did not regard it as his mission to promulgate a new God or to teach new ideas about God, but rather to summon his fellows to live as God-his God and theirs-would have them live…

> Jesus' idea of God indeed is quite naïve and anthropomorphic, and there is no sign that he was troubled by any speculative problems or difficulties…
>
> God was always strictly personal for Jesus-Ruler, Judge, Master, Lord, Father. He thought of him in *anthropomorphic, not in metaphysical or mystical*, fashion.
>
> Summing it all up, we may say Jesus' idea of God was wholly Jewish. At no point, so far as we can judge from the Synoptic Gospels, did he go beyond his peoples thought about God. His uniqueness, so far as his teaching goes, lay not in the novelty of it, but in the insight and unerring instinct with which he made his own the best in thought of his countrymen.[158]

As we found in the Hebrew Bible, Jesus too could even refer to God as a man, as in John 8:16-18:

> 16 Even if I do judge, my judgment is true, because I am not alone, but I and the Father who sent me. 17 And in your Law it is written that the testimony of two men (δυο ανθρώπν, *duo anthropon*) is true. 18 I am the one who testifies about myself, and the Father who sent me also testifies about me.

Delbert Burkett, in his Ph.D. thesis on the Son of Man concept in John, published in 1991, observes regarding this verse:

> Jesus appeals to the Old Testament law governing the testimony of witnesses in order to support the validity of his own testimony. In referring to that law, however, he makes a significant change in the wording. The law reads, 'At the testimony of two witnesses (עדים)…a case shall be established (Deut. 19.15; cf. 17.6). For the phrase 'two witnesses,' found in both the Hebrew and the Greek, Jesus substitutes 'two men.' In v. 18 he proceeds to apply this law to himself and his Father: he and the Father are the 'two Men' who testify. Thus as Jesus uses the phrase 'two Men' here, it paradoxically designates not two human beings, but two divine beings.
>
> In this passage Jesus does precisely the opposite of what one would expect. The natural expectation would be that if a law spoke of 'two men' and Jesus wanted to apply it to himself and

[158] A. McGriffert, ***The God of the Early Christians*** 1924 (New York: Charles Scribners Sons, 1924) 3,17.

God, he might change "two men' to 'two witnesses' to avoid speaking of god as a man. In the present case, he could have simply retained the original wording of the law to avoid so speaking. Instead, he does the reverse. He apparently goes out of his way to apply the phrase 'two Men' to himself and God.[159]

3.2. *Anthropomorphism and the Early Church*

Jesus is the likely source of the early and widespread Christian belief in an embodied Father God. David L. Paulsen, in his enlightening article, "Early Christian Belief In A Corporeal Deity," observes,

> The view that God is incorporeal,* without body or parts, has been the hallmark of Christian orthodoxy, but in the beginning it was not so...(The) ordinary Christians for at least the first three centuries of the current era commonly (and perhaps generally) believed God to be corporeal. The belief was abandoned (and then only gradually) as Neoplatonism became more and more entrenched as the dominant world view of Christian thinkers.[160]

Grace Jantzen, in ***God's World, God's Body***, agrees:

> The idea that God is not embodied has been the stock-in-trade of theological orthodoxy for so long that it comes as a surprise to find that 'FROM THE BEGINNING IT WAS NOT SO.' In the first efforts towards theological understanding in the patristic period, the Fathers of the Church were divided on the question of whether or not God was embodied. Some of them, like Tertullian...clearly thought that he was. Irenaeus is less explicit, but the idea that God has a body could easily be taken as the logical consequence of his line of reasoning.[161]

---

[159] Delbert Burkett, ***The Son of the Man in the Gospel of John*** (JSNT Supplement Series 56, 1991), 108.

[160] Paulsen, D.L., "Early Christian Belief in a Corporeal Deity," ***HTR*** 83:2 (1990), 105. See also idem, "Reply to Kim Paffenroth's Comment," ***HTR*** 86:2 (1993): 235:239; idem, "The Doctrine of Divine Embodiment: Restoration, Judeo-Christian, and Philosophical Perspectives," ***BYU Studies*** 35 (1995-96): 7-95.

[161] Jantzen, ***God's World***, 21. On Christian anthropomorphism see also Carl W. Griffin and David L. Paulsen, "Augustine and the Corporeality of God," ***HTR*** 95 (2002): 97-118; Gilles Quispel, "The Discussion of Judaic Christianity," in idem, ***Gnostic Studies*** II (Istanbul: Nederlands Historisch-Archaeologisch Institute, 1975) 146-158; idem,

Adolph Harnack, in his ***History of Dogma***, confirms that the early Christians believed in a anthropomorphic God. He says of the first century community,

> God was naturally conceived and represented as corporeal by uncultured Christians,[162] though not by these alone, as the later controversies prove...In the case of the cultured, the idea of Corporeality may be traced back to Stoic influences; in the case of the uncultured, popular ideas co-operated with the sayings of the Old Testament literally understood, and the impression of Apocalyptic images.[163]

He notes also that, "in the second century...realistic eschatological ideas no doubt continued to foster in wide circles the popular idea that God had a form and a kind of corporeal existence."[164] Harnack identifies the source of the Christian belief that God was a material being with a form to "popular ideas," the Bible, and Stoic thought. Stoicism was the Greek philosophy which rivaled Platonism. The Stoics believed that the only reality is a material reality. They postulated that God was a material being. Those "cultured" Christians obviously refer to the Christians who were influenced by Greek thought. On the other hand, so-called 'uncultured' Christians, the non-Hellenists, continued the ancient, 'popular' tradition of the anthropomorphic god of Scripture.

Celsus, a second century philosopher, wrote a critique of Christianity in AD 178 entitled ***Alethes Logos*** (True Doctrine). The work was suppressed and destroyed, but we know of it today through the quotes of Origen, the second century Christian Father. Celsus argues "at length" against what he believes to be the Christian understanding that God "is corporeal by nature and has a body like the human form."[165] Iraneus, Bishop of Lyons, writing in that same period

---

"Ezekiel 1:26," *op. cit.*; Fossum, "Jewish-Christian Christology," *op. cit.*; Alexander Colitzin, " 'The Demons Suggest an Illusion of God's Glory in a Form': Controversy Over the Divine Body and Vision of Glory in Some Late Fourth, Early Fifth Century Century Monastic Literature," ***Studia Monastica*** 44 (2002): 13-42; idem, "The Vision of God and the Form of Glory: More Reflections on the Anthropomorphite Controversy of AD 399," in John Behr, Andrew Louth and Dimitri Conomos (edd.), ***Abba: The Tradition of Orthodoxy in the West. Festschriift for Bishop Kallistos (Ware) of Diokleia*** (Crestwood, New York: St. Vladimer's Seminary Press, 2003) 273-297.

[162] Meaning those uninfluenced by Greek intellectualism.

[163] A. Harnack, ***History of Dogma*** (New York: Dover, 1961), 1: 180 n. 1

[164] Ibid., II: 225 n. 5

[165] Paulsen, "Early Christian Belief,"113.

acknowledges the same among the Christians.[166] Robert P. Casey notes that it was the influence of Greek thought which prompted the change:

> The period in which (the) revival of Platonism took place saw the beginning of Christianity, and in the second century it became apparent that Christian theology, if it were to survive, must justify itself philosophically. In doing so it had to make choices between the materialism of Stoa and the immaterialism of Plato. That it ultimately chose the latter may in part be attributed to the influence of men like Philo and Numenius...[167]

Justo L. Gonzalez, in ***Christian Thought Revisited***, also traces the influence that Greek philosophy has had on Christian doctrine. He notes that Clement of Alexandria (d. c. AD 216), writing in the second century was one of the first to bring Plato's god into the Church.

> Thus Clement of Alexandria...turned Platonism into one of his main instruments for understanding Scripture. In consequence... Clement...came to the conclusion that all Scripture concerning God must be understood in such a manner that it is compatible with what the philosophers had said about the Supreme Being.[168]

It was Origen (AD 185-253) though, who gave Clement's incorporeal deity a permant place in Christian tradition. He was a Hellenistic Christian philosopher also from Alexandria, Egypt whose polemic against the popular anthropomorphism became the hallmark of Christianity. He is the first Christian to use the word *asomatos*, meaning "incorporeal," in the orthodox Greek sense to describe God. He acknowledged that the doctrine of God's immateriality was at his time a new doctrine.[169] He also acknowledged that in the period in which he was writing (middle of third century), the issue of God's corporeality had not yet been settled in the Church. He says that, "how God Himself is to be understood-whether as corporeal, and formed according to some shape, or of a different nature from bodies" is "a point which is not clearly indicated in our teachings."[170] Origen thus

---

[166] R.P. Casey, "Clement of Alexandria And The Beginnings of Christian Platonism," ***Harvard Theological Review*** 18 (1925) 86 n.138
[167]Ibid., 45.
[168] J.L. Gonzalez, ***Christian Thought Revisited*** (Nashville.: Abingdon Press, 1989) 40.
[169] Casey, "Clement of Alexandria," 82.
[170]Paulsen, "Early Christian Belief,"109.

decides to settle the issue himself. In his *Homily III*, Origen says that, "the Jews indeed, but also some of our people, suppose that God should be understood as a man, that is adorned with human members and human appearance."[171] He attempts to correct this notion because "the philosophers despise these stories as fabulous and formed in the likeness of poetic fictions."[172] Guy Stroumsa acknowledges that, although Origen refers to these Christians who believe God to be in human form as *akeriotatoi* or "simple persons," many of these are not unsophisticated at all.[173] Melito, Bishop of Sardis in Lydia, who died probably in AD 197, was a learned and prolific writer, composing eighteen works. Origen identifies him as among the "orthodox" Christians who taught that God has a human form and body. Melito wrote a book entitled *The Discourse on the Corporeality of God.*[174] Gennadius, writing in the fifth century, corroborated Origen's claim and says Melito was responsible for a body of Christians who also believed God had a human body.[175] Robert Casey thus concludes:

> Henceforward Christian Platonism with its idea of God as an immaterial, intellectual substance, its charecteristc piety, and its fine mystism was a permanent element in Christian theology…In the century following Origen's death his teachings became the center of a storm of theological debate…Many of his views, such as the periodic conflagration of the world and the impossibility of the fleshy resurrection, were condemned, but his belief about the divine nature emerged triumphant. While the anthropomorphists fought earnestly against the banishment of their material God whose piercing gaze no act of theirs escaped, whose throne was the heavens, and upon whose glorious form their eyes would one day be permitted to rest, the Christian doctrine of God was becoming inextricably involved in a Trinitarian theory, the substance and form of which would have been impossible bur for Clement and Origen, whose immaterialist teaching it presupposed…Even in the Scholastic period, when the philosophy of Aristotle gave new directions to Christian theology, the doctrine of God did not lose the Platonic stamp first deeply impressed upon it by Clement of Alexandria." [176]

---

[171]Ibid., 110-111
[172] Ibid.
[173] Stroumsa, "Incorporeality of God," 346.
[174] Paulsen, "Early Christian Belief,"112.
[175] Ibid.
[176] Casey, "Clement of Alexandria,"100.

Clement and Origen were the first to attempt the overthrow of the popular corporeal understanding of the God of the Scripture among the Christians. But their influence was geographically as well as temporally limited. In the African Church, for instance, the majority of Christians rejected Origen and his immaterial deity. As Roland J. Teske points out, "There was no clear doctrine of the spiritual nature of God in the African Church." [177] He notes that, "until the time of Augustine there simply was not present in the Western Church a concept of the spiritual in the sense of a non-corporeal substance."[178] It was left to Agustine to once and for all jettison the anthropomorphic God of Religion from the church and nail in place the *□ell philosophorum*, the god of philosophy.

3.3. *St. Augustine and the Eclipse of God*

St. Augustine (AD 354-430), born in Thagaste in North Africa, is one of the pivotal Fathers of the Church. His many works have influenced Christian thought probably more than any other person. At the time he was writing, the popular belief among Christians, particularly the Christians of North Africa, was that God was anthropomorphic. In fact, he says this is the reason it took him so long to accept Christianity. In his *Confessions*, St. Augustine shares how he was turned off in his youth because the Christians he knew, including his African mother Monica, believed that God was in the form of a man. As a result, he aligned himself with another group he would later come to anathematize: the Manichean sect. Because they too fought the Christian majority's belief in anthropomorphism, he succumbed to their logic. He says,

> For...that which really is I knew not; and was, as it were through sharpness of wit, persuaded to assent to foolish deceivers (Manichees), when they would ask me:...'is God bounded by a bodily shape, and has hairs and nails?'...At which, I in my ignorance, was much troubled...because as yet...I knew not God to a Spirit, not one who hath parts extended in length and breadth, or whose being was bulk...And what might that should be in us by which we were

---

[177] Roland J. Teske, S.J., "The Aim of Augustine's Proof that God truly Is," ***International Philosophical Quarterly*** 26 (1986): 55.
[178] Teske, "Aim of Augustine's Proof," 55.

> like God, and might be rightly said to be after the image of God, I was altogether ignorant.[179]

He continues:

> I despaired of finding the truth...in Thy Church, O Lord...and it seemed to me very unseemly to believe Thee to have the shape of human flesh, and to be bounded by the bodily lineaments of our members. For when my mind endeavored to recur to the Catholic faith, I was driven back...And I seemed to myself more reverential, if I believed God...Thee, my God...[to be} unbounded...than if..I should imagine Thee bounded by the form of a human body...[180]

The Catholic faith of North Africa, as late as the fourth century, taught that God was a man, at least in form. St. Augustine's mother Monica was one of those believers. And for this reason he rejected the Christian faith. His career as a teacher of rhetoric, however, took him later on in life to Milan, Italy. While there, he met Bishop Ambrose who introduced him to the Latin translations of the writings of Plato and the "purely spiritual" concept of God. Paulsen says:

> Augustine accepted this view of God and, with his long-standing stumbling block to Christian doctrine removed, he was converted to the faith in 386 and the following year, at age thirty-two, was finally baptized.[181]

After discovering this new Neoplatonic interpretation of the faith, he rejoiced:

> But when I understood withal that 'man, created by Thee, after Thine own image,' was not understood by Thy spiritual sons...as though they believed and conceived of Thee as bounded by human shape...with joy I blushed at having SO MANY YEARS barked not against the Catholic faith, but against the fictions of carnal imaginations...For Thou, Most High...hast not limbs some larger, some smaller, but art wholly every where and no where in space, art not of such corporeal shape...Thy Catholic Church...I NOW DISCOVERED...not

---

[179] ***The Confessions of St. Augustine***, trans. Edward B. Pusey (New York: Random House, 1949) 44.
[180] Ibid., 89
[181] "Early Christian Belief," 115

> to teach that for which I had grievously censured her. So I was confounded, and converted; and I joyed.[182]

It is clear that, up even until the time of Augustine, there were two strands of Christianity, exclusive of each other. One in Africa, where it spread from the Apostles first, and one in Europe, which was interpreted through the writings of the Greek philosophers. The God of the African strand of Christianity was the God of Religion: a God in human form. The God of the European strand of Christianity was the God of Philosophy: an abstract, immaterial being. Augustine, though he was an African himself, rejected the faith and the God of his native land, and embraced the God of a foreign land.

3.4 *The Uproar in Egypt*

The issue of God's corporeality came to an explosive head in Egypt in AD 399. Even at that late date, the indigenous Egyptian Christians believed God the Father to have, from the beginning, manifested Himself in human form. The anthropomorphic theophanies of the Bible were interpreted literally by the Egyptian majority. Owen Chadwick refers to the "literalist Egyptian Majority."[183] Because of Origen and Augustine, there was a small group of "Origenist" in the city of Nitria who believed in the God of the Philosophers. But Elizabeth Clark, in ***The Origenist Controversy***, notes that "the sources more representative of the indigenous Egyptian tradition...reveal the distrust felt by the native Egyptian clientele of Origen's views."[184] George Florvosky, in his ***Aspects of Church History***, notes also that the literalists, or so-called "Anthropomorphites," were in the majority in Egypt and thus represented the Egyptian "Orthodox Christian Doctrine."[185] It is not the case that this Egyptian majority was "simple" and "ignorant" and for this reason believed as they did, as Florvosky pointed out:

> Nor should the 'literalism' of the alleged 'Anthropomorphites' be attributed to their 'ignorance' and 'simplicity'...The 'Anthropomorphites' could quote in their support an old and

---

[182] ***Confessions***, 99-100.

[183] G. Florvosky, ***Aspects of Church History*** (Belmont, Massachusetts: Norland Publishing, 1975) 90.

[184] E. Clark, ***The Origenist Controversy*** (New Jersey: Princeton University Press), 57. See also idem, "New Perspectives on the Origenist Controversy: Human Embodiment and Ascetic Strategies," ***Church History*** (1990): 145-62.

[185] Florvosky, ***Aspects of Church History***, 90-91.See also Colitzin, "The Demons Suggest an Illusion," and idem, "The Vision of God and the Form of Glory."

> venerable tradition, which could not be summarily discarded by the charge of 'ignorance'...The 'Anthropomorphite' monks stood in a venerable tradition. The conflict in the Desert was not just a clash between the 'ignorant' and the 'learned.' It was a conflict between two traditions: Evangelical realism and 'Originistic' symbolism...[186]

Theophilus was at that time the Bishop of Alexandria. In the festal letter, which is written and read aloud each Easter Day by the Bishop of Alexandria, Theophilus remarked that "God ought to be regarded as incorporeal, and alien to human form."[187] He stated that Man was not today in the Imago Dei or Image of God. This caused the monks of Scete, Egypt to riot. Leaving their monastic retreat, the monks stormed to Alexandria in droves and even threatened to kill Theophilus.[188] At the time Theophilus had his letter read, not only were the monks angered, but three of the four priests of the Churches at Scete were angered by his heretical pronouncement. Bishop Epiphanius of Slamis was of the same view of the monks regarding God.[189]

One of the monks was a wise and pious man by the name of Apa Aphou of Pemdje. He was a monastic that was early in his career a part of a community which contained members who were themselves taught by "disciples of the Apostles."[190] Thus, he presumably had access to the teachings of the Apostles themselves. As it was Aphou's custom to journey from his monastery retreat to the town of Pemdje once a year to hear the paschal letter read aloud to the congregation, he was then present when Bishop Theophilus's inflammatory letter was read. Upon hearing it, he was greatly disturbed and was ordered by the Lord to "go to Alexandria to set this aright."[191]

Thus, Aphou traveled and waited three days outside the Bishop's gate. When he was finally permitted entrance, he was given an audience with the Bishop at which point, after having the Bishop read his letter to him, Aphou challenged his statement that man was not in the image of God. I will quote the discussion, as it is reported in a Coptic text and repeated by Florvosky.

---

[186] Ibid., 91, 96.
[187] Ibid., 117.
[188] Clark, ***Origenist Controversy***, 45.
[189] Ibid.
[190]Florvosky, ***Aspects of Church History***, 109.
[191] Ibid., 113.

The Archbishop said: "How could you say of an Ethiopian that he is in the image of God, or of a leper, or of a cripple, or of a blind man?"

Blessed Aphou replied: "If you proclaim that in such fashion, you will be denying that which He said, namely, 'Let us make man in our likeness and in our image'...

The Archbishop replied: "Far be it! But I believe that Adam alone was created in His likeness and image, but that his children whom he begot after him do not resemble him." Apa Aphou replied, saying: "Moreover, after God had established the covenant with Noah following the flood, He said to him: 'whoever sheds human blood, his own will be shed in return, for man had been created in the image of God'(Gen. 9:6)."

The Archbishop said: "I hesitate to say of an ailing man ...that he bears the image of God, Who is impassable and self-sufficient, while (the former) squat outside and perform his necessities...How could you think of him (as being one) with God, the true light whom nothing can surpass?"

Aphou said to him: "...If we think, for example, of a king who will give orders and a likeness will be painted, and all will proclaim that it is the image of the king, but at the same time all know that it is wood and colors, for it does not raise it's nose (head), like man, nor its ears are those of the king's countenance, nor does it speak like the king. And all these weaknesses which belong to it nobody remembers out of respect for their king's judgment, because he has proclaimed: 'it is my image.' On the contrary, if anyone dare deny it...on the plea that it is not the king's image, he will be executed...for having slighted it. Furthermore, the authorities are mustered concerning it and give praise to bits of wood and to colors, out of respect to the king. Now if such things happen to an image which has no spirit, neither does it stir, being...delusive...how much more, then, (to) man, in whom ABIDES THE SPIRIT OF GOD, and who is active and honored above all animals which are upon the earth; but because of the diversity of elements and colors...and of weaknesses which in us are...for us on account of our salvation; for it is not possible for any of these latter to slight the glory which God has given us, according to Paul: "As for man, it is not proper that he cover his head (because he is the image and glory of God)'(I Cor. 11:7)."

When he heard these words, the blessed Archbishop arose and bent his head saying: "This is fitting that instruction come from those who search in solitude, for, as the reasoning of our hearts are mixed in us, to the point that we err completely in ignorance."

And immediately he wrote within all the country, retracting the phrase, saying: "It is erroneous and proceeds from my lack of intelligence in this respect."(End.)[192]

After writing to every region repudiating his former statement, he visited the monks and said to them, "In seeing you, I behold the face of God."[193] The monks required that he repudiate and burn the writings of Origen, which the repenting Bishop is reputed to have done. Three years later, Theophilus appointed Aphou to Bishop of Pemdje.

Thus, all the way into nearly the fifth century, the Africans still held on to the orthodox Christian position that God manifested Himself in human form as is taught in the Scriptures of Moses, Ex. 15:3 "The Lord is a Man of War."

The god that is worshipped in the Synagogues and Churches of today is not the God that was originally worshipped there. The God of the Patriarchs and Prophets has been pushed out of these holy sanctuaries, and the god of the Philosophers has replaced Him. Casey concludes,

It is easy to see what Platonism brought into the partnership (religion and philosophy), for it supplied Christianity with an immaterialist philosophy...Henceforward Christian Platonism with its idea of God as an immaterial, intellectual substance...was a permanent element in Christian theology.[194]

Maurice Wiles notes also:

the image of God with which the (Church) Fathers worked was not drawn exclusively, or even primarily, from Scripture. Its primary source was the Graeco-Roman world to which they belonged and to which they were concerned to speak...God,

---

192 Ibid., 114-116.
193 Ibid., 126.
194 Casey, "Clement of Alexandria," 101

declares the first article of the Church of England (Thirty-nine Articles) is 'without body, parts or passions.' It is not the sort of description of God which arises naturally or spontaneously from the Bible taken by itself. It comes straight from this Platonic tradition which the Fathers shared with the most thoughtful of their pagan contemporaries.[195]

[195] ***The Christian Fathers*** (London: Hodder and Stoughton, 1966) 13, 17.

Chapter IV:

Allah the Original Man: God in the Qur'ān and Sunnah

4. *Introductory Summary*

Islam is considered the religion *par excellence* of divine transcendence.* God, according to Muslim theologians, is absolutely 'Other.' He is immaterial, possesses no body or form, and invisible. This god, however, does not derive from the Qur'ān or Sunna, but derives from later Greek-inspired interpretations of the Qur'ān and Sunna. Like the God of the Bible, the God of the Qur'ān and Sunna is transcendently anthropomorphic: he has a human form, but one unlike that of man's in that it is dangerously luminous and eternal. The Qur'ān specifically describes God as a delimited being (*shay'*, e.g. 6:19) with human physical characteristics (e.g. a face, two hands, eyes, leg, side, a soul, a spirit). The Sunna specifically refers to God as a person with a body (*shakhṣ*) and according to early 'orthodox' Sunni tradition God appeared to Muḥammad in the form of a man (*shābb*). The early Muslims understood these passages to be literal descriptions of God. It was non-Sunni Muslim groups such as the Jahmiyya and Mu'tazila, influenced by Greek philosophy, who first rejected the anthropomorphism of the God of the Qur'ān and Sunna. Later, Islam's own 'philosophers' would work to bring the God of Islam in line with the god of Greek philosophy.

4.1. *Divine Transcendence and the Religion of Islam*

Islam is often viewed as the religion *par excellence* of divine transcendence.[196] God is *khilāf al-'ālam*, "the absolute divergence from

[196] See e.g. William A. Graham, "Transcendence in Islam," in Edwin Dowdy (ed.), ***Ways of Transcendence; Insights From Major Religions and Modern Thought*** (Bedford Park, South Australia: Australian Association 1982) 7-23. See also W.M. Watt's comments ("Some Muslim Discussions of Anthropomorphism," in idem, ***Early Islam: Collected articles*** [Edinburgh: Edinburgh University Press, 1990] 87): "We in the West tend to speak of Islam as stressing the transcendence of God, but it has to be remembered that, while for the West the chief aspect of transcendence is probably God's might and majesty, for Islam it is rather His otherness from His creatures. This aspect is

the world," and this characteristically Islamic doctrine of *mukhālafa*, "(divine) otherness," precludes the attribution to God of anything like corporeality* and anthropomorphism.[197] But such a model of divine transcendence which precludes anthropomorphism is Hellenistic, as we saw above, not Semitic*. The Semitic, and the ancient Near Eastern model in general, embraced both divine 'otherness' and anthropomorphism: the gods were 'transcendently anthropomorphic,' to use Ronald Hendel's term.[198] That is to say, the gods possessed a form of human shape but of divine substance and quality. [199]

Ancient Near Eastern/Semitic 'transcendent anthropomorphism'* stands in stark contrast to popular Islamic notions of transcendence, which precludes corporeality* and anthropomorphism. This disparity becomes more acute when one considers the insistence, by Islamic tradition and Western scholarship, that the deity is the same in the three monotheistic traditions: "The monotheists not only worship one God; he is the same god for all. Whether called Yahweh or Elohim, God the Father or Allah, it is the selfsame deity who created the world out of nothing."[200] This insistence is of course qur'ānic.[201] But Yahweh, Elohim, and God the Father are a transcendent man. What about Allah? Syllogistic logic demands that Allah be a transcendent man as well.[202] Why the disparity? The answer was already provided by Fazlur Rahman:

---

present in the Old Testament…but in the Muslim outlook its relative importance is greater." See also Samuel M. Zwemer. "The Allah of Islam and the God of Jesus Christ," ***Theology Today*** 3 (1946): 64-77; H.U. Weitbrecht Stanton, ***The Teaching of the Qur'an*** (London: Central Board of Missions and Society for Promoting Christian Knowledge; New York: The Macmillian Company, 1919): 35.

[197] J. Windrow Sweetman defined the principle of *mukhālafa*, to which "the majority (of Muslims) adhered": "all that is said of God is said with a difference and it has become proverbial that nothing the mind can devise can convey anything about Allah… there can be no doubt that the rejection of the corporeality of God is essential." ***Islam and Christian Theology*** 2 vols. (London: Lutterworth Press, 1947), 1. 2:34, 36. See also Gardet, ***Encyclopedia of Islam*** (Second Edition; hereafter ***EI²***) 1:410f., s.v. "Allāh."

[198] Hendel, "Aniconism and Anthropomorphism."

[199] See above.

[200] F.E. Peters, ***The Children of Abraham: Judaism, Christianity, Islam*** Princeton and Oxford: Princeton University Press, 2004) 1. See also Sachiko Murata and William C. Chittick, ***The Vision of Islam*** (New York: Paragon House, 1994) xviii: "The Koran, the Hadith, and the whole Islamic tradition maintain that the God of the Jews, the Christians, and the Muslims is a single God."

[201] See 29:46; 42:14, 2:130-136

[202] Yahweh, Elohim and God the Father is a transcendent man
Yahweh, Elohim, God the Father and Allah are the same God
Therefore, Allah is a transcendent man

> It has been generally held that the God of Islam is uncompromisingly transcendent and that this is shown by the tremendous emphasis Islam puts on the unity of God, His majesty, awesomeness, etc. This picture, however, does not emerge from the Qur'ān, but from later theological development in Islam."[203]

This 'later theological development' included the appropriation of Hellenistic concepts in order to interpret the Qur'ān and Sunnah.*[204] Duad Rahbar correctly drew attention to the "difference between Hellenized Islamic theology…and the simple Semitic atmosphere of the world-view of the Qur'an."[205] The qur'ānic deity is indeed transcendent, but this is a Semitic transcendence: he is transcendently anthropomorphic.

4.2. *Divine Transcendence in the Qur'ān*

D.B. MacDonald, in his article on 'Allāh' in the ***Encyclopedia of Islam***, made this observation:

> The (Qur'ānic) descriptions (of God) are at first sight a strange combination of anthropomorphism and metaphysics…With only a little ingenuity in one-sidedness an absolutely anthropomorphic deity could be put together, or a practically pantheistic, or a coldly and aloofly rationalistic (deity)."[206]

This "strange combination of anthropomorphism and metaphysics" is what characterizes the transcendently anthropomorphic deities of the ancient Near East and Israel.[207] Like the Bible, the Qur'ān affirms that God is both like and unlike man. He is a being, *shay'* (6:19), which, by definition, is delimited and characterized.[208] Some of the mentioned characteristics or 'attributes' (Arabic *ṣifāt*, sing. *ṣifa*) of God indicate an anthropomorphic deity.[209] As a delimited being God possess a face

---

[203] Fazlur Rahman, "The Qur'ānic Concept of God, the Universe and Man," ***IS*** 6(1967): 1-19.
[204] See below.
[205] Daud Rahbar, "Relation of Muslim Theology to the Qur'ān," ***MW*** 51 (1961): 44-49.
[206] D.B. Macdonald, ***Encyclopedia of Islam*** (First Edition; hereafter ***EI¹***) 1:303, 306, s.v. "Allāh."
[207] See above.
[208] See below.
[209] On Islamic anthropomorphism, its sources, history and influences, see: Richard C. Martin, ***The Encyclopedia of the Qur'ān*** (Leiden: Brill, 2001)(hereafter ***EQ***), s.v. "Anthropomorphism," 1: 106ff; Daniel Gimaret, ***Dieu à l'image de l'homme: les***

(*wajh*, 55:26) with eyes (20:39; 11:37); two hands (*yadayya*, 38:75; 5:64), a leg (*sāq*, 68:42), side (*janb*, 39:56) a soul (*nafs*, 3:28, 5:116) and a spirit (*rūḥ*, 66:12); He is in the heavens (67:16) established (*istawā*) on his throne (7:54). From there he will "come" to earth (2:210). The qur'anic God also has some human behaviors: he gets angry (1:7, 2:61, 3:112 and 162, 4:93, etc.); he is cunning (3:54, 8:30, 10:21, 13:42, etc.); he pokes fun (2:15).

Rahbar called attention to the fact that God's 'Most Beautiful Names,' *al-Asmā' al-Ḥusna*, can be divided into "anthropomorphic" or "dispositional" names, i.e. names in which God is disposed towards and likened to man, and "metaphysical" or non-dispositional names - names which seem inappropriate as designations for man.[210] Despite

anthropomorphismes de la sunna et leur interprétation par les théologiens (Paris: Patrimoines, 1997). On Islamic anthropomorphism, its sources, history and influences, see also; Gerhard Böwering, ***EQ***, s.v. "God and His Attributes," 2:316-331; Josef van Ess, ***Theologie und Gesellschaft im 2. und 3. Jahrhundert Hidschra*** (hereafter ***TG***), 6 vols. (Berlin: Walter de Gruyter, 1992), particularly vol. 4. ; idem, "Ta<u>sh</u>bīh wa-Tanzīh," ***EI²*** 10: 341-344; idem. "The Youthful God: Anthropomorphism in Early Islam," The University Lecture in Religion at Arizona State University, March 3, 1988 (Tempe: Arizona State University, 1988); Claude Gilliot, "Muqātil, Grand Exégete, Traditionniste Et Théologien Maudit," ***Journal Asiatique*** 179 (1991): 39-84; *EI, s.v.* "Ta<u>sh</u>bīh," by R. Strothmann, 4:685f; Michel Allard, ***Le probl"eme des attributs divins dans la doctrine d'al-As'ar¸i et de ses premiers grands disciples***. (Beyrouth, Impr. catholique; 1965); Helmut Ritter, ***Das Meer Der Seele*** (Leiden: E. J. Brill, 1955), 445-503 (=Helmut Ritter, ***The Ocean of the Soul: Man, the World and God in the Stories of Farīd al-Dīn 'Aṭṭār***, trns and ed. John O'Kane and Bernd Radtke (Leiden, Boston: Brill, 2003), 448-519; Kees Wagtendonk, "Images in Islam: Discussion of a Paradox" in ***Effigies Dei***, ed. Dirk van Der Plas (Leiden: E.J. Brill, 1987) 112-129; J.M.S. Baljon, "Qur'anic Anthropomorphisms," ***Islamic Studies*** 27 (1988): 119-127;W. Montgomery Watt, "Some Muslim Discussions of Anthropomorphism" and "Created in His Image: A Study in Islamic Theology," in his ***Early Islam*** (Edinburgh: Edinburgh University Press, 1990), 86-93, 94-100; Georges C. Anawati, "Attributes of God: Islamic Concepts" in ***Encyclopedia of Religion*** 1:513-519; A. Al-Azmeh, "Orthodoxy and Hanbalite Fideism." ***Arabica*** 35 (1988): 253-266; Robert M. Haddad, "Iconoclasts and *Mu'tazila*: The Politics of Anthropomorphism." ***The Greek Orthodox Theological Review*** 27 (Summer – Fall 1982): 287-305; W. Madelung, "The Controversy Concerning the Creation of the Koran." in idem, ***Religious Schools and Sects in Medieval Islam***. London: Variorum Reprints, 1985. V; Binyamin Abrahamov, ***Anthropomorphism and Interpretation of the Qur'ān in the Theology of Al-Qasīm Ibn Ibrahim*** (Leiden: E. J. Brill, 1996); idem, ***Al-Kāsim b. Ibrāhīm on the Proof of God's Existence*** (Leiden: E.J. Brill, 1990), 25ff; J. Windrow Sweetman, ***Islam and Christian Theology*** 2 vols. (London: Lutterworth Press, 1947), 1.2:27-47; Merlin Swartz in ***A Medieval Critique of Anthropomorphism: Ibn al-Jawzī's* Kitāb Akhbār aṣ-Ṣifāt, *a Citical Edition of the Arabic Text with Translation, Introduction and Notes*** (Leiden: Brill, 2002); Wesley Williams, "Aspects of the Creed of Ahmad Ibn Hanbal: A Study of Anthropomorphism is Early Islamic Discourse," ***International Journal of Middle East Studies*** 34 (2002): 441-463.

[210] See below.

the prominence given the latter by Muslim theologians, these amount to only a half dozen of the ninety-nine names; *Al-Quddūs*, the Holy; *Al-Khāliq*, the Creator; *Al-Laṭif*, the Subtle; *Al-Badī*, the Incomparable; *Al-Ghānī*, the Independent; *Al-Nūr*, the Light. These are completely dwarfed, however, by Names that could just as easily, and in some cases more easily, be applied to man. God, like man, is *Al-Mu'min*, the Faithful; *As-Sāmi*, the Hearer; *Al-Baṣir*, the Seer; *Al-Wadūd*, the Loving; *Al-Hayy*, the Living; *Al-Wājid*, the Finder; *Al-Ẓāhir*, The Evident; *Al-Barr*, the Righteous; *Al-Ṣabūr*, the Patient etc. The rest of the Names can just as easily be descriptions of man.

The Qur'ān in fact gives some of these very names to men. In surah 2:225, Allah is called *Al-Hayy* (the Living). In Sura 30:19, this same attribute is applied to men: "*He brings out the living (hayy) from the dead, and brings the dead from the living.*" Sura 4:58 says "*Allah is Sami (the Hearing) and Basir (the Seeing).*" Likewise, in Sura 76:2, "*Verily, We have created man from drops of mixed semen…and made him sami (hearing) and basir (seeing).*" In 22:65, Allah is called *ar-Ra'uf* (*the One Full of Kindness*) and *ar-Rahim* (the Most Merciful). In 9:128, we read: "*Verily, there has come to you a Messenger from amongst yourselves…for the believers, he is ra'uf, rahim.*" The difference between the names as applied to God versus as applied to man is indicated by the definite article (*al*). While man can be merciful (*rahim*), God is 'most merciful' (*al-Rahim*). His are the attributes of perfection (*Ṣifāt al-Kamāl*), whereas man's comprise imperfections.[211] In this regard, the qur'ānic Allah is like the biblical Yahweh/Elohim.

4.2.1. *None Like Him*

The pivotal verse wherein God's otherness is most forcefully and (it would seem) clearly articulated is *Al-Shūrā* 42:11: *Laysa kamithlihi shay'*, "There is none like Him." This verse is said to reject "all anthropomorphism." [212] However, a review of the interpretive history of this verse reveals that in fact it was first employed by those who affirmed God's anthropomorphism, not by those who denied it.[213] It was still in the service of the 'anthropomorphists' in Ibn al-Jawzī's time

---

[211] See below.

[212] Abdoldjavad Falaturi, "How Can a Muslim Experience God, Given Islam's Radical Monotheism," in ***We Believe In One God: The Experience of God in Christianity and Islam*** ed. Annemarie Schimmel and Abdoldjavad Falaturi (New York: Seabury Press), 78.

[213] Van Ess, ***TG*** 4:378; Gilliot, "Muqatīl," 57. According to Ahmad b. Hanbal, in his ***Ar-Radd***, 96, Jahm b. Safwan (d. 746) was the first to use this verse in an anti-anthropomorphist manner.

(c. 1190).[214] This seems quite amazing. What is it about *Laysa kamithlihi shay'* that lent itself to the exegetical needs of those who affirmed for God a human form?

The answer to this riddle lies in the grammar of the verse, which could be read in two ways. The most obvious reading is to take the *ka* (***ka**mithlihi*) as a non-expletive, thus: "There is nothing like (*ka*) His likeness (*mithlihi*)." As Ibn al-Jawzī noted, "taken literally (*ẓāhir*) these words indicate that God has a *mithl*, likeness, which is like nothing and like which there is nothing." [215] Ibn al-Jawzī cites this verse as one of the proof-texts relied upon by those who affirmed a human form for God. They took the *mithl*, likeness, here anthropomorphically. But how so? The root *m-th-l* means "to be like, compare," *mithl* "similar, image," *tamthīl* "assimilation, likening." The *mithl* of 42:11 was understood in these circles as a reference to God's form, *ṣūra*, which term is a synonym of *mithāl*.[216] His *mithl*, 'likeness,' Ibn al-'Arabi informs us, is Adam, the Perfect Man (*al-Insān al-Kāmil*).[217] Adam was made "according to the *ṣūra/mithāl* (form/image) of God" according to a *ṣaḥīḥ** prophetic tradition.[218] God has an *aḥsan ṣūra*, "most beautiful form,'[219] which was exegetically associated with Adam's *aḥsan taqwīm*, "most beautiful stature" (95:4).[220] God's and Adam's forms are therefore alike. *Surat al-Shūrā* 42:11 is thus read as, "There is nothing like His Likeness (Adam)."

Syntactically, the comparative particle *ka* could also be read as a syndetic relative cause (*ṣila*) added for emphasis, in which case the reading would be something like, "There (really) is nothing like Him," or simply as an expletive and read "There is nothing like Him." Such a reading, however, does not preclude anthropomorphism, for in the qur'ānic context a denial of 'likeness' is not necessarily a denial of anthropomorphism. "And the blind and the seeing are not alike (*lā yastawī* 35:19)." The verbal root used here, *s-w-y*, denotes "equality, sameness, to be equivalent." The man who can see (presumably the truth of revelation) is contrasted with the man who cannot. It is certainly not to be inferred that one of the men is embodied while the other is not. The difference, that which constitutes their "unlikeness" or "otherness," lies elsewhere. Likewise, 33:32: "O wives of the

---

[214] ***Kitāb Akhbār al-Ṣifāt***, ed. and trns. Merlin Swartz in ***A Medieval Critique of Anthropomorphism***, 29 (Arabic), 148 (English).
[215] Ibid.
[216] Lane, ***Arabic Lexicon***, s.v. ṣūra.
[217] On Ibn al-'Arabī's '*al-Insān al-Kāmil*' see John T. Little, "*Al-Insān Al-Kāmil*: The Perfect Man According to Ibn al-'Arabī," ***Muslim World*** 77 (1987): 43-54.
[218] Bukhārī, ***Ṣaḥīḥ***, *isti'dhān*, 1. and below.
[219] See below.
[220] See below.

Prophet, you are not like (*ka*) any other women." Whether or not the difference lies in the other women's lower order of merit, as Ignaz Goldziher thought, the issue of corporeality/incorporeality is certainly not raised here.[221]

A denial of *tamthīl* (or *tashbīh, siwan, ka, kufu'*) "likeness" to God is therefore not *de jure* a denial of anthropomorphism, God in the form of a man. God could have a human form but still be unlike man. The same expression ('there is none like him') was used for anthropomorphic deities prior to the qur'ānic revelation. It was found already in ancient Egyptian temple inscriptions of the Ptolemaic period.[222] In this context, it meant neither that nothing was similar to God in any way nor did it presuppose monotheism. It meant simply that there is no other god like that god. As Josef van Ess observed, "The statement (*Al-Shūrā* 42:11) did not decide the question whether dissimilarity between God and man was absolute or relative...Why should not the intention of the Quranic verse not be satisfied when God is merely considered to be different, perhaps by his dimensions, or by the matter He is composed of, or by the consistency of the matter?"[223] Van Ess is not being rhetorical here. Indeed, Islam's most notorious advocates of an anthropomorphic Allah, Muqatīl b. Sulaymān (d. 767) and Dāwūd al-Jawāribī, who affirmed for God a flesh and blood body, also affirmed that "Nothing is like Him nor is He like anything else."[224] How is He different? "*bi-qudra*," ("in power") said Muqatīl.[225] The anthropomorphic God differs from man in His power. Or, as explained by the Nābita, an early orthodox Sunni group that affirmed for God a human form[226]: *huwa shay' lā ka-al-ashyā' min jihat al-qidam* ("He is a being unlike beings in respect of sempiternity (eternity backwards)."[227] Early Muslim readers of the Qur'ān thus saw no problem harmonizing their belief in an anthropomorphic God with the qur'ānic demand that there is none like Him. They coined the early

---

[221] Ignaz Goldziher, ***Introduction to Islamic Theology and Law*** trans. by Andras and Ruth Hamori (New Jersey: Princeton University Press, 1981) 93.

[222] Ederhard Otto, ***Gott und Mensch nach den agyptischen Tempelinschriften der griechich-romischen Zeit*** (Heidelberg, 1964) 11ff.

[223] Van Ess, "The Youthful God," 3.

[224] Al-Ash'arī, ***Maqālāt al-Islāmiyyīn***, ed. Helmut Ritter (Istanbul, 1929-33), 209.

[225] Muqatīl b. Sulaymān, ***Tafsīr***, 4 vols. Ed. Mahmud Sahata (Cairo: al-Hay'a, 1980-88), 3:465.

[226] See Wadad Al-Qadi, "The Earliest 'Nabita' and the Paradigmatic 'Nawabit'," ***Studia Islamica*** LXXVIII, 27-61; I. Alon, "Farabi's Funny Flora: al-Nawabit as 'Opposition'," ***Journal of the Royal Asiatic Society*** (1988), pp. 222ff.

[227] Wilferd Madelung and Paul Walker, ***An Ismaili Heresiography: The "Bāb al-Shayṭān" from Abū Tammām's* Kitāb al-shajara** (Leiden: Brill, 1998), 63 (Arabic).

formula, *jism lā ka 'l-ajsām*, God has "a body unlike bodies."[228] Muqatil b. Sulayman said:

> God is a body in the form of a man, with flesh, blood, hair and bones. He has limbs and members, including a hand, a foot, a head, and eyes, and He is solid. Nonetheless, He does not resemble anything else, nor does anything resemble Him.[229]

Muhammad b. Sa'dun, better known as Abu Amir al-Qurahi (d. 524/1130), famous Andalusian theologian, said also:

> The heretics (who deny God's anthropomorphism) cite in evidence the Qur'an verse 'Nothing is like Him,' but the meaning of this verse is only that nothing compared to God in His divinity. In form, however, God is like you and me.[230]

To fully understand this reading and use of surat *al-Shūrā* 42:11, one has to take proper notice of some early Muslim discussions of *tashbīh*, which is usually translated (often incorrectly) as "anthropomorphism." The verbal root *sh-b-h* means literally "to liken (s.o. or s.t. to s.o/t. else)," thus *shibh*="similar to," *shabah*="likeness, resemblance," and *tashbīh*= "assimilation/making similar." This term is not used in the Qur'ān except once, in reference to the death of Jesus (4:157). Now, Muslim theologians of all eras and persuasions were unanimous in regarding *tashbīh*, that is to say, "likening God to creation," as condemnable. But *tashbīh* is not synonymous with anthropomorphism; some of Islam's most explicit anthropomorphists have been as adamant against *tashbīh*, 'likening' God, as the "transcendentalists" (*munazzihūn*) who absolutely rejected anthropomorphism.[231]

At the heart of this semantic issue is the nature and degree of the "likeness," *shabah*, affirmed or denied of God: absolute likeness or only relative likeness. Thus, Taqī al-Dīn b. Taymiyya (d. 728/1328) argued that the term *tashbīh* can denote a proper degree of likeness between Creator and created (i.e. relative likeness), and it can also denote an improper degree of similarity (absolute likeness/identity) whose

---

[228] Ibn Khaldun, ***The Muqaddimah***, 3 vols., trans. by Franz Rosenthal (New York: Pantheon Books, 1958), 3:45ff.; Wolfson, ***Philosophy of the Kalam*** 5ff.

[229] Al-Ash'ari, ***Maqalat al-Islamiyyin***, 152f. On Muqatil cf. below.

[230] Cited by Goldziher, ***Introduction***, 93.

[231] See below.

disallowance is mandatory.[232] That is to say, while *tashbīh* in the sense of positing an exact likeness/identity between Creator and creation is error, *tashbīh* in the sense of acknowledging a relative and limited likeness between Creator and creature, man in particular, is appropriate. This nuance is most clearly articulated by the Ḥanafī *qāḍī* (judge) ʿAlī b. ʿAlī b. Abī al-ʿIzz (d. 792/1390) in his ***Sharh al-ʿaqīda al-Ṭaḥāwīya***. Ibn Abī al ʿIzz begins by noting that the term *tashbīh* had become with the people "rather vague (*lafẓ mujmal*)."[233] He too suggests that there is an improper *tashbīh*, prohibited by the Qurʾān, wherein an *identity* is posited between Creator and created (i.e. God and man are *identical* in their attributes), and there is a proper *tashbīh* wherein only a *general* or *limited* correspondence is affirmed (i.e. the attributes of God and man are similar in *some* respects, while they *differ* in others). Whoever denies the latter (*viz.* general or limited likeness) is as guilty as he who affirms the former (*viz.* identity): "It is clear…that the Creator and the created are similar in some respects and differ in others (*ittifāquhumā min wajhi wa ikhtilāfuhumā min wajh*). And whoever denies what is common between them is a negator and is surely mistaken. On the other hand, whoever makes them homogeneous (*mutamāthilayni*) is a *mushabbih* (likener) and is equally mistaken. And Allah knows best. That is because, even though they are called by the same name, they are not *identical* (*mā ittafaqā fīhi*)."[234]

Ibn Abī al ʿIzz demonstrates this correspondence between God and man by citing qurʾānic verses wherein man is called by the names of God (e.g. 30:19, *ḥayy*; 51:28, *ʿalīm*, ect.). He argues that these are not mere homonyms, such as the Arabic word *mushtarī* (which means both buyer and the planet Jupiter), similar in name only; the attributes of God and man share a common element denoted by the *Ṣifa* or Attribute.[235] They differ in that God's are attributes of perfection (*Ṣifāt al-Kamāl*), whereas man's comprise imperfections.[236] Harry Wolfson argued that the early Muslims applied the legal principle of analogy (*qiyas*) to this theological argument, allowing partial similarity between man and God while rejecting a complete or total identity.

---

[232] Ibn Taymiyya ***Darʾ taʿāruḍ al-ʿaql wa al-naql***, 10 vols. ed. Muḥammad Rashād Sālim (Riyāḍ, 1979), 1:115f, 248f. See also Sherman Jackson's discussion, "Ibn Taymiyyah on Trial in Damascus," ***JSS*** 39 (1994): 41-84, esp. 51ff.

[233] Ibn Abī al ʿIzz, ***Sharh al-ʿaqīda al-Ṭaḥāwīya*** 2 vols. Ed. ʿAbd Allāh b. ʿAbd al-Muḥsin (Beirut, 1408/1987), 1:57 (=***Commentary on the Creed of aṭ-Ṭaḥāwī by Ibn Abī al-ʿIzz***, trns. Muhammad ʿAbdul-Haqq Ansari [Riyadh, Saudi Arabia, 2000], 23).

[234] Ibn Abī al ʿIzz, ***Sharh***, 1:62 (=***Commentary***, 27).

[235] Ibn Abī al ʿIzz, ***Sharh***, 1:63 (=***Commentary***, 28).

[236] Ibn Abī al ʿIzz, ***Sharh***, 1:93ff (=***Commentary***, 44ff).

> The explanation that naturally suggested itself to them (the early Muslims) was that the likeness which is implied in the anthropomorphic verses in the Koran is not to be taken to mean a complete likeness in every respect but that the likeness which is explicitly prohibited in the Koran (42:11) is to be taken to mean a complete likeness in every respect…in their attribution to God these terms are only in some respect like the same terms when attributed to men; in all other respects there is no likeness between them. It is noted, however, that they do not try to explain in what respect they are unlike (*sic*). They are quite satisfied with the simple assertion that the likeness implied is not a likeness in every respect.[237]

Understanding *Al-Shūrā* 42:11 to prohibit only absolute likeness/identity, but allow for relative likeness between Creator and creature, allowed Muslims to both disavow *tamthīl/tashbīh* and affirm a human form for God.

Maimonidees, in his ***Moreh Nebukim*** (ca. 1190), makes reference to "people," presumably Muslims according to Harry A. Wolfson[238] who "came to believe that God has the form (*ṣūrah*) of man, that is to say, man's figure and shape…However, He is, in their opinion, the greatest and most splendid (of bodies) and also His matter is not flesh and blood."[239] We can in fact identify patricians of such a tradition. One hails from 10th century Khurasan, Muḥammad b. Isḥāq b. Khuzayma (d. 924), the most prominent Shāfiʿī in Nishapur at the time. Born in Nīshāpur, Ibn Khuzayma would later be described as the "chief of the ḥadīth scholars (*ra's al-muḥaddithīn*)."[240] Many eminent scholars (*fuḥūl al-ʿulamāʾ*) heard from him, including al-Bukhārī, "the Commander of the Faithful in ḥadīth." A Shāfi'ite *faqīh* (jurisprudent), he was *salafī al-ʿaqīda*, that is to say he understood the qur'ānic and prophetic statements about God according to their apparent meaning, without metaphorical interpretation of the ambiguous verses (*ẓāhirihā bi-dūn ta' wīl li-mutashābihihā*) and without alteration of their apparent meaning (*lā taḥrīf li-ẓāhirihā*)[241] Ibn Khuzayma's most important work is his ***Kitāb al-tawḥīd wa-ithbāt ṣifāt al-Rabb***, a collection of ḥadīth reports touching on the various Attributes of God. According to

---

237 Harry A. Wolfson, ***Philosophy of the Kalam*** (Massachusetts: Harvard University Press, 1976) 14-15.

238 ***Philosophy of the Kalam***, 102-3.

239 ***Moreh***, I, I, p. 14, 11.5-II, translated by Wolfson, ***Philosophy of the Kalam***,102-103.

240 Muḥammad Khalīl Harrās, ed. of Ibn Khuzayma's ***Kitāb al-tawḥīd***, "alif".

241 Ibid., "ḥā'."

Muḥammad Khalīl Harrās, editor of this work, ***Kitāb al-tawḥīd*** enjoyed great respect among the traditionalists of his day, almost being dubbed "*Ṣaḥīḥ* Ibn Khuzayma." It even nearly surpassed the two *Ṣaḥīḥ*'s.[242] Some scholars preferred "*Ṣaḥīḥ* Ibn Khuzayma" to ***Ṣaḥīḥ Bukhārī*** and ***Ṣaḥīḥ Muslim***. In his ***Kitāb al-tawḥīd*** Ibn Khuzayma takes up the charge that the ḥadīth scholars and Sunni orthodox were "likeners (*mushabbiha*)" because they affirmed the literal meaning of the revealed attributes of God (*Ṣifāt al-Akhbār*). Discussing their affirmation that God truly has a face (*wajh*), against the "ignorant Jahmiyya" who claim that God's face in the Qur'ān is really His essence (*dhāt*), Ibn Khuzayma writes:

> His face is that which He described with splendor (*jalāl*) and venerability (*ikrām*) in His statement, "The face of you Lord remains, possessor of Splendor, Venerability." (God) denied that it perishes (*nafy ʿanhu al-halāk*) when His creatures perish. Our Lord is exalted above anything from His essential attributes (*min ṣifāt dhātihi*) perishing…God has affirmed for Himself a Splendid and Venerable face, which He declares is eternal and non-perishable. We and all scholars of our *madhhab* (school of thought) from the Hijaz, the Tihama, Yemen, Iraq, Syria, and Egypt affirm for God (the) face, which He has affirmed for Himself. We profess it with our tongues and believe it in our hearts, without likening (*qhayr an nashabbiha*) His face to one from His creatures. May our Lord be exalted above our likening Him to His creatures…Listen now, O you who understand what we mentioned regarding the manner of speaking common among the Arabs (*jins al-lugha al-sāʾira bayn al-ʿarab*): Do you apply the name *mushabbiha* to the ḥadīth scholars and followers of the Sunna? We and all our scholars in all our lands say that the one we worship has a face…And we say that the face of our Loud (radiates) a brilliant, radiant light (*al-nūr wa al-ḍiyāʾ wa-bahāʾ*) which, if His veil is removed the glory of His face will scorch everything that sees it. His eyes are veiled from the people of this world who will never see Him during this life...The face of our Lord is eternal …
>
> Now God has decreed for human faces destruction and denied them splendor and venerability. They are not attributed the light, brilliance or splendor (*al-nūr wa al-ḍiyāʾ wa-bahāʾ*) that He described His face with. Eyes in this world

---

[242] Ibid., "ẓāʾ"

> may catch human faces without the latter scorching so much as a single hair...Human faces are rooted in time (*muḥdatha*) and created...Every human face perishes…Oh you possessors of reason (*dhawā al-ḥijan*), could it ever really occur to any one with sense and who knows Arabic and knows what *tashbīh* (means) that this (transient and dull human) face is like that (splendidly brilliant face of God)?[243]

Ibn Khuzayma here adamantly argues for God's possession of a true face, but one dangerously radiant and non-perishable, in contrast to man's perishable and dull face: transcendent anthropomorphism! He asks, in short, 'Can one who acknowledges these differences be charged with *tashbīh*?' Certainly not according to the language of the Arabs! We have again both the affirmation of anthropomorphism and the disavowal of *tashbīh*. We have, in short, transcendent anthropomorphism.

4.3. *The Qur'ān's Anthropomorphic Deity*

The Qur'ān therefore fails to substantiate the existence of a wholly transcendent "other." On the contrary, the Qur'ān describes Allah with vivid anthropomorphism. Against the philosophic notion of the immaterial "no-thing" or non-being, Allah is specifically described as a شيء *shay'* "thing." "Say: What thing (*shay'*) is mightiest in testimony? Say: Allah. (6:19)." *Shay'* literally means "thing,"[244] but in the theological context meant "being."[245] The God of the Qur'an is a being. A *shay'* by definition is a delimited and circumscribed entity, not a formless abstraction. As Abu Said ad-Darimi (d. 895), ḥadīth scholar from Herat, points out:

> Every one without exception is in agreement concerning the term *shay'*, namely that a *shay'* cannot exist with neither limit nor attribute (*hadd wa-ṣifa*) and that there is no *shay'* which has neither limit nor attribute.[246]

---

243 Ibid., 10f, 22f.

244 "*shay'*", Hans Wehr, ***Arabic-English Dictionary*** ed. J. M. Cowan (Ithaca: Spoken Language Services, Inc., 1994), 579.

245 R.M. Frank, "The Neoplatonism of Gahm Ibn Safwan," ***Le Museon*** 78 (1965), 399.

246 Ad-Darimi, ***Radd 'ala Jahmiyya*** ed. Gosta Vitestam, ***Kitab ar-radd 'ala l-gahmiya des Abu Sa'id b. 'Uthman b. Sa'id ad-Darimi*** (Lund/Leiden, 1960), 62.

According to ad-Darimi it was Jahm b. Safwan (d. 746)[247] who introduced into Islam the uncircumscribed deity. In his ***Radd 'alā Bishr,*** ad-Darimi argues:

> the obstinate heretic (Jahm) further alleges that God has no boundary (*ḥadd*), no limit, and no term; this is the foundation on which Jahm built all his errors and from which he derived all his falsehoods and is a statement in which, so far as we know, none preceded Jahm...Allah certainly has a limit... and so has His place, for He is on His Throne above the heavens, and these are two limits. Any person who declares that Allah has a limit and that His place has a limit is more knowledgeable than the Jahmis.[248]

Allah is thus a *shay'* or being with some physical limit (though not necessarily with any metaphysical limits). This *shay'* possesses hands, feet, eyes, a face, etc. After creating Adam and calling the angels to make obeisance to him, Allah said to the defiant *Iblis*, "O Iblis, what prevented thee from submitting to him whom I created with MY TWO HANDS *(bi-yadayya)?* (38:75)." Sura 5:64 says, "And the Jews say: The hand of Allah is tied up. Their own hands are shackled and they are cursed for what they say. Nay, BOTH HIS HANDS ARE SPREAD OUT." Allah also has a face and eyes according to the Qur'an. "Every one on it (the earth) passes away-And there endures for ever THE FACE *(wajh)* OF THY LORD, the Lord of glory and honor (55:2)." In Sura 20:39 Allah says, "Put him (Moses) into a chest, then cast it into a river...there an enemy to Me and enemy to him shall take him up. And I shed on thee love from Me; and that thou mayest be brought up before MY EYES." With these eyes Allah sees, and He is thus called *Al-Basir* "The One Who Sees," (17:1) as well as *As-Sami* "One Who Hears," (2:121).

The God of the Qur'ān is not only a living "being" with a face, eyes and hands, but He possesses a soul (*nafs*) as well. In Sura 5:116, Jesus says to Allah, "Thou (Allah) knowest what is in my soul (*nafs*), and I know not what is in Thy soul." Also, in 6:112 it reads, "He has decreed mercy from His soul *(nafs).*" Allah is not a spirit but a being that possesses a spirit or soul.[249]

Neither does the Qur'ān described Allah as a being that exists everywhere (omnipresent). He is instead seated on His Throne. The

---

[247] On Jahm b. Safwan cf. below.

[248] Ad-Darimi, ***Radd 'ala Bishr*** (Cairo 1358 H), p. 23.

[249] On the development of the concept of spirit in Islam cf. D.B. Macdonald, "The Development of the Idea of Spirit in Islam," ***Acta Orientalia*** IX: 307-351.

Throne of Allah has a very significant and exalted place in the Qur'an.[250] It is called the Throne of Grace (23:117), the Mighty Throne of Power (23:86), and the Glorious Throne of Power (83:15). The Arabic word *'arsh*, according to Maulana Muhammad Ali, literally means "a thing constructed for shade" or "anything roofed."[251] The court or sitting place of the king is called *'arsh.*

The most famous of these Throne passages describe Allah anthropomorphically sitting Himself on the *'arsh.* In Sura 57:4 it reads, "He it is who created the heavens and the earth in six days, THEN HE MOUNTED THE THRONE (*thumma 'stawa 'ala l-'arsh*)." Sura 20:5 reads: "*Ar-Rahman 'ala-'l-'arsh istawa*," meaning "The Beneficent One has sat down firmly on the Throne." Allah's angels are said to encircle the Throne (39:75) and hold it up, "Those who bear the Throne of Power and those around it" (Sura 40:7).

According to the early Muslims (*Salaf* or Pious Ancestors) the Throne is material, separate from the rest of creation and not to be understood as an allegorical expression for the creation of heaven and earth.[252] As Allah sits firmly on the Throne of Power, His feet are said to rest on the *Kursi* or stool that accompanies the Throne. Though *Kursi* can signify seat in a very general sense, it usually meant a seat with no back or armrests, a stool.[253] *Kursi* is mentioned only twice in the Qur'ān, but several times in the sayings of the Prophet. In Sura 2:255 it is stated, "His (Allah's) 'Kursi' extends over the heavens and the earth."

From the Throne, Allah comes and goes as He pleases. In Sura 89:22 we read, "Nay, when the earth is made to crumble to pieces, And thy Lord comes with the angels, ranks on ranks..." Also, 2:210, "What do they have to wait for, if not that Allah should come to them in the shadows of the clouds with the angels..." This displacement of God described in the Qur'ān, His ability to "come to" where He wasn't before, makes the notion of a transcendent deity that exists everywhere (or nowhere) difficult to maintain.[254]

---

[250] Cf. Thomas J. O'Shaughnessy, "God's Throne and Biblical Symbolism in the Qur'an," ***Numen*** 20 (1973), 202-221.

[251] ***Holy Qur'an***, trans. by Maulana Ali (Chicago: Specialty Promotions, 1973), 329 n. 895.

[252] For a look at the early traditionalist interpretation of the *'arsh* narratives cf. Gosta Vitestan, "*'Arsh and Kursi:* An Essay on the Throne Traditions in Islam," in ***Living Waters*** Scandinavian Orientalistic Studies ed. by Egon Keck, Svend Sondergaad, and Ellen Wulff (Copenhagen: Museum Tusculanum Press, 1990), 372.

[253] "Kursi," ***EI2***, 509.

[254] J. M. S. Baljon, "Qur'anic Anthropomophisms," ***Islamic Studies*** 27:2 (1988), p. 122. The author argues that there is a Qur'anic basis for interpreting these passages allegorically. His arguments, however, are unconvincing.

Certain verses in the Qur'ān would appear to support the idea of an omnipresent deity. Sura 50:16 "We are nearer than the jugular vein" and Sura 57:4 "He is with you wherever you are" were favorites of transcendentalist Muslims. But for the people of the Sunnah, these verses are to be understood differently. Ahmad b. Hanbal (d. 855), leader of the nascent 'Sunni orthodox movement' of the ninth century, said in his *'Aqida*:

> God created seven heavens (skies) one above another, and seven earths one below another…There was water above the highest heaven; and the Throne of the Merciful was above the water, and God was on the Throne; and the *Kursi* was the place of His feet…He is on His Throne high above the Seventh Heaven...If an innovator and opponent tries to prove (the opposite) by God's words such as: "We are nearer than the jugular vein (50:16)" or "He is with you wherever you are (57:4)"...and similar ambiguous (passages) of the Qur'ān, then say to him (in reply): What this signifies is knowledge (which is everywhere), for God is on the Throne above the seventh and highest heaven, and separate from His creatures, but his knowledge embraces everything…God is on the Throne, and the Throne has bearers carrying it.[255]

Shayk ad-Din Ibn Taymiyya (d. 1328), one of the greatest scholars of Islam, following Ibn Hanbal's tradition, also understands omnipresence as omniscience:

> An essential element of faith in God…is the conviction that while God is above the heavens on His throne…He is also, at the same time, with them wherever they may be and knows what they do…"He is with you wherever you are, for God sees what you do" (57:4). The phrase "and He is with you" does not mean, however, that He is diffused throughout (*mukhtalit*) His creation. Indeed, such an interpretation is an evident contradiction of what the Fathers (*Salaf*) have affirmed…Nay the moon...one of the smallest of Allah's creations, is both placed in the heaven (*mawdu`un fi al-sama'*) and present with the traveler and the non-traveler wherever they may be. And the

---

[255] Ahmad b. Hanbal, ***Aqida I*** trans. by Michel Allard, ***Le Probleme des Attributs Divins dans la Doctrine d'al-As'ar'i et de ses Premiers Grands Disciples***. (Beyrouth: Impr. Catholique, 1965), pp. 99f.

> Exalted is on the Throne, as a watchful guardian of His creatures and their protector Who is cognizant of them.[256]

According to Sunni scholars, then, God can be spatially located on His Throne above the Seven Heavens in an anthropomorphic manner and yet still be with all the Believers wherever they are. There is thus no contradiction between an enthroned and spatially placed God and an omnipresent deity.[257]

4.4. *The Man-God of the Sunnah*

The qur'ānic description of God in no way supports the claim made by extreme Muslim "transcendentalists." For sure, the qur'ānic anthropomorphisms pale in comparison to Biblical anthropomorphisms,[258] and are therefore inconclusive. What is certain, however, is that the Qur'ān nowhere precludes an anthropomorphic deity. There is nothing in the Book which does violence to the Honorable Elijah Muhammad's anthropomorphist theology. It is also true that the Qur'ān nowhere unequivocally attests to an anthropomorphic deity. If the Qur'ān alone is taken as the criterion of the faith, the most that could be said is that Elijah Muhammad's *tafsir* or interpretation of the Qur'ān is one legitimate option among many and in no way puts him outside the pale of Islam.

The Sunnah of the Prophet was said by the early Muslims (*Tabi'un* [Successors to the Companions] and the *Tabi at-Tabi'in* [Successors to the Successors]) to explain and clarify the Qur'ān [259]. The Qur'an, in particular the qur'ānic description of God, can be understood only with the aid of the reliably transmitted word of the Prophet. And the Sunnah is unbelievably clear. Whereas the Qur'ān has both clear and ambiguous verses, making the qur'ānic description of God equivocal on the surface, the Sunnah suffers from no such ambiguity. The hadith literature is literally flooded with anthropomorphisms.[260] What is most

---

[256] Ibn Taymiyya ***Al-Aqidah al-Wasitiyah*** trans. Merlin Swartz, "A seventh-century (A.H.) Sunni Creed: The 'Aqida Wasitiya of Ibn Taymiya," ***Humaniora Islamica*** I (1973), p. 117.

[257] For a look at omnipresence and an embodied (anthropomorphic) deity cf. Grace M. Dyck, "Omnipresence and Incorporality," ***Religious Studies*** 13, pp. 85-91.

[258] Baljon, "Qur'anic Anthropomorphisms," 119.

[259] Ibn Hanbal argued "the Sunnah explains and clarifies the Qur'an." ***Usul us-Sunnah*** *apud* Ibn Abī Ya'lā. ***Ṭabaqāt al-Hanābila***, edited by Muḥammad Ḥāmid al-Fīqī (2 vols. Cairo: Maṭba'at al-Sunna al-Muḥammadīya, 1952) 1:294.

[260] See especially Daniel Gimaret, ***Dieu à l'image de l'homme: les anthropomorphismes de la sunna et leur interprétation par les théologiens*** (Paris: Patrimoines, 1997). For different treatments of the anthropomorphisms in the Qur'ān and Sunnah see: Ibn Khuzaymah, ***Kitāb al-tawḥīd wa-ithbāt ṣifāt al-Rabb***.

astonishing is that there is absolutely no abrogating or mitigating hadith that would serve to balance out or tone down this blatantly anthropomorphic presentation of deity. The Ash'arite theologian and writer al-Suyuti unwittingly demonstrates this most convincingly in his ***ad-Durr al-mantur,***[261] a commentary of the Qur'ān by the hadith. He reports on each verse all of the relevant traditions. But lo! The passage concerning 42:11, "There is none like Him," is *desperately empty.* This is astonishing because al-Suyuti himself completely rejected anthropomorphism. What is more, there are no exegetical* traditions for this verse from the first generation of qur'ānic exegetes.[262] Tabari XXV, p. 12 doesn't cite any, nor does Qurtubi in his ***al-Jami' li-ahkam al-Qur'an*** XVI, pp. 8-9.

4.4.1. *The Form of God*

Al-Bukhari and Muslim report a hadith from the Prophet on the authority of the Companion Al-Mughīra b. Shuʿba: "No *shakhṣ* is more jealous than Allah; no *shakhṣ* is more pleased to grant pardon than He; no *shakhṣ* loves praiseworthy conduct more than He."[263] Allah is thus a *shakhṣ*. The term *shakhṣ* is usually translated as 'corporeal person.' It connotes "the bodily or corporeal form or figure or substance (*suwād*) of a man," or "something possessing height (*irtifāʿ*) and visibility (*ẓuhūr*)," Ibn Manzūr informs us in his *Lisān al- 'Arab* (7, 45, 4-11).[264] Ibn al-Jawzī, in his *Kitāb Akhbār al-Sifāt* 53-4, admits as well that Śthe term *shakhṣ* implies the existance of a body (*jism*) composed of parts, for one terms something a *shakhṣ* because it possesses corporeality (*shukhūs*) and height (*irtifāʿ*)." God, we are thus informed, is a person with a physical body.

Edited by Muḥammad Khalīl Harrās (Cairo: 1968); Ibn al-Jawzī, ***Kitāb Akhbār al-Ṣifāt***, ed. and trns. Merlin Swartz in ***A Medieval Critique of Anthropomorphism: Ibn al-Jawzī's* Kitāb Akhbār aṣ-Ṣifāt, *a Citical Edition of the Arabic Text with Translation, Introduction and Notes*** (Leiden: Brill, 2002)

261 Beirut, 1411/1990.

262 Gilliot, *art. cited,* 57.

263 Bukhārī, ***Ṣaḥīḥ***, *tawḥīd*, 20:512; Muslim, ***Ṣaḥīḥ***, *liʿān,* 17; Ibn Ḥanbal, ***Musnad*** IV:248; Nisā'ī, ***al-Sunan***, *nikāḥ*, 37, 3.

264 See also Lane, ***Arabic Lexicon***, 2:1517.

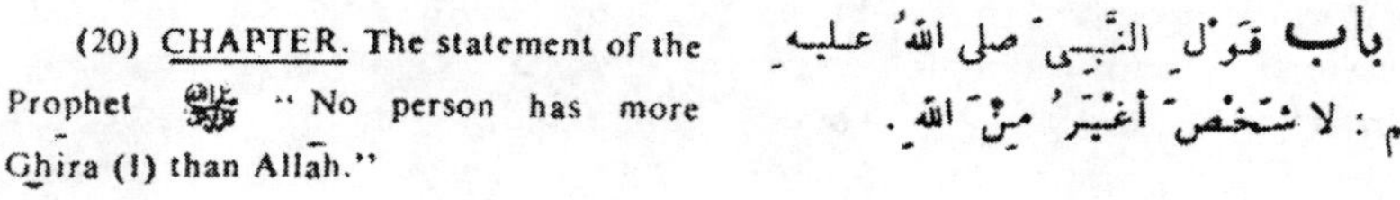

(20) CHAPTER. The statement of the Prophet ﷺ "No person has more Ghira (1) than Allah."

بابُ قَوْلِ النَّبِيِّ صلى اللهُ عليهِ وسلَّم : لا شَخْصَ أغْيَرُ مِنَ اللهِ .

Figure 5

Ṣaḥīḥ Bukhārī *shakhṣ*-report

As a *shakhṣ* the God of the Sunna has a visible form (*ṣūra*), and it is anthropomorphic. According to a *ṣaḥīḥ* (sound) report Adam's form is a likeness of this divine form.

> God created Adam according to His form (*khalaqa llahu Adama 'ala suratihi*), his size being of sixty cubits. Then, once He created him, He said to him: "Go greet this group of angels seated [over there], and listen well in what way they will respond to you. Because such will be [in what follows] your way of greeting—yours and your descendants." [Adam] went, and said [to them]: *as-salamu 'alaykum*. They answered [him]: *as-salamu 'alayka wa rahmatu llah*. They had thus added: *wa rahmatu llah*. All those who will enter into Paradise will have the same form as Adam, their size [theirs also] will be sixty cubits. [But here below,] after [Adam], [the size of] creatures have up to this day not ceased to diminish.[265]

> Do not make your face ugly (*la tuqabbihu l-wajh*)! Because the son of Adam was created according to the form of al-Rahman (*Fa-inna bna Adama khuliqa 'ala surati r-Rahman*).[266]

God thus has a form similar to that of Adam's, though different in some respects. While the transcendentalists used various devices to interpret the 'form' away from God, the Sunni doctors were bitterly opposed to such tricks. Ibn Hanbal says in his *'Aqida* V, "Adam was

---

[265] Bukhārī, ***Ṣaḥīḥ***, *isti'dhān*, 1; Muslim, ***Ṣaḥīḥ***, *birr*, 115; Ibn Ḥanbal, ***Musnad*** II: 244, 251, 315, etc. For a discussion on this hadith and its variants cf. Gimaret, ***Dieu a l'image de l'homme*** 123-136; Watt, "Created in His Image," 94-100.
[266] Ibid.

created in the image of the Merciful, as comes in a report from the Messeger of God transmitted by Ibn Umar..."[267] He said in another creed reported by Ibn Abi Ya'la, "Any one who does not say that God created Adam in the form of the Merciful is a Jahmite (heretic*/disbeliever)."[268] Abū Muḥammad b. Qutayba declared as well: "God possesses an actual form, though it is not like other forms, and He fashioned Adam after it."[269] The reason therefore the Qur'an can say that Adam was made in the best make (*aḥsani taqwīm*) is because he was made according to the form of God himself. This Black Adam looks like God, as we saw above.

4.4.2. *The Prophet's Vision of God*

According to a great number of reports deemed sound (*sahih*) by the hadith scholars, God came to Muhammad in a vision and Muhammad saw His form. One of the most popular of these narratives is reported on the authority of the Companion of the Prophet, Muʿadh b. Jabal:

> [Muʿadh] narrates: One morning, the Messenger of God took a long time to come join us for the dawn prayer, until the moment where we were on the point of seeing the sun come up. The Prophet then came out hurriedly. They did the second call to prayer, and the Messenger of God did the prayer, but his prayer was short. When he had pronounced the final salutation, he shouted to us: "Remain in rows as you are!" Then he turned towards us and said: "I am going to tell you what made me late this morning. I got up last night [to pray]. I did the ablution, I prayed what destiny wished that I pray; then while I was praying, sleepiness took me, and I fell asleep. And there, in front of me, was my Lord, under the most beautiful form (*fī ahsani ṣūrati*). He said [to me]: 'Oh Muḥammad!' –'[Yes] Lord, here I am!' He said [to me]: 'Over what does the Exalted Council dispute?' –'I do not know, Lord,' I responded. He posed [to me] again two times the same question. Then I saw Him putting His palm between my shoulder blades, to the point that I felt the coolness of His

---

[267] Trans. by Watt, ***Islamic Creeds***, p. 31.
[268] Ibn Abi Ya'la, ***Tabaqat al-Hanabila*** I:212,19.
[269] Quoted by Ibn al-Jawzi, *Kitab Akhbar as-Sifat*, 175 (Eng.)

fingertips (*anāmilihi*) between my nipples, and from that moment everything became evident and known to me," etc.[270]

This report and its variants is narrated on the authority of 12 Companions: Mu'adh b. Jabal, Jābir b. Samura,[271] Abū Hurayra,[272] Anas b. Mālik,[273] Abū Umāma,[274] Abū 'Ubayda b. al-Jarrāḥ,[275] 'Abd al-Raḥman b. 'A'is,[276] Thawbān, *mawla rasūli llah*,[277] 'Abd Allāh b. 'Umar,[278] Abū Rāfi',[279] 'Abd al-Raḥman b. Sābiṭ,[280] and 'Abd Allāh b. 'Abbās.[281] Ḥadīth scholars Ibn Ḥanbal, Al-Tirmidhī, Abī Ya'lā al-Mawṣilī (d. 919), 'Abd Allāh b. 'Abd al-Raḥmān al-Dārimī (d. 869), 'Uthman al-Dārimī (d. 895)[282] Ibn Abī 'Āṣim (d. 900), al-Ṭabarānī (d. 971), Al-Lālikā'ī (d. 1027), Nūr al-Dīn al-Haythamī (d. 1405), Ibn Ḥajar al-'Asqalānī (d. 1449), and al-Suyūṭī (d. 1505) all reported the *ḥadīth*. Khaldūn Aḥdab declared, "The *ḥadīth* is *ṣaḥīḥ*. It was reported by a group of Companions, among them: Mu'ādh b. Jabal, Ibn 'Abbas, 'Abd al-Raḥmān b. 'Ā'is, Ibn 'Umar, Abū Hurayra, and Anas, may God be pleased with them."[283] Ibn Mandah, in his ***Al-Maṣdar al-Sābiq*** said also: "This *ḥadīth* is reported from ten (sic) Companions of the Prophet; and the Imāms of the countries, from the people of the east to the west,

---

270 Ibn Ḥanbal, ***Musnad¹***, 5:243; al-Tirmidhī, ***Jāmi' al-Ṣaḥīḥ***, *apud* al-Mubārakfūrī, ***Tuḥfa***, 9: 106ff, #3288; al-Suyūṭī, ***Tafsīr al-Durr al-manthūr***, 7:203.

271 Al-Suyūṭī, ***Tafsīr al-Durr al-manthūr***, 7:203, *sūra Ṣad*.

272 Al-Lālikā'ī, ***Sharḥ uṣūl*** 2: 520; al-Suyūṭī, ***Tafsīr al-Durr al-manthūr***, 7: 203.

273 Al-Suyūṭī, ***Tafsīr al-Durr al-manthūr***, 7: 204.

274 Al-Suyūṭī, ***Tafsīr al-Durr al-manthūr***, 7: 204; Nūr al-Dīn al-Haythamī, ***Kitāb majma' al-baḥrayn fī zawā'id al-mu'jamayn*** (Riyāḍ: Maktabāt al-Rushd, 1992), 370; Ibn Abī 'Āṣim, ***Al-Sunna***, 1: 326, #475.

275 Khaṭīb al-Baghdādī, ***Ta' rīkh Baghdād***, 14 vols. (Cairo, 1931), 8: 151; Al-Suyūṭī, ***Tafsīr al-Durr al-manthūr***, 7: 205.

276 Ibn Ḥanbal, ***Musnad²***, 27: 171, #16621; 'Abd Allah b. 'Abd al-Raḥmān al-Dārimī, ***Sunan al-Dārimī***, 2 vols. (Cairo: Dār al-Ḥadīth, 2000), 1: 606f; Al-Lālikā'ī, ***Sharḥ uṣūl*** 2: 514; Al-Bayhaqī, ***Al-Asma' wa al-Ṣifāt***, 2: 63; Ibn Abī 'Āṣim, ***al-Āḥād wa al-mathānī*** (Riyāḍ, 1991), 5: 48; al-Haythamī, ***Kitāb majma'***, 366.

277 Ibn Abī 'Āṣim, ***Al-Sunna***, 1: 328, #479; al-Suyūṭī, ***Tafsīr al-Durr al-manthūr***, 7: 205; al-Haythamī, ***Kitāb majma'***, 367.

278 Al-Haythamī, ***Kitāb majma'***, 369, #11743.

279 Al-Ṭabarānī, ***Al-Mu'jam al-kabīr*** (Baghdād: al-Dār al-'Arabīyah lil-Ṭibā'ah, 1978) (hereafter ***Al-Mu'jam¹***), 1: 296, #938.

280 Ibn Abī Shaybah, ***al-Kitāb al-muṣannaf fī al-aḥādīth wa-al-āthār*** (Beirut: Dār al-Kutub al-'Ilmīya, 1989), 7:424.

281 Ibn Ḥanbal, ***Musnad¹***, 3:437, #3483; Al-Tirmidhī, ***Jāmi' al-Ṣaḥīḥ***, *apud* al-Mubārakfūrī, ***Tuḥfa***, 9:101ff, #3286; Abū Ya'lā al-Mawṣilī, ***Musnad Abī Ya'lā al-Mawṣilī***, ed. Ḥusayn Salim Asad (Damascus: Dār al-Ma'mūn lil-Turāth, 1984-), 4: 475, #281.

282 Al-Dārimī, ***Naqḍ***, 2: 733ff.

283 Khaldūn Aḥdab, ***Zawā'id Tārīkh Baghdād 'ala al-kutub al-sittah*** (Damascus: Dār al-Qalam, 1996), 6: 253.

relayed it from them."[284] Al-Tirmidhī judged it *ḥasan ṣaḥīḥ* and said: "I asked Muḥammad b. Ismā'īl (al-Bukhārī) about this *ḥadīth* and he said: *hadhā ṣaḥīḥ* ("This is sound")."[285] Ibn Ḥanbal judged it *ṣaḥīḥ*[286] and Muḥammad b. 'Abd Allāh Ḥākim al-Nīsābūrī (933-1014) declared the *isnād* of Ibn 'A'is *ṣaḥīḥ* in his ***al-Mustadrak.***[287] Al-'Awzā'ī[288] and Mukḥūl[289] transmitted the report. Ma'mar, 'Abd al-Razzāq, Ayyub al-Sikhtiyānī (d. 748), Mu'āwiyah b. Ṣāliḥ (d. 775),[290] in short, the *muḥaddithūn* or ḥadīth scholars generally accepted the ḥadīth as sound.

Here is a most explicit portrayal of the corporeal deity of the Sunnah. The Prophet not only sees God in his vision in a corporeal, and clearly anthropomorphic, form, he physically feels His hand and fingertips. Ignaz Goldziher saw in this report "flagrant anthropomorphism."[291] Indeed, the physical contact between Lord and Prophet here described is not only the "summit of intimacy" as Josef van Ess has described it,[292] but the summit of corporeal expression as well. Such a report offended the sensibilities of those transcendentalist theologians who rejected anthropomorphism. They therefore subjected the report to de-anthropomorphizing interpretations; that is to say, they attempted to interpret it in such a way as to disassociate the 'beautiful form' from God.[293] Ibn Fūrak, for example, recounts in his ***Mushkil al-ḥadīth wa bayānuh*** several interpretations advanced by the theologians: either the "most beautiful form" refers to the Prophet who saw God while in this state, or it refers to a created form used by God to communicate to His Prophet, or even the form of an angel in which God inheres.[294] The *muḥaddithūn* or ḥadīth scholars violently rejected these hermeneutics. Al-Dārimī (d.

---

[284] *Apud* Al-Dārimī, ***Naqḍ***, 2:734.

[285] Al-Tirmidhī,***Jāmi' al-Ṣaḥīḥ***, *apud* al-Mubārakfūrī, ***Tuḥfa***, 9: 106ff, #3288.

[286] 'Abd Allāh b. 'Abī, ***Al-Kāmil fī ḍu'afā' al-rijāl***, 7 vols. (Beirut: Dār al-Fikr, 1984), 6: 2344.

[287] See. Al-Bayhaqī, ***Al-Asma' wa al-Ṣifāt***, 2:74.

[288] Al-Bayhaqī, ***Al-Asma' wa al-Ṣifāt***, 2:73ff.

[289] Al-Baghawī, ***Tafsīr***, 4:69; Ibn Abī 'Āṣim, ***Al-Sunna***, 1: 326.

[290] Ibn Abī 'Āṣim, ***Al-Sunna***, 1: 328, #479; al-Suyūtī, ***Tafsīr al-Durr al-manthūr***, 7: 205.

[291] Goldziher, ***Introduction*** 107.

[292] Josef van Ess, "Le *MI'RĀĞ* et la Vision de Dieu dans les Premières Spéculations Théologiques en Islam," in ***Le Voyage Initiatique en Terre D'Islam***, ed. Mohammad Ali Amir-Moezzi (Louvain-Paris: Peeters, 1991),48.

[293]For a discussion of this *ḥadīth v.* Gimaret, ***Dieu à l'image de l'homme***, 143ff; idem, "Au Cœur du *MI'RĀĞ*, un Hadith Interpolé," in ***Le Voyage Initiatique en Terre D'Islam***, op. cited, 67-82.

[294] Abū Bakr b. Fūrak, ***Mushkil al-ḥadīth wa-bayānuh*** (Cairo: Dār al-Kutub al-Ḥadītha, 1979?), 70f.

كتفيّ. قد وجدت برد أنامله بين ثدييّ فتجلّى لي كل شيء وعرفت
فقال يا محمد. قلت لبيك رب، قال فيم يختصم الملأ الأعلى؟
قلت في الكفارات، قال ما هن؟ قلت مشي الأقدام إلى الجماعات،
والجلوس في المساجد بعد الصلاة، وإسباغ الوضوء في المكروهات، قال
ثم فيم؟ قلت إطعام الطعام، ولين الكلام، والصلاة بالليل
والناس نيام. قال سل، قلت اللهم إني أسألك فعل الخيرات،
وترك المنكرات، وحب المساكين، وأن تغفر لي وترحمني، وإذا
أردت فتنة في قوم فتوفني غير مفتون، وأسألك حبك وحب من
يحبك وحب عمل يقرب إلى حبك. قال رسول الله صلى الله عليه وسلم
إنها حق فادرسوها ثم تعلموها » قال أبو عيسى هذا حديث حسن
صحيح. سألت محمد بن إسماعيل عن هذا الحديث فقال هذا
صحيح وقال هذا أصح من حديث الوليد بن مسلم عن عبد الرحمن
ابن يزيد بن جابر قال حدثنا خالد بن اللجلاج حدثني عبد الرحمن
ابن عائش الحضرمي قال قال رسول الله صلى الله عليه وسلم فذكر

(قالها ثلاثا) أي قال الله تعالى هذه المقولة ثلاثا (فتجلى لي) أي ظهر وانكشف
لي (وأسألك حبك) قال الطيبي: يحتمل أن يكون معناه أسألك حبك إياي أو
حبي إياك وعلى هذا يحمل قوله وحب من يحبك (إنها) أي هذه الرؤيا (حق)
إذ رؤيا الأنبياء وحي (فادرسوها) أي فاحفظوا ألفاظها التي ذكرتها لكم في
ضمنها أو أن هذه الروايات (حق فادرسوها) أي اقرأوها (ثم تعلموها) أي
معانيها الدالة هي عليها قال الطيبي: أي لتعلموها فحذف اللام. قوله (هذا حديث
حسن صحيح) وأخرجه أحمد والطبراني والحاكم ومحمد بن نصر في كتاب الصلاة

Figure 6

Page from al-Tirmidhī's ***Jāmiʿ al-Ṣaḥīḥ*** quoting al-Bukhārī's authentification of the 'hadith of the beautiful form'

895) argued in his ***Naqḍ ʿalā al-Marīsī***: "Woe to you! It is not possible that this is Gabriel, or Mīkā'l, or Isrāfīl; it is not possible that this (form) is other than Allāh."[295]

A most interesting exegesis* was advanced by Ibn Ḥanbal according to his son Aḥmad:

> My father reported to me...from ʿAbd al-Raḥmān b. ʿA'is from some of the companions of the Prophet: "He came out to them one morning while in a joyous mood and a radiant face. We said [to him]: 'Oh Messenger of God, here you are in a joyous mood and a glowing face!' --'How could I not be?' he answered. 'My Lord came to me last night under the most beautiful form, and He said [to me]: "'O Muḥammad!'..." And my father (Ibn Ḥanbal) reported to us, ʿAbd al-Razzāq from Maʿmar from Qatāda [from the Prophet], "Allāh created Adam according to His form." My father reported to us, ʿAbd al-Razzāq from Maʿmar from Qatāda, "'in the best stature (*fī aḥsani taqwīm*)' meaning 'in the most beautiful form (*fī aḥsani ṣūrati*)'." Ibrāhīm b. al-Hajjaj reported to us, Ḥammād (b. Salama) reported to us...that the Prophet said, "Allāh is beautiful (*jamīl*) and He loves beauty."[296]

The implication of this collection of *ḥādīths* is unmistakable. The "most beautiful form" is first identified with that form of God according to which Adam was said to be created. This identification is further supported by the Imām's interpretation of *sūra al-Tīn*, "Surely We created man in the best stature (*fī aḥsani taqwīm*) (95:4)." Ibn Ḥanbal accepts the *tafsīr* or exegesis of Qatāda identifying man's "best stature" with God's "most beautiful form."[297] Such an interpretation can amount to nothing short of anthropomorphism. The question still remains, what exactly did Muḥammad see? What does this "beautiful form" of God actually look like? Surprisingly, the *ḥadīth* corpus provides a rather detailed answer to this otherwise blasphemous question.

The important 10th century *ḥadīth* scholar, al-Dāraquṭnī, in his ***Kitāb al Ru'ya*** (Book concerning the Vision of God), reports a *ḥadīth* on the authority of the Companion Anas b. Mālik:

> [The Messenger of God said]: "I saw [my Lord] in His most beautiful form (*aḥsani ṣūratihi*) like a young man (*shābb*) with long hair (*muwaffar*), sitting on the Throne of Grace, around Him a gold

---

[295] Al-Dārimī, ***Naqḍ***, 2: 737.
[296] Aḥmad b. Ḥanbal ***Kitāb al-Sunna*** (Mecca: n.p., 1349 H), 159.
[297] ʿAbd Allāh, ***Kitāb al-Sunna***, 2:490.

carpet. He put His hand between my shoulders and I felt its coolness in my liver. He spoke to me etc.[298]

A provocative report indeed. Similar reports were narrated on the authority of Umm al-Ṭufayl (wife of 'Ubayy b. Ka'b, d. 642),[299] Mu'adh b. 'Afrā',[300] Ibn 'Umar, [301] Ibn 'Abbās,[302] and even 'Ā'isha.[303] *Shābb* is the intermediate stage between a boy before puberty (*ṣabī*, 15-18 years old) and a mature man (*kahl*, 30-33 years old). In the Imāmī (Shi'ī) versions of this *ḥadīth*, however, the *shābb* is specifically described as 30 years old.[304] The divine youth is here described as *muwaffar*. According to Ibn Manẓūr in his ***Lisān al-'Arab***, *wafra* denotes hair that reaches down to the earlobe or even further.[305] The hair of God is black, exceedingly so.[306] The term *muwaffar* gave rise to a number of eccentric readings: *mawfūr* (opulent), *muwaqqar* (venerated), *munawwar* (luminous) and even *muwaffaq* ("assisted by God," i.e. "perfect").[307] And while it is not explicitly stated in this *ḥadīth*, the youthful God's black hair was soon contrasted with His "white skin."[308] For the Rāfiḍite (Shi'ī) theologian Hishām al-Jawalīqī (d. c. 820) God was a "youth in his best years," His body white light and His hair black light.[309] Such a description of God is reminiscent of certain mystical trends in Judaism which identified God with the beloved in the Song of Songs who is

---

[298] al-Dāraquṭnī's ***Kitāb al-ru'ya***, ms. Escorial 1445, fol. 153a; Helmut Ritter, ***Das Meer Der Seele*** (Leiden: E. J. Brill, 1955), 445.
[299] Al-Ṭabarānī, ***Al-Mu'jam al-kabīr*** (Cairo: Maktaba Ibn Taymīyya, n.d) (hereafter ***Al-Mu'jam²***), 25: 143; Ibn Abī 'Āṣim, ***Al-Sunna***, 1:328; al-Bayhaqī, ***Al-Asma' wa al-Ṣifāt***, 2:368; Al-Suyūtī, ***Al-La'āli'***, 28f; 'Alā' al-dīn al-Muttaqī al-Hindī, ***Kanz al-'ummāl fi sanan al-aqwāl wa 'l-af'āl***, 18 vols. (Haydar Abād al-Dakan: Dā'irat al-Ma'ārif al-'Uthmāniya, 1945), I:58; al-Haythamī, ***Kitāb majma'***, 370.
[300] Al-Suyūtī, ***Al-La'āli'***, 30; Ibn Fūrak, ***Mushkil al-ḥadīth***, 387.
[301] Al-Bayhaqī, ***Al-Asma' wa al-Ṣifāt***, 2: 361f, #934; Ibn Fūrak, ***Mushkil al-ḥadīth***, 386.
[302] Ibn 'Adī, ***Al-Kāmil***, 2:677; Al-Bayhaqī, ***Al-Asma' wa al-Ṣifāt***, 2:363; Khaṭīb al-Baghdādī, ***Ta' rīkh Baghdād***, 11: 214; al-Suyūtī, ***Al-La'āli'***, 29f; al-Muttaqī, ***Kanz***, I:58.
[303] Al-Suyūtī, ***Al-La'āli'***, 30.
[304] Ibn Bābawayh al-Qummī, ***Kitāb al-tawḥīd*** (Ṭihrān : Maktabat al-Būzarjumahrī Muṣṭafavī, 1955), 28; Muhammad b. Ya'qūb al-Kulaynī, ***al-Kāfī fī 'Ilm al-dīn***, ed. 'Alī Akbar al-Ghaffārī, 8 vols. (Ṭihrān, 1955-), 100f.
[305] Ibn Manẓūr, ***Lisān al-'Arab***, 15 vols. (Beirut, 1955-1956), 5:288.
[306] Al-Ash'arī, ***Maqālāt al-Islāmiyyīn***, ed. Helmut Ritter (Istanbul, 1929-33), 209.
[307] Gimaret, ***Dieu à l'image***, 154.
[308] Al-Qāsim b. Ibrāhīm, ***Kitāb al-Mustarshid***, ed. and trns. Binyamin Abrahamov in ***Anthropomorphism and Interpretation of the Qur'ān in the Theology of Al-Qāsim Ibn Ibrāhīm*** (Leiden: E. J. Brill, 1996), 133.
[309] Al-Ash'arī, ***Maqālāt***, 209; van Ess, "The Youthful God," 8, 11.

"white and ruddy" and whose "locks are bushy and black as a raven."[310]

Most important is the report by the Prophet's cousin and famed "Interpreter of the Qur'ān," 'Abd Allāh b. 'Abbās: "The Messenger of God said: 'I saw my Lord under the form of a young man (*shābb*) beardless (*amrad*) with curly hair (*ja'd*) and clothed in a green garment (*ḥulla*)."[311] This *ḥadīth* introduces more elements to the beauty of God. In stark contrast to the elderly creator-deity of Judaism and the ancient Near East, white haired and gray bearded, the youthful God of Islam is beardless. Now the Islamic morale advocates wearing a beard. The people of Paradise, however, are beardless, except Mūsā.[312] Adam, too, was created beardless. It was his sons who grew beards due to their father's sin.[313] The beard is thus the mark of the fall of man; beardlessness the mark the righteous in the Hereafter.

Also distinctive in this report is the youthful god's hair. Contrary to the ḥadīth of Anas b. al-Mālik where God is described as having straight hair that reaches to the earlobe or longer, God in this report has curly/wavy hair (*ja'd*). His dress was of considerable significance to the reporters as well. *Ḥulla*, according to Ibn Manẓūr, designates, not a particular clothing item, but an ensemble of two or three items constituting a complete suit.[314] Most of the reports describe the *ḥulla* as green. It is a green *ḥulla* that Gabriel adorns and Muḥammad on the Day of Resurrection will likewise be so attired.[315]

The *isnād* or chain of transmitters of this report is Ḥammād b. Salama (d. 784) < Qatāda d. Di'āma (d. 735) < 'Ikrima (d. 724) < Ibn 'Abbās. While this *ḥadīth* would become very controversial latter, particularly with those who were offended by the explicit anthropomorphism of the text, it gained wide acceptance by the *ḥadīth* scholars and was even invoked in creeds. Ibn Ḥanbal,[316] 'Abd Allāh b. Aḥmad,[317] Ibn Abī 'Āṣim,[318] 'Abd Allah b. 'Adī,[319] al-Ṭabarānī,[320] al-

---

310 *See.* below.

311 Ibn 'Adī, ***Al-Kāmil***, 2:677; Al-Bayhaqī, ***Al-Asma' wa al-Ṣifāt***, 2:363; Khaṭīb al-Baghdādī, ***Ta' rīkh Baghdād***, 11: 214; al-Suyūtī, ***Al-La'āli'***, 29f; al-Muttaqī, ***Kanz,*** I:58.

312 Al-Tirmidhī, ***al-Jāmi' al-ṣaḥīḥ***, *janna* 8 and 12.

313 *V.* C. Shöck, ***Adam im Islam*** (Berlin, 1993), 121f.

314 Ibn Manẓūr, ***Lisān al-'Arab***, XI: 172.

315 Aḥmad b. Ḥanbal, ***Musnad***, ed. Aḥmad Muḥammad Shākir (Egypt: Dār al-Ma'ārif, 1949-) (hereafter ***Musnad³***), 3:456.

316 Ibn Ḥanbal, ***Musnad²***, 4:350f, #2580.

317 'Abd Allāh, ***Kitāb al-Sunna***, 2: 484, 503, #'s 1116, 1117, 1168.

318 Ibn Abī 'Āṣim, ***Al-Sunna***, 1:307, #442.

319 Abd Allah b. 'Adī, ***Al-Kāmil***, 2:677.

320 Al-Ṭabarānī, ***Kitāb al-sunna***, *apud* al-Muttaqī, ***Kanz,*** I:58.

Lālikā'ī,[321] and Abū Bakr al-'Ajurī[322] reported it in full or *mukhtaṣar* (abridged). Aḥmad Muḥammad Shākir (d. 1958), editor of Ibn Ḥanbal's ***Musnad*** and clearly the "greatest traditionalist of his time,"[323] declared: "the *ḥadīth* in its essence is *ṣaḥīḥ*."[324] It was primarily the heretical Mu'tazila, influenced as they were by Greek philosophic ideas,[325] who rejected this report. Abū Bakr b. Ṣadaqa reported hearing Abū Zur'a al-Rāzī (d. 878) say: "The *ḥadīth* of Qatāda from 'Ikrima from Ibn 'Abāss in the Vision is sound (*ṣaḥīḥ*). Shādhān and 'Abd al-Ṣamad b. Kaysān and Ibrāhīm b. Abī Suwayd reported it and none denies it except the Mu'tazila."[326] Aḥmad b. Ḥanbal, around whom Sunni orthodoxy originally consolidated,[327] likewise argued in his *'Aqīda III* that one of the fundamental principles of the Sunna (*uṣūl al-sunna*) is:

> To have faith in the Beatific Vision on the Day of Judgment…and that the Prophet has seen his Lord, since this has been transmitted from the Messenger of God and is correct and authentic. It has been reported from Qatāda, from 'Ikrima, from Ibn 'Abbās…And the *ḥadīth*, in our estimation, is to be taken upon its apparent meaning (*'alā ẓāhirihi*), as it has come from the Prophet. Indulging in *Kalām* with respect to it is an innovation. But we have faith in it as it came, upon its apparent meaning, and we do not dispute with anyone regarding it."[328]

In his *'Aqīda V*, Aḥmad argued that, "Belief in that (*ḥadīth al-shābb* or the report of the Young Man) and counting it true is obligatory" for Muslims. [329] The general acceptance of this *ḥadīth* among the *ḥadīth* scholars is therefore well attested. Consequently, the description of God found therein had a significant effect on the community's ideas of God at that time. The Mu'tazilī Qāḍī 'Abd al-Jabbār noted that this report (*ḥadīth al-shābb*) along with "God created Adam according to Him Form," was the basis of the doctrines of the popular *mushabbiha*

---

[321] Al-Lālikā'ī, ***Sharḥ uṣūl*** 2: 512.
[322] Abū Bakr al-'Ajurī, ***al-Sharī'a***, ed. Muhamma Hāmid al-Fiqī (Cairo: 1950), 491f.
[323] G.H. A. Juynboll, "Aḥmad Muḥammad Shākir (1892-1958) and his edition of Ibn Ḥanbal's ***Musnad***," ***Studies on the Origins and Uses of Islamic Ḥadīth*** (Brookfield, Vt.: Variorum, 1996), 222.
[324] Ibn Ḥanbal, ***Musnad³***, 4:201, #2580, 2634.
[325] See below.
[326] Al-Suyūṭī, ***Al-La'ālī'***, 30.
[327] See Williams, "Aspects of the Creed."
[328] Ibn Ḥanbal, *'Aqīda III, apud* Ibn Abī Ya'lā, ***Ṭabaqāt*** 1:246.
[329] Ibn Ḥanbal, *'Aqīda V, apud* Ibn Abī Ya'lā, ***Ṭabaqāt*** 1:312.

("likeners" or anthropomorphists).[330] But who were these *mushabbiha*? The Zaydī imām and scholar al-Qāsim b. Ibrāhīm (d. 860), who wrote several treaties against the *mushabbiha*, noted in his ***Kitāb al-Mustarshid***:

> The Muslims (lit. those who pray) have agreed with us that the glances will not perceive God, except for a group of the *Rāwafiḍ*, and the *Ḥashwīya* which agree with them. They said the Prophet had seen his Lord white-skinned and dark-haired. They related in another way that He had been seen in the form of an adolescent whose hair was cut off. Some of them claimed that this seeing was with the heart, and some others claimed that it was with the eyes.[331]

For al-Qāsim, "*ḥashwīya*" denoted the pro-Umayyad *ḥadīth* scholars who accepted Aḥmad b. Ḥanbal as their principle authority.[332] Binyamin Abrahamov, editor of al-Qāsim's works, translates the term "*ḥashwīya*" as "scholars of the masses," indicating the general acceptance of these ideas among the community.[333] The Muʿtazilite essayist al-Jāḥiẓ (d. 869), writing around the same time, describes the same doctrinal trend among the early (proto-)Sunnis. He characterizes Ibn Ḥanbal's supporters as *Nābita*,[334] that is "contemptable, suddenly powerful, irritating sprouters on the scene."[335] According to al-Jāḥiẓ the *Nābita* insisted that God "is a body, and they ascribed a form (*ṣūra*) and limits to Him and declared anyone who believes in *al-Ru'ya* (Seeing God) without *tajsīm* (ascribing a body to God) and *taṣwīr* (ascribing a form to

---

[330] Qāḍī ʿAbd al-Jabbār, ***Faḍl al-iʿtizāl***, ed. Fu'ād Sayyid (Tunis, 1974), 149.
[331] Al-Qāsim b. Ibrāhīm, ***Kitāb al-Mustarshid***, 133.
[332] Al-Qāsim b. Ibrāhīm, ***Kitāb al-Dalīl al-Kabīr***, ed. and trns. by Binyamin Abrahamov in ***Al-Kāsim B. Ibrāhīm on the Proof of God's Existence*** (Leiden: E.J. Brill, 1990), 188; Abrahamov, ***Anthropomorphism and Interpretation***, 133, n. 160.
[333] Op. cited.
[334] Ch. Pellat ***EI***, *s.v.* "Nābita," 7:843.
[335] Wadad al-Qadi, "The Earliest 'Nābita' and the Paradigmatic 'Nawābit'," ***Studia Islamica*** 78 (1993), 59. On the *nābita/ḥashwīya v.* also A. S. Halkin, "The Ḥashwiyya" ***JAOS*** 54 [1934], 1-28): ***EI***, *s.v.* "Ḥashwiyya," by ed., 3:269; G. van Vloten, "Les Hachwia et Nabita," ***Actes du Onzième Congrès International des Orientalistes, Paris, 1897*** Paris, 1899, 99-123; M. Th. Houtsma, "Die Ḥashwiya," ***Zeitschrift für Assyriologie*** 26 (1912), 196-202; Fritz Steppat, "From *ʿAhd Ardasir* to Al-Ma'mūn: A Persian Element in the Policy of the Miḥna," in ***Studia Arabica et Islamica: Festschrift for Ihsan ʿAbbas***, ed. Wadad al-Qadi (Beirut: American University of Beirut, 1981), 451ff; Ch. Pellat, "La 'nābita'de Djahiz," ***Annales de l'institut d'études orientales*** (Alger), 10 (1952): 302-325; I. Alon, "Farabi's Funny Flora: al-Nawābit as 'Opposition'," ***Journal of the Royal Asiatic Society*** 37 (1988), 222-25; W. Madelung, ***Der Imam al-Qasim ibn Ibrahim*** (Berlin: Walter De Gruyter & Co., 1965), 223ff.

God) to be a *kāfir* (disbeliever)."[336] The *ṣūra* that the *Nābita* attributed to God was undoubtedly that of a *shābb*, "young man," judging from al-Qāsim's contemporary report and from later polemics against the group.[337] Al-Jāḥiẓ informs us that, because of Ibn Ḥanbal and the concurrence with him of "the masses, the pious recluse, the jurists, and the ḥadīth people,"[338] the prevailing trend (*ghālib*) of the community was anthropomorphism and determinism.[339] Ninth century Sunnism, that is to say earliest Sunnism, was therefore characterized by belief in an anthropomorphic deity, a belief based in part on *ḥadīth al-shābb* (the report of the Youthful God).[340]

4.4.2.1. *The Orthodox Rejects 'Ā'isha's Rejection*

While the Prophet's vision of God is reported on the authority of a great multitude of Companions, the solitary witness against it is 'Ā'isha, the Prophet's favorite wife.[341]

> (Masrūq said): I was sitting back in 'Ā'isha's house when she said: 'O Abū 'Ā'isha, there are three things, whoever says any of which, he is lying about Allāh in the most hateful manner. I asked: 'Which things?' She said: [First,] whoever tells you that Muhammad saw his Lord, he is lying about Allāh in the most hateful manner.' I was sitting back, so I sat up and said: 'O Mother of the Faithful! Give me a moment and do not rush me. Did not Allāh Almighty say "Surely he beheld him on the clear horizon (53:7)?"' She replied: 'I was the first in the entire community to have asked Allāh's Messenger about this, and he

---

[336] Al-Jāḥiẓ, ***Risāla fī al-Nabīta,*** *apud* Al-Jāḥiẓ ***Rasā'il al-Jāḥiẓ***, 4 vols., ed. 'Abd al-Salam Muḥammad Harūn (Cairo: Maktabāt al-Khanjī, 1964-1979), 2:18.

[337] *See* for example the rescript of the Caliph al-Rāḍi in 935.

[338] Al-Jāḥiẓ, ***Kitāb fī khalq al-Qur'ān***, *apud* al-Jāḥiẓ, ***Rasā'il al-Jāḥiẓ***, 3:297

[339] Al-Jāḥiẓ, ***Risāla fī al-Nābita***, *apud* al-Jāḥiẓ, ***Rasā'il al-Jāḥiẓ***, 2:20.

[340] On anthropomorphists trends within 9th century Sunni movements *v.* also Wesley Williams, "Aspects of the Creed of Ahmad Ibn Hanbal," 450ff; Nimrod Hurvitz, "Miḥna as Self-Defence," ***Studia Islamica*** 92 (2001): 98ff.

[341] It is sometimes stated that, along with the Mother of the Faithful, *ru'yat Allāh* was likewise denied by Abū Hurayra and 'Abd Allāh b. Mas'ūd (*V.* for example Gibril Fouad Haddad's, "The Vision of Allah in the World and the Hereafter," in his partial translation of al-Bayhaqī, ***Al-Asma' wa al-Ṣifāt*** [Damascus: As-Sunna Foundation of America, 1998], 78). There is, however, no evidence that either denied Muḥammad's vision of God. This claim is probably based on the fact that both are recorded as interpreting *sūrat al-Najm* as visions of Gabriel. But this hardly precludes an affirmation of a vision, say, on another occasion. Abū Hurayra in fact explicitly affirmed a Vision of God by the Prophet according to certain reports. See al-Lālikā'ī, ***Sharḥ uṣūl***, 2:520; al-Suyūtī, ***Tafsīr al-Durr al-manthūr***, 7:203.

said: "It is but Gabriel, I did not see him in the actual form in which he was created other than these two times. I saw him alighting from heaven, covering it all. The magnitude of his frame spans what lies between the heaven and the earth."' Then she said: 'Did you not hear Allāh say: "Vision comprehends Him not, but He comprehends all vision. He is the Subtle, the Aware (6:103)?" Did you not hear Allāh say: "And it is not (vouchsafed) to any mortal that Allāh should speak to him except by revelation or from behind a veil, or (that) He sends a messenger to reveal what He will by His leave. Lo! He is Exalted, Wise (42:51)?"' She continued: '[Second,] whoever claims that Allāh's Messenger concealed any part of Allāh's Book, he is lying about All§h in the most hateful manner when Allāh is saying: "O Messenger, make known that which has been revealed unto you from your Lord, for if you do it not, you will not have conveyed His Message (5:67)."' She continued: '[Third,] whoever claims that he can tell what shall happen tomorrow, he is lying about Allāh in the most hateful manner, since Allāh is saying: "Say: None in the heavens and the earth knoweth the Unseen save Allāh [and they know not when they will be raised again (27:65)".'[342]

This report seems pretty categorical. But there are reasons to doubt the authenticity of the above rejection, at least as presented in this report. Being the youngest and favorite wife of the Prophet, 'Ā'isha was used by later groups and tendencies as label and pretense.[343] Reports bearing her name therefore must be treated skeptically. Richard Bell has demonstrated how a single statement of 'Ā'isha can balloon into a full narrative with embellishments of later reporters.[344] Such embellishments are evident in the above report as well. While enumerating the "enormous lies," 'Ā'isha mentions those who claim that Muḥammad "concealed anything of what he was commanded." The idea that the Prophet concealed portions of the revelation, such as the succession of 'Alī, was distinctly Shī'ite,[345] in particular Saba'ite. As these groups did not come on the scene until long after 'Ā'isha's time, this statement is best explained as a later attribution to the favorite wife

---

342 Muslim, ***Ṣaḥīḥ***, 1:111, #337.

343 Josef van Ess, "Muhammad's Ascension and the Beginnings of Islamic Theology," unpublished lecture, 1998, University of Michigan, 19.

344 Richard Bell, "Mohammed's Call," ***The Muslim World*** 24 (1934), 13ff.

345 Moojan Momen, ***An Introduction to Shi'I Islam*** (New Haven: Yale University Press, 1985), 16ff.

of the Prophet.[346] There is also evidence suggesting 'Ā'isha at one time countenanced a vision of God by Muḥammad. There is a *ḥadīth al-ru'ya* (report of the Prophet's seeing God) attributed to her[347] and the earliest versions of the Prophet's 'Call Report' on her authority describe the Prophet's encounter with *al-Ḥaqq*, i.e. God.[348]

The treatment by *ḥadīth* scholars of this rejection by 'Ā'isha varied. According to Ibn Taymīya, the "people of knowledge" reject as lies this narration from her along with a similar report claiming that Abū Bakr likewise asked the Prophet who said "I saw Him."[349] On the whole, though, the early Sunni scholars, while not going as far as Ibn Taymīya in labeling the report of 'Ā'isha a lie, did dismiss her as unqualified to speak on this matter. This attitude was probably based on a report from 'Abd al-Razzāq b. Ḥammām (d. 826). The latter mentioned the *ḥadīth* of 'Ā'isha to Ma'mar b. Rāshid (d. 770), the famous Yemenite *muḥaddith* (ḥadīth scholar), who said, "'Ā'isha is not with us more knowledgeable (in this matter) than Ibn 'Abbās."[350] The Shāfi'ite *muḥaddith* Ibn Khuzayma (d. 924), who would later be described as the "chief of the hadith scholars (*ra's al-muḥaddithīn*),"[351] declared in his ***Kitāb al-tawhīd***: "The agreement of the Tribe of Hāshim (that Muhammad saw his Lord) is...more appropriate than 'Ā'isha's isolated statement/doctrine (that he did not)."

Another element of the controversy was whether the Prophet saw his Lord while awake or asleep. 'A'isha seems to have denied a physical viewing of God by the Prophet or a vision during the nocturnal journey (*isrā' / mi'rāj*). Abd Allah b. Abbas reported that the Prophet saw Him in a dream/vision on a night which had nothing to do with the nocturnal journey. He suggested that the vision occurred *fi l-manam*, "during the sleep." In the report of Mu'ad we find *fa-statqaltu*,

---

346 Van Ess, "Le *MI'RĀĞ*," 50.

347 Al-Suyūtī, ***Al-La'āli'***, 1:30. The *isnād* is Ibn Jurayj < Safwān b. Sulaym < 'Ā'isha. Being that Safwān died in 132 H while 'Ā'isha died in 58 H, this *isnād* would understandably be considered "weak."

348 In az-Zuhrī's account of Muḥammad's Call allegedly on the authority of 'Ā'isha, she gives the following narrative: "The beginning of revelation for the Messenger of God (God bless and preserve him) was a true vision. It used to come like the breaking of dawn. Afterwards solitude became dear to him, and he would go to a cave on Ḥīra to engage in *tahannuth* there for a certain number of nights...At length unexpectedly *Al-Ḥaqq* came to him and said, "O Muḥammad, thou art the Messenger of God." See Watt, ***Muhammad at Mecca***, 40. *Al-Ḥaqq* is of course a name God. Its usage here, according to Watt, supports the view that Muḥammad originally took the visions of *sūrat al-Najm* as visions of God. Al-Ṭabarī, ***The History of al-Ṭabarī***, trns. W. Montgomery Watt and M. V. McDonald (New York: State University of New York Press, 1988),6:67 n. 96. *V.* Watt's comments.

349 Ibn Taymīya, ***Minhāj al-sunna al-nabawīya*** (Cairo,1964), 2: 511.

350 Ibn Khuzayma, ***Kitāb al-tawhīd***, 229.

351 Muḥammad Khalīl Harrās, ed. of Ibn Khuzayma's ***Kitāb al-tawḥīd***, "alif".

"then I fell asleep." In the version found in Ibn Hanbal's ***Musnad***, on the other hand, there is the explicit statement to the contrary: *hatta stayqaztu fa-ida ana bi-rabbi*, "then I woke up, and there in front of me was my Lord." Nonetheless, a consensus developed later that the Vision took place during the Prophet's sleep; he saw Him with his heart.[352] Ibn Ḥanbal,[353] al-Darimī,[354] and al-Ash'arī[355] would have preferred it.

That Muḥammad's vision of God occurred during his sleep in no way mitigated the force of the theophany as far as the *muḥaddithūn* or ḥadīth scholars were concerned.[356] It was a true vision of the heart. "The heart lied not about that which it saw (53:11)." When asked concerning this matter, Ibn Ḥanbal would have responded: "Yes, he saw Him in reality (*rā'hu ḥaqqan*), for the visions of the prophets are real."[357] For al-Ash'arī too the Vision was a *ru'ya ḥaqīqa* (true vision), not a dream delusion (*takhayyul*).[358] In support of this position, the traditionalists could cite 'Ā'isha who claimed that "the first revelation granted to the Messenger of Allāh was the true dream in a state of sleep, so that he never dreamed a dream but the truth of it shone forth like the dawn of the morning,"[359] as well as Mu'ādh who said: "That which the Prophet saw in his sleep and while awoke, it is truth."[360] Al-Ḍaḥḥāk b. Muzāḥim (d. 723) reported that Muḥammad said, "I looked at Him with my heart until I was sure that He was present and that I really saw Him."[361] Though the heart was the instrument of the vision, Muḥammad "really saw Him."

---

[352] *See* Ibn Abī 'Āṣīm, ***al-Sunna***, 1: 324; Al-Lālikā'ī, ***Sharḥ uṣūl*** 2:519; Ibn Taymīya, ***Al-Qawl al-Aḥmad fī bayān ghalāt man ghaliṭa 'alā al-Imām Aḥmad*** (Riyaḍ: Dār al-'Āṣimah, 1998), 133; Ibn Qayyīm al-Jawzīya, ***Zād al-ma'ād***, 3:28f; al-Haythamī, ***Kitāb majma'***, 366f.

[353] The Imām was reportedly asked, "In which way do you believe Muḥammad saw his Lord?" to which he replied, "The way (mentioned in) the *ḥadīth* of A'mash from Ziyād b. al-Ḥaṣīn from Abī al-'Ālīya from Ibn 'Abbās: The Prophet saw his Lord with his heart." Al-Lālikā'ī, ***Sharḥ uṣūl*** 2:519.

[354] Al-Dārimī, ***Naqḍ***, 2:738.

[355] Op. cited.

[356] The transcendentalists of course took a different position. For them the Vision was an imaginary dream. Ibn Fūrak quotes the saying of one exegete: (The theologians) say that the dream is an imaginary vision (*wahm*) that God creates in the one sleeping to signify to him a thing which will be or which was, by means of interpretation of dreams. Now the imaginary visions (*awhām*) can represent the imagined otherwise than it is in reality." Ibn Fūrak, ***Mushkīl al-ḥadīt***, 23.

[357] Ibn Qayyīm al-Jawzīya, ***Zād al-ma'ād***,3:29.

[358] Ibn Fūrak, ***Mujarrad***, 86.

[359] Maualana Muhammad Ali, ***A Manual of Hadith***, (Lahore: The Ahmadiyya Anjuman Ishaat Islam), 3f.

[360] Ibn Abī 'Āṣim, ***Al-Sunna***, 1:325, #473.

[361] *V.* below n. 208.

4.4.2.2. *The Hon. Elijah Muhammad's Rejection*

We have then early Sunni acknowledgement of a report unequivocal in its anthropomorphism: God appeared in the form of a man. While the prophet's vision of God may be comfortably situated in the history of Islamic dogma, its place in the teachings of the Honorable Elijah Muhammad is, ironically, less obvious. The Hon. Elijah Muhammad seemed to have categorically rejected the Prophet's vision of God. He stated in ***Our Savior Has Arrived***: "In fact Muhammad (the Prophet) never saw the God. Muhammad only Heard His Voice." [362] He goes on to say, "The Muhammad of the prophecy of the Holy Quran teaches and prophesies of a Muhammad who would get his Word from the Mouth of Allah (God) and not through visions of talking to Him and never seeing the Speaker." Relevant to these passages is one found in ***Message to the Black Man***. The Messenger says, "The Holy Qur'an refers to the Days of Allah, meaning in the years of resurrection, and it often repeats that the people will meet with Allah in person, NOT IN VISION."[363]

It appears that, according to the Honorable Elijah Muhammad, there are two Muhammads: one who will experience Allah only in visions, and another who will experience Allah in Person. This latter will not be communicated to through the veil of visions. He will speak to God "face to face, as a man speaketh to his friend." Many of the Prophets experienced God. But, as the Messenger states, they did so only through the veil of a vision. Micaiah the prophet had a vision of God as reported in I Kings 22:19: "And he said, Hear thou therefore the word of the Lord; I saw the Lord sitting on his throne, and all the host of heaven standing by him on his right hand and on his left." Isaiah also reports a vision of God; "In the year that the king Uzziah died I saw also the Lord sitting upon a throne, high and lifted up (Isaiah 6:1)." Without a doubt, the most important is that reported by the Prophet Ezekiel. In his so-called "Inaugural Vision," the prophet reports, "And above the firmament (I saw) the likeness of a throne, as the appearance of a sapphire stone: and upon the likeness of the throne was the likeness as the appearance of a man above upon it…(Ez. 1:26)." These experiences that the prophets of old had are referred to in Hebrew as *Re'uyot Yahweh* or Visions of Yahweh. These prophets saw and experienced God only in a vision.

Prophet Muhammad did not see God in the Person. He did not speak to Him "face to face, as a man speaketh to his friend." He only

---

[362] (Chicago: Muhammad's Temple of Islam No. 2, 1974.) 135.

[363] Muhammad, ***Message to the Black Man***, 189.

experienced Allah in a Vision, according to early Islamic tradition, the same way the prophets before him experienced the Divine-behind the veil of a vision. It is the Most Honorable Elijah Muhammad who experienced God in the flesh. He did so for three and one half years. This is why he is not referred to as a *nabi* or prophet. Prophets prophesy of the coming of the God whom they experienced only in a vision. The Honorable Elijah Muhammad, on the other hand, proclaimed that he represents the physical presence of God in the world.

4.5. *Literal or Metaphorical*

The God of the Sunnah is unquestionably anthropomorphic. The Qur'ān and Sunnah speak of His eyes, ears, arms, legs, hands, feet, chest, elbows, loins, fingers, palms, etc. He is blatantly stated to have appeared to the Prophet "in the form of a young man." The question undoubtedly raises itself, "Did the Prophet mean these descriptions literally?" The topic was taken up by Daniel Gimaret in his study of anthropompomorphism in the Suuna, ***Dieu a' l'image de l'homme***. The French scholar concludes:

> (A) reason in favor of a literal interpretation is that, quite simply, nothing attests to the Prophet ever being opposed to it. Nowhere in the innumerable mass of traditions that are attributed to him, do we see the least guarding against what one will call later the sin of "assimiliationism" (*tashbih*)...One finds in the *sunnah*—it is, moreover, clearly about apocryphal traditions—the anticipated condemnation of diverse heterodox sects: the *qadariyyas* (Free-Willers), the *murgi'as*, the *zindiqs* (Manechaeans); (but) there is never a (condemnation) of the *mushabbihas* (anthropomorphists).[364]

I believe we can take this a step farther. There are indeed reports that indicate that the Prophet intended these descriptions to be understood literally. In a tradition narrated by Abd Allah and found in Bukhari, the Prophet contrasts the two eyes of Allah with the one eye of *ad-Dajjal*. In the process and obviously for clarity purposes, he points to his eyes so the people will make no mistake as to what type of eye he is referring:

---

[364] 25.

Narrated Abd Allah: Ad-Dajjal was mentioned in the presence of the Prophet. The Prophet said: "Allah is not hidden from you; He is not one-eyed," and pointed with his hand towards his eye, adding, "While Al-Masih Ad-Dajjal is blind in the right eye and his eye looks like a protruding grape."[365]

Another relevant ḥadīth is reported on the authority of Abu Hurayra and found in Abu Dawud.

[Abu Yunus] said: I heard Abu Hurayra recite the verse "Surely God commands you to make over trusts to those worthy of them, and that when you judge between people, you judge with justice. Surely God admonishes you with what is excellent. Surely God is ever Hearing, Seeing." Then he said: «I saw God's messenger [when he recited these last words] put his finger on his ear, and the next finger on his eye.» Abu Hurayra says: «I saw God's messenger, when he recited this [verse], he [so] put his two fingers. »[366]

Tabarani and Abd Allah b. Ahmad also report a tradition from Uqba b. 'Amir:

['Uqba b. 'Amir] said: I saw God's messenger, when he recited the verse that is at the end of Surat *an-Nūr*, put his two fingers under his two eyes while saying *bi - kulli say'in basīr* (Allah is Observer of every thing.)

These physical gestures made by the Prophet clearly suggest that his intent was for the descriptions to be taken in the physical sense. According to a tradition on the authority of Jubayr b. Mutim and found in Abu Dawud, Ibn Khuzayma, at-Tabarani and others, God sits on the Throne like a man sitting on a leather saddle and makes it creak.

[Jubayr b. Mut'im] narrates: A Bedouin came to find the Messenger of God and said to him: "O Messenger of God, the men are all in, the women and the children perish, the resources are growing thin, the beasts are dying. Pray then to God in our favor so it rains! We ask of you to intercede for us

---

[365] Al-Bukhārī, ***Ṣaḥīḥ*** 9:371

[366] Abu Dawud as-Sijistani, ***as-Sunan***, ed. M. Muhyi d-din 'Abd al-Hamid, 4 vol., (Cairo, 1339/1920; repr. Beirut n.d.) 18, 4728; Ibn Khuzayma, ***Kitāb al- Tawḥīd*** 42, 16s.

> alongside God, and we ask of God to intercede for us alongside of you." "Unfortunate one!" answered the Messenger of God, "do you know what you're saying?" Then he started to say *subhana llah*, and did not stop repeating it so long as he didn't see his Companions doing as much. Then he said [to the Bedouin]: "Unfortunate one! One does not ask God to intercede alongside any one of His creatures! God is very much above this! Unfortunate one! Do you know who God is? (God is on His Throne, which is above His heavens, and heavens are above His earth,) like this"—and the Messenger of God put his fingers in the shape of a tent—*and it creaks under Him like the creaking of the saddle under the rider*."[367]

The Prophet compares Allah sitting on the Throne and making it creak to a man sitting on a saddled horse and making the saddle creak. The anthropomorphism is blatant. The Prophet's physical gesturing hardly allows us to see in this report anything other than a physical description of God's "establishment" on the Throne.

Indeed, the early Muslims took these descriptions as literal representations of the Godhead. A.S. Tritton, ***Revelation And Reason In Islam***, noted:

> From earliest Islam there had been a strong preference...to take these descriptions literally.' It was said that God, when he grows angry, grows heavier and the throne groans under his weight like a camel saddle. Others explained that it was the throne that grew heavier, not God."[368]

Ahmad b. Hanbal (d. 855) affirmed the Attributes must be understood according to their literal meaning. In his ***A Description of the Believer From Ahl as-Sunnah wal-Jama'ah*** reported on the authority of Muhammad b. al-Andarani, Ibn Hanbal argues: "That he (the Believer) confirms everything that the Prophets and Messengers came with and that he believes in it resolutely, according to the apparent and manifest [meaning]."[369] Al-Khattabi (d. 338H) said "The way (*madhhab*) of the Salaf with regard to the Ṣifāṭ is to affirm them as they are *'ala ẓahīr'* (with their apparent meaning), negating any *tashbīh* to them, nor *takyīf* (asking how)."[370] To affirm the literal meaning of these Qur'anic and narrated descriptions is to affirm a

---

[367] Abu Dawud, ***as-Sunan***, 18 §4726; Ibn Khuzayma, ***Kitāb al- Tawḥīd*** 103: 6ff.
[368] (London: George Allen & Anura Ltd., 1957) 21.
[369] *Apud* Ibn Abī Ya'lā. ***Ṭabaqāt***,
[370] ***Al-Ghuniyah 'an Kalam wa Ahlihi*** as quoted in ***Mukhtasir al-Uluww***, no. 137.

concept of God not too different from that expounded by the Honorable Elijah Muhammad. It is to be acknowledged that there are some differences in the anthropomorphic ideas (for early Islam God was massive and lacked a stomach cavity while Muhammad's God was completely human in body), yet these differences are no more severe than those which existed within the early Islamic community.[371] Again, the evidence shows that Elijah Muhammad's theology is well within the pale of Islam.

4.6. *Muqatil b. Sulayman, the Hon. Elijah Muhammad, and Point Number 12*

A wonderful opportunity to examine the place of the Honorable Elijah Muhammad's doctrines in the history of Islamic theology is found in an analysis of the doctrine of an early qur'ānic exegete, Muqatil b. Sulayman (d. 150/767) from Balkh. Herbert Berg has already suggested a similarity between the two.[372] Muqatil, like Elijah Muhammad, is known for an explicit and unabashed anthropomorphic theology. Al-Ash'ari, in his ***Maqalāt al-Islamīyin***, described Muqatil's views as follows:

> God is a body; He has hair, He has the form of a man; He has flesh, blood, hair and bone; He has limbs and organs, such as hand, foot, head, eyes. It is [a] dense (*muṣmat*) [body]. And in spite of this, He resembles nothing and nothing resembles Him.[373]

This bold description of God has negatively colored Muqatil's image with posterity and in the academic literature.[374] There has recently been some debate, however, over the accuracy of this charge. The publication of his exegetical works did little to bring clarity to Muqatil's doctrines in this regard. Claude Gilliot's lengthy study of the question yielded no conclusive answer.[375] Binyamin Abrahamov concluded that a survey of Muqatil's exegesis shows that he was not a

---

[371] The differences, for example, between Muqatil b. Sulayman and Dawud al-Jawaribi (cf. van Ess, "Youthful God…" 3ff.). Hisham al-Jawaliqi, Ali b. Mithani, Hisham b. al-Hakam, Al-Mughira b. Said, and Bayan b. Sim'an all had varying concepts of the Godhead, though all were anthropomorphist.
[372] *Art. cited*, 345.
[373] *Op. cited.*
[374] Cf. M. Plessner's article, "al-Mukatil B. Sulaiman," ***EI2***, 711-12.
[375] Gilliot, *art. cited*, 83.

mushabbiha (anthropomorphist).[376] Josef van Ess,[377] on the other hand, as well as Claud Gilliot, have demonstrated that, while figurative interpretations to qur'ānic anthropomorphisms can certainly be found in the various recensions of Muqatil's ***Tafsir***, literal interpretations to these anthropomorphisms are not at all lacking. There exists in the material itself ample justification for believing the reports of Muqatil's anthropomorphist theology. Not only does he explain the "hand" (*yad*) of God anthropomorphically, he applies the same exegetical method to the "leg" (*saq*), the "descent" (*nazul*), the "vision" (*ru'ya*) and the "establishment on the Throne." (*'istawa ala l-arsh*).[378] That Muqatil was a *mujassima* or corporealist who attributed a body to God is clearly attested in his exegesis of Surat *al-Ikhlāṣ*. He understands *as-ṣamad* (112:2) as dense, not hollow and as "he who has no [hollow stomach] similar to the hollow (stomach) of creatures."[379] God is thus massive in his body and differs from creatures in that he lacks a stomach cavity.

The most revealing passage is found in the extensive extract of Muqatil's ***At-tafsir fi mutashabih al-Qur'an*** preserved in Malati's (d. 377/987) ***Kitab at-tanbih wa ar-radd.***[380] We read there the incredible statement: "Everywhere it is said in the Qur'an, 'and He sat Himself (*wa-stawa'*) is meant: He is 32 years old, and settles, istaqarra."[381] Muqatil's description of God as 32 years old means that God appears to the people in the ideal shape of a man of that age.[382] This is obviously based on the hadith of the "youthful God." Instead of using the designation *shābb* as found in most versions of the hadith Muqatil uses *kahl* which indicates a man who has reached his maturity but has not yet begun to gray.[383] That this is the ideal age according to Muqatil is shown by the fact that he gave the "virgins of Paradise" of Sura 56:37 this same age.[384]

---

[376] Binyamin Abrahamov, ***Al-Kasim B. Ibrahim on the Proof of God's Existence: Kitab al-Dalil al-Kabir*** (Leiden: E. J. Brill, 1990) 5.

[377] Van Ess, ***TG*** II, pp. 529f.; Gilliot, *art. cited,* 54ff.

[378] Cf. Gilliot, *art. cited,* 54ff.

[379] Ibid., 55. Gilliot correctly observes that, as density and "mass" are characteristic of bodies, this interpretation betrays a corporealist orientation. Nevertheless, he is incorrect in suggesting that Muqatil's refusal to attribute a *jawf* or stomach to God "rules out" an anthropomorphist interpretation (55). As we have shown above (37ff.), the absence of the stomach cavity was a part of the anthropomorphist doctrine. Dawud al-Jawaribi, a generation later, propagated an even cruder anthropomorphist doctrine which likewise denied God a stomach cavity; van Ess, ***TG*** II: 432ff.

[380] Ed. by Sven Dedering ("Bibliotheca Islamica" IX [Istanbul, 1936]).

[381] ***Tanbih*** 60, 12/75.

[382] Van Ess, ***TG*** II:530.

[383] Ibid.; idem., "Youthful God", 11.

[384] ***Tanbih*** 60, 7f./75, 5f.

The "charge" of anthropomorphism is thus substantiated. It seems appropriate here to cite the parallels between the doctrines of Muqatil and the Honorable Elijah Muhammad. For the latter, God is also a man of flesh and blood. In a famous speech in Atlanta, the Hon. Elijah Muhammad stated:

> God is a man, a flesh and blood being, but He is a Divine Being. Why do we call God a Divine Being? Because He is a Being like we are but His wisdom, power and other capacities and attributes are Supreme, making Him the Highest Power...He has the Divine Power to will whatever He wishes and to bring it into existence with His Divine Will.[385]

The Hon. Elijah Muhammad's description of the difference between God as a flesh and blood man, a Divine Being, and regular humans is paralleled in Muqatil's exegesis of Sura 42 and the so-called 'anti-anthropomorphic injunction,' "There is none like Him." As we saw above, Muqatil concludes his description of God as a man of flesh and blood with the words: "*And in spite of this, He resembles nothing and nothing resembles Him.*" This is no doubt to conform to the Qur'anic mandate to acknowledge a difference between God and His creation. But wherein lies the difference? In his exegesis of this passage as found in his ***Tafsir***, Muqatil comments: "in power" (*bi-l-qudra*).[386] God differs from man "in power."

Muqatil and the Hon. Elijah Muhammad likewise agree in their physical description of God. Muqatil's God is in the image of the youths of Paradise, beardless (*amrad*).[387] He has rich, black hair,[388] not curly (*ja'd*) as the traditions of the "youthful God" going back to Ibn Abbas maintain. Muqatil describes the hair as *muwaffar*:[389] it goes to the earlobe or even farther.[390] God's black hair, as we saw above, was contrasted with His white skin.[391] Muqatil's God was a young man, around 32-33 years old, with white skin and black hair that goes to his earlobes or beyond. He is beardless. If one were to glance at a picture of Fard Muhammad, God Himself according to the Honorable Elijah Muhammad, one would instantly recognize the similarity. Fard is a young man, 33 years old when He first arrived in America in 1910.

---

[385] As quoted in Louis Lomax, ***When the Word is Given*** (Cleveland: World Publishing Company, 1962) 127f.

[386] Muqatil b. Sulayman, ***Tafsir***, III:465; cf. also Gilliot, *art. cited*, 56.

[387] Cf. Gimaret, ***Diea a l'image***, 157 n. 2.

[388] Al-Ash'ari, ***Maqalat,***153, 1.

[389] Van Ess ***TG*** IV:381.

[390] Gimaret, ***Diea a l'image***, 157 n. 2.

[391] See above. Cf. van Ess ***TG*** I:342ff.

His rich black hair that reaches to His earlobes outlines His white skin. (Figure 6). His beardless face is a conspicuous departure from the wearing of beards that has become characteristic of Muslims since the Prophet's time. It is as if Muqatil's God has appeared in America.

Figure 7

Master Fard Muhammad

Descriptions of God paralleling those articulated by the Honorable Elijah Muhammad are thus found articulated in the early period of Islam. With Muqatil, we are talking about the end of the Umayyad period[392] and the beginning of the era of theological discourse in Islam. The question that remains is whether this anthropomorphist theology was as anathema* to Muqatil's contemporaries as it will be to later theologians. To answer this question, we must take a look at the theological milieu of the time.

4.6.1. *Anthropomorphism and Pre-Sunni Islam*

In order to properly comprehend dogmatic development in Islam, it is first necessary to do away with notions of "orthodoxy*" and "heresy*." Neither term has much significance in early Islam.[393] During the period with which we are dealing, the later Umayyad period, there was no "orthodox" Islam as such. The consolidation of Sunnite Islam was a post-*Mihna* phenomenon.[394] Under the Umayyads, we can only speak of a "general religious movement" composed of men from the various centers-Medina, Damascus, Basra, and Kufa-whose primary interests were theology, mysticism, asceticism and law.[395] Nor was this a monolithic body. The general religious movement of early Islam consisted of many individuals and groups holding different opinions.[396] Some held the doctrine of free will, while others adhered to the dogma of *irja* (deferring judgement). There were also men with Shiite tendencies. Anthropomorphism was in no way absent from this body.[397] Some of the most important names of this movement have been associated with anthropomorphist doctrines: Ikrimah (d. 723), Qatada (d. 735), Muk'hul (d. 731), az-Zuhri (d. 742), Amr b. Harith (d. 712-65), and Abu Qilabah Abd Allah b. Yazid (d. 104/723). All of these men were reported to have acknowledged that

---

[392] The Umayyad period was c. 661-749 AD.

[393] Cf. Alexander Knysh, "'Orthodoxy' and 'Heresy' in Medieval Islam: An Essay in Reassessment," ***The Muslim World*** 83 (1993), 48f.; W.M. Watt, "The Great Community and the Sects," in ***Early Islam***, 173f.

[394] The *Mihna* was the Inquisition instituted by the Caliph al-Ma'mun (d. 833) and cancelled by al-Mutawakil (d. 861). On the maturing of Sunnite Islam cf. W. M. Watt, ***The Formative Period of Islamic Thought*** (Edinburgh: Edinburgh University Press, 1998), 279f.

[395] Watt, ***Islamic Philosophy and Theology***, 72; idem., ***Formative Period***, 63f.

[396] Ziauddin Ahmed, "A Survey of the Development of Theology in Islam," ***Islamic Studies*** 11 (1972) 105; Watt, ***Formative Period***, 69.

[397] Watt, "Some Muslim Discussions ," 86-93; A.S. Tritton, ***Muslim Theology*** (London: Luzac & Company LTD., 1947), 48ff.

the Prophet saw God in His most beautiful form, the form of a young man.[398]

Anthropomorphist ideas were not restricted to the grass roots, however. In 743, the Umayyad Caliph Hisham had Ja'd b. Dirham executed for heretical views. Little is known of Ja'd[399]. According to a semi-legendary account reported by ad-Darimi and Abu Bakr al-Khallal (d. 311/923), the governor of Iraq, Khalid al-Qarisi, publicly slaughtered Ja'd on the day of the Feast of Sacrifices because he asserted that "God has not taken Abraham as his friend, nor has he spoken to Moses."[400] According to Wilfred Madelung, these assertions were an attack on the "anthropomorphic, personifying God of the traditionalist Sunnism."[401] Indeed, Ja'd was denying a report handed down on the authority of Ibn Abbas that speaks of a tripartite gradation between Abraham, Moses and Mohammad: "Abraham is the Friend of God (*khalil* Allah), Moses spoke to God (*kalim* Allah), and Mohammad saw God."[402] Those who rejected an anthropomorphic God could not accept the implications of this gradation. God could not speak to Moses because, according to Ja'd and the later Jahmiyya, speech is a human attribute requiring organs of sound. God could not take Abraham as friend (*khalil*) because a *khalil* is needy (from *khalla*-need). Exalted is God above such human characteristics, thought Ja'd. For this attack on the anthropomorphic deity of early Islam, the Caliph had him killed. The common ideas at this stage, the end of the Umayyad period, are clearly anthropomorphist.

Ja'd was the first true anti-anthropomorphist for whom any substantive information is known. His rejection of anthropomorphism was apparently enlarged upon and systematized by his student Jahm b. Safwan (d. 746), regarded as the first systematic theologian of Islam.[403] Jahm initiated a dogmatic crisis unseen in Islam up to that point. He accused "the main body of the faithful and the 'orthodox' doctors of...'tashbih'...as it is usually translated, anthropomorphism."[404]

The central tenet of Jahm's doctrine was the denial of the attributes of God.[405] "That which characterizes the Jahmiyya is

---

[398] Gimaret, ***Diea a l'image***, 155f.; Ritter, ***Das Meer***, 445ff.
[399] Frank, *art. cited*, 398.
[400] Quoted from Madelung, "The Origins of the Controversy," V:505.
[401] Ibid., 507.
[402] Ibn Khuzayma, ***Kitāb al-tawhīd*** 130, 1.
[403] J. van Ness, "Early Development of Kalam," in ***Studies on the First Century of Islamic Society*** (5), ed. G.H.A. Juynboll, Southern Illinois University Press, 118. He argues that "theology properly speaking did not exist before Jahm."
[404] Watt, ***Early Islam***, 86.
[405] Seal, *op. cited*, 45.

fundamentally…their anti-anthropomorphism."[406] His ministry was aimed against the "anthropomorphists" and the "hitherto established convention of literal interpretation so loyally followed by his predecessors."[407] Jahm's contemporaries, particularly those who concerned themselves with the study of tradition (*muhaddithun*) "took these verses (on the Attributes) on their face value"[408] and "recognized as genuine and interpret literally the crudely anthropomorphic traditions."[409] The protest against Jahm from the *muhaddithun* or hadith scholars was immediate. Ibrahim b. Tahman (d. 163/747) of Khurasan wrote one of the first refutations of Jahm b. Safwan.[410] Muqatil was another who wrote against Jahm's transcendent deity. Dhahabi, in his ***Mizan***, quotes al-Abbas b. Mus'ab al-Marwazi: "Muqatil came to Merv and there wed the mother of Abu Isma Nuh b. a. Maryam. He preached in the mosque. Jahm came to see him and conversed with him. They got worked up and each between them wrote a work in which each attacked the other."[411] According to Ibn Hazm, the dispute was over anthropomorphism: "While Jahm held that Allah, exalted be He, was neither something nor naught, exalted be He, being the creator of everything, and nothing existed but that was created, Muqatil opined that Allah was a body, flesh and blood in the form of a man."[412]

Muqatil's anthropomorphism does not seem to have caused much stir among his contemporaries. Indeed, he gained fame in *tafsir* (qurŞānic interpretation) and polemics.[413] Though criticized by posterity for his divergence from the rules of hadith transmission, Muqatil was highly praised for his extensive knowledge of Qur'an and as "a man who lived the Book of God."[414] Abbad b. Kathir al-Basri (d. 140-50 H) stated that in his generation there was no one more learned

---

406 Gimaret, ***Diea a l'image,*** 28.

407 Abdus Abdus Subhan, "Al-Jahm bin Sawan and His Philosophy," ***Islamic Culture*** 11 (1937) 222, 227.

408 J. Schacht, "Ahl al-Hadith," ***EI2***, 412.

409 "Hashwiyya," ***EI2,*** 269.

410 Muhammad Tahir Mallick, "The Traditionists and the Jahmiyya," ***Hamdard Islamicus*** 3:3 (1980): 31-45.

411 Adh-Dhahabi, ***Mizam al-I'tidal***, 4:173.

412 Ibn Hazm, ***Kitab al-Fasl fi al-Milal wa'l-Ahwa wa'l-Nihal*** (Cairo 1317-21 H), 4:205.

413 Isaiah Goldfeld, "Muqatil Ibn Sulayman," ***Arabic and Islamic Studies*** Vol. II ed. by Jacob Mansour (Ramat: Bar-Ilan University Press), XVII. For a look at ***Tafsir Muqatil*** cf. Kees Versteegh, "Grammar and Exegesis: The Origins of Kufan Grammar and the *Tafsir Muqatil*," ***Der Islam*** 67:2 (1990), 206-242.

414 Goldfeld has assembled the various opinions of Muqatil by his contemporaries. Cf. also Nabia Abbot, ***Studies in Arabic Literary Papyri II: Qur'anic Commentary and Tradition*** (Chicago: University of Chicago Press, 1967) 92ff.

in the Qur'an than Muqatil. In 745, the Umayyad governor Nasr b. Sayyar sent him and his namesake Muqatil b. Hayyan as experts on Qur'an to represent him during the negotiations with Harith b. Suraj.[415] The Caliph al-Mansur sought Muqatil out for his understanding of "why God created flies."[416] The crown prince al-Mahdi patronized Muqatil for his knowledge of *tafsir.*[417] Sufyan at-Thawri (d. 777), Sufyan b. Uyainah (d. 813), ash-Shafi'I (d. 820), Ahmad b. Hanbal (d. 855) and Ibrahim b. Ishaq al-Harbi (d. 198-285/813-99) all spoke positively of Muqatil's knowledge of Qur'an.[418]

At least one contemporary criticized Muqatil's ideas of God: Abu Hanifa (d. 150/738). This, however, turns out to be the exception that proves the rule. Abu Hanifa censured both Muqatil and Jahm as "extremists."[419] Muqatil's "extremism" was of course *tashbih.* But there is reason to believe that the problem was not *tashbih* per se, but extreme *tashbih* as the account explicitly states. For one, in spite of Abu Hanifa's reliance on *ra'y* (personal opinion) in legal matters, he was far from free of anthropomorphist tendencies in his theology. He affirmed that God was seated on His Throne above the Seventh Heaven and doesn't exist everywhere.[420] He is also reported to have affirmed that God can be seen with the eyes in this world and the next.[421] This implies the positing of a corporeal existence for God.

It could therefore not have been anthropomorphism per se that engendered this censure from Abu Hanifa. A more plausible source of condemnation would be Muqatil's "extreme" anthropomorphism; the mention of flesh, blood, bones, stomach, etc. Not that these items aren't necessarily implied by positing a "form of a young man" to God, but most of the hadith scholars maintained that it was unlawful to discuss any attribute not explicitly mentioned in Qur'an or Hadith.[422] Thus, it is sound to speak of God's eyes, ears, hair, face, mouth, uvula, molar teeth, chest, heart, arms, elbows, hands, palms, fingers, fingertips, loins, legs, thighs, feet, breath, beautiful form and form of a young man; all of these were revealed in the *Shari'a.* To discuss

---

[415] Goldfeld, "Muqatil Ibn Sulayman," XVII.
[416] Abbot, ***Studies***, 106.
[417] Ibid.
[418] Goldfeld, *art. cited,* XXIX.
[419] al-Baghdadi, ***Tarikh Baghdad***, 13:164.
[420] Cf. A. J. Wensink ***The Muslim Creed*** (New Delhi: Oriental Reprint, 1932, 1979) 121.
[421] Reported in Majlisi's ***Tadhkiratu'l-A'imma***,130. Cf. also Dwight M. Donaldson, ***The Shi'ite Religion*** (London: Luzac & Company, 1933), 133ff.
[422] Ibn Taymiyya argued: "*Allah shall be qualified only with those Attributes with which He has qualified Himself or His Messenger has qualified Him. Nothing should be said beyond the Qur'an and the Hadith.*" (Ibn Taymiyya, ***Majmu' Fatawa Ibn Taymiyya***, 36 vols. [Cairo, 1404 H], 5:26.)

anything outside of the *Shari'a* is an innovation. It is lawful to discuss the *sura* or form/image of God, but it is not lawful to speak of the *jism* or body of God. The objection is not substantive but semantical. Ibn Taymiyya made this point in his ***Majmu' al-Fatwa***:

> Indeed, the term body (*jism*), organs (*'arad*), extent (*mutahayyiz*) and their like are newly-invented terminologies. We have mentioned many a time before that the *Salaf* and the Imams have not spoken about such things, neither by way of negation or by way of affirmation. Rather, they declared those who spoke about such maters to be innovators and went to great lengths to censure them.[423]

Further support of this suggestion is the lack of condemnation of a contemporary of Muqatil and Abu Hanifa, Ubayd b. Mihran al-Muktib al-Kufi. Ubayd is believed to have been a student of Mujahid (d. 721) along with Muqatil.[424] Ash-Shaharastani lists him as an anthropomorphist for whom God "is in the likeness of a man."[425] Ubayd justifies this claim with the hadith, "*God created Adam after the form of the Merciful.*" In spite of this, Ubayd's contemporaries considered him trustworthy as a *muhaddith.* None objected to his anthropomorphism, not even Abu Hanifa.[426]

Thus, Muqatil's anthropomorphism seems to have fit in well with the theological milieu of the time, his extremism not withstanding. The description of God as presented by the Honorable Elijah Muhammad was therefore acceptable in early Islam. There would come a time when this is no longer the case. Transcendentalism will ultimately win the dogmatic struggle.[427] It is sufficient to note that the concept of God as a young man with rich black hair played a very important part in the development of Islamic theology.

4.7. *The Dogamatic Crises*

> The problems implicit in the anthropomorphic conceptions of the Qur'an did not begin to thrust themselves upon the awareness of Muslim thinkers till towards the close of the

---

423 Ibid., 3:306ff, 13:304f.

424 Watt, ***Early Islam,*** 197, n. 152.

425 Shahrastani, M ***Kitab al-Milal wa 'l-Nihal***. trns. by A. K. Kazi and J. G. Flynn in ***Muslim Sects and Divisions*** (London: Kegan Paul International, 1984),120.

426 Van Ess, **TG** I:212f.

427 Rahbar, *art. cited*; Valerie Jon Hoffman, ***The Theological Development of the Concept of the Unity of God in Islam From A.D. 750 to 950***, MA Thesis, University of Chicago, 1979.

second century after the Hijra. The point was apparently raised first by the heterodox* groups of the Mu'tazila and the Jahmiyya, and they raised it...by accusing the main body of the faithful and the 'orthodox' doctors of ...'tashbih'...as it is usually translated, anthropomorphism. The Mu'tazila and the Jahmiyya-at this point probably not entirely distinct from one another-had come under the influence of Greek philosophy.

W.M. Watt, ***Early Islam***

By early Abbasid[428] times, the community of Islam was divided along theological lines. One of the central issues was the nature of God.[429] While several groups competed for doctrinal hegemony, the two main groups arguing over the Attributes of God were the hadith advocates (*Ashab al-Hadith* or "the people of Traditions") and the Mu'tazila. The latter disparagingly referred to the former as a*l-Hashwiyya*.[430] The exact meaning of *Hashwiyya* is unknown but it is clearly used in a derogatory way. The term is usually rendered "vulgarists."[431] Marshall Hodgson argues that the preferred meaning is "men of the people, of the majority; they were not verbose, a secondary notion, but populistic."[432]

Evidence presented by A.S. Halkin supports this interpretation. In his article, "The Hashwiyya," Halkin states, "We learn also that the name is by no means applicable to a well defined group, including as it does virtually the whole community.[433]

Ibn Qutayba, in his ***Mukhtalif al Hadith*** noted that the *Ashab al-Hadith* or hadith-advocates "were nicknamed Hashwiyya, Nabita,

---

428 The Abbasids were the second dynasty of Islam (750-1258) following the fall of the Umayyads.

429 J. Pavlin, "Sunni Kalam and Theological Controversies," in ***History of Islamic Philosophy*** ed. S H Nasr and O Leaman, (London, 1996) Vol I., 105-117.

430 A. S. Halkin, "The Hashwiyya," ***Journal of the American Oriental Society***, 54 (1934), pp. 1-28; "Hashwiyya," ***EI2***, III, p. 269; G. Van Vloten, "Les Hachwia Et Nabita," ***Actes du Onzieme Congres International des Orientalistes, Paris, 1897*** Paris, 1899, pp. 99-123; M. Th. Houtsma, "Die Hashwiya," ***Zeitschrift fur Assyriologie*** 26, (1912), pp. 196-202; Fritz Steppat, "From *'Ahd Ardasir* to Al-Ma'mum: A Persian Element in the Policy of the Mihna", in ***Studia Arabica et Islamica: Festschrift for Ihsan 'Abbas***, ed. By Wadad Al-Qadi (Beirut: American University of Beirut, 1981) pp. 451ff..

431 Halkin, *art. cited*, 2.

432 Hodgson, ***Venture of Islam***, I:392.

433 Halkin, *art. cited*., 6.

Mujabbira."[434] Abu Muhammad al-Hasan an-Nawbakhti (d. 922), in his *Firaq ash-Shia,* described the Hashwiyya as the masses:

> These comprise the vast majority: the *ahl al-Hashw,* the followers of the kings, and the supporters of the victorious, I mean those who joined Mu'awiya.[435]

Doctrinally, the Hashwiyya were noted for their literal acceptance of the Qur'an and traditions, particularly the anthropomorphic descriptions of God.[436] Hodgson notes,

> For however much the Hadith folk might in principle reject such things, anthropomorphism in tales of God, presenting Him in the image of a human being...served to support a sense of personal contact with the divine presence in revelation. The Qur'an teemed with anthropomorphic images...which the Hadith folk found no reason to tone down so long as they served to exalt the glory of God and the honor of His prophets.[437]

The anthropomorphism of the *Ashab al-Hadith* was opposed by the Mu'tazila. According to P. Hoodbhoy "the Mu'tazila doctrine rejected the anthropomorphic representations of God popular at that time..."[438] The school of the Mu'tazila was actually a loose association of thinkers primarily from Basra and Baghdad who differed widely among themselves on important points.[439] Wasil b. Ata and Amr b. 'Ubayd, after separating from the circle of al-Hasan al-Basri, founded the school in the early part of the ninth century. They were later joined and succeeded by Abu al-Hudhayl and an-Nazzam. In Baghdad, a branch of the Mu'tazila formed around Bishr b. al-Mu'tamir. The Caliph Harun ar-Rashid temporarily jailed Bishr for his views.

The Mu'tazilite affirmations and the subsequent controversy which they caused centered around the unity of Allah or *tawhid. Tawhid* for the Mu'tazila was not just an affirmation of monotheism; all Muslims affirmed such. Theirs was a special "philosophic" concept that called into question the anthropomorphism of the *Ashab al-Hadith.* The

---

[434] Ibn Qutayba, ***Ta'wil muhtalif al-hadith*** ed. M. Zuhri an-Naggar (Cairo, 1386/1966; repr. Beirut, 1393/1972), 96.
[435] An-Nawbakhti, ***Firaq ash-Shia*** ed. H. Ritter (Leipziq, 1931) 96.
[436] Anawati, "Attributes of God," 513.
[437] Hodgson, ***Venture of Islam***, 391.
[438] P. Hoodbhoy, ***Islam and Science*** (London: Zed Books Ltd, 1991), 97.
[439] F.E. Peters, ***Allah's Commonwealth***, (New York: Simon & Schusler, 1973), 183.

Mu'tazila denied the worth of hadith in interpreting the Qur'an. They believed reason was superior to Tradition and more authoritative. This is called *Kalam*. The Mu'tazila therefore invented a grammatical system of exegesis (*ta'wil*) allowing them to interpret away the anthropomorphisms of the Qur'an in a philosophical fashion.

It was this school that gave the current Muslim world its allegorical mode of exegesis. Where the Qur'an speaks of the faithful 'seeing God,' it really means they would 'know' Him, according to this method of reading scripture. The hand of Allah meant 'grace' and His face was rendered His 'essence.' Just as their Jewish and Christian predecessors, the Mu'tazila applied Hellenistic rationalism to strip away the references of Allah that disagreed with the god of Greek philosophy. ***The Encyclopedia of Islam*** observes that "the Mu'tazilite schools...wished to justify dialectically the Muslim notion of God, in the face of the Greek-inspired 'God of the philosophers'.[440] F.E. Peters, in ***Allah's Commonwealth***, notes as well:

> The intrusion of these new constructs and novel modes of understanding are first perceptible in the work of Jahm ibn Safwan, a far more likely sire to the Mu'tazila than Wasil. Jahm had before him some vision of the world and God rationalized on a Neoplatonic* model, and he proceeded to explain Allah in terms of that understanding. The Mu'tazilites followed in his path, not with one but with many world views, some of them crossed with non-Greek themes, but NONE of them even remotely resembling the (world view) that lay behind the Qur'an.[441]

The result was the introduction into Islam of a totally new and foreign view of the nature of God. Al-Ash'ari describes the Mu'tazilite concept of God:

> Allah...is no body, nor object, nor volume, nor form, nor flesh, nor blood, nor person, nor substance, nor 'accidents,' nor provided with color, taste, smell, touch, heat, cold, moistness, dryness, length, breadth, depth...Neither is He provided with parts, divisions, limbs, members, with directions, with right or left hand...no place encompasses Him...He cannot be described by any description which can be applied to creatures...He can not be described by measure, nor by

440 "Allah," ***EI***, 1960, 412
441 Ibid., p. 185.

movement in a direction...The senses do not reach Him, nor can man describe Him by analogy. He does not resemble the creatures in any way...Nothing of what occur to any mind or can be conceived by fantasy resembles Him...Eyes do not see Him...nor can He be heard by ears. [442]

According to Henri Masse, in his ***Islam***, "the Mu'tazilites considered Allah to be Pure Spirit and consequently they rejected all those attributes of God..."[443] The Mu'tazila ideas were revitalized with the rise of the *falsafa* (philosopher) movement of the 10th century. Hitti observes that, "After (Ash'ari) the scholastic attempt to reconcile religious doctrine with Greek thought became the supreme feature of Moslem intellectual life as it was of medieval Christian life."[444] The Arabic translations of the Greek Hellenistic writings gave Plato and Aristotle a considerable following in the Arab world. Speaking of the philosophic movement in Islam, Fazhur Rahman, in his ***Islam***, notes that "The materials with which this philosophical system was constructed were either Greek or deduced from Greek ideas; in its material or content aspect, therefore, it is Hellenistic throughout."[445]

Muslim intercourse with Greek ideas had the same effect that it did on the Judeo-Christian traditions: the God of Religion was gradually being supplanted by the God of Philosophy. Rahman observes,

On the basis of the Plotinian idea of the ultimate ground of Reality, the One of Plotinus...the philosophers re-interpreted and elaborated the Mu'tazilite doctrine of the Unity of God. According to the new doctrine, God was represented as Pure Being without essence or attributes, His only attribute being necessary existence.[446]

The Encyclopedia of Islam (1961) agrees,

Another influence was Greek philosophy. The students of it in Islam...with it (Greek Philosophy) as guide...attacked the problem of the nature of Allah. Unity (tawhid), religiously and philosophically, they had to preserve; but, in preserving it, the

---

[442] Wensinck, ***Muslim Creed***, 73f2.
[443] Masse, ***Islam***, 206.
[444] P.K. Hitti. ***History of the Arabs***. (London: .Macmillian, 1970) 431.
[445] Rahman, ***Islam***, p. 117.
[446] Ibid., p. 118

> nature of Allah Himself was gradually reduced to a bare, undefinable something...[447]

The Mu'tazilite 'heresy' produced the ninth century 'dogmatic crises' in Islam. The intensity of the crises equaled that of the Arius-Athanasis feud which resulted in the Nicean Creed of Christianity. Unlike Christianity, Islam had no machinery comparable to the Ecumenical Councils, which could say authoritatively what constitutes 'right doctrine.'[448] By the time a wide area of agreement or consensus (*ijma*) was reached, transcendentalist notions had saturated the doctrinal soil. Shibli Nu'mani describes the final outcome for anthropomorphism in Islamic thought in his ***'Ilm ul Kalam***:

> In the first stage (of the development of Islamic theology) God is held to be corporeal, seated on the Throne, possessing hands, feet and face. God set His hand on the shoulder of Mohammmad and the Prophet felt that it was cold. In the second stage God is still held to be corporeal, having hands and face and legs, but all these are not like ours. In the third stage God is conceived to have neither body, hands nor face. Such words in the Qur'an have not the real meaning at all but are metaphorical and allegorical. God is Hearer, Seer, and Knower but all these attributes are in addition to His quiddity (*mahiya*). In the fourth stage God's attributes are neither identical with His essence nor alien to it (*la 'ayn wa la ghayr*). In the fifth stage God's essence is absolutely simple. In it there is no sort of multiplicity whatever. His essence is Knowing, Seeing, Hearing, Powerful, etc. In the sixth and last stage God is conceived of as Absolute Existence, i.e., His existence is His very quiddity. This takes the form of the Oneness of Existence (*Wahdat ul Wujud*), where we arrive at the point where philosophy and Sufism meet. It must not be supposed that these stages represent a chronological order in which the later superseded the earlier. Representatives of the different points of view were contemporaneous and still are."[449]

---

[447] "Allah," ***Encyclopedia of Islam*** (1961), p. 37.

[448] Watt, ***Formative Period***, 5f.

[449] Shibli Nu'mani, ***'Ilm ul Kalam***, 26f quoted in J. Windrow Sweetman, ***Islam and Christian Theology*** Part I, II:13.

Conclusion One

Poray Casimier claimed to have 'exposed' the "abundant doctrinal inconsistencies with Scripture"[450] of the NOI's teaching that God is a man. We have, I believe, proven him wrong. The anthropomorphism which characterizes the theology of the Honorable Elijah Muhammad is not contrary to the spirit or letter of the Bible, the Qur'ān or the Sunnah. On the contrary, these sources describe God in terms most compatible with the teachings of the Honorable Elijah Muhammad. The Bible explicitly calls God a man, and the Sunnah states that God is a corporeal person (*shakhṣ*) who appeared to Muhammad in the form of a man, a young man (*shābb*). We can now see the humor in Mustafa El-Amin's statement,

> As the reader can clearly see, the concept of God in the Religion of Al-Islam is extremely different than that of the Nation of Islam. Over one billion Muslims and others believe and accept the concept of Allah (God) as it is presented in the Religion of Al-Islam and the Holy Qur'an. Only a few thousand believe and accept the concept of God as it is presented by the Nation of Islam.[451]

Z. Ansari made a similar statement in 1981:

> When all these various characteristics are pieced together in order to obtain an integrated view of the 'Nation of Islam's' concept of God, the concept that emerges does not even remotely resemble the one to which the Muslims all over the world subscribe.[452]

The irony here is that the concept of God as presented by the Muslim world today-that invisible, incorporeal deity-is foreign to Islam as laid down by the Qur'ān and Sunnah. It is an import from Greece. The Honorable Elijah Muhammad is closer to the God of Islam with his anthropomorphic deity than the current Muslim world is with their immaterial 'other'. If Prophet Muhammad was not "un-Islamic" for

[450] ***Islamic Impostors***, XX.
[451] El-Amin, *op. cited*, 5f.
[452] Ansari, *art. cited,* 147.

saying God came to him in the form of a man, why then should Elijah Muhammad be condemned for saying the same?

The God of Scripture was a divine man who possessed a holy, human form. Scripture explicitly calls him so: *'îš* (man), *gibbôr* (mighty man), *shakhṣ* (physical person/man) and *shābb* (young man). This transcendent anthropomorphism characterizes the God of the Bible and the God of the Qur'ān and Sunnah. Such a deity lacks human frailty, and exemplifies the perfection of human strengths. Such a deity differs both from the abstract deity of Greek philosophy and the anthropomorphic deities of the Greek pantheon, the latter characterized much by human weaknesses. The Immaterial Deity of the philosophers replaced the Man-God of Scripture in Judaism, Christianity and Islam. The Honorable Elijah Muhammad therefore represents a turning back to 'the God of Old.'

Part Two

The Bible, the Qur'ān, and the Secret of the Black God

Chapter V:

The Black God and the Ancient Mysteries

5. *Introductory Summary*

The religious texts of the ancient East, i.e. the hieroglyphic writings of ancient Kemet (Egypt), the cuneiform writings of ancient Sumer (Chaldea/Mesopotamia), and the Sanskrit writings of ancient India, record the history of God as a divine Black man. According to these texts, God was originally a luminous, formless essence hidden within a primordial* substantive darkness called 'waters'. At some point, this divine luminosity concentrated itself within the darkness and produced the atom or first particle of distinct matter, the 'golden egg' of ancient myth*. From this first atom there emerged many atoms, which the God used to build up his own luminous body. This body was anthropomorphic and thus this God was the first man in existence, a self-created man. This was a brilliantly luminous man, represented by the so-called 'sun-gods' of ancient myth. Indeed, the sun in the sky was said to be only a sign of the luminous anthropomorphic body of the creator-god.

This God's initial attempts at creation proved unsuccessful, as the brilliant luminosity of the divine form scorched material creation. As a solution the God veiled his luminosity with a body made from that same primordial dark substance from which he initially emerged. This divine black body refracted the divine light as it passed through the hair pores covering the body. This black body is therefore referred to in later literature as God's 'shadow' as it shades creation from the scorching heat of the 'sun' or luminous body of God. As the light passed through the hair pores of this divine black body it produced a dark-blue iridescence or glow. The ancients symbolized this visual effect by the semiprecious stone sapphire or lapis lazuli, which was a dark blue stone with golden speckles throughout. The God's body at this stage was thus depicted dark blue and said to be made of sapphire/lapis lazuli. Veiled in this (blue-)black body, the God successfully produced the material cosmos. The creator-gods of ancient myth were thus often painted dark blue.

Animals were used by the ancients to represent or symbolize various characteristics or attributes of the gods. The so-called 'attribute animal' of this black-bodied creator-god was the black bovine,* usually a bull. The bull symbolized the strength and fecundity of the creator-god. It also associated the God with the primordial dark waters, which the bull was believed to personify. As the God's black body was made from this primordial darkness, the black hide of the bull represented the black skin of the creator-god. This black body of God symbolized by the black bull was at the center of the 'mystery of God' in the ancient Mystery Systems. In ancient Kemet (Egypt), for example, the greatest mystery concerned the union of the sun-god Rēʿ, i.e. the luminous body of God, with the black god Osiris, the personification of the divine black body.

5.1. *The Black God in Antiquity*

Godfrey Higgins, in his still prodigious work, ***Anacalypsis***, observed:

> We have found the Black complexion or something relating to it whenever we have approached the origin of nations. The Alma Mater, the Goddess Multimammia, the founders of the Oracles, the Memnon of first idols, were always Black. Venus, Jupiter, Apollo, Bacchus, Hercules, Asteroth, Adonis, Horus, Apis, Osiris, and Amen: in short all the...deities were black. They remained as they were first...in very ancient times.[453]

Though made over a century ago, current History-of-Religions scholarship only confirms Higgins' observation. The major deities of Egypt, India, Asia, the Near East, Greece and Central and South America were indeed black. Of special note we may mention, in addition to those listed above, Min of Egypt,[454] Viṣṇu and Kriṣṇa India,[455] Buddha of Asia,[456] 'Il/'El/Al of the Near East,[457] and

---

[453] ***Anacalypsis, an Attempt to Draw Aside the Veil of the Saitic Isis, or, An Inquiry Into the Origins of Languages, Nations, and Religions*** (1836; Brooklyn: A&B Book Publishers, 1992) 286.

[454] On Min and black gods of Egypt in general see Terence DuQuesne, ***Black and Gold God: colour symbolism of the god Anubis with observations on the phenomenology of colour in Egyptian and comparative religion*** (London: Da'th Scholarly Services, Darengo Publications, 1996) *passim*, esp. 18-23; Edmund S. Meltzer, " 'Who Knows the Color of God?'" ***Journal of Ancient Civilizations*** 11 (1996): 123-129; Jules Taylor, "The Black Image in Egyptian Art," ***Journal of African Civilization*** 1 (April, 1979) 29-38.

[455] On Viṣṇu and Kṛṣṇa see below.

[456] See photos of black Buddhas and some relevant data in Runoko Rashidi and Ivan Van Sertima, ***African Presence in Early Asia***(New Brunswick: Transaction Publishers, 1995 [Tenth Anniversary Edition]), e.g. 51-53, 82, 116, 118, 322, 335.

[457] Werner Daum, ***Ursemitische Religion*** (Stuttgart: W. Kohlhammer, 1985) and below.

Quetzalcoatl of the early Americas.[458] The blackness of these deities did not necessarily indicate that they were chthonic (associated with death and the underworld) or in any way malevolent. Indeed, in the various ancient traditions, it was the king of the gods, the creator deity himself, who was black.[459] The blackness of the creator deity, that is to say the creator deity's black *body*-how it originated, of what substance(s) it was composed, why it was black, etc.-was at the center of the 'mystery of God' in ancient Egypt, India, and Sumer/Akkad. We will analyze this "mystery of the black god" and explore its relation to biblical myth and theology.

---

[458] The anthropomorphic creator-god of Central Mexico, *Ehecatl Quetzalcoatl*, was black (Figure 8). See H. B. Nicholson, "The Deity 9 Wind 'Ehecatl-Quetzalcoatl' in the Mixteca Pictorials," ***Journal of Latin American Lore*** 4 (1978): 61-92; Eloise Quiñones Keber, "Topiltzin Quetzalcoatl in Text and Images," MA Thesis, Columbia University, New York, 1979; Fray Bernardino De Sahagan, ***A History of Ancient Mexico***, trans. Fanny R. Bandelier (Glendale, California: The Arthur H. Clark Company, 1932) 1:26. It is necessary to distinguish the historical-legendary figure, *Topiltzin Questzalcoatl* from the mythological-cosmological figure, Ehecatl-Quetzalcoatl. The ethnic identity of the former has been a matter of speculation. While a number of scholars cling to the post-Conquest myth of the legendary figure as a "bearded, white" foreigner (e.g. Graham Hancock, ***Fingerprints of the Gods*** [New York: Three Rivers Press, 1995] 102-05; Thor Heyerdahl, "The Bearded Gods Speak," in Geoffrey Ashe et al [edd.], ***The Quest for America*** [London: Pall Mall Press, 1971] 199-238; Constance Irwin, ***Fair Gods and Stone Faces*** [New York: St. Martin's Press, 1963] 33-47), the Totec ruler was likely either a native or maybe an African immigrant (B.C. Hedrick, "Quetzalcoatl: European or Indigene?" in Carroll L. Riley et al [edd.], ***Man Across the Sea: Problems of Pre-Columbian Contacts*** [Austin and London: University of Texas Press, 1971] 255-265; Ivan Van Sertima, "Among the Quetzalcoatls," in idem, ***They Came Before Columbus: The African Presence in Ancient America*** [New York: Random House, 1976] 71-89; Negel Davies, ***The Aztecs: A History*** [Norman: University of Oklahoma Press, 1980] 258-9). But regardless of the ethnic identity of the legendary figure, the mythological creator-god, Ehecatl-Quetzalcoatl, was black, as is shown, for example, in the cosmological narrative of Vindobonensis Obverse and the Codex Vaticanus. See Jill Leslie Furst, ***Codex Vindobonensis Mexicanus I: A Commentary*** (Albany: State University of New York, 1978) 100, 123-26; Eduard Seler, ***The Tonalamatl of the Aubin Collection: An Old Mexican Picture Amnuscript in the Paris National Library*** (Berlin, 1901) 45-7; idem, ***Codex vaticanus nr. 3773 (codex vaticanus B) eine altmexikansiche bilderschrift der Vatikanischen bibliothek*** (Berlin, 1902) 1:7 figure 1. Indeed, according to post-Conquest pictorial representations, the historic-legendary figure, as Totec priest, often dressed up as the god Ehecatl. In so doing, he painted his body black. See De Sahagan, ***A History***, Back; Keber, "Topiltzin," 65, 79, 86. On pre- and post-Conquest pictorials of Topiltzin Quetzalcoatl see Eloise Quiñones Keber, "The Aztec Image of Topiltzin Quetzalcoatl," in J. Kathryn Josserand and Karen Dakin (edd.), ***Smoke and Mist: Mesoamerican Studies in Memory of Thelma D. Sullivan*** (BAR International Series 402[i], 1988) 329-343. On the relation of the two Quetzalcoatls see Henry B. Nicholson, "Ehecatl-Quetzalcoatl vs. Topiltzin Quetzalcoatl of Tollan: a Problem in Mesoamerican Religion and History" in ***Actes du XLIIe Congrès international des amâricanistes. Congrès du centenaire: Paris, 2-9 septembre 1976*** (Paris: Socièlè des amèricanistes, 1976) 35-47.

[459] See below.

Figure 8

Ehecatl Quetzalcoatl, Black creator-God of Central America lifting the Primordial* Sky (from H.B. Nicholson, "The Deity 9 Wind 'Ehecatl-Quetzalcoatl' in the Mixteca Pictorials," 1978)

5.2. *The Black God and his Black Bull*

In antiquity various aspects of the gods were represented zoomorphically. That is to say, different animals were used to symbolize distinct characteristics or attributes of a deity,[460] who was otherwise anthropomorphic. The paramount 'attribute animal' of the black creator-god was the black bovine*, usually a bull. The bull represented potency, fecundity, and primordial materiality, all essential characteristics of the creator-god.[461] The color of the bull was not

---

[460] On the 'attribute animal' of ancient Near Eastern religion see Erik Hornung, ***Conceptions of God in Ancient Egypt: the One and the Many*** (Ithaca: Cornell University Press, 1982)109-25; P. Amiet, ***Corpus des cylinders de Ras Shamra-Ougarit II: Sceaux-cylinres en hematite et pierres diverses*** (Ras Shamra-Ougarit IX; Paris: Éditions Recherche sur les Civilisations, 1992) 68; "Attribute Animal" in idem, ***Art of the Ancient Near East***, trans. J. Shepley and C. Choquet (New York: Abrams, 1980) 440 n. 787.

[461] On the symbolism of the bull see Mircea Eliade, ***Patterns in Comparative Religion***, translated by Rosemary Sheed (1958; Lincoln and London: University of Nebraska Press, 1996) 82-93; Karel van der Toorn, Bob Becking and Pieter W. van der Horst (edd.), ***Dictionary of Deities and Demons in the Bible***, 2nd Edition (Leiden and Grand Rapids, MI.: Brill and Eerdmans, 1999) s.v. "Calf," by N. Wyatt, 180-182; ***ERE*** 2:887-889 s.v.

arbitrary. As René L. Vos pointed out, "Color reflected the nature of a god" and thus the skin color "constituted the vehicle of the divine nature of a sacred animal."[462] Over against the golden lion or falcon, which symbolized morning/midday sunlight, the black bovine symbolized night and materiality.[463] The black bovine was associated with the black primordial waters from which the creator-god emerged;[464] it thus came to symbolize the black material body that the creator-god will form for himself,[465] the black skin of the bovine

---

Bull, by C.J. Caskell. See also René L. Vos, "Varius Coloribus Apis: Some Remarks of the Colours of Apis and Other Sacred Animals," in Willy Clarysse, Antoon Schoors and Harco Willems (edd.), ***Egyptian Religion: The Last Thousand Years***, **Part 1.** ***Studies Dedicated to the Memory of Jan Quaegebeur*** (Leuven: Uitgeverij Peeters en Departement Oosterse Studies, 1998) 715, who notes that the bulls of Egypt "materialize upon the earth the creative forces of the hidden demiurge (creator-god)."

[462] "Varius Coloribus Apis," 711.

[463] Asko Parpola, "New correspondences between Harappan and Near Eastern glyptic art," ***South Asian Archaeology*** 1981, 178 notes: "Indeed, the golden-skinned hairy lion is an archetypal symbol for the golden-rayed sun, the lord of the day...Night...is equally well represented by the bull, whose horns connect it with the crescent of the moon." On the bull and the moon-god in ancient Near Eastern mythology see also Tallay Ornan, "The Bull and its Two Masters: Moon and Storm Deities in Relation to the Bull in Ancient Near Eastern Art," ***Israel Exploration Journal*** 51 (2001) 1-26; Dominique Collon, "The Near Eastern Moon God," in Diederik J.W. Meijer (ed.), ***Natural Phenomena: Their Meaning, Depiction and Description in the Ancient Near East*** (North-Holland, Amsterdam, 1992) 19-37. On the falcon as symbol of the sun-god see J. Assmann, ***Liturgische Lieder an den Sonnengott. Untersuchungen zur ägyptischen Hymnik I*** (MÄS 19; Berlin, 1969) 170-1.

[464] Parpola, "New correspondences," 181 suggests that "the dark buffalo bathing in muddy water was conceived as the personification of the cosmic waters of chaos". In the *Ṛg Veda* the cosmic waters are cows (e.g. 4.3.11; 3.31.3; 4.1.11) and in *Pañcaviṃśa-Brāmana* 21.3.7 the spotted cow Śabalā is addressed: "Thou art the [primeval ocean]." On water and cows in Indic tradition see further Anne Feldhaus, ***Water and Womanhood. Religious Meanings of Rivers in Maharashtra*** (New York and Oxford: Oxford University Press, 1995) 46-47. The black bull (*k'km*) of Egypt, Apis, personified the waters of the Nile which was regarded as a type of Nun, the dark, primeval watery mass out of which creation sprang (See Émile Chassinat, "La Mise a Mort Rituelle D'Apis," ***Recueil de travaux relatifs a la philology et a l'archeologie egyptiennes et assyriennes*** 38 [1916] 33-60; E.A. Wallis Budge, ***The Egyptian Book of the Dead (The Papyrus of Ani). Egyptian Text Transliterated and Translated*** [New York: Dover Publications, Inc. 1967] cxxiii). See also the Babylonian Enki (Figure 9), called *am-gig-abzu*, 'black bull of the Apsû (primordial waters)." See W.F. Albright, "The Mouth of the Rivers," ***AJSL*** 35 (1991): 161-195, esp. 167. The Babylonian Tiamat (primordial salt-waters) seems also to have been presented as a bovine in the *Enūma Elish*: see B. Landsberger and J.V. Kinnier Wilson, "The Fifth Tablet of Enuma Elis," ***JNES*** 20 (1961): 175 [art.=154-179]. On the black bull and the black waters of creation see also Vos, "Varius Coloribus Apis," 715, 718.

[465] Thus the Buchis bull of Armant, whose name means something like "who makes the *ba* dwell within the body." See Dieter Kessler, "Bull Gods," in Donald B. Redford (ed.), ***The Ancient Gods Speak: A Guide to Egyptian Religion*** (Oxford: Oxford University Press, 2002) 30.

signaling the black skin of the deity.[466] Thus, the hide of the sacrificial bull of ancient Sumer/Akkad, which was required to be 'black as asphalt (Figure 10),' was ritually identified with the skin of the Sumerian/Akkadian creator-deity Anu.[467] This association between divine and bovine skin is explicitly articulated, for example, in the Indic[468]* scripture *Śatapatha-Brāhmaṇa*[469] with regard to the black *tārpya* garment worn by the king during the Indic royal consecration ceremony called *Rājasūya*. During this ceremony the king ritually impersonated the creator-god and divine king Prajāpati-Varuṇa.[470] The black *tārpya* garment worn by the king represented the body of the royal creator-god (Prajāpati-Varuṇa) whom the king impersonated here.[471]

---

[466] See e.g. the black skin of the Egyptian deity Min (Figure 14), the 'creator god *par excellence*," and his black bovines (H.Gauthier, ***Les fêtes du dieu Min*** 2 vols. [Le Caire, 1931; IFAO. Recherches d'Archéologie] 2:55-57; ***DDD*** s.v. "Min," 577 by K. van der Toorn; Veronica Ions, ***Egyptian Mythology*** [Middlesex: The Hamlyn Publishing Group Ltd., 1968] 110; G.A. Wainwright, "Some Aspects of Amūn," ***Journal of Egyptian Archaeology*** 20 [1934]: 140 [art.=139-53]), the black-skinned Osiris and the black bull Apis (Vos, "Varius Coloribus Apis," 716; idem, "Apis," ***DDD*** 70) as well as the Indic Yamā with his black skin and black buffalo [P. van Bosch, "Yama-The God on the Black Buffalo," in ***Commemorative Figures*** [Leiden: E.J. Brill, 1982] 21-64). In contrast, but making the same point, see the white-skinned Śiva and his white bull Nandi.

[467] In one description of the Babylonian *kalū*-ritual the slaying and skinning of the black bull is mythologized as the god Bēl's slaying and flaying of the god Anu, whose characteristic attribute animal was the black bull. See Daum, ***Ursemitische Religion***, 204; E. Ebeling, ***Tod und Leben nach den Vorstellungen der Babylonier*** 2 vols. (Berlin-Leipzig, 1931) 1:29; C. Bezold, ***Babylonisch-assyrisches Glossar*** (Heidelberg: C. Winter, 1926) 210 s.v. sugugalu; Georgia de Santillana and Hertha von Dechend, ***Hamlet's Mill: An essay on myth and the frame of time*** (Boston: Gambit, Inc., 1969) 124. On Anu see further Herman Wohlstein, ***The Sky-God An-Anu*** (Jericho, New York: Paul A. Stroock, 1976).

[468] I will use 'Indic' throughout this work to refer to the traditions of ancient India, as opposed to 'Indian,' which is popularly, though erroneously, associated with the indigenous groups of the early Americas.

[469] Brāhmanas are Vedic texts dealing with priestly sacrifices and rituals.

[470] See J. Gonda, "Vedic Gods and the Sacrifice," ***Numen*** 30 (1983): 1-34; Walter O. Kaelber, "'Tapas,' Birth, and Spiritual Rebirth in the Veda," ***History of Religions*** 15 (1976): 343-386; Johannes Cornelis Heesternman, ***The Ancient Indian Royal Consecration: The rājasūya described according to the Yajus texts and annotated*** (The Hague: Mouton & Co., 1957).

[471] See Heesternman, ***Ancient Indian Royal Consecration*** on the somatic significance of the ritual garments. Specifically, the black antelope skins represent the black skin of the divine king Varuṇ[a,] who personifies the primordial waters. On the black skinned Varuṇ[a] see *Śatapatha- Brāhmana* [11.6.1]. On Varuṇ[a] and the black sacrificial garments see further Alfred Hillebrandt, ***Vedic Mythology***, trans. from the German by Sreeramula Rajeswara Sarma, 2 vols. (Delhi: Motilal Banarsidass Publishers, 1999; reprint) 2: 41, 44-45. On Varuṇ[a] in Indic mythology generally see ibid. 2:1-47; Alain Daniélou, ***The Myths and Gods of India*** (1964; Rochester, Vermont: Inner Traditions International, 1985) 118-121; F.B.J. Kuiper, ***Varuṇ[a] and Vidūṣaka. On the Origin of the Sanskrit Drama*** (Amsterdam/Oxford/New York: North-Holland Publishing Company, 1979); Sukumari

Figure 9

Ancient seal depicting the Sumerian/Akkadian creator-god Enki/Ea (enthroned), the "black bull of the Apsû (primordial fresh-waters)"

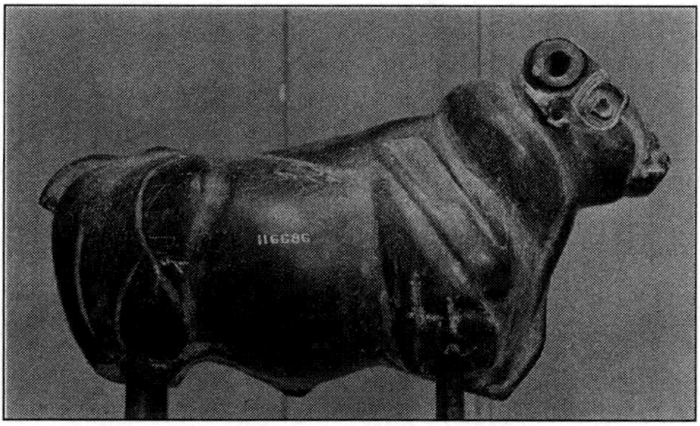

Figure 10

Image of Sacrificial Bull, "black as asphalt" used to represent the Sumerian/Akkadian king of the gods, An/Anu (from Elizabeth Lansing, ***The Sumerians: Inventors and Builders*** [New York: McGraw-Hill Book Company, 1971])

Bhattacharji, ***The Indian Theogony: A Comparative Study of Indian Mythology From the Vedas to the Purāṇas*** (Cambridge: Cambridge University Press, 1970) Chapter One.

Regarding the *tārpya* garment and by implication its divine counterpart, *Śatapatha-Brāhmaṇa* 3, 1, 2, 13-17 notes:

> it (i.e. the *tārpya* garment) is indeed his (i.e. king's) own skin he thereby puts on himself. Now that skin which belongs to the cow was originally on man. The gods spake, 'Verily, the cow supports everything here (on earth); come, let us put on the cow that skin which is now on man; therewith she will be able to endure rain and cold and heat. Accordingly, having flayed man, they put that skin on the cow, and therewith she now endures rain and cold and heat. For man was indeed flayed; and hence wherever a stalk of grass or some other object cuts him, the blood trickles out. They then put that skin, the (*tārpya*) garment, on him; and for this reason none but man wears a garment, it having been put on him as his skin...Let him, then, not be naked in the presence of a cow. For the cow knows that she wears his skin, and runs away for fear lest he should take the skin from her.[472]

In explaining the relation between the black ritual garment and the black cow skin, it is here recalled that the latter actually was once man's own skin, who lost it to the cow (man was 'flayed'). This black bovine skin apparently once covered man's fleshy skin as an exterior layer, according to this mythical account. In place of this lost exterior layer, man was given the black *tārpya* garment. Now whenever the cow sees a naked man it flees in fear of him trying to retrieve his original 'garment,' the black skin that now protects the cow from inclement weather. It must be kept in mind that the Vedas are the literary work of the invading Indo-Aryan tribes, and this description of the flaying of man's black skin reflects the actual experience of the indigenous 'black, snub-nosed' Dasyus tribes who were indeed flayed by the Aryan hordes. This historical flaying is mythologized in the *Ṛg Veda* (I. 130-8) where the Aryan deity Indra is described as tearing off the black skin of the Asura, the gods of the pre-Aryan black tribes.[473] In this *Rājasūya* or

---

[472] Trans. J. Eggeling, ***The Śatapatha- Brāhmana according to the text of the Mādhyandina school***. I-V. ***Sacred Books of the East*** (Oxford, 1882-1900) II: 9f.

[473] On the historical conflict between the invading Aryans and the indigenous black tribes of India, and its mythic portrayal in the Vedas as the conflict between the Devas and the Asuras, see Ram Sharan Sharma, ***Sūdras in Ancient India. A Social history of the lower order down to circa A.D. 600*** (Delhi: Molilal Banarsidass, 1980) Chapt. II; Daniélou, ***Myths and Gods of India***, 139-146. On the racial background of the Asuras see also R. Ruggles Gates, "The Asurs and Birhors of Chota Nagpur," in T.N. Madan and Gopāla Śarana (edd.), ***Indian Anthropology. Essays in Memory of D.N. Majumdar*** (New York: Asia Publishing House, 1962) 163-184.

consecration ritual the human king is impersonating the divine king, God, whose skin is represented by the bovin skin. The black garment/bovine skin represents the black skin of the pre-Aryan black gods. Asko Parpola has demonstrated that both the *tārpya* garment and its divine analogue, the 'sky garment' of the gods (i.e. the divine body), are associated with the skin of the mythic 'bull of heaven.'[474]

5.3. *The Blue-Black Creator-God*

In his *Praeparatio Evangelica* (III, 115a, 7) the fourth century church historian Eusebius of Caesarea quoted from Porphyry's (ca. 233-309) lost work, *Concerning Images*, a note on an Egyptian view of the Creator: "The Demiurge (creator-god), whom the Egyptians call Cneph, is of human form, but with a skin of dark blue, holding a girdle and a scepter, and crowned with a royal wing on his head."[475] While we have by now come to expect the divine human form, the dark blue skin requires some explanation. Indeed, the leading gods of the ancient Near East were not just black, but blue-black. This dark 'blueness' of the divine body had profound significance. It was not just any blue, but sapphire blue.[476] In biblical tradition and in ancient and medieval texts generally the term 'sapphire' denoted the semiprecious stone lapis lazuli.[477] Considered the "ultimate Divine substance," sapphire/lapis

---

[474] ***The Sky-Garment: A Study of the Harappan religion and its relation to the Mesopotamian and later Indian religion*** (SO 57; Helsinki, 1985); idem, "The Harappan 'Priest-King's' Robe and the Vedic Tārpya Garment: Their Interrelation and Symbolism (Astral and Procreative)," ***South Asian Archaeology*** 1983, vol. 1, 385-403. On the garments of the gods in ancient Near Eastern tradition see A. Leo Oppenheim, "The Golden Garments of the Gods," ***Journal of Near Eastern Society of Columbia University*** 8 (1949): 172-193; Herbert Sauren, "Die Kleidung Der Götter," ***Visible Religion*** 2 (1984): 95-117; David Freedman, "Ṣubāt Bāšti: A Robe of Splendor," ***JANES*** 4 (1972): 91-5. See also Alan Miller, "The Garments of the Gods in Japanese Ritual," ***Journal of Ritual Studies*** 5 (Summer 1991): 33-55.

[475] Trans. E.H. Grifford, 1903.

[476] The dark blue skin of the anthropomorphic deities of Egypt was *jrtyw* or *ḫsbḏ* (lapis lazuli), which is a blue-black: See Caroline Ransom Williams, ***The Decoration of the Tomb of Per-Nēb*** (New York: The Metropolitan Museum of Art, 1932) 52f; J.R. Harris, ***Lexicographical Studies in Ancient Egyptian Minerals*** (Berlin: Akademie-Verlag, 1961) 226.

[477] Michel Pastoureau, ***Blue: The History of a Color*** (Princeton: Princeton University Press, 2001) 7, 21f; ***The Interpreter's dictionary of the Bible: an illustrated encyclopedia identifying and explaining all proper names and significant terms and subjects in the Holy Scriptures, including the Apocrypha, with attention to archaeological discoveries and researches into life and faith of ancient times*** 5 vols. (George Arthur Buttrick et al [edd.]; New York: Abingdon Press, 1962-76) s.v. "Sapphire," by W.E. Stapes; ***Dictionary of the Bible***, ed. James Hastings (New York: MacMillian Publishing Company, 1988) 497, s.v. "Jewels and Precious Stones," by J. Patrick and G.R. Berry.

lazuli possessed great mythological significance in the ancient Near East.[478] In its natural state lapis lazuli is dark blue with fine golden speckles[479] recalling the "sky bedecked with stars"[480]; thus the visible heaven is often said to be sapphiric.[481] This sapphiric heaven, called the 'sky- garment' of the gods,[482] was associated with the divine body,[483]

---

[478] F. Daumas, "Lapis-lazuli et Régénération," in Sydney Aufrère, ***L'Univers minéral dans la pensée Égyptienne***, 2 vols. (Le Caire: Institut Français d'Archéologie Orientale du Caire, 1991) 2:463-488; John Irwin, "The Lāṭ Bhairo at Benares (Vārāṇasī): Another Pre-Aśokan Monument?" ***ZDMG*** 133 (1983): 327-43 [art.=320-352].

[479] On Lapis Lazuli see Lissie von Rosen, ***Lapis Lazuli in Geological Contexts and in Ancient Written Sources*** (Partille: Paul Åströms förlag, 1988); idem, ***Lapis Lazuli in Archaeological Contexts*** (Jonsered: Paul Åströms förlag, 1990); Rutherford J. Gettens, "Lapis Lazuli and Ultramarine in Ancient Times," ***Alumni de la Fondation universitaire*** 19 (1950): 342-357.

[480] See Irwin, "Lāṭ Bhairo," 332.

[481] Exod. 24:10; Ez. 1:26 (LXX); William Brownlee notes "This dome (of heaven) was thought of as sapphire in color, and as crystalline and transparent." ***Ezekiel 1-19*** (Waco, TX: Word Books, 1986), 13. Nut, the ancient Egyptian sky goddess, "glistens like lapis lazuli." See Assmann, ***Liturgische Lieder***, 314ff. text III 4. The association of the heavens with precious stones is found in Babylonian cosmologies as well, which may have influenced biblical cosmology. According to W.G. Lambert, the Babylonians associated their three heavens (upper/middle/lower) with stones, the lower deriving its blue from the jasper stone ("The Cosmology of Sumer and Babylon," in Carmen Blacker and Michael Loewe (edd.), ***Ancient Cosmologies*** [London: George Allen & Unwin Ltd, 1975] 58). In rabbinic literature, the firmament is often made of crystal, whench the heavens derive their light (See Louis Ginzberg, ***The Legends of the Jews*** [7 vols; Baltimore: John Hopkins University Press, 1911, 1939], vol. 1, 13).

[482] See especially Parpola, ***Sky-Garment***; idem, "Harappan 'Priest-King's' Robe"; Oppenheim, "Golden Garments." This designation arises from the golden star-like ornaments or appliqué work sewn into the garment recalling the star-spangled night sky.

[483] Amun-Re is "beautiful youth of purest lapis lazuli (*ḥwn-nfr n-ḫsbḏ-m3ʿ*) whose "body is heaven" (*ḫt. K nwt*). See J. Assmann, ***Sonnenhymnen in thebanischen Gräbern*** (Mainz: a.R., 1983) 5, #6:5; 124, # 43:14; A.I. Sadek, ***Popular Religion in Egypt During the New Kingdom*** (Hildsheim, 1987) 14. See also Grey Hubert Skipwith, " 'The Lord of Heaven.' (The Fire of God; the Mountain Summit; The Divine Chariot; and the Vision of Ezekiel.)," ***JQR*** 19 (1906-7): 693-4 and illustrations in Othmar Keel, ***The Symbolism of the Biblical World. Ancient Near Eastern Iconography and the Book of Psalms*** (London: SPCK, 1978) 33-4. In Manichaean tradition, the Mother of Life spread out the heaven with the skin of the Sons of Darkness according to the testimony of Theodore bar Khonai, *Liber Scholiorum* XI, trns. H. Pognon in ***Inscriptions Mandaïtes des coupes de Khouabir***, II (Paris: Welter, 1899) 188. In the *Greater Bundahišn*, 189, 8 the cosmic body is said to have "skin like the sky." See also the anthropomorphic body of Zurvan, called *Spihr*, which is associated with both the blue firmament and a blue garment: see R.C. Zaehner, ***Zurvan, A Zoroastrian Dilemma*** (Oxford, 1955; rep. 1972), 11f, 122. The stars covering the garment signified rays of celestial light emanating from the hair-pores of the divine skin (see below). Thus, in some depictions of this 'sky-garment,' the garment itself is missing and the stars are painted on the very skin of the anthropos. See e.g. the golden statue found in Susa and published by R. de Mecquenem, ***Offrandes de fondation du temple de Chouchinak***, (Paris, 1905) vol. II, Pl. XXIV 1*a*. See also Oppenheim, "Golden Garments," 182 Fig. 2.

'garment' being an ancient and widespread metaphor for body.[484] Thus, the leading deities of the ancient Near East had sapphiric-blue bodies. This is particularly the case with deities associated with fecundity or creation.[485] In Egypt, "The traditional colour of (the) gods' limbs (was) the dark blue lapis lazuli."[486] The ancient Near Eastern cult statue, which was considered the earthly body of the deity,[487] was ideally made of a wooden core platted with red gold or silver, overlaid with sapphires,[488] all of which signified substances from the body of the

---

[484]Geo Widengren, ***The Great Vohu Manah and the Apostle of God: Studies in Iranian and Manichaean Religion*** (Uppsala: A.-B. Lundequistska Bokhandeln, 1945) 50-55, 76-83; J.M. Rist, "A Common Metaphor," in idem, ***Plotinus: The Road to Reality*** (London: Cambridge University Press, 1967) 188-198; Dennis Ronald MacDonald, ***There is no Male and Female: The Fate of a Dominical Saying in Paul and Gnosticism*** (Philadelphia: Fortress Press, 1987), 23-25.

[485] John Baines, ***Fecundity Figures: Egyptian Personification and the Iconology of a Genre*** (Wiltschire: Aris & Phillips and Chicago: Bolchazy-Carducci, 1985) 139-142.

[486] Lise Manniche, "The Body Colours of Gods and Man in Inland Jewellery and Related Objects from the Tomb of Tutankhamun," ***Acta Orientalia*** 43 (1982): 5-12 (10). On the color of the god's skin as indicative of its status and role, with the sapphiric-bodied deity as 'king of the gods' see Robins, "Color Symbolism," in Redford ***Ancient Gods Speak***, 58-9; Monika Dolińsks, "Red and Blue Figures of Amun," ***Varia aegyptiaca*** 6 (1990): 5-6 [art.=3-7]. On the association of a deities skin color and character see also John Baines, "Color Terminology and Color Classification: Ancient Egyptian Color Terminology and Polychromy," ***American Anthropologists*** 87 (1985): 284 [art.=282-97]

[487] On the ancient Near Eastern cult of divine images see Neal H. Walls (ed.) ***Cult Image and Divine Representation in the Ancient Near East*** (American Schools of Oriental Research Books Series 10; Boston: American Schools of Oriental Research, 2005); Zainab Bahrani, ***The Graven Image: Representation in Babylonia and Assyria*** (Philadelphia: University of Pennsylvania Press, 2003); Michael B. Dick (ed.), ***Born in Heaven, Made on Earth: The Making of the Cult Image in the Ancient Near East*** (Winona Lake, Indiana: Eisenbrauns, 1999); idem, "The Relationship between the Cult Image and the Deity in Mesopotamia," in Jiří Prosecký (ed.), ***Intellectual Life of** the **ancient Near East: Papers Presented at the 43rd Rencontre assyriologique international, Prague, July 1-5, 1996*** (Prague: Oriental Institute, 1998) 11-16; T. Jacobsen, "The Graven Image," in P.D. Miller Jr., P.D. Hanson and S.D. McBride (edd.), ***Ancient Israelite Religion: Essays in Honor of Frank Moore Cross*** (Philadelphia: Fortress Press, 1987) 15-32, esp. 16-20;

[488] When King Nabu-apla-iddina of Babylon (ca. 887-855 BC) restored the image (*ṣalmu*) of the god Shamash, it was made of "red gold and clear lapis lazuli": L.W. King, ***Babylonian Boundary-Stones and Memorial-Tablets in the British Museum: With Atlas of Plates*** (London: British Museum, 1912) 120-127, #36 IV 20. Lugal-zagesi, *ensi* (governor) of Ummah, during his sack of Lagash (ca. 2340 B.C.E.) is said to have plundered the temple of the goddess Amageštin and robed her "of her precious metal and lapis lazuli, and threw her in the well." H. Steible, ***Die altsumerischen Bau- und Weihinschriften*** (Freiburger Altorientalische Studien 5; Wiesbaden: F. Steiner, 1982): Ukgagina 16:6:11-7:6. The reference is likely to the goddesses cult statute. See Michael B. Dick, "The Mesopotamian Cult Statute: A Sacramental Encounter with Divinity," in Walls, ***Cult Image***, 49. See also the lament of Ninšubur on the occasion of Inanna's 'Descent to the Netherworld" (II. 43-46):

O Father Enlil, let no one in the Netherworld kill your child!

deity: "his (i.e. Rē'"s) bones are silver, his flesh is gold, his hair genuine lapis-lazuli."[489] But the hair too was a metaphor for rays of light emanating from the hair-pores covering the body[490] and lapis lazuli was considered 'solidified celestial light'.[491] The deity's whole body was therefore depicted blue.[492] Mediating between the gold flesh and lapis lazuli 'hair' of the creator deity is the divine black skin signified by the bull hide. The black bull, Ad de Vries informs us, "mediated between fire (gold) and water (lapis lazuli), heaven and earth" (inserts original).[493]

> Let no one smelt your fine silver along with crude ore! (on the translation of this line see A.R. George, "Observations on a Passage of 'Inanna's Descent'," ***JCS*** 37 [1985]: 109-13)
> Let no one cleave your fine lapis lazuli along with the lapidary's stones!
> Let no one cut up your boxwood along with the carpenter's timber!
> Let no one in the Netherworld kill the young woman Inanna!

Inanna's statue is thus made of boxwood (*taškarinnu*), plated with silver and overlaid with lapis lazuli. Cf. the *eršemma* of Ningirgilu (*CT* 15 23). On the above passage as a reference to Inanna's cult statue see also Giorgio Buccellati, "The Descent of Inanna as a Ritual Journey to Kutha?" ***Syro-Mesopotamian Studies*** 3 (1982): 3-7. On Egyptian cult statues and lapis-lazuli see Daumas, "Lapis-lazuli et Régénération," 465-67. On the materials used for the construction of divine images see Victor Hurowitz, "What Goes In Is What Comes Out – Materials for Creating Cult Statues" in G. Beckman and T.J. Lewish (edd.), ***Text and Artifact – Proceedings of the Colloquium of the Center for Judaic Studies, University of Pennsylvania, April 27-29, 1998***, Brown Judaic Series, 2006 (in press).

489 Gay Robins, "Cult Statues in Ancient Egypt," in Walls, ***Cult Image***, 6; idem, "Color Symbolism," 60; Claude Traunecker, ***The Gods of Egypt***, translated from the French by David Lorton (Ithaca and London: Cornell University Press, 2001) 44; Dmitri Meeks, "Divine Bodies," in Dimitri Meeks and Christine Favard-Meeks, ***Daily Life of the Egyptian Gods***, translated by G.M. Goshgarian (Ithaca and London: Cornell University Press, 1996) 57; Hornung, ***Conceptions of God***, 134.

490 Ad de Vries, ***Dictionary of Symbols and Imagery*** (Amsterdam and London: North-Holland Publishing Company, 1974) 39 s.v. Beard; Marten Stol, "The Moon as Seen by the Babylonians," in Diederik J.W. Meijer (ed.), ***Natural Phenomena: Their Meaning, Depiction and Description in the Ancient Near East*** (North-Holland, Amsterdam, 1992) 255.

491 On lapis lazuli as "solidified celestial light" see Robins, "Color Symbolism," 60. On rays of light emanating from the divine hair pores see for example *Śatapatha-Brāhmaṇa* 10, 4, 4, 1-2: "When Prajāpati was creating living beings, Death, that evil, overpowered him. He practiced austerities for a thousand years, striving to leave evil behind him. 2. Whilst he was practicing austerities, lights went upwards from those hair-pits of his; and those lights are those stars; as many stars as there are, so many hair-pits there are." Translation by Eggeling. See also below. On ancient Near Eastern parallels see Parpola, ***Sky-Garment***, 74.

492 Thus the blue bodied deity Amun. See Traunecker, ***Gods of Egypt***, 44; Wainwright, "Some Aspects of Amūn"; Dolińsks, "Red and Blue Figures of Amun."

493 ***Dictionary of Symbols and Imagery***, 69 s.v. Bull. As the 'bull of heaven' the bovine has sapphiric associations as well. See e.g. the statuette from Uruk, Jemdet Nasr period (c. 3200-2900 BC) with trefoil inlays of lapis lazuli: H. Schmökel, ***Ur, Assur und Babylon: Drei Jahrtausende im Zweistromland*** (Stuttgart, 1955), plate 8, top. In the *Epic of Gilgamesh* (Old Babylonian Version, Tablet IV 170-3) the Bull of heaven has

The light of the 'golden flesh' passing through the hair-pores of the divine black skin therefore produced a sapphiric 'surrounding splendor.'[494]

5.4. *The Self-Created Blue-Black Creator*

Before creating the cosmos, according to ancient Near Eastern tradition, the black god created himself, or, rather, his body: "O Rēʿ who gave birth to righteousness, sovereign who created all this, who built his limbs, who modeled his body, who created himself, who gave birth to himself."[495] Ancient Indic and ancient Egyptian tradition give fairly detailed mythic accounts of the self-creation of the black god.[496]

---

horns of lapis lazuli. Nanna-Sin, moon-god of Sumer and Babylon, is the 'frisky calf of heaven' and the 'lapis lazuli bull.' See Ornan, "The Bull and its Two Masters," 3; Stol, "The Moon," 255. On Nanna-Sin see further ***DDD***, s.v. Sîn 782-3 by M. Stol. See also the sapphiric bearded bull in Jeremy Black and Anthony Green, ***Gods, Demons and Symbols of Ancient Mesopotamia: An Illustrated Dictionary*** (London: British Museum Press, 1992) 44 s.v. bison.

[494] See e.g. A. Massy, *Le Papyrus de Leiden I $_{347}$* (Ghent, 1885) 2 where an Egyptian deity is described as "robed in brilliance and wrapped in turquoise." See further Meeks, "Divine Bodies," 57.

[495] From Theb. Tomb 157: translation from J. Zandee, "The Birth-Giving Creator-God in Ancient Egypt," in Alan B. Lloyd (ed.), ***Studies in Pharaonic Religion and Society, in Honour of J. Gwyn Griffiths*** (London: The Egypt Exploration Society, 1992) 175 [art.=168-185]. See also the hieratic Coffin Text 714: "I (Atum) created my body in my glory; I am he who made myself; I formed myself according to my will and according to my heart." Translation from John D. Currid, in his ***Ancient Egypt and the Old Testament*** (Grand Rapids, Michigan: Baker Books, 1997), 58.

[496] On theo-cosmogony in Indic tradition, see, besides the primary Indic texts: David Leeming with Margaret Leeming, ***A Dictionary of Creation Myths*** New York and Oxford: Oxford University Press, 1994) s.v. Indian Creation, 139-144; Daniélou, ***Myths and Gods of India***; S.S. Dange (ed.), ***Myths of Creation. Papers read at the Seminar on 17th March, 1985*** (Bombay, 1987) Chapters 1-5; J. Gonda, " "In the Beginning," ***Annals of the Bhandarkar Oriental Research Institute*** 63 (1982): 453-62; F.B.J. Kuiper, ***Ancient Indian Cosmogony*** (ed. John Irwin; New Delhi: Vikas Publishing House, 1983); Wendy Doniger O'Flaherty, ***Hindu Myths: A Sourcebook Translated from the Sanskrit*** (London: Penguin Books, 1975); Bruce Lincoln, "The Indo-European Myth of Creation," ***HR*** 15 (1975): 121-145; Bhattacharji, ***Indian Theogony***; W. Norman Brown, "The Creation Myth of the Rig Veda," ***JAOS*** 62 (1942): 85-98. In Egyptian tradition, besides the standard accounts in treatments of Egyptian myth: Françoise Dunand and Christiane Zivie-Coche, ***Gods and Men in Egypt: 3000 BCE to 395 CE***, translated from the French by David Lorton (Ithaca and London: Cornell University Press, 2002) Chapter Two ("Cosmogonies, Creation, and Time"); Richard J. Clifford, ***Creation Accounts in the Ancient Near East and the bible*** (CBQMS 26; Washington, DC; Catholic Biblical Association of America, 1994) Chapter Four; J.P. Allen, ***Genesis in Egypt: The Philosophy of Ancient Egyptian Creation Accounts*** (YES 2; New Haven: Yale University, 1988). On Sumerian/Akkadian accounts of creation see Clifford, ***Creation Accounts***, Chapters Two and Three; Alexander Heidel, ***The Babylonian Genesis*** (2nd edition; Chicago and London: The University of Chicago Press, 1963); J. van Dijk, "Le motif cosmique dans la pensée sumérienne," ***Acta Orientalia*** 28 (1964): 1-59; Morris

Most amazing is the remarkable similarity of these accounts. While one nation deriving its account from the other is improbable, it is likely that the similarities evince a widespread ancient Near Eastern mythic tradition concerning a self-created black creator-deity.[497]

According to this mythic tradition there was in the beginning only darkness, material darkness universally described as 'water.'[498] Hidden within this dark primordial water was the deity in a formless, luminous* state.[499] This primordial 'water' was characterized by what the Indic texts call *jāmi*, the unproductive state of non-differentiation of its constituent elements. All potential dualities (e.g. light/darkness, spirit/matter, male/female), which are a prerequisite to the generative process, lay undistinguished and negatively homogeneous; the ancient Egyptians called it the "state in which did not yet exist 'two things'." Creation begins with the distinguishing and separation of these elements.[500] How long this primeval,* homogeneous mass with its

---

Jastrow, Jr., "The Sumerian View of Beginnings," ***JAOS*** 36 (1916): 122-135; idem, "Sumerian and Akkadian Views of Beginnings," ***JAOS*** 36 (1916): 274-299.

[497] Speaking more broadly K.K.A. Venkatachari ("Babylonian, Assyrian and Other Accounts" in Dange, ***Myths of Creation***, 34) notes: "The myths regarding the creation of the universe and life, as found in the literature of the ancient civilizations bear remarkable similarity which is not easy to explain away, considering the lack of communication in the olden days and the fact that there was no print or other media as we have now."

[498] "At first there was only darkness (*tamas*) wrapped in darkness. All this was unillumined water." *Ṛg Veda* 10.129.1-6. An ancient Egyptian Coffin Text (Spell 80) mentions "the darkness *(kkyt)* of Nun." See Helmer Ringgren, "Light and Darkness in Ancient Egyptian Religion," in ***Liber amicorum. Studies in honour of Professor Dr. C.J. Bleeker. Published on the occasion of his retirement from the chair of the history of religions and the phenomenology of religion at the University of Amsterdam*** (SHR 17; Leiden: E.J. Brill, 1969) 143 [art.=140-150]. On the waters in Indic tradition see H.W. Bodewitz, "The Waters in Vedic Cosmic Classifications," ***Indologica Taurinensia*** 10 (1982): 45-54. In Egyptian tradition see Clifford, ***Creation Accounts***, 101-104; R.T. Rundle Clark, ***Myth and Symbol in Ancient Egypt*** (London: Thames and Hudson, 1959) 54-55. On the primordial waters in ancient myth see also Tamra Andrews, ***Legends of the Earth, Sea, and Sky: An Encyclopedia of Nature Myths*** (Santa Barbara, California: ABC-CLIO, 1998) s.v. Primordial Sea, 181-82; Eliade, ***Patterns***, Chapter Five; Philip Freund, ***Myths of Creation*** (New York: Washington Square Press, Inc, 1965) Chapter Four.

[499] For example the spiritual and featureless Brahman (neuter), which existed within the Indic primordial waters, was "brilliant, without body, sinewless": see E. Osborn Martin, ***The Gods of India: A Brief Description of their History, Character & Worship*** (London and Toronto: J.M. Dent and Sons, Ltd. And New York: E.P. Dutton and Co., 1914) Chapter 1; T.S Maxwell, ***The Gods of Asia: Image, Text, and Meaning*** (Delhi: Oxford University Press, 1997), 30; Kurian Mathothu, ***The Development of the Concept of Trimurti in Hinduism*** (Pali, India, 1974) 31-42. S.S. Dange, "Ṛgvedic Accounts," in Dange, ***Myths of Creation***, 10 notes: "In all the mythical accounts of Creation in the (Ṛg Veda), Water and Heat (i.e. a 'ray of light') seem to be the basic principles."

[500] Hans-Peter Hasenfratz, "Patterns of Creation in Ancient Egypt," in Henning Graf Reventlow and Yair Hoffman (edd.), ***Creation in Jewish and Christian Tradition*** (JSOTSup 319; Sheffield: Sheffield Academic Press, 2002) 174 [art.=174-178]; John

hidden divine luminosity existed is not indicated. At some point, however, God's luminosity concentrated itself within the primordial waters into a single point, producing the first distinguishable particle of luminous matter,[501] the mythical 'golden germ' or fiery a-tom,[502] the quark of modern-day quantum physics.[503] This soon developed into an atom,[504] described mythically as the 'golden egg.'

5.4.1. *The Cosmogonic Egg and the Primordial Atom*

In ***Our Savior Has Arrived***, the Hon. Elijah Muhammad makes an astute observation:

> Take a magnifying glass and start looking at these little atoms out here in front of you. You see they are egg-shaped and they are oblong. You crack them open and you find everything in them that you find out here.[505]

Irwin, " 'Asokan' Pillars: The Mystery of Foundation and Collapse," in Gilbert Pollet (ed.), ***India and the Ancient World: History, Trade and Culture Before A.D. 650*** (OLA 25; Leuven: Departement Oriëntalistiek, 1987) 87-93.

[501] Dunand and Zivie-Coche, ***Gods and Men in Egypt***, 51 note: "Matter was already in Nun, waiting to be coagulated to a point where the dry contrasted with the unformed matter."

[502] In Indic tradition the *Hiraṇya-Garbha* or 'Golden Germ"; see e.g. *Ṛg Veda* 10.121.7; *Atharva Veda* 10.7.28; *Matsya Pūraṇa* 2.25ff. On the golden germ see Daniélou, ***Myths and Gods of India***, 237-38; J. Gonda, "Background and variants of the Hiraṇyagarbha Conception," in Perala Ratnam (ed.), ***Studies in Indo-Asian Art and Culture***, III (Delhi, 1974) 39-54; Mircea Eliade, "Spirit, Light, and Seed," ***HR*** 11 (1971): 1-30; Bhattacharji, ***Indian Theogony***, 330-1; F.B.J. Kuiper, "The Golden Germ," in idem, ***Ancient Indian Cosmogony***, 22-40; F.D.K. Bosch, ***The Golden Germ, An Introduction to Indian Symbolism*** (The Hague: Mouton, 1960). On the cosmogonic egg in Egyptian tradition see Clifford, ***Creation Accounts***, 106, 112; Clark, ***Myth and Symbol***, 56. On the Sumerian creator-god An/Anu planting the primordial seed see Clifford, ***Creation Accounts***, 26-29 and 39, where the author quotes an ancient Sumerian text entitled *Bird and Fish*, where mention is made of "the life-giving waters that begat the fecund seed."

[503] The *Hiraṇya-Garbha*, according to Daniélou, ***Myths and Gods of India***, 234, is a "ball of fire from which the universe develops" and Von Franz, in her discussion of cosmogonic "Germs and Eggs" appropriately describes the mythical germ as "an enormous concentration of energy in...one center," ***Creation Myths***, 232. These descriptions identify the 'golden germ' with the quark (a-tom) of modern physics, the fundamental particle of matter, which is also a "ball" and "center of (fiery) energy." See Lawrence M. Krauss, ***Atom: An Odyssey from the Big Bang to Life on Earth...And Beyond*** (Boston: Little, Brown and Company, 2001); Leon Lederman with Dick Teresi, ***The God Particle: If the Universe is the Answer, What is the Question*** (New York: Dell Publishing, 1993); Isaac Asimov, ***Atom: Journey Across the Subatomic Cosmos*** (New York: Truman Talley Books, 1992).

[504] On the relation of the a-tom (quark) and the atom see sources cited above n. 502.

[505] Elijah Muhammad, ***Our Savior Has Arrived***, 1974, 73.

Ancient tradition also described the primordial atom, in which everything (including God) was originally contained and out of which everything (including God) emerged, as an egg.[506] This 'Cosmogonic*' or 'Mundane' Egg symbolized the key to the mystery of Origins. Manley P. Hall, world-renowned scholar of the Occult, in his book ***MAN: The Grand Symbol of The Mysteries,*** observes:

> The whole mystery of origin and destiny is concealed in the symbolism of that radiant gold egg…It was declared that such as understood this mystery had risen above all temporal limitations.[507]

Madame H.P. Blavatsky, Matriarch of Theosophy, says also:

> The 'Mundane Egg' is, perhaps, one of the most universally adopted symbols…Whence this universal symbol? The Egg was incorporated as a sacred sign in the cosmogony of every people on the Earth, and was revered both on account of its form and its inner mystery…It was known as that which represented most successfully the origin and secret of being. The gradual development of the imperceptible germ within the closed shell; the inward working, without apparent outward interference of force, which from a latent 'nothing' produced an active 'something,' needing naught save heat;

---

[506] On the cosmogonic egg see Marie-Louise von Franz, ***Creation Myths*** revised edition (Boston and London: Shambhala, 1995), Chapter Eight ("Germs and Eggs"); de Vries, ***Dictionary***, 158-9 s.v. egg; ***ER*** 5:36-7 s.v. Egg by Venetia Newall; idem, ***An Egg at Easter: A Folklore Study*** (Bloomington: Indiana University Press, 1971) Chapter One; Eliade, ***Patterns***, 413-416; Anna-Britta Hellbom, "The Creation Egg," ***Ethnos*** 1 (1963): 63-105; Robert Wildhaber, "Zum Symbolgehalt und zur Ikonographie des Eies,' ***Deutsches Jahrbuch für Volkskunde*** 6 (1960): 7ff; H.J. Sheppard, "Egg Symbolism in Alchemy," ***Ambix*** 6 (August, 1958): 140-148; Freund, ***Myths of Creation***, Chapter Five; Martti Haavio, ***Väinämöinen: Eternal Sage*** (Helsinki, 1952) 45-63; Franz Lukas, "Das Ei als kosmogonische Vorstellung," ***Zeitschrift des Vereins für Volkskunde*** (Berlin, 1894) 227-243; James Gardner, ***The Faiths of the World: A Dictionary of All Religions and Religious Sects, their Doctrines Rites, Ceremonies and Customs***, 2 vols. (Edinburgh: A. Fullarton & Co., 1860) 1:797-8 s.v. Egg (Mundane). In Indic tradition see further F.B.J. Kuiper, "Cosmogony and Conception: A Query," ***HR*** 10 (1970): 100-104 [art.=91-138]; Gonda, "Background"; H. Lommel, "Der Welt-ei-Mythos im Rig-Veda," ***Mélanges Bally*** (Geneva, 1939) 214-20. On the cosmic egg as *prima materia* see also C.G. Jung, ***Psychology and Alchemy*** (2nd ed.; Princeton: Princeton University Press, 1968) 202. On the golden cosmogonic egg and the primordial atom see Freund, ***Myths of Creation***, Chapter 15; True Islam, ***The Book of God: An Encyclopedia of Proof that the Black Man is God*** (Atlanta: All in All Publishing, 1999) 148-151.

[507] Manley P. Hall, ***MAN - The Grand Symbol of the Mysteries***, 1972, 69.

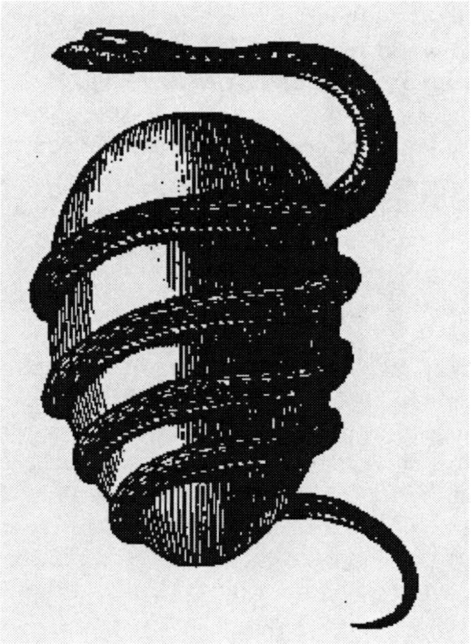

Figure 11

The Mundane Egg (Primordial Atom) born from the Cosmic Serpent (Divine Spirit/Latent Energy/God-Force

> and which, having gradually evolved into a concrete, living creature, broke its shell, appearing to outward senses of all a self-generated and self-created being-must have been a standing miracle from the beginning."[508]

The Egg symbolized *prima material*,[509] that 'primeval* substance in creation,'[510] or 'progenitive germ,'[511] from which the world evolved. As Philip Freund pointed out in 1965, this cosmogonic egg is the same as

[508] Blavatsky, ***The Secret Doctrine*** 1:65,365.
[509] Jung, ***Psychology and Alchemy***, 202.
[510] Hillbom, "Creation Egg," 64.
[511] Freund, ***Myths of Creation***, 49.

the 'primordial atom' of modern scientific theories on the origin of the universe.[512] In fact, the primordial atom, first proposed by Abbé Georges Lemaître, physicist at Louvain University, has since been called by scientists "Lemaître's Egg" in recognition of its relation to the cosmogonic egg of the ancients. Isaac Asimov, for example, in his ***Atom: Journey Across the Subatomic Cosmos***, describes the beginning of the universe from a scientist's perspective in a way that radically approaches the beginning as described by these ancient religious texts:

> there was a time when the matter and energy of the Universe were literally squashed together into one exceeding dense mass. (The Belgian astronomer Abbé Georges Henri Lemaitre) called it the cosmic egg…If we consider the situation before the cosmic egg was formed, we might visualize a vast illimitable sea of nothingness…The nothingness contains energy…The Pre-Universe…had energy, and although all of its properties were otherwise those of a vacuum, it is called a false vacuum. Out of this false vacuum, a tiny point of matter appears where the energy, by blind forces of random changes, just happens to have concentrated itself sufficiently for the purpose. In fact, we might imagine the illimitable false vacuum to be a frothing, bubbling mass, producing bits of matter here and there as the ocean waves produce foam.[513]

Here we have a world-renowned scientist describing the pre-cosmic world in terms of a primordial ocean of matter and a cosmogonic egg, language deriving from the ancient mythic tradition.

---

[512] Ibid., 180.

[513] Asimov, ***Atom***, 304-310 On the congruence between modern quantum physics and ancient Eastern thought see the still insightful Fritjof Capra, ***The Tao of Physics*** (3rd ed.; Boston: Shambhala, 1991).

Figure 12

Indic Creator God Brahmā before emerging out of the Cosmogonic Egg/Primordial Atom (from Manly P. Hall, ***MAN: Grand Symbol of the Mysteries***). The Indic text, *The Laws of Manu*, relates:

> This universe was enveloped in darkness, unperceived, undistinguishable...Then the irresistible, self-existent Lord...seeking to produce various creatures...deposited in them (the primordial waters) a seed (quark). This (seed) became a golden egg (atom), resplendent as the sun, in which he himself was born as Brahmā, the progenitor of the word...Being formed by that first cause...that [Man (Puruṣa)] is called Brahmā...This egg, after the creator had inhabited (it) for a thousand years...burst open, and Brahmā, issuing forth by meditation, commenced the work of creation.

The 'bursting forth' of the Creator God out of the egg/atom signifies that the atoms were used to build up the Creator God's body.

5.4.2. *The Primordial Atom and the Birth of God*

According to these ancient texts this 'egg' or atom (also depicted as a lotus plant)[514] began rotating and moving 'on the waters,' which movement originated time.[515] Within this atom the creator-deity now resided and, eventually, from this atom he emerged as a luminous *anthropos* (man),[516] the so-called sun-god: Atum-Rēʿ of Egypt (Figure 13)[517] and Prajāpati-Brahmā of India (Figure 14).[518]

---

[514] See Bosch, ***Golden Germ***, 56-57.

[515] On the birth of time in Egyptian cosmogonic tradition see Dunand and Zivie-Coche, ***Gods and Men in Egypt***, 64-70.

[516] As von Franz remarks: "the motif of the human form of the first creative being, an anthropos figure…is another very widespread archetypal motif in creation myths." ***Creation Myths***, 34. See also Dunand and Zivie-Coche, ***Gods and Men in Egypt***, 48: "This (creator-)god was autogenous...He modeled his own body, and we must say that this was almost always anthropomorphically". See e.g. *Vādhūla-Sūtra* 6.4.109: "Brahman emitted [out of himself] Agni (the primordial spark of fire) and Prajāpati (a macrocosmic Agni) and he (Brahman) created the latter (viz. Prajāpati) in the form of a man." In ancient Near Eastern and Indic tradition, cosmogony (birth of the cosmos), theogony (birth and evolution of God/gods) and anthropogony (creation of man) are all revealed to be the same evolutionary process described from different perspectives. Thus, in Egyptian and Indic wisdom embroyogony, i.e. the development of the human embryo in the womb, recapitulates and therefore gives insight into the theo-cosmogonic process. See David Leeming and Margaret Leeming, ***A Dictionary of Creation Myths*** New York and Oxford: Oxford University Press, 1994) 31-33 s.v. Birth as Creation Metaphor; Jan Assmann, ***Egyptian Solar Religion in the New Kingdom. Re, Amun and the Crisis of Polytheism***, translated from the German by Anthony Alcock (London and New York: Kegan Paul International, 1995) 175; Ragnhild Bjerre Finnestad, ***Image of the World and Symbol of the Creator. On the Cosmological and Iconological Values of the Temple of Edfu*** (SOR 10; Wiesbaden: Otto Harrassowitz, 1985); F.B.J. Kuiper, "Cosmogony and Conception: A Query," ***HR*** 10 (1970): 91-183 [=***Ancient Indian Cosmogony***, 90-137]; Mircea Eliade, "Cosmogonic Myth and 'Sacred History'," ***Religious Studies*** 2 (1967): 171-83; Manly P. Hall, ***Man: Grand symbol of the Mysteries. Thoughts in occult anatomy*** Los Angeles: The Philosophical Research society, 1972). On the motif of the man-cosmos-God isomorphism see also Klaus Klostermaier, "The Body of God: Cosmos – Avatara – Image," in Robert B. Crotty (ed.), ***The Charles Strong Lectures 1972-1984*** (Leiden: E.J. Brill, 1987) 103-120; Alex Wayman, "The Human Body as Microcosm in India, Greek Cosmology, and Sixteenth-Century Europe," ***HR*** 22 (1982): 172-190; Brenda E.F. Beck, "The symbolic merger of Body, space and cosmos in Hindu Tamil Nadu," ***Contributions to Indian Sociology***, n.s. 10 (1976): 213-243; Leonard Barkan, ***Nature's Work: The Human Body as Image of the World*** (New Haven and London: Yale University Press, 1975); George P. Conger, "Cosmic Persons and Human Universes in Indian Philosophy," ***Journal and Proceedings of the Asiatic Society of Bengel*** n.s. 29 (1933): 255-270.

[517] "there was in the beginning neither heaven nor earth, and nothing existed except a boundless primeval mass of water which was shrouded in darkness and which contained within itself the germs or beginnings, male and female, of everything which was to be in the future world. The divine primeval spirit which formed an essential part of the primeval matter felt within itself the desire to begin the work of creation, and its word woke to life the world, the form and shape of which it had already depicted to itself. The first act of creation began with the formation of an egg out of the primeval water, from

When the creator-god first emerged, the ancient sources tell us, he lacked the black-body. Indeed, he was light that separated from and emerged out of the darkness.[519] His body, we are told, was originally a body of light described variously as white gold, yellow gold or red gold.[520] The brilliance of this body surpassed that of the sun, which the creator-deity (sun-god) created only as a sign and a 'vicar.'[521] This brilliantly luminous body proved lethal to his future creation. His creatures were perishing at the sight of it and his cosmos was being scorched.[522] The creator-deity decided to cloak his luminosity in a

---

which broke forth Rā, the immediate cause of all life upon earth." Quoted from Budge, ***Egyptian Book of the Dead***, xcviii. See also Zandee, "The Birth-Giving Creator-God," 182: "Atum is 'complete' as an androgynous god. He unites within himself masculinity and femininity. He possesses all conditions to bring forth the all out of him. He was a Monad and made himself millions of creatures which he contained potentially in himself. He was the one who came into being of himself (*ḫpr ḏs.f*), who was the creator of his own existence, the *causa sui*." In a New Kingdom royal inscription Atum is described as he "who generates himself within the egg." See Assmann, ***Egyptian Solar Religion***, 112. Another image used by the Egyptians to depict the primordial atom out of which the creator-god emerged is the primordial mound (*benben*) that raised out of the primordial waters at the beginning of creation (see Clifford, ***Creation Accounts***, 105-6). This mound was the "first solid matter" brought from the bottom of the waters and it was identified with Atum himself (Traunecker, ***Gods of Egypt***, 77; Irwin, " 'Asokan' Pillars," 92. On the Primordial Mound see further idem, "The Sacred Anthill and the Cult of the Primordial Mound," ***HR*** 21 [1982]: 339-360; idem, "The Mystery of the (Future) Buddha's First Words," ***Annali Instituto Orientale di Napoli*** 41 [1981]: 623-664). It is no coincidence that this primordial atom is identified with and personifies Atum, the god born from that atom.

[518]See below and Martin, ***Gods of India***, 86, 87; Kurian Manthothu, ***The Development of the Concept of Trimūrti in Hinduism*** (Pali, Kerala, India, 1974) 54; Wendy Doniger and Brian K. Smith, ***The Laws of Manu*** (London: Penguin Books, 1991): 3-4.On Prajāpati-Brahmā and the cosmic man (Puruṣa) see ***ER*** 2:294 s.v. Brahman by Wendy Doniger; J.Gonda, ***Prajāpati's Relations with Brahman, Bṛhaspati and Brahmā*** (Amsterdam/Oxford/New York: North-Holland Publishing Company, 1989) Chapter IX; idem, "Beginning" 52-53; idem, "Background" 51-2; J.R. Joshi, "Prajāpati in Vedic Mythology and Ritual," ***Annals of the Bhandarkar Oriental Research Institute*** 53 (1972):101-125, esp. 114.

[519] See Ringgren, "Light and Darkness," 141-42

[520]On the golden, anthropomorphic body of Prajāpati-Brahmā see *Śatapatha-Brāhmaṇa* 10.1.4.9; 7.4.1.15; Shanti Lal Nagar, ***The Image of Brahmā in India and Abroad***, Vol. 1 (Delhi: Parimal Publications, 1992), 113, 134-43, 361-370; Km. Rajani Mishra, ***Brahmā-Worship. Tradition and Iconography*** (Delhi: Kanishka Publishing House, 1989) 50-57; Gonda, "Background"; The Egyptian sun-god is "the brilliant one (*ḫ'y*)," "white light (*wḥḫ ḥddwt*." See Ringgren, "Light and Darkness," 145. Rēʿ is "gold of the gods," "white gold" with a body "cast …from gold." See Assmann, ***Egyptian Solar Religion***, 27, 94, 95.

[521] See Budge, ***Egyptian Book of the Dead***, xcvi.

[522] See for example the tales in the *Mahābhārat* (O'flaherty, ***Hindu Myths***, 38-43) of Prajāpati-Brahmā's scorching the primordial creation with his 'fiery energy' and in the *Mārkaṇḍeya Prurāṇa* (Ibid., 66-70) of the sun-god Vivasvat whose form radiated excessive heat, scorching the three worlds. On Egyptian parallels see below. On the

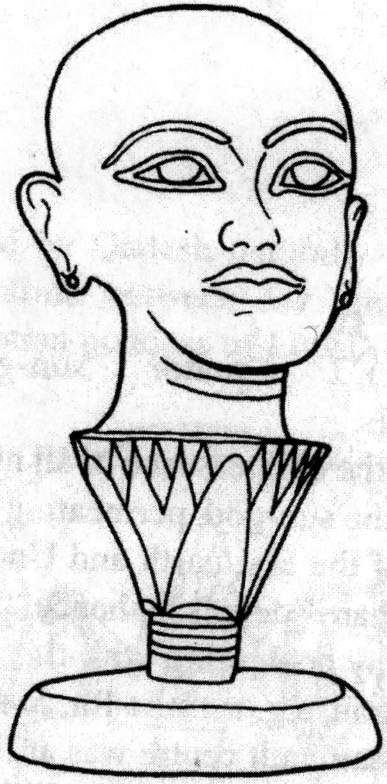

Figure 13

The anthropomorphic creator-god of Egypt, Rēʿ, emerging from the primordial atom, shown here as the mythical Lotus Plant.

lethality of seeing the god's luminous body in Egyptian tradition see also Meeks, "Divine Bodies," 58.

Figure 14

The Indic creator-god Prajāpati-Brahmā (white anthropos) emerging from the lotus plant (primordial "seed" or atom). The lotus is emerging from the navel of Viṣṇu (primordial, universal soul) who is reclining on the primordial serpent Śesa (matter), himself resting on the primordial waters. These images represent the birth of the creator-god out of the primordial matter: "The anthropomorphic figure (Viṣṇu), the serpent coils that form his bed, and the water on which this serpent floats, are triune manifestations of the single divine, imperishable, cosmic substance, the energy underlying and inhabiting all forms of life."[523]

[523] Heinrich Robert Zimmer in Joseph Campbell (ed.), ***Myths and Symbols in Indian Art and Civilization*** (New York: Harper, 1962) 92.

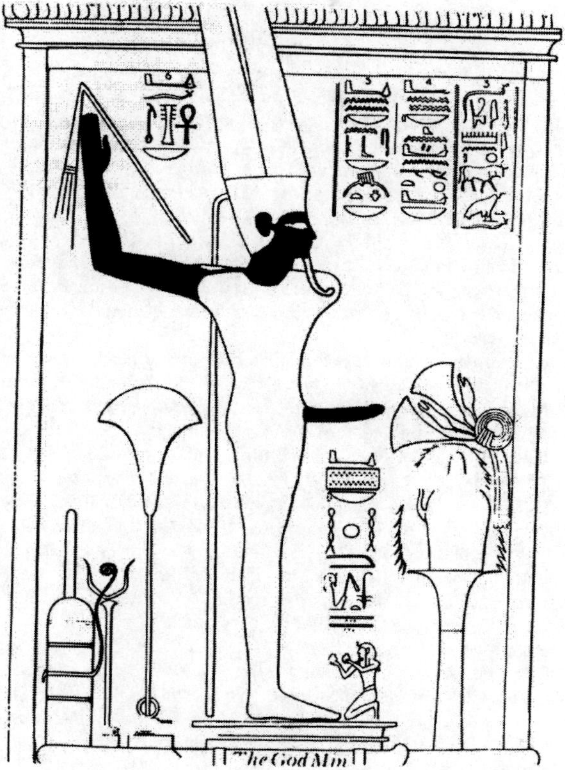

Figure 15

Min, Egyptian black 'creator-god *par excellence*', who emerged from the primordial dark waters, from which his black body was formed

bodily 'veil,' which he made from the primordial waters out of which he emerged. That primordial matter, black and aqueous, became the substance of his new body, which he wore over the luminous form like a garment, concealing its brilliance.[524] But some of this brilliance shown through the hair-pores of the new black body,[525] and this produced a

---

[524] The luminous, anthropomorphic Indic creator-deity Prajāpati-Brahmā is said to have, after the initial creation, wrapped himself in the primordial waters (Vāk/Virāj; see G.H. Godbole, "Later Vedic and Brahmanical Accounts," in Dange, ***Myths of Creation***, 13). He then became *haritah śyāvah*, dark brown (*śyāvah*, like night, *Ṛg Veda* 6.48.6.) with a ting of yellow (a yellow glow, *haritah*). See *Taittirīya Brāhmaṇa* 2.3.5.1; *Śatapatha-Brāhmaṇa* 6.2.2.2. On Vāk and the primordial waters see ibid., 6.1.1.9; *Pañcaavemśa-Brāhmaṇa* 20.14.2; *Ṛg Veda* 10.125.3; *Jaiminīya-Brāhmaṇa* 2.252 (Vāk as primordial cow); Bosch, ***Golden Germ***, 52-53. On Vāk as primordial matter see Nagar, ***Image of Brāhma***, viii; Joshi, "Prajāpati," 113. On Prajāpati-Brahmā's copulation with Vāk as a metaphor for the reuniting of fire (breath) with water see Mishra, ***Brahmā-Worship.*** 11. On the fiery breath (Agni) and the waters see further Kuiper, "Golden Germ," 27-30; Bosch, ***Golden Germ***, 57-62.

In Egypt, Rēʿ transforms (*ḫpr*) his luminous body into a black body symbolized by the gods Atum and Osiris, both of whom had black bulls as their attribute animal; on Atum's black bull Mnevis see George Hart, ***The Routledge Dictionary of Egyptian Gods and Goddesses*** [2nd edition; London and New York: Routledge, 2005] 95 s.v. Mnevis; Ions, ***Egyptian Mythology***, 40). On Rēʿ darkening and transforming into Atum see See Ringgren, "Light and Darkness," 150; Karl W.Luckert, ***Egyptian Light and Hebrew Fire. Theological and Philosophical Roots of Christendom in Evolutionary Perspective*** (Albany: State University of New York Press, 1991) 73. Most often, Rēʿ's black body is identified with the black god Osiris (Figure 16), who represents the black primordial waters of Nun; see Chassinat, "Mise a Mort Rituelle." On black Osiris as the netherworld body of Rēʿ see Hasenfratz, "Patterns of Creation," 176; Jan Assmann, ***The Search for God in Ancient Egypt***, translated from the German by David Lorton (Ithaca and New York: Cornell University Press, 2001) 41; idem, ***Death and Salvation in Ancient Egypt***, translated from the German by David Lorton (Ithaca and London: Cornell University Press, 2005) 188; Clark, ***Myth and Symbol***, 158; Martin Lev and Carol Ring, "Journey of the Night Sun," ***Parabola*** 8 (1983): 14-18; Albert Churchward, ***Signs & Symbols of Primordial Man: The Evolution of Religious Doctrines from the Eschatology of the Ancient Egyptians*** (Brooklyn: A&B Publishers Group, 1994, reprint) 63-66, 274-6, 322.

[525] See above and also *Mahābhārata* 5.129.11 which mentions "rays of light, like the sun's, [shining] from [Kṛṣṇa's] very pores." Translated James W. Lane, ***Visions of God: Narratives of Theophany in the Mahābhārata*** (Vienna 1989) 134. Now Kṛṣṇa, whose name means 'black' (A.L. Basham, ***The Wonder that was India*** [London: Sidgwick and Jackson, 1954] 305) is in many ways the paradigmatic blue-black god. As David R. Kinsley, ***The Sword and the Flute: Kali and Krishna, Dark Visions of the Terrible and the Sublime in Hindu Mythology*** (Berkeley: University of California Press, 1975) noted, Kṛṣṇa with his blue-black complexion is the "quintessence of divine beauty": "His appearance is redeeming in itself...Over and over again we read of his luminous dark complexion, large dark eyes, black curly hair. For devotees of Kṛṣṇa the image of their blue lord is the quintessence of divine beauty. The *Brahma-vaivarta-purāṇa*...describes Kṛṣṇa as emanating a blinding light...But Kṛṣṇa's devotees see within that dazzling light to an even more dazzling and redeeming image of their darling...(the) lovely image of Kṛṣṇa located in the center of this light. He is blue like a new cloud." The "dazzling light" is the light emanating through the hair-pores from the dangerously luminous form within the black body (his 'Universal Form', *viśvarūpadarśana*; see *Bhagavadgītā* 11;

dark-blue iridescence or glow. The result was the sapphiric body of the creator-deity.[526] While the luminous, fiery body was 'terrible' and destructive, the blue-black 'sapphiric' body was beautiful and auspicious, a mercy to the creatures.[527] "Blue as the sky, dark as the

---

Lane, ***Visions of God***, 135-141). The description "luminous dark complexion" nicely captures the divine paradox.

[526] Thus Viṣṇu (Figure 16) is "dark-hued, cloud-hued, sapphire-hued, gem-hued, ocean and sea-hued" (See S. Settar, "Vishnu-Krishna in Nammalvar's Tiruvaymoli [C.7-8th Cent. A.D.]," in G. Kamalakar and M. Veerender [edd.], ***Vishnu in Art, Thought, and Literature*** [Hyderbad: Birla Archaeological & Cultural Research Institute, 1993] 225) and Varuṇa, the "cloud-dark Lord of aquatic creatures," when he appeared to Arjuna was "the color of lapis lazuli, lighting up every direction" (*Mahābhārata* 3.42.5-6). The Viṣṇu of the Purānic Trimūrti or Triad is the creator-god (Prajāpati-)Brahmā with the luminous body cloaked within an aquatic body made from the primordial waters. Therefore, as Viṣṇu, (Prajāpati-)Brahmā is called "he who dwells in the [causal] waters, *Nārāyana*." By assuming this form (Prajāpati-)Brahmā showed mercy on creation. Thus, in his 'Viṣṇu' form he is called auspicious. On Viṣṇu see Daniélou, ***Myths and Gods of India***, Chapters Eleven through Fourteen; Arvind Sharma, "The Significance of Viṣṇu Reclining on the Serpent," ***Religion*** 16 (1986): 101-114; Nanditha Krishna, ***The Art and Iconography of Vishnu-Narayana*** (Bombay, 1980); Kalpana S. Desai, ***Iconography of Viṣṇu (In Northern India, Upto the Mediaeval Period)*** (New Delhi: Abhinav Publications, 1973);F.B.J Kuiper, "The Three Strides of Viṣṇu," in idem, ***Ancient Indian Cosmogony***, 41-55; Bhattachari, ***Indian Theogony***, Chapter Fourteen; Martin, ***Gods of India***, Chapter Three; J. Gonda, ***Aspects of Early Viṣṇuism*** (Utrecht; N.V.A. Oosthoek's Uitgevers Mij, 1954). See also Wendy Doniger O'flaherty, "The Submarine Mare in the Mythology of Śiva," ***JRAS*** 1971 9-27 and below.

In ancient Egyptian tradition see e.g. the famous story of the Withdrawal of Rēʿ to Heaven. After incinerating most humans with his fiery fury personified as his daughter, the ferocious lioness Sekhmet (who, incidentally, got out of hand), Rēʿ re-entered the primordial water (he mounted the back of Nut-Nun personified as the primordial cow). He thus concealed his luminous body within Nut-Nun. He is now "(he) who conceals his image in the body of Nut," "who conceals his image in his heaven." (P. Leiden I 344 v50.I. 4 and viii.7 in J. Zandee, ***Der Amunshymnus des Papyrus Lkeiden I 344***, 3 vols. [Leiden, 1992]. See also Assmann, ***Egyptian Solar Religion***, 70-72]. By concealing his luminous body within the body of Nut, Rēʿ becomes the sapphire-bodied Amun-Re, described as "beautiful youth of purest lapis lazuli (*ḥwn-nfr n-ḫsbḏ-m3ʿ*) whose "body is heaven" (*ḥt. K nwt*)." See above n. 31. In the Leiden Papyrus stored at the museum in Leiden (see Adolf Erman, "Der Leidener Amons-hymnus," ***Sitzungsberichte der Preussischen Akademie der Wissenschaften*** 11 [1923]: 66ff) Rēʿ's dangerously luminous body is described as his 'secret form' hidden within Amun (70-73). On the myth of Rēʿ's Withdrawal see Robert A. Armour, ***Gods and Myths of Ancient Egypt*** (2nd edition; Cairo and New York: American University in Cairo Press, 2001) 87-89; Clark, ***Myth and Symbol***, 181-186; Stephen Quirke, ***The Cult of Ra: Sun-Worship in Ancient Egypt*** (New York: Thames & Hudson, 2001) 35-6; Rudolf Anthes, "Mythology in ancient Egypt," in Samuel Noah Kramer (ed.), ***Mythologies of the Ancient World*** (Garden City, New York: Anchor Books, 1961) 17-22. On Amun's sapphiric body see above.

[527] Śiva too has two forms, his fiery form born from the golden egg called his 'terrible form' and his aquatic form described as "auspicious." See *Mahābhārata* 13.146.4; *Brahmāṇḍa Purāṇa*. See O'flaherty, "Submarine Mare."

Figure 16

Viṣṇu, the blue-black "auspicious" form of the Indic creator-god. Here the deity is depicted in "universal form," which contains within it all creation, and from which all (phenomenal) creation emerged (from Devdutt Pattanaik, ***Vishnu: An Introduction*** [Mumbai: Vakils, Feffer and Simons Ltd. 1999])

rain-cloud…Viṣṇu (Figure 15) was the personification of beauty."[528] The act of cloaking the divinely luminous form in a black body was considered a divine sacrifice[529] - a sacrifice that resulted in the first human being (Allah The Original Man) and which permitted the creation of the (more densely) material world.[530]

This blue-black body of the deity was the most arcane secret of the ancient mysteries. In Egypt it was the mystery of the unity of Rēʿ and his black body Osiris.[531] As one text from a New Kingdom royal tomb associated with the mystery rites reveals: "It is a great mystery, it is Rēʿ and Osiris. He who reveals it will die a sudden death."[532] According to the *Book of Gates* this is the "Mystery of the Great God."[533] In Vedic India, "the central theme of what can be denoted by no other term than Aryan mysticism"[534] is the secret of Agni (fire) hidden in water (Varuṇa), *viz.* the mystery of the luminous Prajāpati-Brahmā (creator-

---

[528] Devdutt Pattanaik, ***Vishnu, An Introduction*** (Mumbai, India: Vakils, Feffer and Simons, Ltd., 1999) 7.

[529] According to the cosmogonic account of Berosses, priest of Bēl-Marduk of Babylon, published in Greek ca. 250 BC, after cleaving the villainous primordial water (Grk. *Omorka*; Baby. *Tiamat*) and creating the cosmos, Bēl-Marduk's luminosity was unbearable for living creatures who were therefore perishing. Bēl-Marduk thus ordered a god to cut off his (i.e. Bēl-Marduk's) head (self-sacrifice); his blood was mixed with earth to form men and animals that could survive. See K.K.A. Venkatachari, "Babylonian, Assyrian and Other Accounts," in Dange, ***Myths of Creation***, 36-37. See also Brian K. Smith, "Sacrifice and Being: Prajapati's Cosmic Emission and Its Consequences," ***Religion*** 32 (1985): 71-87; Gonda, "Vedic Gods and the Sacrifice"; idem, "The Popular Prajapati," ***HR*** 22 (1982): 129-149; Joshi, "Prajāpati in Vedic Mythology and Ritual."

[530] This sacrificial 'incarnation,' if you will, is often represented metaphorically as the creator-god (re-)uniting with his wife/daughter, the celestial ocean (primordial matter) depicted as the primordial cow. When Rēʿ as Bull begets with the Divine Cow, i.e. Nut-Nun, the material world with its planets and humans are produced. Thus, "we are all cattle" (see G.S. Bedagkar, "Egyptian, Hebrew and Greek Accounts," in Dange, ***Myths of Creation***, 33). Prajāpati-Brahmā, (re-)uniting with Vāk (primordial water/primordial cow), produced the *idaṃ sarvam* or "phenomenal, material world," beginning with Manu, the first human, which is only Prajāpati-Brahmā himself in the phenomenal, material world: *Śatapatha-Brāhmaṇa* 6.6.1.19; 9.4.1.12; J. Gonda, "All, Universe and Totality in the Śatapatha-Brāhmaṇa," ***Journal of the Oriental Institute*** 32 (1982): 1-17; Joshi, "Prajāpati in Vedic Mythology and Ritual."

[531] According to Jan Assmann "the most secret Arcanum known to the mysteries of the solar journey" is "the nocturnal union of Re and Osiris." Assmann, ***Egyptian Solar Religion***, 28; Idem, ***Death and Salvation in Ancient Egypt***, trans. from the German by David Lorton (Ithaca and London: Cornell University Press, 2005) 186. On Osiris as the black body of Rēʿ see above.

[532] Assmann, ***Search for God***, 79.

[533] Quoted in Assmann, ***Death and Salvation***, 189.

[534] F.B.J. Kuiper, "The Bliss of Aša," ***Indo-Iranian Journal*** 8 (1964): 124 [art.=96-129;= ***Ancient Indian Cosmogony***, Chapter Four].

god) hidden within the black and aqueous body.[535] The Akkadian 'bull-ritual' likewise associated the pelt of the black bull with the "mystery of Anu, Enlil, Ea(Enki) and of Ninmah," i.e. the black gods of Sumer/Akkad.[536]

Osiris.
From the Papyrus of
Iuâu, Plate XXII.

Figure 17

Osiris, black body of the Sun God Rēʿ (from E.A. Wallis Budge, ***Osiris: The Egyptian Religion of Resurrection*** [New York: University Books, 1961])

---

[535] Kuiper, "Bliss of Aša"; idem, "Remarks on 'The Avestan Hymn to Mithra'," ***Indo-Iranian Journal*** 5 (1961): 36-60; idem, "The Heavenly Bucket," in idem, ***Ancient Indian Cosmogony***, Chapter 6.
[536] Wohlstein, ***Sky-God An-Anu***, 118, 122.

Chapter VI:

The Bible, the Qur'ān, and the Black God

6. *Introductory Summary*

The God of ancient Israel was this same black god represented by the black bull. German scholar Werner Daum and British scholar Julian Baldick have both demonstrated that the god of the 'Proto-Semites', that ancient group from which the Semites (Hebrews, Arabs, Canaanites, Akkadians, etc.) developed, was a black god called 'Il/'El/'Al depicted as an old man and represented by the black bovine. The ancient Hebrews worshipped this same black god under the names 'El ('Elohim) and Yahweh. The God of the ancient Hebrews and Arabs was, like the black god of ancient Near Eastern myth, represented by the bull and black rain cloud, both of which symbolized the black body of the God. This black body veiled the dangerously luminous body, called *kāḇôd* or 'Glory,' of the God of ancient Israel, just as in the ancient Near Eastern myth of the Black God.

6.1. *Black God of Ancient Arabia and Israel*

In 1985, German scholar Werner Daum published an important monograph, ***Ursemitische Religion*** ("Proto-Semitic Religion").[537] By a close study of ancient South Arabian inscriptions and modern Yemeni folktales and ritual practices, Daum was able to produce a convincing reconstruction of proto-Semitic Religion, or at least important aspects thereof. The proto-Semites are believed to have been the original speakers of that language (Proto-Semitic) from which the various Semitic* languages derived (Arabic, Hebrew, Ugaritic, Akkadian, etc.). It has been suggested that these Proto-Semites originated in the areas round the northern frontier of Syria,[538] and began diverging probably around 5000 BC. As these Proto-Semites will eventually evolve into the Semites (Arabs, Hebrews, Canaanites, Akkadians, etc.), proto-Semitic religion will make an important contribution to the development of the Semitic religious tradition, even the Semitic monotheistic traditions (i.e. the so-called 'Religions of the

[537] Stuttgart; Berlin; Köln; Mainz: Verlag W. Kohlhammer, 1985.
[538] ***Ursemitische Religion***, 54.

Book'- Judaism, Christianity, and Islam). Daum suggests that our best evidence for reconstructing the 'Ursemitische Religion' comes from southern Arabia.[539] The most important observation for our purposes is that, according to Daum's reconstruction, the high god of the proto-Semites was a black storm deity, rain being most valued in this part of the world, called 'Il/'El/'Al. Now *'l* is the general appellative meaning 'god' and proper divine name in all the major branches of the Semitic family of languages[540]; from it derived the Hebrew אלוה *'ĕlōah* (thus the biblical אלהים *'ĕlōhîm*, God")[541] and Arabic إلاه *ilāh* (thus the qur'ānic الله *aḻḻāh*, "God").[542] This ancient proto-Semitic deity was depicted as an old, bearded man and associated with the black rain cloud, black bovine (ibex, bull, buffalo) and occasionally the black ostrich. These, Daum tells us, "symbolisiert den dunklen 'Il („symbolized the dark 'Il')."[543] In the ancient Near East and India the black rain-cloud symbolized the god's black body[544] and the hide of the black bull signified the skin of the black god.[545]

The British historian Julian Baldick followed up and expanded upon Daum's research with ***Black God: The Afroasiatic Roots of the Jewish, Christian and Muslim Religions***.[546] Baldick's research suggested that, just as there is an 'Afroasiatic' language group indigenous to North Africa and Arabia (consisting of the Semitic languages, the ancient Egyptian language, Berber, Hausa, and the Kushitic and Omotic languages of the Horn of Africa) there is likewise an 'Afroasiatic' religious tradition indigenous to the same area and peculiar to the same groups. This 'Afroasiatic' religious tradition is characterized by a dualistic logic which emphasizes the male-female dichotomy and by a divine triad consisting of a Black storm god, a goddess, and a young hero god. Baldick notes:

---

[539] Duam points out that "The two Yemens are still that part of the Middle East which most vividly retains the manners and customs of ancient Arabia." "Pre-Islamic Rite in South Arabia," ***Journal of the Royal Asiatic Society*** 1 (1987): 5.

[540] ***TDOT*** 1:242, 244 s.v. אל 'ēl.

[541] Ibid; ***DDD*** s.v. "Eloah" by D.Pardee, 285.

[542] ***EI*** X:1093 s.v. "Ilāh," by D.B. Macdonald; Ulf Oldenburg, "Above the Stars of El: El in Ancient South Arabic Religion," ***ZAW*** 82 (1970): 188-208 (188-198).

[543] ***Ursemitische Religion***, 99.

[544] The Indic Varuṇa is the "cloud-dark Lord of aquatic creatures," and Viṣṇu is "dark-hued, cloud-hued, sapphire-hued, gem-hued, ocean and sea-hued." See above. Kṛṣṇa is also described as possessing "a complexuion beautiful like that of dense raincloud." See Charles S.J. White, "Kṛṣṇa as Divine Child," ***HR*** 10 (1970): 164 [art.=156-177]. See also the Egyptian Min.

[545] See above.

[546] New York: Syracuse University Press, 1997.

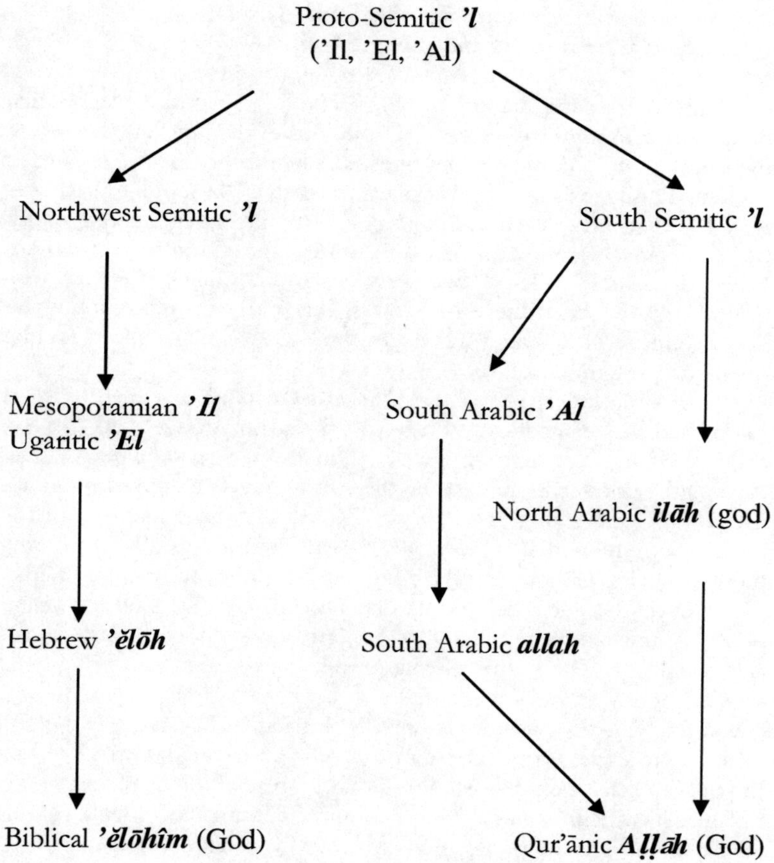
Proto-Semitic ***’l***
(’Il, ’El, ’Al)
Northwest Semitic ***’l***
South Semitic ***’l***
Mesopotamian ***’Il***
Ugaritic ***’El***
South Arabic ***’Al***
North Arabic ***ilāh*** (god)
Hebrew ***’ĕlōh***
South Arabic ***allah***
Biblical ***’ĕlōhîm*** (God)
Qur’ānic ***Aḷḷāh*** (God)

> 'Afroasiatic' logic is in my view particularly dualistic and based on the opposition between male and female...(T)his logic is particularly directed towards obtaining water, and operates by combining a male storm-god, black and violent, with a female deity of the sun, white and vulnerable.[547]

This 'Afroasiatic' paradigm which revolves around a black storm deity can be found in the religious traditions of the Ancient Egyptians, the Oromo and Omotic peoples of Ethiopia, and the South Arabians of Yemen. This black storm god is identified with a Black bull or goat. He is said to descend to earth riding dark clouds and is depended upon for the fertilizing waters of storms. Among the Oromo of southern Ethiopia, God is called *Waqa Quracca* meaning Black (*Quracca*) God (*Waqa*).[548] He rides the dark clouds, has red eyes representing his anger, and is the Creator. The Oromo sacrifice Black sheep to him hoping to procure rain.

This Afroasiatic triad of the Black Storm God, represented by a Black Bull, a sun goddess, and a young warrior god is said to have originated in Northern Syria.[549] The Syrian prototype of this Afroasiatic Triad is thought to be the storm god *Adad*, the sun goddess *Atargatis* and the young god *Asklepios.*[550] Adad, whose name is said to mean 'the only' and also 'holy one,'[551] was depicted as a man wearing bull horns, standing on a bull and holding bolts of lighting in his hands.

This Afroasiatic triad and its Black Storm God is found in ancient South Arabia as well. The Black Storm God of South Arabia was called *'LMQH*. The name and its proper vocalization is a mystery to scholars today who conventionally write it as "Almaqah." He was called the 'Raging' and the 'Ruiner,'[552] indicating his status as the god of the destructive storm. He was said to be an old man symbolized by the bull and the ibex. Baldick notes that "a black bull...figures in rain-making, in which, as in Arabia, the animal is practically identical with an old man, who wears the bulls hide and is himself threatened with murder."[553] Daum and Baldick have convincingly established the identity of 'Almaqah' and the Black Storm God of modern Yemenite folktales. 'Almaqah was joined by the sun goddess *Shams* and the

---

[547] Baldick, ***Black God,*** 4-5.

[548] Baldick, 114.

[549] Ibid., 42.

[550] Helmer Ringgren, ***Religions Religion of the Ancient Near East.*** (Philadelphia:.Westminster Press, 1973.) 155.

[551] Higgins, ***Anacalypsis*** II: 181.

[552] Baldick, ***Black God,*** 20.

[553] Ibid., 110.

young god *Athtar,* completing the divine triad.[554] The power of this Black Storm God of ancient Arabia was not confined to the ability to cause rain. He was all-powerful and infinity rich.[555]

As noted above, the name of the Black Storm God of South Arabia is written today as 'Almaqah.' But this is a purely conventional vocalization of the name written in ancient inscriptions as *'LMQH.* This name, possessing no vowels (as all Semitic languages are consonantal), has long puzzled linguists and historians. Daum and Baldick argue that the name should be written as *'Al Muqa'* which means "The God ('Al) Who Waters Intensively."[556] *'Al* is believed to be the etymological root of the name *Allah*, the God of Islam. In fact, the general term for 'god' in ancient southern Arabia was *'al* and *allah.*[557] The same is true in Syria. Even though the Black Storm God was called 'Adad,' "the Only," the common word for 'god' in Syriac was *allah* and the proper name for God was *Allaha*, 'The God.'[558] Adad's consort, Atargatis, was also called *Allat,*[559] the feminine of and consort to Allah. She was also symbolized by the crescent moon, the symbol of Islam.[560] The god of the Qur'ān (Allah) indeed appears as a storm god. In Surah 13 entitled, "The Thunder" He is specifically described as a fearful storm god.

> 12. He (Allah) it is Who shows you the lightning causing fear and hope and (Who) brings up the heavy cloud.
> 13. And the thunder celebrates His praise, and the angels too for awe of Him. And He sends the thunderbolts and smites with them whom He pleases, yet they dispute concerning Allah, and He is Mighty in prowess…
> 17. He sends down water from the clouds, then watercourses flow according to their measure, and the torrent bears along the swelling foam…

The "heavy cloud" of verse 12 is reminiscent of the dark and heavy cloud upon which the Black Storm God was said to descend to the earth. Allah here is a terrifying God, with thunder and lighting at His disposal which He uses to cause fear and "smite" whom He pleases.

---

[554] Fenegan, ***The Archeology of World Religions***, 471

[555] Baldick, ***Black God***, 21.

[556] Ibid., 25-6.

[557] Th. C. Vriezen, *The Religion of Ancient Israel*, 70.

[558] F.V. Winnet, "Allah Before Islam," ***The Moslem World***, Volume XXVIII, 1938, 247.

[559] "Syrians," ***Encyclopedia of Religion and Ethics***, 1962, 165.

[560] "Syrians," 165.

But on a brighter note, He also sends down life sustaining water (verse 17). This strongly argues for His identity with the ancient Arabian Storm God also called Allah or Al Muqah, "God who Waters Intensively."

6.2. *Sūrat al-Ikhlāṣ and the Black God*

One of the most oft-repeated verses of the Qur'ān is *Al- Ikhlāṣ*: The Unity (Sura 112).

Qul: huwa llahu ahadun
Allahu l-samadu
Lam yalid wa-lam yulad
Wa-lam yakun lahu kufu'an ahad

1 Say: He Allah is One
2 Allah is *aṣ-ṣamad*
3 He begets not, nor is He begotten
4 And none is equal to Him.

Sura 112 is reckoned the single most important chapter in the Qur'ān as it defines Islam's attitude toward Allah.[561] It is no question *al-Ikhlāṣ*, along with *al-Shūrā* 42:11, which is cited most often as proof of the completely non-anthropomorphic nature of God. On the contrary, it is *Al- Ikhlāṣ* where we find the strongest support for an anthropomorphic, at least a corporeal* (embodied) Allah. In this verse the God of the Qur'ān is also connected with the ancient Black God. In verse two, God is referred to as *aṣ-ṣamad*. This word is the *hapax legomenon* of the Qur'ān n. Even today there is no agreement as to what the word means.[562] It is often translated as "Eternal" or "He to whom all depend," but this is not the lexical meaning of the word. By the time of al-Tabari (d. 923) the orthodox reading equated *ṣamad* with *muṣmat*, "solid, of even composition, massive, compact, or not hollow (i.e. without a stomach cavity)."[563] Al-Ash'ari (d. 935), in his ***Maqalāt al-Islāmīyīn*** observed: "Many people say, 'He (God) is solid,' interpreting the word of God *'ṣamad'* to mean solid, i.e., not hollow."[564] The greatest of the *Sahaba* (Companions) and the *Tabi'un* (Successors)

---

561 Gordon Newby, "*Surat Al-'Ikhlas,*" ***Orient and Occident*** 22 (1973): 127.
562 Uri Rubin, "Al-Sammad and the High God: An Interpretation of *sura* CXII," ***Islam*** LXI (1984): 187-217; Franz Rosenthal, "Some minor problems in the Qur'an," in ***The Joshua Starr Memorial Volume*** (New York: Conference on Jewish Relations, 1953) 67-84; van Ess, " Youthful God," 3ff.
563 Ibid.
564 Al-Ash'ari, ***Maqalat***, 34.

attached this meaning to the word: Ibn Abbas, al-Hasan, Sa'id b. Jubayr, Mujahid, ad-Dahhak, Sa'id b. al-Mausayyib, Ikrimah. The great men of the *Salaf* understood this word to mean that God is a massive, solid being, not hollow (i.e. without a stomach cavity).[565] God is thus a physical being.

But this is not all. The Arabs used *aṣ-ṣamad* in pre-Islamic times to designate their tribal chief and the High God who was thought to resemble this human tribal chief.[566] Most importantly, the pre-Islamic High God was called Allah.[567] The grammarian Abū 'Ubayda, in his *Majāz al-Qur'ān* (2, 316), noted: "*aṣ-ṣamad* is he towards whom one directs himself, and no one is above him. This is how the Arabs call their nobles (*ashrāfahā*.)" This clearly demonstrates that *aṣ-ṣamad* does not imply a non-anthropomorphic deity, for the Arabs commonly used the term for both God and men. And it is in the pre-Islamic sense that the word appears in the Qur'ān, as Uri Rubin's extensive study of the verse has shown.[568]

Verse 3 describes God as one who begets not and is Himself unbegotten. This of course, on the surface, appears unmistakable in its rejection of anthropomorphism. Again, analyzing it in its historical context proves otherwise. Four hundred Lihyanite and Dedanite inscriptions dating back to the fifth century BC were found in the area of al-Ulah in Northern Arabia. In these inscriptions are pre-Islamic invocations to Allah. One of the names applied to the pre-Islamic Allah, which distinguished him from the other deities acknowledged and worshipped by the idolatrous Arabs, was '*abtar*' which means he had "no offspring."

> O Allah, God without offspring, greeting…
> O Allah, God without offspring, knower of men…

F.V. Winnet, in his article, "Allah Before Islam," observes:

> Looking back over the texts given above, we find nothing distinctive in the appeals addressed to Allah…But there is one epithet applied to Allah which is not applied to any other god in north Arabic inscriptions and that is '*abtar*' (without offspring). It evidently denotes a quality that was regarded as

---

565 Cf. Tabari, ***Tafsir*** 30:196f.; Rosenthal, *art. cited,* pp. 76ff.
566 Uri Rubin, *art. cited*, pp. 200ff.
567 F. Winnet, ***A Study of Lihyanite and Thamudic Inscriptions*** (Toronto: University of Toronto Press,1937); idem., "Allah Before Islam," ***The Moslem World*** 28 (1938), pp. 239-259.
568 Uri Rubin, *art. cited,* p. 206.

peculiar to Allah alone; it thus forms our chief key to the Allah-theology of the pre-Islamic Arabs.[569]

'Abtar' denoted the quality of not producing offspring. Julian Baldick has shown that the 'Black God' of ancient South Arabia was characterized by this abnormal sexual behavior, i.e. the refusal to beget offspring.[570] This clearly demonstrates that the attributing to a god such a refusal need not indicate a non-anthropomorphic nature. The two descriptions of Allah found in *Al-Ikhlāṣ* – God as *aṣ-ṣamad* and as one who begets not – therefore connects the God of the Qur'ān with the god of pre-Islamic Arabia,[571] the proto-Semitic Black God called *Śal* who was human in form and black. Verse 4 is to be understood in this context. "And none is equal to Him." The word used here is not *mithl* but *kufu'an*. The word *kufu'* means "equal." There is none equal to this anthropomorphic, massive God who chooses not to beget.[572]

The conjunction of blackness, massiveness (*al-ṣamad*), and the form of God is observed in a remarkable report narrated by the famed qur'ānic commentator al-Tabari as part of his explication of sura 2:30.[573] After Adam's body was made from *ḥama'* fermented black mud (see *ḥamma* 'to blacken, become black') wrought into shape (*masnūn*), it was left standing as a hollow, lifeless statue for forty years; Allah did not blow his breath into Adam. During this time, the angels saw Adam and were terrified at the sight, none more than Iblīs, the Devil. Iblīs would strike Adam's body and it would make a hollow ring. He then went into

---

569 Winnet, "Allah Before Islam," 244.

570 Baldick, *op. cited*, 65.

571 Newby, *art. cited,* 130; Uri Rubin, *art. cited*, 206

572 Nor does similarity require that both forms (God's and man's) are created. Frithjoh Schreon (Dilemmas of Theological Speculation: A Muslim Perspective," ***Islamic Quarterly*** XVII [1979] 44f) illustrates this point most lucidly:

> As fallacious reasoning of this sort, taken from the catechism of Fudali, is the following: 'Let us suppose that a temporal thing resembles God, that is to say that God is such that one could attribute to Him qualities that one also observes in temporal creatures: in this case, He too would have to have a temporal origin and consequently need to have a Creator…' This conclusion is false, because the temporal character of things has no connection with their qualities; it simply pertains to their level of manifestation. It is as if one said: There is no resemblance between the moon and its reflection in water, because if there were a resemblance, the moon would have to be liquid like water…

573 ***The** Commentary **on the Qur'ān by Abū Ja'far Muḥammad b. Jarīr al-Ṭabarī; being an abridged translation of Jāmiʿ al-bayān 'an taʿwīl āy al-Qur'ān, with an introduction and notes***, by J. Cooper (Oxford [Oxfordshire]; New York: Oxford University Press, 1987) 214-15.

Adam's hollow body through his mouth, exiting through Adam's rear. Iblīs then said to the frightened angels: "Do not be afraid of this: your Lord is solid (*ṣamad*), but this is hollow. Indeed, if I am given power over it, I shall utterly destroy it."[574] This last statement gives us the reason the angels were terrified: they thought the black Adam-statue was God (Adam, we recall, is God's *mithāl/mithl*, Likeness, according to one reading of sura 42:11). This idea has a Jewish precedent. In the rabbinic text ***Genesis Rabbah***, we read: "Said [Rabbi] Hoshaiah: When the Holy One, blessed be He, came to create the first man, the ministering angels mistook him (viz. Adam) [for God, since man was in God's image,] and wanted to say before him, 'Holy, [holy, holy is the Lord of hosts].'"[575] In the Islamic version, the angels are disabused of this belief once it was learned that Adam's body was hollow; Allah, the angels well knew, has a compact and solid black body.[576]

6.3. *Yahweh-El, Black God of Israel*

The two primary names of God in the Hebrew Bible are *yahweh* ('Jehova') and *'ĕl/'ĕlōhîm*. Scholars now know that Yahweh and El are actually two historically distinct deities hailing from different areas who eventually coalesced in the biblical canon.[577] The Canaanite creator-god El, called 'Bull El (*ṯr 'il*),'was the original deity of Israel.[578] He, like

[574] Translated by Cooper, ***Commentary***, 214-15. On the creation of Adam in Muslim tradition see further Leigh N.B. Chipman, "Mythic Aspects of the Process of Adam's Creation in Judaism and Islam," ***Studia Islamica*** 93 (2001) 5-25; J.-C Vadet, "La creation et l'investiture de l'homme dans le sunnisme ou la légende d'Adam chez al-Kisā'ī," ***Studia Islamica*** 42 (1975): 5-37.

[575] Jacob Neusner, ***The Incarnation of God: The Character of Divinity in Formative Judaism*** (Philadelphia: Fortress Press, 1988) 3.

[576] On this tradition see especially Josef van Ess, ***The Youthful God: Anthropomorphism in Early Islam*** (Tempe, AZ: Department of Religious Studies, Arizona State University, 1988) 1-2.

[577] Bernhard Lang, ***The Hebrew God: Portrait of an Ancient Deity*** (New Haven; London: Yale University Press, 2002) 24-52; Mark S. Smith, ***The Early History of God. Yahweh and the Other Deities in Ancient Israel***, 2nd Edition (Grand Rapids, Mi.: William B. Eerdmans Pub. Co., 2002) 32-43; idem, ***The Origin of Biblical Monotheism*** (Oxford: Oxford University Press, 2001) 135-148; Tryggve N.D. Mettinger, "The Elusive Essence: YHWH, El and Baal and the Distinctiveness of Israelite Faith," in ***Hebräische Bibel und ihre zweifache Nachgeschichte*** (Neukirchen-Vluyn: Neukirchener, 1990) 393-417; idem, "The Study of the Gottesbild.-Problems and Suggestions," ***Svensk exegetisk arsbok*** 54 (1989): 135-145; Conrad E L'Heureux, "Searching for the origins of God," in ***Traditions in transformation: Turning Points in Biblical Faith*** (Winona Lake, IN: Eisenbrauns, 1981)_ 33-57.

[578] Ibid. See also ***DDD*** 274-80 s.v. El by W. Herrmann. On West Semitic El as creator deity see ***DDD*** 280-81 s.v. El-Creator-of-the-Earth by W. Röllig; P.D. Miller, Jr. "El, the Creator of Earth," ***BASOR*** 239 (1980): 43-46.

Figure 18

Black god of Canaan and early Israel,'El (from Prichard, ***ANET***)

the black-god 'Il/'El/'Al of the Proto-Semites, was depicted as an old, bearded man (Figure 18).[579] Also like the ancient Near Eastern and Proto-Semitic black god, the Canaanite El had as his primary attribute animal the black bull.[580] Yahweh, on the other hand, originated in the southern region of present day Palestine and Jordan and only secondarily entered the Israelite pantheon.[581] He was a warrior/storm deity associated with the black storm cloud.[582] Already in early portions of the biblical text the two deities (Yahweh and El) have merged, becoming Yahweh-El.[583]

Like the ancient Near Eastern and Proto-Semitic Black God, Yahweh-El possessed a dangerously luminous anthropomorphic form, called his כבוד *kāḇôd* "Glory"[584] (Figure 21), which, for the protection

---

[579] M. Yon and J. Gachet, "Une statuette du dieu El à Ugarit," ***Syria*** 66 (1989): 349; N. Wyatt, "The Stella of the Seated God from Ugarit," ***UF*** 15 (1983): 271-77; Marvin H. Pope, "The Scene on the Drinking Mug from Ugarit," in Hans Goedicke, ***Near Eastern Studies in Honor of William Foxwell Albright*** (Baltimore: Johns Hopkins Press, 1971) 393-405.

[580] Daum, ***Ursemitische Religion***, 184-188; Baldick, ***Black God***, 38-9.

[581] On the origins of Yahwism see above and further Alberto R.W. Green, ***The Storm-God in the Ancient Near East*** (Winona Lake, Indiana: 2003) Chap. 4; Karel van der Toorn, ***Family Religion in Babylon, Syria and Israel. Continuity and Change in the Forms of Religious Life*** Leiden: E.J. Brill, 1996) 281-286; Erhard S. Gestenberger, ***Theologies of the Old Testament*** (Minneapolis: Fortress Press, 2002) 138-151; Herbert Niehr, "The Rise of YHWH in Judahite and Israelite Religion: Methodological and Religio-Historical Aspects," in Diana Vikander Edelman (ed.), ***The Triumph of Elohim. From Yahwisms to Judaisms*** (Grand Rapids, Mich.: William B. Eerdmans Publishing Company, 1996) 45-72.

[582] See especially Green, ***Storm-God***, 258-280; Victor Hurowitz, "From Storm God to Abstract Being," ***Bible Review*** 14:5 (October 1998): 40-47; P.E. Dion, "Yahweh as Storm-god and Sun-god," ***ZAW*** 103 (1991) 43-71; Jörg Jeremias, ***Theophanie; die Geschichte einer alttestamentlichen Gattung***, (Neukirchen-Vluyn: Neukirchener Verlag des Erziehungsvereins, 1965); idem, "Theophany in the OT," ***The Interpreter's dictionary of the Bible, Supplementary Volume*** (Nashville : Abingdon, 1976) 896-898.

[583] See esp. Smith, ***History of God***, 32-42; idem, ***Biblical Monotheism***, 141-42.

[584] For a tradition-history of the *kābôd* in the HB see especially Carey C. Newman, ***Paul's Glory-Christology: Tradition and Rhetoric*** (Leiden: E.J. Brill, 1992). See also ***TDOT*** 7:23-38 s.v. "כבוד," by Weinfeld; ***TDNT*** 2:238-47 s.v. δοξα: C. כבודin the OT by G. von Rad; J. Morgenstern, "Biblical Theophanies," ***ZA*** 25 (1911): 139-193, 28 (1913-14): 15-60. On the luminous, anthropomorphic *kābôd* see Moshe Weinfeld, ***Deuteronomy and the Deuteronomic School*** (Oxford: The Clarendon Press, 1972) 191-209, esp. 200-206; idem, ***TDOT*** 7:31-33 s.v. כבוד; Mettinger, ***Dethronement of Sabaoth***, Chapters Three and Four; J. E. Fossum, "Glory," ***DDD*** 348-52; A. Joseph Everson, "Ezekiel and the Glory of the Lord Tradition," in Daniel Durken (ed.), ***Sin, Salvation, and the Spirit***, (Collegeville, Minnesota: The Liturgical Press, 1979): 163-176; Moshe Greenberg, ***Ezekiel 1-20*** The Anchor Bible (Garden City, New York: Doubleday & Company, Inc., 1983), 52f; idem, "Ezekiel's Vision: Literary and Iconographic Aspects," in H. Tadmor and M. Weinfeld (edd.), ***History, Historiography and Interpretation*** (Jerusalem and Leiden: The Image Press, the Hebrew University and E.J. Brill, 1983): 159-168; Rimmon Kasher, "Anthropomorphism, Holiness and the Cult: A New look at Ezekiel 40-48," ***ZAW*** 110 (1998): 192-208; Andrei A. Orlov, "Ex 33 on God's Face: A

of his creatures, he concealed within a black material covering, ערפל *'ărāpel.*[585] *'ărāpel* means "thick" or "intense darkness."[586] Like the Proto-Semitic Black God as well, this "intensely dark" covering is described as a "cloud of blackness/darkness," חשך וענן *ḥōšek we-'ānān* (lit.: "darkness and clouds").[587] The reference in most cases is not to actual clouds,[588] but to "a cloudlike covering enveloping and concealing the deity."[589] Thus, ערפל *'ărāpel* "intense darkness" is "associated...with the (veiled) manifestation of God wherever he appears or reveals his presence" and thus "indicates the actual appearance of God."[590] This means that when Yahweh-El is seen he has an "intensely black" appearance, like the Proto-Semitic Black God.

Lesson from the Enoch Tradition," ***SBL Seminar Papers*** 39 (2000): 130-147. On the anthropomorphic *kābôd* in later Jewish mystical tradition see Gilles Quispel, "Ezekiel 1:26 in Jewish Mysticism and Gnosis," ***VC*** 34 (1980): 1-13;Jarl Fossum, "Jewish-Christian Christology and Jewish Mysticism," ***VC*** 37 (1983): 260-287; April D. de Conick, ***Seek to See Him: Ascent and Vision Mysticism in the Gospel of Thomas*** (Leiden: E.J. Brill, 1996) 99-125.

585 See e.g. Ex. 13:21f, 14:19-25, 19:9, 20: 21-23; Deut. 4:11, 5:22f; 2 Sam. 22:8-9; Pss. 18:9-12, 97:2; I Kings 8:12.

586 On ערפל see ***TDOT*** 11:371-75 s.v. ערפל *'ᵃrāpel* by Mulder; Cohen, "The Basic Meaning"; Forest Charles Cornelius, "The theological significance of darkness in the Old Testament," Ph.D diss. Southern Baptist Theological Seminary, 1990, 12-51, 103-110; A.J. Loader, "The Concept of Darkness in the Hebrew Root 'RB/ 'RP," in I.H. Eybers et al (edd.), ***De Fructu Oris Sui. Essays in Honour of Adrianus Van Selms*** (Leiden: E.J. Brill, 1971) 98-107.

587 On the theophanic cloud see ***TDOT*** 11:253-257 s.v. ענן *'ānān*; Paul Allen Smith, "An Investigation of the Relationship of Theophanies to God's Concealment by Clouds in the Old Testament," Ph.D diss. New Orleans Baptist Theological Seminary, 1994; Leopold Sabourin, "The Biblical Cloud: Terminology and Traditions," ***Biblical Theology Bulletin*** 4 (1974): 301; Julian Morgenstern, "Biblical Theophanies," ***Zeitschrift für Assyriologie*** 25 (1911) 139-191

588 In the Torah at least two different cloud-phenomena are associated with Yahweh-El's theophany: Firstly, a locomotive or vehicular *'ānān* by which Yahweh 'descends' (ירד, *yrd*), presumably from 'heaven.' This 'chariot-cloud' is characteristic of E (Exod. 33:7-11; Num. 11:25; 12:5). On the other hand, "the cloud in P and in Ezekiel is the divine envelope which screens the Deity from mortal view. God doesn't *descend* (ירד, *yrd*) in a cloud as in the earlier sources, but *manifests himself* (נראה, *nr'h*) in a cloud (Exod. 16:10; Num. 17:7) so that man may not gaze upon him and die" (Weinfeld, ***Deuteronomy and the Deuteronomic School***, 202). See also Benjamin D. Sommer, "Conflicting Constructions of Divine Presence in the Priestly Tabernacle," ***Biblical Interpretation*** 9 (2001): 41-63; David Frankel, "Two Priestly Conceptions of Guidance in the Wilderness," ***JSOT*** 81 (1998): 31-37; Thomas W. Mann, "The Pillar of Cloud in the Reed Sea Narrative," ***JBL*** 90 (1971): 15-30; Leopold Sabourin, "The Biblical Cloud: Terminology and Traditions," ***BTB*** 4 (1974): 297-303.

589 ***TDOT*** 11:190 s.v. עמוד *'ammûḏ* by Freedman-Willoughby.

590 Mulder, "ערפל *'ᵃrāpel*" 374.

In later Jewish tradition, this black cloud is understood as a symbol of the black body of God.[591]

6.4. *Black Bull of Israel*

Yahweh-El is called *'ăbîr yisrā'ēl*, "Bull of Israel" (Isa. 1:24).[592] In Deut. 33:17 Joseph is described as *běkôr šôr* (MT: *šôrô*), "first-born of the Bull (Yahweh-El)."[593] Yahweh-El possesses the horns of the wild ox, *rě'ēm* (Num. 23:22; 24:8; Ps. 22:22). That Yahweh-El's attribute animal was understood to be a bull is further demonstrated by the story of the golden calf in Exodus 32 and the narrative in I Kings 12:25-30 concerning the bull idols consecrated in the Northern Kingdom of Israel by Jeroboam. These idols did not represent pedestals upon which an invisible deity stood, but were indeed tauromorphic ("bull-form") representations of Yahweh-El.[594] It is likely that these passages in Exodus 32 and I Kings reflect a southern (Judaen) polemic against a northern (Israelite) bull-cult that was every bit legitimate in the eyes of the Northerners (i.e. Israelites).[595] What is more, archeological evidence suggests that at an earlier period tauromorphic representation of Yahweh-El was officially legitimate in the South (Judah) as well.[596] That is to say, the god of the ancient Israelites was the Bull God. "All of this suggests that throughout Israel's history, from exodus to exile, there was a nearly continuous worship of Yahweh as a bull."[597]

---

[591] See Wesley Williams, "Sapphiric God: Esoteric Speculation on the Body Divine in Post-Biblical Jewish Tradition," ***HTR***, forthcoming.

[592] The MT's אביר is likely a cognate of אבּיר. ***BDB*** lists the former as a construct form of the later in Isa. 1:24. See also A.H.W. Curtis, "Some Observations on 'Bull' Terminology in the Ugaritic Texts and the Old Testament," in ***In Quest of the Past; Studies on Israelite Religion, Literature, and Prophetism. Papers Read at the Loint British-Dutch Old Testament Conference*** (Leiden: E.J. Brill, 1990): 17-31.

[593] See also Gen. 49:22-26 and discussion in Korpel, ***Rift in the Clouds***, 532-34.

[594] Curtis, "Bull Terminology," 21-25; John N. Oswalt, "The golden Calves and the Egyptian Concept of Deity," ***Evangelical Quarterly*** 45 (1973) 13-20. *Pace* W.F. Albright, ***From Stone Age to Christianity*** (Anchor Books edition; New york, 1957) 266.

[595] N. Wyatt, "Calf עגל," ***DDD***180-82; idem, "Of Calves and Kings: The Canaanite Dimension in the Religion of Israel," ***Scandinavian Journal of the Old Testament*** 6 (1992): 68-91; George W. Coats ("The Golden Calf in Psalm 22," ***Horizons in Biblical Theology*** 9 [1987]: 1-12) argues that this polemic is reflected in the change in terminology, from the positively connotated *rě'ēm*, "wild ox" to the negative *'ēgel*, "calf."

[596] See esp. G.W. Ahlström, "An Archaeological Picture of Iron Age Religions in Ancient Palestine," ***Studia Orientalia*** 55 (198?): 11, 16

[597] John N. Oswalt, "Golden Calves and the 'Bull of Jacob': The Impact on Israel of Its Religious Environment," in Avraham Gileadi (ed.), ***Israel's Apostasy and Restoration: Essays in Honor of Roland K. Harrison*** (Grand Rapids, Michigan: Baker Book house, 1988)12.

Bull figurines found at Hazor and Dhahrat et-Tawileh (Figure 19), two ancient Israelite sites, may represent the Canaanite-Israelite high-god "Bull El,"[598] but because the figurines are of young zebu bulls it is possible that they represent the storm-god Yahweh still unassimilated to El.[599] The most important evidence of course are the epigraphic finds at Kh. El-Qôm and, especially, Kuntillet 'Ajrud, an ancient way-station in the Sinai.[600] The endlessly controversial drawings and inscriptions on two pithoi (storage jars), particularly Pithos A, likely picture Yahweh-El and his consort (*'šrh*) in composite form: half anthropomorphic, half bovine (Figure 20).[601] We clearly have here a visual depiction of the 'calf of Samaria' that Hosea so zealously polemicised against (Hos. 8:6). As M.D. Coogan observes, "Both figures have...appropriate theriomorphic aspects of the 'bull of Jacob' and his lady."[602] This bull-man *Mischwesen* ("composite being") recalls certain Phoenician stamp seals, also dated from the 8-6 centuries BC, depicting an anthropomorphic god with a bull-head enthroned on a cherubim throne.[603] We are reminded of course of Yahweh-El's characteristic cherubim throne from which he even gets the divine title, ישב הכרבים *yōšēb hakkĕrūbîm* "he who is enthroned above the cherubim."[604] This image also recalls a similar bovine-man *Mischwesen*, the "Black Buffalo"

---

[598] Amihai Mazar, "The 'Bull Site' – An Iron Age I Open Cult Place," ***Bulletin of the American Society of Oriental Research*** 247 (1982): 27-43; Gösta W. Ahlström, "The Bull Figurine from Dhahrat et-Tawileh," ***Bulletin of the American Society of Oriental Research*** 280 (1990): 77-82; Johannes C. DeMoor, ***The Rise of Yahwism: The roots of Israelite Monotheism*** (Leuven: Leuven University Press, 1997): 126-30.

[599] On the significance of the type/age of the bull in its identification with a god see Daniel E. Fleming, "If El is a Bull, Who is a Calf? Reflections on Religion in Second-Millennium Syria-Palestine," ***Eretz-Israel*** 26 (1999): 23-27.

[600] For an overview see Z. Meshel, "Kuntillet 'Ajrud," ***The Anchor Bible Dictionary*** 4 (1992): 103-109.

[601] See especially Brian B. Schmidt, "The Iron Age *Pithoi* Drawings from Horvat Teman or Kuntillet 'Ajrud: Some New Proposals," ***Journal of Ancient Near Eastern Religions*** 2 (2002): 91-125; Baruch Margalit, "The Meaning and Significance of Asherah," ***VT*** 40 (1990): 264-297 (274-78).

[602] "Canaanite Origins and Lineage: Reflections on the Religion of Ancient Israel," in P.D. Miller et al (edd.), ***Ancient Israelite Religion. Essays in Honor of Frank Moore Cross*** (Philadelphia, 1987) 119.

[603] Tallay Ornan, "The Bull and its Two Masters: Moon and Storm Deities in Relation to the Bull in Ancient Near Eastern Art," ***Israel Exploration Journal*** 51 (2001): 23; W. Culican, "The Iconography of Some Phoenician Seals and Seal Impressions," ***Australian Journal of Biblical Archeology*** 1 (1968): 57-60.

[604] See esp. Tryggve N.D. Mettinger, ***The Dethronement of Sabaoth. Studies in the Shem and Kabod Theologies*** (CWK Gleerup, 1982) 19-37; idem, "YHWH SABAOTH-The Heavenly King on the Cerubim Throne," in Tomoo Ishida (ed.), ***Studies in the Period of David and Solomon and Other Essays. Papers Read at the International Symposium for Biblical Studies, Tokyo, 5-7 December, 1979*** (Winona Lake, Indiana: Eisenbrauns, 1982) 109-138.

Figure 19

Yahweh-Bull figurine from Hazor

Figure 20

Bovine image of Yahweh and his Ashera (consort) from Kuntillet`Ajrud

deity depicted on the so-called Proto-Śiva seal from Mohenjo-dara (Figure 21).[605] Yahweh-El is thus part of the broader 'Black Bull' tradition of the ancient Near and Far East. Yahweh-El is, therefore, ancient Israel's Black God. As Julian Baldick notes: "the God of the Bible…come(s) out of the original Semitic black rain-deity".[606] Thus, the root of Jewish, Christian and Islamic tradition is this proto-Semitic Black God.

[605] Alf Hiltebeitel, "The Indus Valley 'Proto-Śiva', Reexamined through Reflections on the Goddess, the Buffalo, and the Symbolism of *vāhanas*," ***Anthropos*** 73 (1978): 767-797; Doris Srinivasan, "The So-Called Proto-Śiva Seal from Mohenjo-Daro: An Iconological Assessment," ***Archives of Asian Art*** 29 (1975): 47-58; Parpola, "New correspondences."

[606] Baldick, ***Black God***, 162.

Figure 21

'Black Buffalo' of ancient Mohenjo-dara

Chapter VII:

The Bible and the Secret of the Black God

7. *Introductory Summary*

Not only was the God of ancient Israel the 'Black Bull' of ancient Near Eastern* mythic tradition, the 'myth* of the Black God' formed part of the secret theology of the Temple in Jerusalem. It was priests associated with this Temple that were responsible for the Torah (Pentateuch or Five Books of Moses) as we know it. A particularly important piece of priestly literature in the Bible is the first chapter of Genesis which, we are told, "contains the essence of Priestly knowledge in a most concentrated form." As an esoteric* or secret priestly text, Genesis I contains two different narratives: (1) exoterically* the text narrates God's creation of the cosmos (2) esoterically the text narrates God's own self-creation and somatic ('bodily') evolution, a process that culminates on Day Six with his creation of and incarnation* within a black body called 'Adam.'

A detailed analysis of the Hebrew of Genesis 1:1-4, 26 demonstrates that the King James English translation of this text is wholly inadequate and that the Hebrew narrative affirms:

- Creation was not 'out of nothing,' but involved the manipulation of a pre-existent triple-darkness – an uncreated dark substance or, better, three distinguished dark substances.
- Prior to the start of creation God existed within this pre-existent triple-darkness as a luminous,* creative spirit or 'breath.'
- Within this triple-darkness also was the 'golden egg' or primordial atom.
- The first act of creation, narrated in Gen. 1:4, was God's own emergence from the triple-darkness as a brilliantly luminous man.
- The Genesis narrative describing God's creation and vivification of Adam is actually, esoterically, a description of God's creation of and incarnation within his own black body.

Thus, the ancient Near Eastern 'myth* of the Black God' lies behind the Hebrew Genesis I narrative. The priests of the Temple even performed this 'myth' theatrically within the Temple during the execution of the liturgies* or religious services. That is to say, the rituals performed by the priests within the Temple actually reenact God's creation of the cosmos and his own self-creation. The high priest in these reenactments played the role of God and his (the high priest's) special garments, dark blue and gold, symbolized the blue-black 'sapphiric' body of Yahweh-Elohim, the God of Israel.

This 'myth of the Black God' is found in Islamic tradition as well. According to the Qur'ān God created the cosmos from a triple-darkness. According to a report on the authority of the Prophet Muḥammad of Arabia God existed within this triple-darkness prior to creation. The Qur'ān, when read in its Arabic and ancient Near Eastern context, affirms, like the Bible, God's creation of and incarnation within a black body named 'Adam.'

7.1. *The Temple of Jerusalem, the Bible, and the Secret of God*

The central institution of ancient Israel was the Temple in Jerusalem. Not only was it the fulcrum of Israel's cult, it was also the architectural embodiment of Israel's ancient mythic-tradition and the stage upon which that mythic-tradition was ritually reenacted. Thus, studies exploring the significance of the 'Temple symbolism' have gone a long way in reconstructing that ancient Israelite mythic-tradition,[607] at the center of which was the myth of the Black God. As this mythic-tradition was the central component of the ancient mysteries, so it was the central component of the esoteric* Temple tradition of Israel.

Biblical scholarship has shown that the Torah or so-called Five Books of Moses (Pentateuch) is a composite of sources written by authors from different time-periods and places.[608] While certain aspects of the "Documentary Hypothesis" have been recently challenged and

[607] See in particular the works of Margaret Barker: ***the Great High Priest: The Temple Roots of Christian Liturgy*** (London: T&T Clark, 2003); "Beyond the Veil of the Temple: The High Priestly Origins of the Apocalypses," ***Scottish Journal of Theology*** 51 (1998): 1-21; ***Great Angel: A Study of Israel's Second God*** (Louisville, Kentucky: Westminster/John Knox Press, 1992); ***The Gate of Heaven: The History and Symbolism of the Temple in Jerusalem*** (London: SPCK, 1991); ***On Earth as it is in Heaven: Temple Symbolism in the New Testament*** (Edinburgh: T&T Clark, 1995).

[608] See the still useful introductions: John H. Hayes, ***An Introduction to Old Testament Study*** (Nashville: Abingdon Press, 1991 [1979]); Richard Elliot Friedman, ***Who Wrote the Bible?*** (New York: Harper & Row, Publishers, 1987).

Figure 22

The Temple of Solomon in Jerusalem (c. 1000 BC – 586 BC)

revised,[609] the fundamental point of multiple-authorship remains firmly established.[610] One of, if not the most important of these authors was the priestly author/editor who is believed to be responsible for large portions of the Torah[611] as well as its final redaction or editing.[612] 'P,'[613] as this priestly author/editor is called by biblical scholars, was likely a member of the Zadokite priesthood, the chief priesthood of Solomon's Temple in Jerusalem and, after some interruption, again in the Second Temple during the Persian period (538-333 BC), the period that saw the formation of the Bible as we know it.[614] It was in fact at the hands of Zadokite priests of this latter period that the Bible is believed to have come together. Nevertheless, the priestly materials found in the Torah represent priestly traditions going back to the pre-exilic monarchy (First Temple: 1000 BC-586 BC).[615] They thus provide important insight into the Temple mythic-tradition of ancient Israel.

The Temple traditions of ancient Israel, as in the ancient Near East generally, constituted an esoteric tradition known, at least in its details, only to the priests.[616] These priestly secrets included the mythico-theological significance of the Temple, the Temple appurtenances, and the Temple rituals.[617] The P material in the Torah likewise constitutes an esoteric 'document,' especially Genesis I.[618]

---

[609] See the summary of recent developments in Robert K. Gnuse ,"Redefining the Elohist," ***JBL*** 119 (2000): 201-220; Mark S. Smith, ***The Pilgrimage Pattern in Exodus*** (JSOTSup 239; Sheffield: Sheffield Academic Press, 1997) Chapter Five.

[610] See especially Richard Elliot Friedman, ***The Hidden Book in the Bible: Restored, Translated and Introduced*** (New York: HarperCollins, 1998) 350-378.

[611] Significant portions of Genesis (including all of Genesis I) and Exodus, virtually all of Leviticus, and three-fourths of Numbers.

[612] On the formation of the biblical canon see Peter W. Flint (ed.), ***The Bible at Qumran: Text, Shape and Interpretation*** (Grand Rapids Michigan and Cambridge, U.K.: William B. Eerdmans Publishing Company, 2001; Eugene Ulrich, ***The Dead Sea Scrolls and the Origins of the Bible*** (Grand Rapids Michigan and Cambridge, U.K.: William B. Eerdmans Publishing Company; Leiden: Brill, 1999); Hayes, ***Introduction***, Chapter One.

[613] 'P' here will stand for both the presumed priestly author(s) as well as the priestly materials in the Torah.

[614] See especially Robert B. Coote and David Robert Ord, ***In the Beginning: Creation and the Priestly History*** (Minneapolis: Fortress Press, 1991) Chapters Three and Four.

[615] Coote and Ord, ***In the Beginning***, 40. Ancient Jewish history is (partly) divided between that which occurred between the building and destruction of the first temple in Jerusalem (b. 1006 BC, d. 586 BC, so-called First Temple Period) and that which occurred during the time of the second temple, built in 515 BC and destroyed in 70 AD (so-called Seconf Temple Period).

[616] Chayim Cohen, "Was the P Document Esoteric," ***JANES*** 1 (1969): 39-44.

[617] On the esoteric rituals within the Tabernacle see Menahem Haran, "The Complex of Ritual Acts Performed inside the Tabernacle," ***Scripta Hierosolymitana*** 8 (1961): 272-302.

[618] Israel Knohl, ***The Sanctuary of Silence: the Priestly Torah and the Holiness School*** (Minneapolis: Fortress Press, 1995) 153; Menahem Haran, "Behind the Scenes of

Gerhard von Rad in his Genesis commentary appropriately put any would-be interpreter of this text on notice:

> Whoever expounds Gen., ch. I, must understand one thing: this is Priestly doctrine-indeed, it contains the essence of Priestly knowledge in a most concentrated form...Nothing is here by chance; everything must be considered carefully, deliberately, and precisely...Nowhere at all is the text only allusive, symbolic, or figuratively poetic. Actually, the exposition must painstakingly free this bundled and rather esoteric doctrine sentence by sentence, indeed, word by word. These sentences cannot be easily over interpreted theologically! Indeed, to us the danger appears greater that the expositor will fall short of discovering the concentrated doctrinal content.[619]

Because Genesis I contains "the essence of Priestly knowledge in a most concentrated form," and this knowledge was esoteric, the Temple traditions represented by P are never explicitly communicated in these materials. Stephen A. Geller has recently taken notice of P's "reticence to verbalize his underlying concepts."[620]

> P certainly has ideas but he rarely presents them openly. His motto seems to be, "Never explain!"...To be sure, glimmers of a theology can be sensed from the structure P impresses on the Pentateuch...But P is more reticent than any other biblical tradition about putting the logic of his theological reasoning into words...The Problem with P is...that this reticence is somehow willed, in some peculiar way intrinsic to his message. P seems to be aiming at a theology of indirection... P, more than any other biblical author, reveals what he has to say by how he says it.[621]

"How he says it"- this is the key to unlocking the esoteric tradition represented by P, the priestly author. Bernhard W. Anderson likewise pointed out that it is the literary *structure* of the P materials that give

---

History: Determining the Date of the Priestly Source," ***JBL*** 100 (1981): 321-333; Cohen, "Was the P Document Esoteric."

[619] Gerhard von Rad, ***Genesis: A Commentary***, translated from the German by John H. Marks (Philadelphia: Westminster Press, 1961) 45.

[620] "Blood Cult: Toward a Literary Theology of the Priestly Work of the Pentateuch," ***Prooftexts*** 12 (1992): 97-124..

[621] Geller, "Blood Cult,"99, 100.

evidence of the priest's theological perspective.[622] Instead of openly verbalizing these theological concepts, P employs a method of 'literary indirection' through placement, juxtaposition, and subtle allusion to impress these unarticulated concepts on the structure of the Torah.[623] Employing the tools of literary analysis has allowed scholars to shed light on a number of these 'esoteric' themes.[624] One such theme is the self-origination and evolution of the black body of God.

7.2. 'How Came the Black God, Mr. Muhammad?' *Biblical Creation and the Secret of the Black God*

The God of the Torah is the ancient Near Eastern Black God. But does the Bible say anything about his origin from an atom in darkness?

There were multiple creation accounts circulating in ancient Israel, the account found in the first chapter of Genesis being only one of them.[625] These accounts were clearly part of the ancient Near Eastern cosmogonic tradition. Indeed, even the myth of the war of the creator-god against the primeval sea (*Chaoskampf*), so characteristic of the so-called 'pagan' cosmogonies, had wide circulation in ancient Israel and is alluded to in several biblical texts (Isa 51:9f.; Ps. 74:12ff.; Job 26:10ff. etc.).[626] But in the Genesis creation narrative, which, we are told, "contains the essence of priestly knowledge in concentrated form," this

---

[622] "A Stylistic Study of the Priestly Creation Story," in G. W. Coats and B.O. Long (edd.), ***Canon and Authority: essays in Old Testament religion and theology*** (Philadelphia: Fortress Press, 1977) 148-162.

[623] Geller, "Blood Cult."

[624] See e.g. Mark S. Smith, "The Literary Arrangement of the Priestly Redaction of Exodus: A Preliminary Investigation," ***CBQ*** 58 (1996): 25-50; Anderson, "A Stylistic Study;" Joseph Blekinsopp, "The Structure of P," ***CBQ*** 38 (1976): 275-292; idem, ***Prophecy and Canon***_(Notre Dame and London: University of Notre Dame, 1977) 56-69; Peter J. Kearney, "Creation and Liturgy: The P Redaction of Ex 25-40," ***ZAW*** 89 (1977): 375-387; Michael Fishbane, ***Text and Texture: Close Readings of Selected Biblical Texts*** (New York: Schocken Books, 1979) 11-13; Joseph Blekinsopp, "The Structure of P," ***CBQ*** 38 (1976): 275-292; idem, ***Prophecy and Canon***_(Notre Dame and London: University of Notre Dame, 1977) 56-69; Peter J. Kearney, "Creation and Liturgy: The P Redaction of Ex 25-40," ***ZAW*** 89 (1977): 375-387; Michael Fishbane, ***Text and Texture: Close Readings of Selected Biblical Texts*** (New York: Schocken Books, 1979) 11-13.

[625] Clifford, ***Creation Accounts***, Part Two; ***ABD*** 1:1162-68 s.v. Cosmogony, Cosmology by Robert A. Oden, Jr.

[626] Fishbane, ***Biblical Myth***, Chapter Two; Carola Kloos, ***Yhwh's Combate with the Sea: A Canaanite Tradition in the Religion of Israel*** (Amsterdam: G.A. van Oorschat and Leiden: E.J. Brill, 1986) John Day, ***God's Conflict with the Dragon and the Sea*** (Cambridge, 1985);

'war-against-chaos' myth is nowhere found.[627] However, another ancient Near Eastern mythic motif* is.

In his commentary on Genesis, Claus Westermann called our attention to an important fact, the recognition of which is critical to a proper understanding of the Genesis creation account and, indeed, the theology behind it.

> The first chapter of Genesis had its origin in the course of a history of tradition of which the written text of P is the last stage, and which stretches back *beyond and outside Israel* in a long and many-branched oral pre-history."[628]

The origin of the Genesis 1 creation narrative does indeed lie outside of Israel, and there can be no doubt as to its general provenance: "That some form or other of the ancient Near-Eastern myth of creation lies behind the Priestly account cannot be denied."[629] The *specific* provenance, however, has been debated. Since the publication of the Babylonian creation account, ***Enūma elīš***, in 1876 by George Smith the similarities between the Babylonian and Hebrew narratives have been often noted.[630] The Babylonian Exile, during which large numbers of Jewish priests were exiled in Babylon, is surely a proper context in which to understand these similarities. But Israel also, earlier and for a longer period of time, were in Egypt. Moses was an Egyptian (Exod. 2:19) 'learned in all the wisdom of Egypt (Act 7:22).' Indeed, while Babylonian influence is discernable in the structure and some of the vocabulary of Genesis 1, scholars have pointed out that this creation account that was edited during the Exile itself derives from the much older Egyptian cosmogonic tradition.[631]

---

[627] David Toshio Tsumura, ***The Earth and Waters in Genesis 1 and 2. A Linguistic Investigation*** (JSOTSup 83; Sheffield: Sheffield Academic Press, 1989) 65; Day, ***God's Conflict***, 53.

[628] Westermann, ***Genesis 1-11***, 83.

[629] Islwyn Blythin, "A Note on Genesis 1^2," ***VT*** 12 (1962): 120 [art.=120-121]. See also Whitley, "Patterns of Creation," 36; Arvid S. Kapelrud, "The Mythological Features in Genesis Chapter 1 and the Author's Intention," ***VT*** 24 (1974): 179 [art.=86]. Susan Niditch (***Chaos to Cosmos: Studies in Biblical Patterns of Creation*** [SPSH 6; Chico, California: Scholars Press, 1985] 18) noted also that "There is no doubt a shared Near Eastern notion of the way the cosmos' order unfolded," and Gen. 1 reflects that shared notion.

[630] See e.g. A. Heidel, ***The Babylonian Genesis*** (Chicago: University of Chicago Press, 1942).

[631] Rikki E. Watts ("On the Edge of the Millennium: Making Sense of Genesis 1," in Hans Boersma [ed.]. ***Living in the LambLight: Christianity and Contemporary Challenges to the Gospel*** [Vancouver: Regent College Publishing, 2001] 138-9 [art.=129-51]) argues that in the light of the time Israel spent in Egypt, the "dominant background against which Genesis 1 is read and heard" should be the Egyptian creation

> When the template of ancient Egyptian creation traditions is held up against the Genesis I creation account there is a quite remarkable correspondence. The conclusion is stark and compelling: ancient Egypt provided the foundation tradition which was shaped and handed down by successive priestly generations...Ancient Egypt proves to be the single, coherent and rich source of the priestly creation tradition. The Nile civilization provides not simply a possible context for odd verses, but again and again accounts for the details of the Genesis I creation narrative and is the key to its common thread.[632]

The first chapter of Genesis is in fact a Hebrew adaptation of an ancient Egyptian cosmogony.[633] As such, the Egyptian original casts an illuminating light on Genesis 1. As Abraham Yahuda noted:

> the Egyptian background...throws full light on the most important and conspicuous points of creation (in Genesis), and explains many features which have always puzzled the interpreters and theologians. In some instances it gives us the key to the solution of problems which were considered insoluble.[634]

Therefore, in order to make since of the enigmatic priestly creation account, we must avail ourselves to not only the biblical priestly materials in the Torah and the Hebrew Bible generally, but also to the Egyptian original of this Hebrew adaptation.[635]

---

accounts: "How does one explain that it happens to be Egyptian stories, he place where Israel had just spent 400 years and which stories antedate considerably Israel's stay in Egypt, whose scattered details on the whole bear a greater resemblance to Genesis 1 than those, for example, of Mesopotamia?" He suggests that "the details of the varied Egyptian accounts...have influenced the language of Israel's creation story (144)."

[632] James E. Atwell, "An Egyptian Source for Genesis I," ***JTS*** 51 (2000): 466-7 [art.=441-77].

[633] Herman Gunkel ("Influence of Babylonian," 44) wrote that Gen. 1 "is merely the Judaic reworking of much older traditional material that originally must have been considerably more mythological in nature," and according to W.F. Albright ("Contributions," 365) P "effaced the original outlines" of the Egypto-Phoenician cosmogonic narrative that he received. On Gen 1 as an "abbreviation" see also McBride, "Divine Protocol," XX.

[634] Abraham Shalom Yahuda, ***The Accuracy of the Bible*** (London: William Heineman Ltd., 1934), 136.

[635] This is not to deny the new and idiosyncratic ways in which Israel may have received, interpreted and utilized these ancient traditions. It is to say, however, that any attempt to

To apply von Rad's cautious and careful methodology of "painstakingly free(ing) this bundled and rather esoteric doctrine sentence by sentence…word by word"[636] to the whole of Genesis 1 will require a full monograph. Our concern here will be verses 1-4, which are profound and profoundly significant not only for a proper understanding of the Genesis creation narrative but also, and most importantly, for an understanding of the God of the Torah.

7.2.1. *Triple-Darkness in the Hebrew Bible*

The opening verses of Genesis reads:

בראשית ברא אלהים את השמים ואת הארץ
והארץ היתה תהו ובהו
וחשך על־פני תהום
ורוח אלהים מרחפת על־פני המים
ויאמר אלהים יהי אור ויהי־אור
וירא אלהים את־האור כי־טוב
ויבדל אלהים בין האור ובין החשך

bĕrē'šît bārā' 'ĕlōhîm 'ēt haššāmayîm wĕ'ēt hā'āreṣ
wĕhā'āreṣ hāyĕtâ tōhû wāb̲ōhû
wĕḥōšek̲ 'al-pĕnê tĕhōm
wĕrûaḥ 'ĕlōhîm mĕraḥephet 'al-pĕnê hammayîm
wayyō'mer 'ĕlōhîm yĕhî 'ôr wayhî 'ôr
wayyar' 'ĕlōhîm 'et hā'ôr kî ṭôb
wayyabdēl 'ĕlōhîm bên hā'ôr ûbên haḥōšek

The King James Version (KJV) of these opening verses reads:

1. In the beginning God created the heavens and the earth;
2a. and the earth was without form, and void;
2b. and darkness was upon the face of the deep.
2c. and the spirit of God moved upon the face of the waters.
3. And God said, Let there be light: and there was light.
4. And God saw the light, that it was good: and God

interpret this text must consider all available source materials that bear on the text, the Egyptian materials included.

[636] ***Genesis***, 45.

divided the light from the darkness.

This translation has a number of theological implications to it, two of which are significant here: (1) that this is a recounting of the 'absolute beginning' of things and that (2) creation was *ex nihilo*, that is to say 'from/out of nothing.' It is now recognized that this is a totally inadequate-indeed inaccurate-rendering of the Hebrew original, in which neither of these two implications are present. Verse 1 in the Hebrew reads:

בראשית ברא אלהים את השמים ואת הארץ

bĕrē'šît bārā' 'ĕlōhîm 'ēt haššāmayîm wĕ'ēt hā'āreṣ

The first word, בראשית *bĕrē'šît* is rendered by the KJV as "In *the* beginning." As pointed out by Peter Ochs, this translation "creates a substantive entity called 'the Beginning'" that is unsupported by the Hebrew.[637] ***bĕrē'šît*** lacks the definite article marker (the Hebrew vowel sign *gameṣ* [ָ] "ā"), which would have given us ***bārē'šît***. Rather, ***bĕrē'šît*** (with a *šewa* [ְ] "ĕ") means literally "in *a* beginning." This means that the text is not recounting the absolute beginning of things.[638] The syntax of the beginning of v.2 (*waw* + subject + verb)

[637] "Genesis 1-2: Creation as Evolution," ***The Living Pulpit*** (April-June 2001): 8 [art.=8-10].

[638] As recognized by Daniel M. Berry, "Understanding the Beginning of Genesis: Just How Many Beginnings were There?" ***Jewish Bible Quarterly*** 31 (2003): 90-93. According to the Hebrew syntax, read in the light of the structural parallel between Gen. 1:1-3 and 2:4b-7, the first line of Genesis I is not an independent sentence but a dependent clause (protasis) subordinated to v. 3 (apodasis or main clause). Verse 2 is a parenthetical clause in between. The word בראשית *bĕrē'šît* is to be read as in construct with the finite verb ברא *bārā'* "create" in the genitive. As such, *bĕrē'šît* would have relative, not absolute, temporal significance, as proved by P. Humbert in his groundbreaking article, "Troise notes sur Genesis 1," ***Norsk Teologish Tidsskrift*** 56 (1955): 85-96 and most recently William P. Brown, ***Structure, Role, and Ideology in the Hebrew and Greek Texts of Genesis 1:1-2:3*** (SBLDS 132; Atlanta: Scholars Press, 1993) 63-66 who successfully defends Humbert's findings against the criticisms of Walther Eichrodt, "In the Beginning. A Contribution to the Interpretation of the First Word of the Bible," in B.W. Anderson and W. Harrelson (edd.), ***Israel's Prophetic Heritage. Essays in Honor of J. Muilenburg*** (New York: Harper & Row, 1962) 1-10 and N.H. Ridderbos, "Genesis I 1 und 2," ***Oudtestamentische Studiën*** 12 (1958): 214-60. See also Humbert's own adequate defense: "Encore le premier mot de la bible,' ***ZAW*** 76 (1964): 121-31. Some have taken v. 2 as the main clause, but as Jack M. Sasson noted ("Time…to Begin," in Michael Fishbane, Emanuel Tov and Wetson W. Fields [edd.], ***'Sha'arei Talmon': Studies in the Bible, Qumran, and the Ancient Near East Presented to Shemaryahu Talmon*** [Winona Lake, Indiana: Eisenbrauns, 1992] 187), that v.1 is a temporal clause subordinate to v. 3 is "really beyond dispute." Nor is it reasonable to take v.1. as a

indicates that the elements described in v. 2 (earth, darkness, water) already existed at the time of the action indicated by the main verb *hāyĕtâ*, "was." This treatment of the Hebrew grammar of Genesis 1 may seem bewildering to a non-specialist but, as Professor Richard Elliott Friedman, biblical scholar from the University of California, San Diego, pointed out, the theological implications of the syntax here are significant.

> Here is a case in which a tiny point of grammar makes a difference for theology. In the Hebrew of this verse, the noun comes before the verb (in the perfect form). This is now known to be the way of conveying the past perfect in Biblical Hebrew. This point of grammar means that this verse does not mean 'the earth was shapeless and formless'-referring to the condition of the earth starting the instant after it was created. This verse rather means that 'the earth *had been* shapeless and formless'-that is, it had already existed in this shapeless condition *prior* to the creation. Creation of matter in the Torah is not out of nothing (*creatio ex nihilo*), as many have claimed. And the Torah is not claiming to be telling events from the beginning of time.[639]

Genesis therefore tells us only about *a certain* beginning; the beginning of a certain phenomenon. The more correct reading is thus: "When God began to create the heavens and the earth (the earth having [previously] been such and such…) God said, Let there be light…"[640]

The Hebrew verb used to describe God's creative activity, ברא *bārā'* 'to create,' does not imply *creatio ex nihilo*.[641] In fact, "the Heb.

---

summary title or "introductory resumé" (*contra* Westermann, ***Genesis 1-11***, 94; Bastiaan Jongeling, "Some Remarks on the Beginning of Genesis 1, 2," ***Folia Orientalia*** 21 [1980]: 27-32; Waltke, "Creation Account," 226; Anderson, ***From Creation***, 52; Von Rad, ***Genesis***, 49). As pointed out by Brown, ***Structure, Role, and Ideology***, 71, nowhere else in the Hebrew Bible does such a title begin with a prepositional phrase. On the syntax of Gen. 1:1-3 see the review by Brown, ***Structure, Role, and Ideology***, 62-77.

[639] Richard Elliott Friedman, ***Commentary on the Torah*** (San Francisco: HarperSanFrancisco, 2001), 6. See also Merrill F. Unger, "Rethinking the Genesis Account of Creation," ***Bibliotheca Sacra*** 115 (1958): 27-35 (27-8).

[640] On this translation see also Harry M. Orlinsky "The New Jewish Version of the Torah: Toward a New Philosophy of Bible Translation," ***JBL*** 82 (1963): 253 [art.=249-64]: "The implications of the new, correct rendering, are clear. The Hebrew texts tells us nothing about creation *ex nihilo* or about the beginning of time."

[641] Lane, "Initiation," 69; Anderson, ***From Creation***, 30; Waltke, "Creation Account," 336; Morgenstern, "Sources," 201;

root *br'* probably has the original meaning 'to separate, divide',"[642] and the verb has come to signify "cutting out," i.e. from existing materials, or to form/shape.[643] It is used in the Hebrew Bible as a synonym to other verbs of making, such as יצר *yāṣar* 'to form' (Isa 43:17; 45:7, 18; Am 4:13) and עשה *'āśāh* 'to make' (Isa 41:20; 43:17; 45:7, 12, 18; Am 4:3), which imply the manipulation of some pre-existing material.[644]

> To the Hebrews...creation was not a philosophical or metaphysical concept; it involved no question of the nature of existence or of the emergence of being from nonbeing. To create meant simply to give shape and form, and all the Hebrew words which are so rendered derive from the vocabulary of handicraft, and refer primarily to the paring of leather, the moulding (*sic*) of clay and the like."[645]

Thus, when the opening verse speaks of God's "creating the heavens and the earth," the Hebrew literally speaks of God's shaping the

---

[642] ***TDOT*** 2:245 [art.=242-49] s.v. ברא *bārā'* by Bernhardt. See also E. Dantinne, "Création et separation," ***Mus*** 74 (1961): 441-51.

[643] Rabbi Louis Jacobs, "Jewish Cosmology," in Carmen Blacker and Michael Loewe (edd.), ***Ancient Cosmologies*** (London: George Allen & Unwin Ltd, 1975) 71: "Nowhere in the Biblical record is the doctrine of *creatio ex nihilo* clearly mentioned. Although the root *bara*, 'to create', is used only of God's activity, never of man's, it does not in itself imply *creatio ex nihilo*; indeed, the root meaning seems to be that of 'cutting out' i.e. of an existing material." See also Westermann, ***Genesis 1–11***, 99; A.A. Bevan, "The Hebrew Verb ברא 'to create,' ***Journal of Philology*** 29 (1904): 263-65.

[644] ***TDOT*** 2:246 s.v. ברא *bārā'* by Bernhardt; Bernhard W. Anderson, ***Creation Versus Chaos. The Reinterpretation of Mystical Symbolism in the Bible*** (New York: Association Press, 1967) 123-26; Waltke, "Creation Account," 337; Herman Gunkel, ***Genesis: Translated and Interpreted***, trans. Mark E. Biddle (Macon, Georgia: Mercer University Press, 1997) 103; Sasson, "Time…to Begin," 186.

[645] Theodor H. Gaster, ***Myth, Legend, and Custom in the Old Testament. A comparative study with chapters from Sir James G. Frazer's*** **Folklore in the Old Testament** (New York and Evanston: Harper & Row, Publishers, 1975) 3.

preexisting materials into the heavens and the earth.[646] Those preexistent materials are described in v. 2.[647]

Edward Young, in his study of Gen 1:2, very keenly observed that v.2 contains three circumstantial clauses that describe a three-fold set of conditions.[648] This three-fold set of conditions, as the Hebrew syntax indicates, existed prior to the beginning of creation. Each clause is packed with information, which can be unpacked only "sentence by sentence...word by word."

---

[646] Friedman, ***Commentary on the Torah***, 6-7: "Now we can appreciate the importance of understanding the Torah's first words correctly: The Torah does not claim to report everything that has occurred since the beginning of space and time. It does not say, 'In the Beginning, God created the skies and the earth.' It rather says, 'In the beginning of God's creating the skies and the earth, when the earth had been shapeless and formless...' That is, there is preexisting matter, which is in a state of water chaos. Subsequent matter-dry land, heavenly bodies, plants, animals-may be formed out of this undifferentiated fluid." See also Robert Luyster, "Wind and Water: Cosmogonic Symbolism in the Old Testament," ***ZAW*** 93 (1981): 7 [art.=1-10]: "In no case...do we find any mention of a creation *ex nihilo*. The cosmos pre-exists; it needs only to be revealed, organized, and defended against further reductions to a chaotic state."

[647] Merrill F. Unger, "Rethinking the Genesis Account of Creation," ***Bibliotheca Sacra*** 115 (January-March 1958): 27-35: "In the original language, Genesis 1:2 consists of three circumstantial clauses, all describing conditions or circumstances existing *at the time of* the principle action indicated in verse 1, or giving reason for the action." See also W. Randall Garr, "God's Creation: ברא in the Priestly Source," ***HTR*** 97 (2004): 83-90 (86-7); Bernhard W. Anderson, ***From Creation to New Creation: Old Testament Perspectives*** (Minneapolis: Fortress Press, 1994) 30; William P. Brown, ***Structure, Role, And Ideology in the Hebrew and Greek Texts of Genesis 1:1-2:3*** (SBLDS 132; Atlanta: Scholars Press, 1993) 76; Waltke, "Creation Account," 142; Herman Gunkel, ***Genesis: Translated and Interpreted***, trans. Mark E. Biddle (Macon, Georgia: Mercer University Press, 1997) 103; Tuvia Freedman, " רוח אלהים - And a Wind from God: Genesis 1:2," ***Jewish Bible Quarterly*** 24 (1996): 9-13 (10); Westermann, ***Genesis 1–11***, 108; Douglass A. Knight, "Cosmogony and Order in the Hebrew Tradition," in Robin W. Lovin and Frank E. Reynolds (edd.), ***Cosmogony and Ethical Order. New Studies in Comparative Ethics*** (Chicago and London: The University of Chicago Press, 1985) 138-9: "There is virtually no sense of *creatio ex nihilo*. Something exists prior to the creation act...Creation out of nothing is not articulated in the Hebrew tradition until ca. 100 B.C.E. in 2 Maccabees 7:28"; Graves and Patai, ***Hebrew Myths***, 21; Arvid S. Kapelrud, "The Mythological Features in Genesis Chapter 1 and the Author's Intentions," ***VT*** 24 (1974): 181[art.=178-86]; Gaster, ***Myth, Legend, and Custom***, 3; Lane, "Initiation," 72; Loren R. Fisher, "Creation at Ugarit and in the Old Testament," ***VT*** 15 (1965): 313-24; C.F. Whitley, "The Pattern of Creation in Genesis, Chapter 1," ***JNES*** 17 (1958): 32-40 (32); Powis Smith, "Syntax and Meaning," 110: "(tohu wabohu): This is the condition or state in which the earth was when God began his creative activity."

[648] See also Roberto Ouro, "The Earth of Genesis 1:2: Abiotic or Chaotic? Part I," ***Andrews University Seminary Studies*** 35 (1998): 261 [259-276]: "Verse 2 presents three clauses that describe three circumstances or conditions that existed at a particular time, which is defined by the verb form of the three clauses."

v. 2a:

והארץ היתה תהו ובהו

wĕhā'āreṣ hāyĕtâ tōhû wāḇōhû

-the earth having (previously) been a mingled mass of unproductive dark substance...

The primordial earth, הארץ *hā'āreṣ*, is here characterized as תהו ובהו *tōhû wāḇōhû*, translated in the KJV as "without form and void." The Hebrew is a compound of two terms that individually carry the meaning 'unproductiveness/desert/formlessness" and "nothingness/emptiness."'[649] Together, however, they form a *farrago*, "wherein two usually alliterative[650] words combine to give a meaning other than their constituent parts."'[651] As William P. Brown and Jack Sasson note, the compound suggests a 'mingled mass,' 'a mixture of heterogeneous ingredients,' a 'hodgepodge.'[652] David Toshio Tsumura has demonstrated that the connotations of תהו *tōhû* suggest an arid, desert-like condition.[653] The compound also suggests a certain darkness. בהו *ḇōhû* has been described as a "dark, formless stuff" and the term has been associated with the Phoenician goddess *Baau*, equated with "Night."'[654] According to the Jewish rabbis, תהו *tōhû* emitted darkness.[655] The primordial earth was therefore an unproductive 'mingled mass' of dark 'stuff.'[656]

---

[649]Ouro. "Earth of Genesis 1:2," 266-76; Katherine M. Hayes, "Jeremiah IV 23: *Tōhû* without *Bōhû*,' *VT* 47 (1997): 247-49; David Toshio Tsumura, ***The Earth and Waters in Genesis 1 and 2. A Linguistic Investigation*** (JSOTSup 83; Sheffield: Sheffield Academic Press, 1989) Chapter 2.

[650] "the repetition of usually initial consonant sounds in two or more neighboring words or syllables (as *w*ild and *w*oolly, *th*reatening *th*rongs)..."***Merriam-Websters Collegiate Dictionary***, Tenth Edition s.v.

[651] Sasson, "Time...to Begin," 188; Brown, ***Structure, Role, And Ideology***, 74.

[652]Brown, ***Structure, Role, And Ideology***, 74-75; Sasson, "Time...to Begin," 188.

[653] ***Earth and Waters***, 156; Ouro, "Earth of Genesis 1:2," 276.

[654] Eusebius, *Praep. Evang.* I.10; Albert L. Baumgarten, ***The* Phoenician History *of Philo of Byblos: A Commentary*** (Leiden: E.J. Brill, 1981) 145; ***ABD*** 1:1166 s.v. Cosmogony, Cosmology by Oden, Jr; von Rad, ***Genesis***, 48; Albright, "Contributions," 366.

[655] Babylonian Talmud *Hag.* 12a. On the relation of *tōhû* to darkness in Isa. 45:19 and Jer. 4:12 see David Toshio Tsumura, "*Tōhû* in Isaiah XLV 19," ***VT*** 38 (1988): 361-64.

[656] "The two words in the Hebrew, *tōhû* and *bōhû*... plus the references to the deep and the water, yields a picture of an undifferentiated, shapeless fluid that had existed prior to creation...All...elements of creation may possibly be formed out of (this) preexisting matter, that is, from the initially undifferentiated chaos." Friedman, ***Commentary on the Torah***, 6.

v. 2b:

וחשך על־פני תהום

wĕḥōšek̠ ʿal-pĕnê tĕhōm

> And the dark, upper waters (חשך *ḥōšek̠*) were opposite the dark, lower waters (תהום *tĕhōm*)

חשך *ḥōšek̠* "darkness" is not here simply the absence of light, but is a material substance.[657] It is an aqueous matter. Psalms 18: 11 [Heb. 12] defines it as חשכת־מים *ḥeškat mayyîm,* "dark waters." This primordial darkness, as Herman Gunkel already observed, "was not explicitly created by God, but rather it was simply there from the beginning."[658]

It is often assumed that this particular darkness, חשך *ḥōšek̠* is 'on the face of' and therefore characterizes the תהום *tĕhōm* or deep (lower waters). This is inaccurate. The cause of the error is the inadequate translation of the preposition על־פני *ʿal-pĕnê* as "on the face of". As T.A. Perry has pointed out, the primary meaning of this preposition is "opposite, over against."[659] The *ḥōšek̠* is not "enveloping" the *tĕhōm* but is situated over against/opposite the *tĕhōm.* The *tĕhōm* are the subterranean waters; they therefore exist below the *ʾāreṣ* or primordial earth, that dark mingled mass.[660] The *ḥōšek̠* are the waters that existed where heaven will eventually be, as Perry has clearly shown by comparison with Gen 2:4 and Jer 4:23.[661] The image is thus one of upper and lower waters not yet separated (that happens on Day 2)

---

[657] Tuvia Freedman, "רוח אלהים – And a Wind From God: Genesis 1:2," ***Jewish Bible Quarterly*** 24 (1996): 11 [art.=9-13]: "the bible regards darkness (חשך), not as a mere absence of light, but as substantial matter"; Brevard S. Childs, ***Myth and Reality in the Old Testament*** 1960, 33: "The darkness does not belong to God's creation, but is independent of it. It cannot be understood merely as the absence of light, but possesses a quality of its own." *Contra* Lambert, "A Study," 7.

[658] Gunkel, "Influence of Babylonian," 27. Isa. 45.7, where Yahweh is called "The one forming (יוצר) light and creating (בורא) darkness," does not contradict this. The two participles are parallel, and the verbs denote the act of shaping and ordering. As Charles noted in his Th. Thesis, ("theological significance," 91 n. 18) Isa. 45:7 is "another witness to the claim that God forms, orders or manipulates the preexistent darkness."

[659] "A Poetics of Absence: The Structure and Meaning of Genesis 1:2," ***JSOT*** 58 (1993): 5 [art.=3-11]. Roberto Ouro, "The Earth of Genesis 1:2: Abiotic or Chaotic? Part II," 37 (1999): 42 [art.=39-53] took no notice of the various nuances of this complex preposition.

[660] On the *tĕhōm* as the subterranean waters see especially Tsumura, ***The Earth and Waters***, Chapter Four.

[661] "A Poetics of Absence,"5-7.

occupying all vertical space.[662] Between them is הארץ *hā'āreṣ*, the primordial earth-mass. In v. 2c the *ḥōšek* and *tĕhōm* are together called 'the waters' (המים *hammayîm*, see below). But the distinction between the two implied by the different names used is important. In Ugaritic (Canaanite) tradition, from which Israelite tradition sprang,[663] both the upper and lower waters are called *thmt* (*tehoms*).[664] Here, however, only the lower waters are *tĕhōm*, while the upper waters are *ḥōšek*. Like *ḥōšek*, the *tĕhōm*-waters are characterized by darkness.[665] Thus, the preexistent chaos of v. 2 consisted of (1) הארץ *hā'āreṣ*, the arid, unproductive dark earth-mass; (2) חשך *ḥōšek*, the dark upper waters; and (3) תהום *tĕhōm*, the dark lower waters. This three-fold condition noticed by Young was therefore a three-fold material darkness-*a triple-darkn*ess, if you will.

v.2c:

ורוח אלהים מרחפת על־פני המים

wĕrû^a^ḥ 'ĕlōhîm mĕraḥephet 'al-pĕnê hammayîm

But the Spirit/Breath of God *mĕraḥepet* (across?)[666] the waters.

---

[662] "A Poetics of Absence," 5.

[663] Michael David Coogan, "Canaanite Origins and Lineage," in Patrick D. Miller, Jr., Paul D. Hanson, and S. Dean McBride (edd.) ***Ancient Israelite Religion: Essays in Honor of Frank Moor Cross*** (Philadelphia: Fortress Press, 1987) 11516 [art.=115-24]: "it is essential to consider biblical religion as a subset of Israelite religion and Israelite religion as a subset of Canaanite religion...To be sure, by the beginning of the first millennium B.C.E. Israel, like its neighbors Phoenicia, Ammon, Moab, Edom, and Aram, had begun to show distinctive traits in religious as well as in other aspects of its life. But this was a development from a Canaanite matrix and can be understood only by the reconstruction of that matrix...and by the analysis of parallel developments in neighboring states." See also Smith, ***Early History of God***, 4.

[664] On the two *thm*-waters in Ugaritic tradition see Tsumura, ***Earth and Water***, 144, 150-53

[665] AS Wensink, "Ocean," 40 shows, in biblical and Jewish tradition *tĕhôm*'s characteristic feature is darkness.

[666] It is not clear to me how the preposition *'al-pĕnê* is to be translated in this verse. Perry ("A Poetics of Absence," 7 n. 7) prefers to translate it "opposite" as in v. 2b. But Brown, ***Structure, Role, And Ideology***, 75-6 has correctly pointed out that the presence in v.2c of the active participle *mĕraḥepet* distinguishes the use of *'al-pĕnê* here from its use in v. 2b. There is thus ambiguity regarding the divine spirit's relationship to the waters. Is it "opposite" the waters, or "on the face/surface of the waters." Because all of the vertical space is filled with the waters, it is difficult to imagine how anything could be 'upon' or 'on the surface' of them, as observed by Perry ("A Poetics of Absence," 5). In v. 20, the birds of Day 5 are said to flutter over the earth *across* (*al-pĕnê*) the firmament of the skies."

Scholars have debated over the precise significance and translation of רוח אלהים *rûᵃḥ ʾĕlōhîm.*[667] The Hebrew רוח *rûᵃḥ* can mean "wind," "breath," "spirit," "person," and more.[668] Translators have rendered *rûᵃḥ ʾĕlōhîm* in Gen. 1:2c variously as "Spirit of God,"[669] "wind from God,"[670] and "terrible storm."[671] While Harry M. Orlinsky's observation that "S/spirit is really a Christian interpretation that originated in the postbiblical period"[672] is on point, the strictly meterological "wind" is out of context in the Priestly corpus.[673] This context suggests instead that רוח אלהים *rûᵃḥ ʾĕlōhîm* "is the very breath of God,"[674] "God's creative force."[675] This creative force of God was there with/in the triple-darkness. As Michael DeRoche aptly put it: "The precreated world may have been unordered, but, according to Gen 1:2c, Elohim was present in it in a state of readiness to create."[676] The waters (המים *hammayîm*) of v.2c, over which (or in which) the *rûᵃḥ ʾĕlōhîm* "acted" (leaving *mĕraḥephet* untranslated for now) are not synonymous with the subterranean *tĕhōm.*[677] Rather, they are the

---

667 See the various discussions by Tuvia Freedman, " רוח אלהים – And a Wind From God: Genesis 1:2," ***Jewish Bible Quarterly*** 24 (1996): 9-13; Roberto Ouro, "The Earth of Genesis 1:2: Abiotic or Chaotic? Part III," ***AUSS*** 38 (2000): 59-64 [art.=59-67]; Brown, ***Structure, Role, And Ideology***, 75-77; Westermann, ***Genesis 1-11***, 106-7; Michael DeRoche, "The *rûaḥ ʾĕlōhîm* in Gen. 1:2c: Creation or Chaos," in Lyle Eslinger & Glen Taylor (edd.), ***Ascribe to the Lord: Biblical & other studies in memory of Peter C. Craigie*** (JSOTSup 67; Sheffield: Sheffield Academic Press, 1988) 303-318; Robert Luyster, "Wind and Water: Cosmogonic Symbolism in the Old Testament," ***ZAW*** 93 (1981): 1-10; P.J. Smith, "A Semotactical Approach to the Meaning of the Term *rûaḥ ʾĕlōhîm* in Genesis 1:2," ***JNSL*** 8 (1980): 99-104; Edward J. Young, "The Interpretation of Genesis 1:2," ***Westminster Theological Journal*** 23 (1961): 174-78 [art.=151-178]; Orlinsky, "New Jewish Version," 254-57; Sabatino Moscati, "The Wind in Biblical And Phoenician Cosmogony," ***JBL*** 66 (1947): 307-309; William H. McClellan, S.J., "The Meaning of ruah 'Elohîm in Genesis 1,2" ***Biblica*** 15 (1934): 517-27; John P. Peters, "The Wind of God," ***JBL*** 30 (1911): 44-54.

668 ***TDNT*** 6:359-67 s.v. πνευμα by Baumgärtel; William Ross Schoemaker, "The Use of רוח in the Old Testament and πνευμα in the New Testament. A Lexicographical Study," ***JBL*** 13-14 (1904-1905): 13-67.

669 E.g. KJV. See also Roberto Ouro, "the Earth of Genesis 1:2: Abiotic or Chaotic, Part III," ***Andrews University Seminary Studies*** 38 (2000): 65 [art.=59-67]

670 Ridderbos, "Gen I:1 und 2," 245; Westermann, ***Genesis***, 107-08.

671 Taking *ʾĕlōhîm* not as a name of God but as a superlative. See W.H. Schmidt, ***Die Schöpfungsgeschichte der Priesterschrift*** (WMANT 17; Neukirchen-Vluyn, 1973) 83; von Rad, ***Genesis*** 47.

672 "New Jewish Version," 255.

673 Brown, ***Structure, Role, And Ideology***, 76-77; DeRoche, "The *rûaḥ ʾĕlōhîm*," 317.

674 Brown, ***Structure, Role, And Ideology***, 77; G. Wenham, ***Genesis 1-15*** (WBC; Waco, 1987) 2.

675 Freedman, " רוח אלהים" 13.

676 "The *rûaḥ ʾĕlōhîm*," 315.

677 *Contra* Westermann, ***Genesis*** 106; Lambert, "A Study," 7.

collective waters filling all vertical space-that is, they are both the *ḥōšek*-waters (upper waters) and the *tĕhōm*-waters (lower waters) together, still undivided.[678]

7.2.2. *The Primordial Atom*

We have postponed translating מרחפת *mĕraḥephet* because of its significance and its difficulty. Great disagreement exists among scholars regarding the term.[679] However, the difficulty does not lie in the term itself, but rather in the attempt to harmonize its lexical meanings and its mythological implications with certain (erroneous) presuppositions brought to the text regarding the religion of ancient Israel. If one approached the text without these presuppositions, however, the available evidence in fact allows us to make reasonable sense of the word and the passage.

מרחפת *mĕraḥephet* is the Pi'el[680] feminine singular active participle of the Hebrew verb *rāḥapha*, meaning "to hover, fly, flutter."[681] The term refers to the activity of birds.[682] The Syriac cognate may be translated "brooding" and suggests the activity of a mother bird incubating her eggs.[683] On this basis many early translations of Gen 1:2c had "And the Spirit of God brooded over the waters."[684] This

---

[678] Perry, "A Poetics of Absence," 5.

[679] S.R. Driver, ***A Critical and Exegetical Commentary on Deuteronomy*** (New York: Charles Scribner's Sons, 1909) 356-358; John P. Peters, "The Wind of God," ***JBL*** 30 (1911): 44-54; William H. McClellan, "The Meaning of Ruah 'Elohim in Genesis 1,2," ***Bib*** 15 (1934) 526-27; Edward J. Young, "The Interpretation of Genesis 1:2," ***Westminster Theological Journal*** 23 (1961): 151-178 [172-3]; Islwyn Blythin, "A Note on Genesis 1 2," ***VT*** 12 (1962): 120-21; Theodor Herze Gaster, ***Myth, legend, and custom in the Old Testament; a comparative study with chapters from Sir James G. Frazer's* Folklore in the Old Testament** (New York, Harper & Row, 1969) 5; D.F. Payne, "Approaches to Genesis i 2," ***Transactions of the Glasgow University Oriental Society*** 1972: 67-69; Robert Luyster, "Wind and Water: Cosmogonic Symbolism in the Old Testament," ***ZAW*** 93 (1981): 8; Roberto Ouro, "The Earth of Genesis 1:2: Abiotic or Chaotic? Part III," ***AUSS*** 38 (2000): 64-65.

[680] Pi'el is the name of one of the seven major Hebrew verbal stems.

[681] Westermann, ***Genesis 1–11***, 107;

[682] Robert Graves and Raphael Patai, ***Hebrew Myths. The Book of Genesis*** (Garden City, New York: Doubleday & Company, Inc., 1963) 31: "The hovering of the Spirit of God over the waste of waters in *Genesis* 1. 2 suggests a bird." See also Tuvia Freedman, "רוח אלהים – And a Wind From God: Genesis 1:2," ***Jewish Bible Quarterly*** 24 (1996): 10 [art.=9-13]. On avian imagery and the deity in the Bible see Meredith G. Kline, "The Feast of Cover-Over," ***JETS*** 37 (1994): 497-510.

[683] See discussion in T. Jansma, " '*And the Spirit of God Moved Upon the Face of the Waters*' Some Remarks on the Syro-Hexaplaric Reading of Gen. I 2," ***VT*** 20 (1970): 16-24.

[684] Thus ***Brown-Drivers-Briggs*** רחף, translates: "hovering over the face of the waters, or perhaps brooding (and fertilizing)."

avian imagery suggested to a number of commentators the cosmogonic egg. Thus August Dillman,[685] Franz Delitzsch[686] and Hermann Gunkel[687] saw in Gen. 1:2c a "distant allusion" to the cosmogonic egg myth. Gunkel noted: "We may well assume that the basic meaning of the word (רחף) is related to the Syriac 'to brood' and surmise that the ancient and widespread speculation concerning the world egg echoes here…this view (i.e. the world egg) is…to be considered the original intention of the Israelite cosmogony underlying this texts."[688] Julian Morgenstern likewise argued in 1920: "Certainly the Phoenician cosmogonic myth of the origin of the world from a great egg lies at the bottom of 1:2*b* (sic). The רוח אלהים(Spirit of God) is here conceived as a gigantic female bird, which hovers or broods upon the surface of the waters, and from which the universe egg is ultimately hatched."[689]

This reading was supported by a number of scholars.[690] However, objections to this mythological reading of 1:2c were raised early.[691] The principle objection has been that the meaning "to brood" is secondary with the Syriac verb and the Hebrew verb suggests more of a sense of motion rather than rest (brooding).[692] John Peters, for example, argued on the basis of Deut. 32:11, the only other biblical instance of the Pi'el form of the verb *rāḥapha*, that *mĕraḥephet* indicates a violent rushing of

---

685 A. Dillmann, ***Genesis Critically and Exegetically Expounded***, trans. W.B. Stevenson (Edinburgh: T&T Clark, 1897) 59;

686 ***New Commentary on Genesis***, trans. Sophia Taylor (Edinburgh: T&T Clark, 1888) 81.

687 ***Schöpfung und Chaos in Urzeit und Endzeit. Eine religionsgeschichtliche Untersuchung über Gen 1 und Ap Joh 12*** (Göttingen: Vandenhoeck und Ruprecht, 1895); ***Genesis***, 105-06.

688 Gunkel, ***Genesis***, 106.

689 Julian Morgenstern, "The Sources of the Creation Story-Genesis 1:1-2:4," ***AJSL*** 36 (1920): 196.

690 John Skinner, ***A critical and Exegetical Commentary on Genesis*** (2nd Edition; Edinburgh: Clark, 1980, 1930) 17: "…the divine Spirit, figured as a bird brooding over its nest"; Edward P. Arbez, "Exegetical Notes on Genesis 1:1-2" ***CBQ*** 10 (1948) 147-8: "Back of the figure used by the author we may, with modern writers, discern the image of the world-egg, the myth regarding which is to be found among the Egyptians, Phoenicians, etc." A. Jeremias, ***Das AT im Lichte des AO*** (Lpg.: 1930) 24f; See also Haavio, ***Väinämöinen*** 56; Hellbom, "Creation Egg" 66.

691 John P. Peters, "The Wind of God," ***JBL*** 30 (1911): 44-54; idem, "The Wind of God (Part II)," ***JBL*** 33 (1914): 81-86; idem, ***Bible and Spade*** (New York: Charles Scribner's Sons, 1922) 53-59; W.F. Albright, "Contributions to Biblical Archaeology and Philology," ***JBL*** 43 (1924): 363-369; Leroy Waterman, "Cosmogonic Affinities in Genesis 1:2," ***AJSL*** 43 (1927): 182-184; J.M. Powis Smith, "The Syntax and Meaning of Genesis 1:1-3," ***AJSL*** 44 (1927/1928) 112-113.

692 Powis Smith, "Syntax and Meaning," 113: "In all three of the passages in which the Hebrew verb appears some vigorous motion is required." William H. McClellan, "The Meaning of Ruah 'Elohim in Genesis 1,2," ***Bib*** 15 (1934) 526-27;

the bird into the nest to force the younglings out in order to fly.[693] But as has been pointed out by several scholars, neither the Hebrew, Ugaritic or Syriac supports such an interpretation.[694] In any case, the violent action of the bird/spirit/wind would not preclude the cosmogonic egg myth; in a number of such myths the wind blows violently on the egg, causing it to break open and reveal the cosmos.[695]

D.F. Payne, in a review of all the relevant data, concludes that the root meaning of the word suggests a bird "poised either to aid its young or attack its victim...There seems also to be a consistent implication of waiting for the right moment – for the nestling to falter and fall, for the victim to become weak and helpless, for the egg to hatch out."[696] In Genesis, "The picture (is) of God's Spirit poised in bird-like fashion."[697] The biblical text allows us to be more precise. As William H. McClellan rightly pointed out, Deut. 32:11, the only other biblical instance of the Pi'el form of the verb, is "our best source for the true interpretation of *m^e rahefeth* in Gen 1.2".[698] Accordingly, the image is not that of a predator bird ready to attack its prey, but of a mother bird hovering over her younglings.

The important point of these discussions is this: whether we understand *mĕraḥephet* as the activity of a bird brooding over eggs, hovering over hatchlings or rushing at young nestlings, the avian image remains, and thus does the presence of the egg.[699] Whether the egg is unhatched (and thus the brooding bird) or recently hatched (thus the rushing/hovering bird), it still exists in the background of the imagery. Therefore, regardless of which translation of מרחפת *mĕraḥephet* one

---

[693] See above n. See also the Septuagint (LXX) or Greek translation of the Hebrew Bible: מרחפת is there rendered επεφερετο, "to rush at, strike."

[694] McClellan, "The Meaning of Ruah 'Elohim," 524-27; Sabatino Moscati, "The Wind in Biblical And Phoenician Cosmogony," ***JBL*** 66 (1947): 307-309; On Deut. 32: 11 see also S.R. Driver, ***A Critical and Exegetical Commentary on Deuteronomy*** (New York: Charles Scribner's Sons, 1909) 356-358.

[695] Haavio, ***Väinämöinen***, 59-60.

[696] "Approaches to Genesis i 2," ***Transactions of the Glasgow University Oriental Society*** 1972, 68.

[697] Sabatno Moscati, "The Wind in Biblical and Phoenician Cosmology," ***JBL*** 66 (1947): 307 [art.=305-10]: "the participle appears to express a protective action."

[698] "The Meaning of ruah 'Elohîm in Genesis 1,2" ***Biblica*** 15 (1934): 525 [art.=517-27].

[699] Thus the error of Claus Westermann's claim that the cosmic egg's "appearance in Gen 1:2 relies solely on the interpretation of רחף as 'brood'." ***Genesis 1-11: A Commentary*** Minneapolis: Augsburg Publishing House, 1984) 107. William Albright's discussion on *mĕraḥepet* nicely illustrates the point I am making. Albright mistakenly assumed that because *rḥp* may mean 'flap wings, flutter, hover," instead of 'brood,' that "the world-egg theory...falls to the ground completely" ("Contributions," 368). Yet he is forced to admit: "The verb *rāḥāf*, which is particularly applied to the fluttering of birds, suggests that the *rû^a ḥ elôhîm* was conceived of originally in the form of a bird, like the Egyptian b_3 *nṯr*" (Ibid., 368 n. 10). As long as the bird image remains, the egg necessarily remains.

adopts, the presence of the egg is implied. Genesis 1:2 gives us no indication of the exact *stage* in the cosmogonic development we are observing-i.e. whether the egg/atom is still lying dormant in the waters (thus the 'brooding' spirit), or whether the cosmos has already, though quite recently, begun emerging out of it (thus the protective, hovering bird);[700] it is thus not necessary here to pinpoint the exact avian activity. It is sufficient to note that the use of מרחפת *mĕraḥephet* in Genesis 1 necessarily implies the presence of the cosmogonic egg, much as Dillman, Delitzsch, Gunkel and others have argued. *It therefore necessarily implies the presence of the primordial atom within the three-fold darkness.*

This is in fact the traditional Jewish and Christian interpretation of the term.[701] The authoritative Jewish exegete Rashi gives the received Jewish view-"as a dove that broods over the nest."[702] The antiquity of this Jewish interpretation is indicated by Jerome (*Heb. Qu. In Gen., PL* 23, 939) whose Jewish informers related that מרחפת *mĕraḥephet* suggested the incubation of eggs. The Babylonian Talmud explicitly confirms the existence of the cosmogonic egg: God, we are told, took two halves of an egg, fertilized them, and created the world from them.[703] This of course is reminiscent of the Indic creation account: "the world's egg divided itself into two parts, the one of silver, the other of gold. The silver part became the earth, the golden part the sky. The outer cover of the egg became the mountains; the inner cover, the clouds and the snow; the inside veins became the rivers, the liquid in the egg became the ocean (*Chāndogya Upaniṣad* 3.19.1-4)." Venetia Newell, in her study of the cosmogonic egg motif observed that "the self-induced fracture of the egg resembles the cataclysmic splitting of the atom."[704] This, of course, agrees with the Hon. Elijah Muhammad, who says of the Primordial Atom(s): "You see they are egg-shaped and they are oblong. You crack them open and you find everything in them that you find out here."[705]

This reading is confirmed by the Egyptian/Phoenician background of the Hebrew passage. As pointed out above, a number of scholars have recognized that Genesis I is a Hebrew version of an ancient

---

[700] Thus, even if Leroy Waterman is correct that "the whole of the Genesis account lies beyond that point in the myth where a fertilization motive could any natural place," it is not true that "Consequently...(the) world-egg theory unquestionably falls to the ground." "Cosmogonic Affinities in Genesis 1:2," ***AJSL*** 18 (1927): 177-184 (183).
[701] Peters, "Wind of God," 45-46.
[702] M. Jastrow, ***Dictionary of the Targumim, the Talmud Babli and Yerusalami, and the Midrashic Literature*** (2 vols.; New York: Title, 1943) 2:1468 s.v. רחף.
[703] Hellbom, "Creation Egg."
[704] ***An Egg at Easter***, 12.
[705] Elijah Muhammad, ***Our Savior Has Arrived***, 1974, 73.

Egyptian cosmogony. As also pointed out above, an examination of the Egyptian original sheds light on the Hebrew abbreviation.

The Egyptian original is no doubt the Hermopolitan creation account.[706] Hermopolis was the Greek name for the ancient city of Unet in Upper Egypt. The Hermopolitan priests in their narrative of creation personified the characteristics of the pre-cosmic chaos in four pairs of male and female gods (called the Ogdoad, 'Eight'): Nun and his female compliment Naunet (primordial waters); Huh and Hauhet (boundlessness/'spatial infinity');[707] Kuk and Kauket (darkness); and Amun and Amaunet (breath/concealed dynamism).[708] As the goddesses had no independent existence,[709] the pre-cosmic chaos had four characteristics, and these correspond exactly to the pre-cosmic chaos of Gen 1:2.[710]

> ...striking is the likeness between the terms in which the primeval chaos is described in the Hermopolitan and Hebrew cosmogonies. The (Ogdoad) was composed of a formless deep, an illimitable chaos, darkness, and a breath; the Hebrew cosmogony begins with a formless (*tohû*) deep, illimitable chaos (*bohû*), darkness, and breath.[711]

Rudolf Kilian, in his article "Gen 1 2 und die Urgötter von Hermopolis ("Gen 1:2 and the Primordial Gods of Hermopolis") demonstrated the close correspondence between the ancient Egyptian and Hebrew descriptions of the primordial chaos and before him Gustav Jéquier ("Les Quatre Cynocéphales" [The Four Dog-faced Baboons"]) was already convinced that these correspondences prove the dependence of Gen 1:2 on the Hermopolitan account.[712] James K. Hoffmeier has nicely summarized these correspondences:[713]

---

[706]As A.H. Sayce ("The Egyptian Background on Genesis 1," in ***Studies Presented to F.Ll. Griffith*** [London: Egypt Exploration Society, 1932] 420, 422 [art.=419-423]) observed: "Between this Hermopolitan cosmogony and that of the first chapter of Genesis the resemblance is obvious and striking...a resemblance which is too close to be fortuitous." He argued that P "adopted the Egyptian cosmogony" (421).

[707] Clifford, ***Creation Accounts***, 112; Luckert, ***Egyptian Light***, 97; Hoffmeier "Thoughts on Genesis 1 & 2," 43; Kilian, "Gen. 1 2," 421-422;

[708] See Clifford, ***Creation Accounts***, 112; Luckert, ***Egyptian Light***, 98; Kilian, "Gen. 1 2," 422-25;

[709] Clifford, ***Creation Accounts***, 112.

[710] James E. Atwell, "An Egyptian Source for Genesis 1," ***JTS*** 51 (2000): 450-55 [art.=441-77]; Hoffmeier "Thoughts on Genesis 1 & 2"; Kilian, "Gen. 1 2."

[711] A.H. Sayce, "The Egyptian Background on Genesis 1," in ***Studies Presented to F.Ll. Griffith*** (London: Egypt Exploration Society, 1932) 423 [art.=419-423]

[712] in Samuel A.B. Mercer (ed.), ***Egyptian Religion*** (New York, 1934) 2:78-86.

[713] "Thoughts on Genesis 1 & 2," 43-44.

Nun = *tĕhōm* (Primordial waters)
Huh = *tōhû wāḇōhû* (Boundlessness)
Kuk = *ḥōšeḵ* (Darkness)
Amun = *rû^{a}ḥ ʾĕlōhîm* (Divine breath)[714]

According to the Hermopolitan priests, from these four qualities of the primordial chaos was produced the cosmic seed (quark), then the cosmic egg (atom), from which sprang the creator-god: "You [the Ogdoad] made a seed (quark) from a fluid expelled from you…You put it in Nun, condensed it into a single form (egg/atom)[715] and your descendant (creator-god) is born radiant in the form of an infant."[716] The Phoenician cosmogony as recorded by Philo of Byblos,[717] which is rooted in the Hermopolitan account[718] and has influenced the Hebrew account,[719] likewise features the cosmogonic egg.[720] Thus, the sources of the Hebrew account feature the egg; the early Jewish and Christian readers of the Hebrew account recognized therein the egg; and the Hebrew account itself alludes to the egg. This very brevity of the allusion speaks to the familiarity with the cosmogonic egg motif that

---

[714] On Amun and the *rû^{a}ḥ ʾĕlōhîm* "spirit of God" see Hans-Peter Hasenfratz, "Patterns of Creation in Ancient Egypt," in Henning Graf Reventlow and Yair Hoffman (edd.), ***Creation in Jewish and Christian Tradition*** (JSOTSup 319; Sheffield: Sheffield Academic Press, 2002) 175. Atwell, "An Egyptian Source," 455 notes: "In all likelihood it is Amun who is the source of the imagery of רוח אלהים (*rû^{a}ḥ ʾĕlōhîm*, Spirit of God) in Genesis 1:2."

[715] In the Harris Magical papyrus, an ancient Egyptian manuscript of the New Kingdom Period (1569-1085 BC) this form is specified as the egg: "Oh Egg of the water, source of the earth, product of the Ogdoad…" This is in fact the earliest known reference to the cosmogonic egg. See ***ER*** 5:36 s.v. Egg by Newall,

[716] Ritual text quoted by Clifford, ***Creation Accounts***, 112.

[717] He is not to be confused with Philo of Alexandria, Egypt, who gave us insight above into the esoteric tradition of the Jerusalem priesthood.

[718] On the Egyptian origin of Philo's cosmogony see Baumgarten, ***Phoenician History***, 110ff; R.A. Oden, Jr. "Philo of Byblos and Hellenistic Historiography," ***Palestine Exploration Quarterly*** (1978): 126.

[719] According to Oden, ***ABD*** 1:1166 s.v. Cosmogony, Cosmology, such Poenician speculation likely played a role in helping Israel to formulate the Priestly creation account (Gen 1). Freund, ***Myths of Creation***, 49 noted: "The Hebrew *Genesis*, it would seem, owes much to the Phoenician cosmogony, as found in Philo of Byblus." Clifford, ***Creation Accounts***, 141recognizes a Phoenician prototype for Gen 1:2. See also Albright, "Contributions," 366; O. Eissfeldt, "Das Chaos in der biblischen und in der phönizischen Kosmogonie," ***Forschungen und Fortschritte*** 16 (1940) 1-3; Moscati, "Wind in Biblical And Phoenician Cosmogony"; Frank Moore Cross, "The 'Olden Gods' in Ancient Near Eastern Creation Myths," in Frank Moore Cross, Werner E. Lemke, and Patrick D. Miller, Jr. (edd.), ***Magnalia Dei, the mighty acts of God: essays on the Bible and archaeology in memory of G. Ernest Wright*** (Garden City, N.Y.: Doubleday, 1976) 335-36.

[720] See e.g. Baumgarten, ***Phoenician History***, 115-116; Eissfeldt, "Das Chaos."

the priestly author assumed on behalf of his listeners/readers. "Just as the briefest mention of words and phrases like the Pilgrims, the Founding Fathers, or the Gettysburg Address will resonate widely to an American audience,"[721] so too the very sparse use of מרחפת *mĕraḥephet* will have called forth for an Israelite audience the entire myth.

The second verse of Genesis therefore says that before creation began there existed a three-fold material darkness, consisting of earth and water mingled. Within this three-fold or triple-darkness was the cosmogonic egg or primordial atom. This primordial atom was either 'unhatched,' meaning it still lay dormant in the waters, or recently 'hatched,' meaning the initial stages of creation had begun; the text does not allow us to specify. Within this triple-darkness and acting in some way upon the egg/atom was the creative Breath of God.

7.2.3. *Primordial Triple-Darkness in the Qur'ān*

Surat al-Anʿām (6):1 reads:

> All praises belong to God, who created (*khalaqa*) the heavens and the earth, and made (*jaʿala*) the darkness (*al-ẓulumāt*) and the light (*al-nūr*).

Like the Hebrew equivalents, the Arabic words of creation are actually verbs of *making*, implying some pre-existent material. خلق *khalaqa* is literally the "creation of a thing after measuring and designing it, often after the measure of another pre-existent thing; to determine a thing's measure."[722] Thus sura 6:2 "(Jesus says): He it is who created you (خلقكم *khalaqakum*) from clay." Likewise جعل *ja'ala* is "to make a thing into a particular state or condition, or constituting or appointing it for a definite purpose." The verb implies the changing of a thing from one state or condition to another. Thus Surat al-Anbiyā' (21):31: "and We made (جعلنا *ja'alnā*) from water every living thing." The two verbs خلق *khalaqa* and جعل *ja'ala* imply the taking of a pre-existent thing and shaping/fashioning it into a state or condition with which Allah is pleased. Surat al-Anʿām (6):1 therefore does not affirm *creation ex nihilo*, the absolute creation of all material existence from nothing. This notion is absent from the Qur'ān.[723] Instead, the Qur'ān posits in the beginning a single, black, aquatic cloud-like mass, called دخان *dhuhān*

---

[721] Robert A. Oden, Jr, in ***ABD*** 1:1165 s.v. Cosmogony, Cosmology, speaking with regard to the Genesis biblical allusions to theomachy.

[722] See Lane, ***Lexicon***, s.v. خلق

[723] Maurice Bucaille, ***The Bible, the Qur'an and Science: The Holy Scriptures Examined in the Light of Modern Knowledge*** (Paris: Seghers, 1989) 139-155.

(41:11).[724] The heavens (*al-samāwāt*) and earth were initially joined together (*ratq)* in this black mass until God separated them (*fatq*; 21:30), forming the seven heavens, the earth, "what is between them," and "every living thing out of the water" (2:29; 50:38).

The statement "and (God) made (*ja'ala*) the darkness (*al-ẓulumāt*)" means God fashioned the pre-existent darkness into a new state pleasing to him, a state appropriate to an ordered cosmos. The term used for 'darkness' here, *al-ẓulumāt,* is plural indicating that this pre-existent darkness was multiple. Surat al-Nūr (24):40 specifies that this was a triple darkness (*zulumāt thalātha*), described as a بحر لجي *bahrin lujjīyin* "deep sea" composed of "(a layer of) water above which is (a layer of) water above which is a cloud (*mauj min fauqihi mauj min fauqihi sahāb*)." The *zulumāt* therefore consists of two *amwāj* (pl. of *mauj,* "billow, wave") over which is a *sahāb*, "cloud." This cloud, the top layer of this triple-darkness, corresponds to the دخان *dhuhān*, the pre-cosmic heavens in their original state as a dark cloud, and it corresponds to the Hebrew *ḥōšek*, the top layer of triple-darkness described in Genesis 1:2. This three-layered darkness is called in later Arabic sources *al-Bahr al-Muẓlim*, the Dark Ocean.

According to a report on the authority of the Companion Abū Razin, found in Tirmidhi, *Jāmia' al-Sahih*, sura 11:1; Ibn Mājah, *Sunan*, 1, # 182; Ibn Hanbal, *Musnad* 12:17-20;and Tabari, *Tafsir*, 11:7, the Prophet was asked: "Where was our Lord before he created the heavens and the earth?" The Prophet replied: "He was in a cloud, with(out) air above him or below him. Then he created his throne on the water." Thus, GOD HIMSELF EXISTED IN THIS PRIMORDIAL BLACK CLOUD PRIOR TO CREATION! The Qur'ān therefore concurs with the Hebrew Bible on this matter.

7.2.4. *'Let There Be Light'*

Back to Genesis. The first creative act actually recored in Genesis is in vv.3-4, the creation of light

vv.3-4

ויאמר אלהים יהי אור ויהי־אור
וירא אלהים את־האור כי־טוב
ויבדל אלהים בין האור ובין החשך

[724] دخان *dhuhān* derives from the verb *dhakhina*, "to become dusky or dingy of color, inclining toward black.' See Lane, ***Lexicon***, s.v. دخن

wayyō'mer 'ĕlōhîm yĕhî 'ôr wayhî 'ôr
wayyar' 'ĕlōhîm 'et hā'ôr kî ṭôb
wayyabdēl 'ĕlōhîm bên hā'ôr ûbên haḥōšek

And God said, "Let there be light," and there was light
And God saw the light, that is was good
And God separated between the light and the dark
upper waters

According to the Egyptian original of this Hebrew creation account, after the Ogdoad or eight (read: four) 'chaos' gods came together and produced the egg, light sprang from out of the darkness.[725] That light was the luminous creator-god himself emerging from the dark waters.[726] The Hebrew adaptaion, as found in the priestly materials of the Hebrew Bible, says the same.

Contrary to popular assumptions Genesis I does not describe creation by divine *fiat* or creation by the word of God alone. This misconception is based on an inattentive reading of the Hebrew text (and some theologically motivated eisegesis as well). *Ĕlōhîm* (God) does indeed begin some of his creative activity with the command, "Let there be X," in Hebrew X... יהי *yĕhî*...X. For example: "And let there be a firmament...," יהי רקיע, *yĕhî rāqî^{a}'* (v. 6). But this divine command itself does not result in the desired creation. The command is usually followed by the declaration that God himself fulfilled his own command by *making* the desired creature: "and God made (עשה *'āśāh*) the firmament (v.7)." This is the well-known command-fulfillment formula characteristic of the priestly materials: the objective is stated, and then carried out.[727] Accordingly, as Prof. Friedman points out, "we cannot understand these things to be formed simply by the words 'Let there be'."[728] In Genesis I this command (יהי *yĕhî* "Let there be...") is given three times (vv. 3, 6, 14), twice conspicuously followed by a verb indicating how the command was fulfilled (vv. 7, 16). In vv. 7 and 16, which describe the making of the firmament and the luminaries (sun and moon) respectively, the fulfillment verb is עשה *'āśāh* "to make." As pointed out above, this verb implies the fashioning of a thing from pre-existing materials, which, in the case of Genesis I, is the dark primordial matter. "Subsequent matter - dry land, heavenly bodies,

[725] Ringgren, "Light and Darkness," 141.
[726] See above.
[727] Brown, ***Structure, Role, and Ideology***, 81-88.
[728] ***Commentary on the Torah***, 7.

plants, animals - may be formed out of this undifferentiated fluid," as Friedman observes.[729]

This command-fulfillment formula is usually accompanied by the important phrase ויהי־כן *wayhî kēn*, translated in the KJV as "and it was so (vv. 7 and 15; see also vv. 9, 11, 24, 30)." This is an inadequate translation.[730] The phrase serves two primary purposes in Genesis I. When it occurs after the description of the fulfillment of the command, as in v. 7b, it serves to emphasize and confirm the manner of fulfillment as a divine activity.[731]

Command: v. 6 "Let there be a firmament…"
Fulfillment: v.7a "So God made a firmament and divided…"
Confirmation: v.7b *wayhî kēn*, "and indeed, it happened thusly."

The emphasis is on God's actual construction of the firmament and dividing of the waters.[732] God here is not a magician that 'poofs' objects into existence by his mere word. *Wayhî kēn* calls special attention to this fact by highlighting and confirming Elohim's divine handicraft.[733]

On the other hand, when the phrase comes between the command and the fulfillment, as in v. 15 (and 11, 24), it serves a different, though similar purpose. It plays the role of a transition marker introducing the description of *how* the command is to be fulfilled, which immediately follows.[734]

Command: "Let there be luminaries…"
Transition: *wayhî kēn*, "It happened as follows:.."
Fulfillment: "God made the two great lights…"

Wayhî kēn in this context indicates that what follows is a description of the *manner* in which the command is fulfilled (i.e. "God *made* the two lights). Again, this demonstrates that the command itself does not generate the created object; it only initiates the generative process. This is not creation by divine fiat. *Wayhî kēn*'s characteristic feature is thus to call special attention to the divine activity that accomplishes and

[729] Friedman, ***Commentary on the Torah***, 7.
[730]See especially O.H. Steck, ***Der Schöpfungsbericht der Priesterschrift: Studien zzur literarkritischen und überlieferungsgeschichtlichen Problematik von Genesis I,I-2,4a*** (FRLANT 115; Göttingen, 1981)32-39.
[731] Brown, ***Structure, Role, and Ideology***, 83, 85-87, 125-27.
[732] Brown, ***Structure, Role, and Ideology***, 87.
[733] See Brown, ***Structure, Role, and Ideology***, 86.
[734] Brown, ***Structure, Role, and Ideology***, 121; Steck, ***Der Schöpfungsbericht***, 32-39.

fulfills the divine command, either by introducing the description of that activity or by confirming and emphasizing it after it has succeeded.

Verses 3–4 are to be understood in this context. The divine command, יהי אור *yĕhî ʾôr*, "Let there be light," is followed immediately by ויהי־אור *wayhî ʾôr*, which is to be understood as a variant of the *wayhî kēn* formula[735] and translated, "and light appeared in this manner:.." instead of simply, "and there was light." *Wayhî ʾôr* is likely as transition marker, as in v. 15, introducing the manner by which light came into existence.

> And God saw the light, that is was good
> And God separated (יבדל *yabdēl*) between the light and the dark upper waters

The light already existed within the darkness.[736] The verb of fulfillment here is בדל *bādal* "to divide, separate." After seeing the light within the darkness and recognizing its value (it was "good"), Elohim separated it from the *ḥōšek*, the dark upper waters where it apparently was localized.[737] Thus, as in the ancient Near Eastern and Indic creation accounts, the first creative act is to divide the primordial elements.[738]

7.2.5. *Primordial Light and the Luminous Body of God*

What is the nature of this light that emerged from darkness?[739] It is clearly unrelated to the sun, which was not created until Day Four and which is a tool refracting the primordial light to the earth.[740] Ed Noort

---

[735] Schmidt, ***Schöpfungsgeschichte***, 58; Wenham, ***Genesis***, 6.

[736] Nicolas Wyatt, "The Darkness of Genesis I 2," ***VT*** 43 (1993): 547-48 [art.=543-54]; Gunkel, ***Genesis***, 107: "God separated light and darkness, that is, he determined that they would no longer intermingle with one another"; M. Lambert, "A Study of the First Chapter of Genesis," ***HUCA*** 1 (1924): 6 [art.=3-12]: "In truth, the separation of the light from the darkness is explicable only if the two things are coexistent."

[737] Perry, "Poetics of Absence," 7-8

[738] Friedman, ***Commentary on the Torah***, 7: "Initially there is only watery chaos: shapeless and formless. The creation is the making of distinctions."

[739] On the "surprising implication that light proceeds from the darkness" see Wyatt, "Darkness of Genesis I 2," 548.

[740] As revealed by P's widely noted recognized paralleling of the Days 1-3 and 4-6 (See Umberto Cassuto, ***A Commentary on the Book of Genesis***, trns. Israel Abrahams, 2 vols. [Jerusalem: Magnes Press, 1961] 17; Rikki E. Watts, "On the Edge of the Millennium: Making Sense of Genesis 1," in Hans Boersma [ed.], ***Living in the LambLight: Christianity and Contemporary Challenges to the Gospel*** [Vancouver: Regent College Publishing, 2001] 129-151). Jacob Milgrom, in a brief but highly insightful article ("The Alleged 'Hidden Light'," in ***The Idea of Biblical Interpretation: Essays for James Kugel*** [Lieden: Brill, 2004]:41-44) has demonstrated that this noted parallel implies that

correctly perceived that the light of v.3 is presented as an attribute of Elohim himself.[741] Nicolas Wyatt, in a close study of the poetic form of Gen 1:2 observes that

> the logical structure of the verse indicates that a process is being identified within the verse. The process involves the initial stages in the self-manifestation of the deity. *It is, in somewhat unusual form, an account of a theophany.*[742]

This initial theophany actually begins at v. 3 with the emergence of divine light from the darkness of v.2. As in the Egyptian original, the emergence of light from the darkness was the emergence of the creator-god, in his luminous form, from darkness. While this is only implicit in Genesis I - for the priest was an esotericist - it is made explicit in other Temple materials. Ben Zion Wacholder has recently argued that Ezekiel's vision of the כבוד יהוה *kābôd yhwh* (Ezek. 1) was an interpretation of Gen. 1:3, the light of Day One represented by the luminous anthropomorphic form of God seen by the priest-prophet.[743] Most important is Psalms 104. That this is a Temple psalm is clear. Paul Humbert in a seminal article argued that both Gen I and Psalm 104 originally served as librettos in the Jerusalem Temple.[744] The Psalm is an interpretation/version of the creation account recorded in Genesis I[745] and, as such, "provides us with a tool for reflecting on Genesis 1:1-

---

the luminaries created on the fourth day actually do not shine with their own light, but instead refract and funnel to the earth the light of Day One (Gen. 1:3).

741 "The Creation of Light in Genesis I:1-5: Remarks on the Function of Light and Darkness in the Opening Verses of the Hebrew Bible," in George H. van Kooten (ed.), ***The Creation of Heaven and Earth: Re-Interpretations of Genesis I in the Context of Judaism, Ancient Philosophy, Christianity, and Modern Physics*** (Leiden: Brill, 2005)3-20.

742 Wyatt, "Darkness of Genesis I 2," 550.

743 "Creation in Ezekiel's Merkabah: Ezekiel 1 and Genesis 1," in Evans, ***Of Scribes and Sages***, 15-32.

744 "La relation de Genèse et Psaume 104 avec la liturgie du Nouvel-An israélite," in idem, ***Opuscules d'un hébraïsant*** (Neuchâtel: Université de Neuchâtel, 1958) 60-83.

745 James Luther Mays, ***Psalms: Interpretation*** (Louisville: John Knox Press, 1994) 331: "Both (Gen 1 and Ps 104) are surely expressions of the same theology of creator and creature." Levenson, ***Creation***, 57 saw a "genetic relation between Genesis 1 and Psalm 104." On the relation between Genesis I and Psalm 104 see further Samuel Terrien, ***The Psalms: Strophic Structure and Theological Commentary*** Grand Rapids, MI and Cambridge, U.K.: William B. Eerdmans Publishing Company, 2003) 710, 718-19; J. Day, ***Psalms*** (Sheffield, 1990) 41ff; Atwell, "An Egyptian Source," 461-62; Levenson, ***Creation***, Chapter Five; Arch Rutherford, "The Relationship of Psalm 104 to the Doctrine of Creation," M.A. thesis, Dallas Theological Seminary, 1971; Humbert, "La relation de Genèse et Psaume 104"; Kemper Fullerton, "The Feeling for Form in Psalm in Psalm 104," ***JBL*** 40 (1921): 43-56.

2:4."[746] As Arch Rutherford put it: "As a Biblical commentary on Genesis One a great deal can be learned from its (Ps. 104) contents."[747] Psalm 104 is the more significant because scholars have recognized that it, like Genesis I, is rooted in Egyptian cosmogonic tradition.[748] According to James E. Atwell, "Psalm 104 and Genesis I (are) witnesses to a single common Egyptian-inspired tradition."[749]

Psalm 104 is a hymn extolling the creator through reflection on his creation. The stanzas of the hymn follow the first five days of Genesis I.[750] Verse 2 of Psalm 104 is an interpretation of the emergence of light on the first day and the creation of the heavens of the second:

> 1. Bless the Lord, O my soul
> O Lord my God, you are very great.
> You are clothed with honor (הוד *hôd*) and majesty (הדר *hādār*)
> 2. Wrapped in light as with a garment (עטה - אור כשלמה *'ōteh 'ôr kaśśalmāh*)
> You stretch out the heavens like a tent

Here the light of Gen 1:3 is interpreted as God's own 'garment.'[751] הוד *hôd* (glory) and הדר *hādār* (majesty) are synonyms of כבוד *kābôd*, Yahweh's luminous, anthropomorphic form.[752] The light of Day One that emerges from the darkness is therefore understood in this Temple hymn as the luminous anthropomorphic form of God (Figure 21). Of special significance is the verb עטה *'ōteh*, "to wrap or envelope oneself." Its Akkadian cognate *eṭû* means "to be dark."[753] Describing God's wrapping himself with light through a verb meaning "to darken" is no contradiction but a divine paradox, as recognized by Samuel Terrien:

> The verb translated 'wrapping himself' or 'enveloping himself' is related to an Akkadian root meaning 'to be

---

[746] Atwell, "An Egyptian Source," 461.
[747] "Relationship," 13.
[748] Atwell, "An Egyptian Source," 461-62; Clifford, ***Creation Accounts***, 114; Mays, ***Psalms***, 331-32; Levenson, ***Creation***, 57-65.
[749] Atwell, "An Egyptian Source," 461.
[750] See Terrien, ***The Psalms***, 710; Levenson, ***Creation***, 53-56; Rutherford, "Relationship"; Humbert, "La relation"; Fullerton, "Feeling for Form," 51-56.
[751] "Light was the first thing created (Gen. 1:3) and it is in that Jehovah shrouds Himself, veiling His hidden glory from his creation." Woodrow Michael Kroll, ***Psalms: The Poetry of Palestine*** (Lanham, MD: University Press of America, 1987) 302. See also
[752] See above n.
[753] ***BDB*** 741 s.v.

darkened,' and the poet may have attempted to express the ineffable when he said that God 'darkens himself with light.[754]

Rutherford expressed it aptly as well:

> In one sense the light of the first creative day covers the infinite brightness of the glory of God, while in another sense it reveals the glory of God to all creation...The upholder of nature at once conceals his true being and discloses his presence through the light which can be seen and yet is too dazzling for human sight.[755]

This Temple tradition of the light of day one signifying Yahweh's own luminous form that somehow 'darkens' him even in its luminosity was also expounded by the first century Jewish exeget Philo of Alexandria. Philo was of priestly lineage and,[756] so argues Margaret Barker, is an important source with which to understand Second Temple priestly tradition.[757]In his *Opif.* 31 Philo discusses the light of Day One, which he identifies with the Logos, who, in his hellenizing interpretation of the Torah, is Yahweh himself.[758]

> Now that invisible light (of Gen. 1:3) perceptible only by mind has come into being as an image of the divine (Logos)...It is a supercelestial star, fount of the perceptible stars, such as it would not be inappropriate to call it 'all-brightness' to signify that from which the sun and moon, and all the other planets and fixed stars draw, in accordance with the capacity of each, the [degrees of] light befitting them; for that unmixed and pure

---

[754] ***The Psalms and Their Meaning for Today*** (New York: The Bobbs-Merrill Company, Inc., 1952) 57.
[755] "Relationship," 14, 56.
[756] D.R. Schwartz, "Philo's Priestly Descent," in F.E. Greenspahn, E. Hilgert, and B.L. Mack (edd.) ***Nourished with Peace*** (Chico, 1984) 155-171.
[757] "Temple Imagery in Philo: An Indication of the Origin of the Logos?" in William Horbury (ed.), ***Templum Amicitiae. Essays on the Second Temple presented to Ernst Bammel***, (JSOT Supplement Series 48; Sheffield: Sheffield Academic Press, 1991) 71-102.
[758] On Philo's identification of the Logos with the anthropomorphic Yahweh see Barker, ***Great Angel***, 144-133; N.A. Dahl and Alan Segal, "Philo and the Rabbis on the Names of God," ***JSJ*** 9 (1978): 27 [art.=1-28].

Figure 23

The 'Kābôd' (Glory) of Yahweh, as depicted in Kaballah (Esoteric Judaism): the letters of the name Yahweh (YHWH) forming a fiery human figure. This is, according to Kaballah, the first human form God assumed after he emerged as an *anthropos* (man) from triple-darkness

radiance *is dimmed* (*amauroumenès*) as soon as it begins to experience the change which is involved in the passage from intelligible (*viz.* the incorporeal) to sensible (*viz.* the visible); for nothing in the realm of sense is absolutely pure.

According to Philo, the light of Day One is the luminous image, *eikon*, of the Logos. From it the heavenly bodies draw their own luminosity. The radiance of the Logos *dimmed* however as soon as it entered the sense-perceptible world. As John Dillon has pointed out, in its progressive descent into the cosmos this archetypal light "becomes somehow mixed with the 'darkness' of matter, which leads to its becoming sense-perceptible (*i.e.* visible)".[759] Thus, as soon as the light emerged from hiddenness and enters the sphere of sense-perception, it begins its journey of 'darkening' that will culminate with the black body of Adam on Day Six (see below).

Another important priestly witness of the recognition of the light of Gen. 1:3 as the anthropomorphic form of God is the Prologue to the Gospel of John (vv. 1-18) in the New Testament, specifically the first five verses.

> 1a. In the beginning was the Word (λόγος *Logos*),
> 1b. and the Word was with God (ό θεος *ho theos*)
> 1c. and the Word was divine (θεος *theos*)
> 1. He was in the beginning with God
> 3a. All things came into being through him
> 3b. Without him not one thing came into being
> 3c. What has come into being
> 4. in him was life, and the life was the light of all people
> 5. The light shines in the darkness, and the darkness did not overcome it.

The Gospel of John dates to the period after the destruction of the Second Temple (70 AD), probably written around 100 AD.[760] The author of this gospel was likely a Palestinian Jew connected with the Jerusalem priesthood;[761] his gospel is saturated with Temple symbolism.[762] The Prologue and its *Logos* theology are themselves

759 Dillon, "*Asômatos*," 105.
760 See John B. Gabel, Charles B. Wheeler and Anthony D. York (edd.), ***The Bible as Literature: An Introduction*** (4th ed.; Oxford: Oxford University Press, 2000) 217-18 and the standard commentaries.
761 See above.
762 See especially Coloe, ***God Dwells with Us***.

rooted in first-century Jewish traditions of biblical interpretation,[763] as was Philo's. In particular, in a series of articles Peder Borgen demonstrated that the first five verses of John's Prologue is an interpretive (he uses the term 'targumic') paraphrase of the first three verses of Genesis 1.[764] The light אור *ôr* of Gen. 1:3-4 is the light φως *phōs* of John 1:4-5, which is the *Logos*, i.e. the pre-incarnate Christ.[765] In the Jewish and early Christian tradition that underlies this identification in John's Prologue, the *ôr/phōs/Logos* that emerged on Day One was a luminous *anthropos* (the Greek φως *phōs* means both 'light' and 'man'): a primordial man made of and surrounded by light.[766] This luminous *anthropos* was the creator-god: "all things came into being through him (Jhn. 3a)." He shinned in the darkness (σκότος *skotos*= חשך *ḥōšek*), but the darkness did not overcome him.

We therefore have sufficient evidence of the priestly identification of the light of Gen 1:3-4 with the creator-god or that god's luminous, anthropomorphic form. Psalms 104, Philo, and the Gospel of John, all with priestly/Temple associations, help us better understand the esoteric

---

763 Daniel Boyarin, "The Gospel of the *Memra*: Jewish Binitarianism and the Prologue to John," ***HTR*** 94:3 (2001) 243-84; W.D. Davies, "Aspects of the Jewish Background of the Gospel of John," in R. Alan Culpepper and C. Clifton Black (edd.), ***Exploring the Gospel of John: In Honour of D. Moody Smith*** (Louisville: Westminster John Knox Press, 1996) 46-52Craig A. Evans, ***Word and Glory: On the Exegetical and Theological Background of John's Prologue*** (JSOTSup 89; Sheffield: Sheffield Academic Press, 1993); David Runia, ***Philo in Early Christian Literature: A Survey*** (Minneapolis, 1993) 78-83; Thomas H. Tobin, S.J., "The Prologue of John and Hellenistic Jewish Speculation," ***CBQ*** 52 (1990): 252-269;

764 "Observations on the Targumic Character of the Prologue of John," ***NTS*** 16 (1970): 288-295; "Logos was the True Light: Contributions to the Interpretation of the Prologue of John," ***NTS*** 14 (1972): 115-30; "The Prologue of john-as Exposition of the Old Testament" in idem, ***Philo, John and Paul: New Perspectives on Judaism and Early Christianity*** (BJS, 131; Atlanta: Scholars Press, 1987) 75-102. See more recently John Painter, "Rereading Genesis in the Prologue of John?" in David E. Aune, Torrey Seland and Jarl Henning Ulrichsen (edd.) ***Neotestamentica et Philonica: Studies in Honor of Peder Borgen*** (Leiden and Boston: Brill, 2003) 179-201; Coloe, ***God Dwells with Us***, Chapter One; idem, "The Structure of the Johannine Prologue and Genesis 1," ***Australian Biblical Review*** 45 (1997): 40-55; Evans, ***Word and Glory***, 77-79.

765 Painter, "Rereading Genesis," 182-83; Elaine H. Pagels, "Exegesis of Genesis 1 in the Gospels of Thomas and John," ***JBL*** 118 (1999): 477-496; Tobin, "Prologue of John," 262-65; Borgen, "Logos was the True Light." See also Elizabeth R. Achtemeier, "Jesus Christ, the Light of the World: The Biblical Understanding of Light and Darkness," ***Int*** 17 (1963): 439-449.

766 Pagels, "Exegesis of Genesis 1"; April D. de Conick, ***Seek to See Him: Ascent and Vision Mysticism in the Gospel of Thomas*** (Leiden: E.J. Brill, 1996) 65-79; Jarl Fossum, "The Image of the Invisible God: Colossians 1.15-18a in the Light of Jewish Mysticism and Gnosticism," in idem, ***The Image of the Invisible God. Essays on the Influence of Jewish Mysticism on Early Christology*** (GöttingenVandenhoeck & Ruprecht, 1995) 13-39; idem, ***Name of God***, 280; Gilles Quispel, "Ezekiel 1:26 in Jewish Mysticism and Gnosis," ***VC*** 34 (1980): 1-13.

doctrine of the priestly author of Genesis I with regard to the appearance of light out of the darkness on Day One. Herbert Gordon May already in 1939 recognized that Gen. 1:3-5 must be understood against the backdrop of the biblical references to Yahweh's own luminous being.[767] When we also consider the Egyptian original to this Hebrew creation account, which also described the first appearance of light as the emergence of the luminous creator-god out of the primordial darkness, we have a firm basis from which to proceed in interpreting Gen. 1:3-4:[768] these verses described the emergence of God himself, in a brilliantly luminous form, out of the primordial dark matter.

We can summarize Gen. 1-4 as follows: At some unspecified time ('in a beginning') long ago the cosmos consisted only of a triple-darkness: (1) an arid, dark mingled mass called הארץ *hā'āreṣ*, "the earth" (2) over which was חשך *ḥōšek*, dark (upper) waters and (3) below which was תהום *tĕhōm*, dark (lower) waters. Within this triple-darkness was the luminous, creative breath of God (רוח אלהים *rû^{a}ḥ 'ĕlōhîm*) either hovering over, brooding on, or (doubtfully) rushing upon the primordial atom or its recently 'hatched' elements. When creation officially begins in v. 3, God himself emerges from the triple-darkness as a luminous *anthropos*. It is likely that he emerged in this form directly from the primordial atom. Not only is the suggestion supported by the Egyptian originals of this Hebrew creation account, but we also have material proof that some Israelites indeed understood Yahweh to have emerged from the primordial atom, just as Re' of Egypt and Brahma of India had done. On an inscribed Hebrew seal from the northern kingdom of Israel (Judah) dated to the 8th cent. BC (Figure 24) is an image of a young solar deity sitting upon a lotus plant. The seal bears the name 'Abiyahu ("Yahweh is my father"), servant/minister (*'ebed*) of 'Uzziah. 'Uzziah was the King of Judah (773-735 B.C). 'Abiyahu was thus a 'high official' of the royal court. As Othmar Keel and Christoph Uehlinger point out, the image is likely a representation of the god of Israel.[769] Thus, Yahweh is here depicted as the sun god emerging from the lotus plant, just as Re' and Brahma had done

[767] "The Creation of Light in Genesis 1 $_{3-5}$," ***JBL*** 58 (1939): 203-11.
[768] Giovanni Garbini's argument ("The Creation of Light in the First Chapter of Genesis," ***Proceedings of the Fifth World Congress of Jewish Studies*** [1969] 1:2 [art.=1-4]) that the high place given to the creation of light in Gen 1:3-5 is the result of Iranian influence is based on his false claim that "Such an essential function of light is completely absent from Mesopotamian, Egyptian or Canaanite cosmogonies" and therefore must be rejected. As we saw, the emergence of light from darkness at the start of creation is a central theme in Egyptian cosmogonies.
[769] ***Gods, Goddesses and Images of God in Ancient Israel*** [Minneapolis: Fortress Press, 1998], 249, 401.

previously. The lotus plant, like the cosmogonic egg, symbolized the first piece of distinguishable matter, viz. the primordial atom. Here, then, is the evidence that at least some persons in Israel, connected with the court itself, thought Yahweh emerged from the primordial atom. This luminous form of God that emerged from the darkness on Day One is likely the same as the *kāḇôd* or Glory of Yahweh, the latter's brilliantly luminous form.

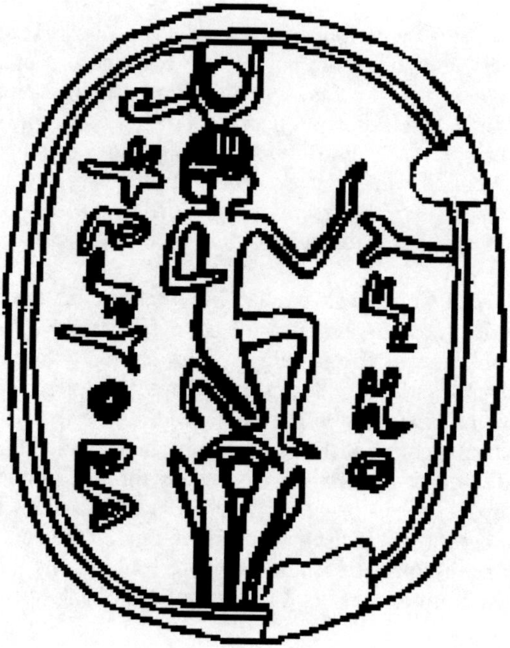

Figure 24

7th century BC Hebrew depiction of Yahweh as a solar deity emerging from the Lotus Plant/Primordial Atom (from Othmar Keel and Christoph Uehlinger, ***Gods, Goddesses, and Images of God in Ancient Israel*** [Augsburg Fortress Publishers, 1998])

7.3. *Adam, the Black Body of God*

Day One was thus the beginning of God's visible, *corporeal* manifestation. He existed before Day One, of course, but as a 'creative breath' hidden in the darkness. When light emerged from the darkness, God emerged as a luminous *anthropos*, according to the priestly tradition underlying Genesis I. According to the esoteric tradition of Judaism, called *Kabbalah*, the biblical story of creation in six days is both a cosmogony and a *theogony*,* that is an account of God's own corporeal birth and self-evolution:

> the work of creation as described in the first chapter of Genesis has a twofold character: Insofar as it represents, in a mystical sense, the history of God's self-revelation and His unfolding...the description is a theogony...and only in so far as it brings the "nether" world into being, i.e. creation in the strict sense...can it be described as cosmogony...Theogony and cosmogony represent not two different acts of creation, but two aspects of the same.[770]

The six days of Genesis chronicle not only the birth of different aspects of the physical cosmos, but also the six evolutionary forms God himself assumed on each of the six days, culminating with man on day six, God's most 'beautiful' and 'perfect' shape.[771] Our examination of Day One confirms that this kabbalistic reading of the Genesis creation account as an account of theogony is justified by the text itself and thus originated with, or at least was shared by the priesthood of Solomon's Temple. Space does not permit us to discuss each of these six days. Instead, the following discussion will focus on the culminating event on Day Six: the birth of Adam. A close look at this passage confirms that the real point of Genesis I is the evolution of the body of God.

7.3.1. *Adam as Cult Statue*

Adam's creation on Day Six was the crown of God's creative activity.

---

[770] Gershom Scholem, ***Major Trends in Jewish Mysticism*** (New York: Schocken Books, 1995) 222, 223. On the Kabbalistic doctrine of the evolution of the biblical God see also Arthur Green, ***A Guide to the Zohar*** (Stanford: Stanford University Press, 2004), 101-108; Isaiah Tishby, "The Account of Creation," in Fischel Lachower and Isaiah Tishby, ***The Wisdom of the Zohar, An Anthology of Texts***, trns. From the Hebrew by David Goldstein, 3 vols. (Portland, Oregon: Oxford, 2002), II: 549ff

[771] S.L.M. Mathers, ***The Kabbalah Revealed*** (London: Arkana Books, 1991) 43-46, 77.

And God said: Let us make Adam/man as our image (צלם *ṣelem*), according to our likeness (דמות *dĕmût*) [772] (Gen. 1:26)

Adam was thus made to be the image of God, צלם אלהים, *ṣelem 'ĕlōhîm*. A closer look at P's *imago Dei* concept will further elucidate the esoteric tradition of the Jerusalem Temple. Scholarly interpretations of Gen.1:26-7 are numerous and divergent.[773] The Hebrew צלם *ṣelem*

---

[772] The *beth* in בצלמנו *bĕṣalmēnû*, usually translated "*in* our image" is to be read as *beth essentiae*, "*as* our image (*ṣelem*). See ***TLOT*** 3:1082 s.v. "צלם," by Wildberger; ***TDOT*** 12:394 s.v. "צלם" by Stendebach; D.J.A. Clines, "The Image of God in Man," ***TynBul*** 19 (1968): 76-80. On *beth essentiae* see J.H. Charlesworth, "The *Beth Essentiae* And the Permissive Meaning of the Hiphil (Aphel)," in H.W. Attridge, J.J. Collins and T.H. Tobin (edd.), ***Of Scribes and Scrolls: Studies on the Hebrew Bible, Intertestamental Judaism, and Christian Origins, Presented to John Strugnell on the Occasion of His Sixtieth Birthday*** (Lanham: University Press of America, 1990) 67-78; Cyrus H. Gordon, " 'In' of Predication or Equivalence," ***JBL*** 100 (1981) 612-613; Lawrence N. Manross, "Bêth Essentiae," ***JBL*** 73 (1954): 238-9. On the other hand, we understand the כ in כדמותנו *kidĕmûthēnû* as *kaph* of the norm (according to our likeness). Clines' ("Image of God in Man," 76-80, 90-93) argument is still persuasive: „...there is no reason why בצלמנו and כדמותנו should be equivalent, and a perfectly satisfactory interpretation is gained by taking בצלמנו as 'as our image, to be our image' and כדמותנו not as synonymous with בצלמנו, but a explanatory of the 'image', that it is an image made כדמותנו, 'according to our likeness, like us…דמות then specifies what kind of image it is: it is a 'likeness'-image, not simply an image; representational, not simply representative (77, 91)." See also Ivan Golub, "Man – Image of God (Genesis 1:26): A New Approach to an Old Problem," in "***Wünschet Jerusalem Friedmen": Collected Communications to the XIIth Congress of the International Organization for the Study of the Old Testament, Jerusalem 1986*** (Frankfurt am Main: Peter Lang, 1988) 227-28.

[773] The literature is of course too vast to do justice to in a short note. For a history of interpretations up to 1982 *v.* Gunnlaugur A. Jónsson, ***The Image of God: Genesis 1:26-28 in a Century of Old Testament Research*** (CB.OT, 26; Stockholm: Almquist & Wiksell International, 1988) and the research cited there. Of special note see also sources sited above, esp. nn. 50-1 and further: R.McL. Wilson, "The Early History of the Exegesis of Gen. 1.26," ***Studia Patristica*** 1 (1957): 420-37; J. Jervell, ***Imago Dei: Gen. 1:26 in Spätjudentum, in Gnosis und in den paulinischen Briefen*** (FRLANT 76; Göttingen: Vandenhoeck & Ruprecht, 1960); George Arthur Buttrick et al (edd.), ***The Interpreter's Dictionary of the Bible*** (New York: Abingdon Press, 1962; hereafter ***IDB***) 2:682-684 s.v. "Image of God," by N.W. Porteous; Meredith G. Kline, "Creation in the Image of the Glory-Spirit," ***Westminster Theological Journal*** 39 (1977): 250-72; Maryanne Cline Horowitz, "The Image of God in Mam-Is Woman Included?" ***HTR*** 72 (1979): 175-206; Jarl Fossum, "Gen. 1,26 and 2,7 in Judaism, Samaritanism, and Gnosticism," ***JSJ*** 16 (1985): 202-239; Byron L. Sherwin, "The Human Body and the Image of God," in Dan Cohn-Sherbok (ed.), ***A Traditional Quest: Essays in Honour of Louis Jacobs*** (Sheffield: University of Sheffield, 1991) 74-85; Johannes C. de Moor, "The Duality in God and Man: Gen. 1:26-27 as P's Interpretation of the Yahwistic Creation Account," in ***Intertextuality in Ugarit and Israel*** (OTS, 40; Leiden; Boston: Brill, 1998) 112-125; W.Randall Garr, " 'Image' and 'Likeness' in the Inscription from Tell Fakhariyeh," ***IEJ*** 50 (2000): 227-234; Dearman, "Theophany, Anthropomorphism, and the Imago Dei"; Yair Lorberbaum, ***Image of God, Kabbalah and Aggadah*** (Tel Aviv: Schocken Publishing House, 2004) [Hebrew].

means primarily "statue"[774] and *ṣelem 'ĕlōhîm* is a cognate of the Akkadian *ṣalam ili/ilāni*, the common Mesopotamian term for god-statues.[775] Scholars have now seen that this terminological congruence contains conceptual congruence as well: P's *ṣelem* (image) is the Mesopotamian *ṣalmu* (cult-image), thus Adam was created to be the living statue of the deity, the deity's very presence on earth.[776]

> Gen 1:26…can only be understood against the background of an ancient Yahweh statue…Here the terms *ṣlm* and *dmwt* are used as synonyms denoting 'statue'. Humans are thus created to be the living statues of the deity. The ritual of vivifying the cult statue was transferred to man in Genesis 2. There was no further need of a divine image because…humans represented Yahweh, as a statue would have done…[777]

---

[774] Ludwig Koehler and Walter Baumgartner, ***The Hebrew and Aramaic Lexicon of the Old Testament*** (hereafter ***HALOT***) (5vols.; Leiden: E.J. Brill, 1994-) 3:1028-29, s.v. צלם.
[775] ***The Assyrian Dictionary*** (hereafter ***CAD***; Chicago: Oriental Institute of the University of Chicago, 1962) 16: 78b-80a, 84b-85a, s.v. Ṣalmu; E. Douglas Van Buren, "The *ṣalmê* in Mesopotamian Art and Religion," ***Orientalia*** 5 (1936): 65-92.
[776] See above nn. 50-1; ***HALOT*** 3:1028-1029; ***DDD*** s.v. "Image," by A. Livingstone, 448-450; Samuel E. Loewenstamm, "'Beloved is Man in that he was created in the Image'," in idem, ***Comparative Studies in Biblical and Ancient Oriental Literatures*** (AOAT, 204; Kevelaer: Butzon & Bercker; Neukirchen-Vluyn: Neukirchener Verlag, 1980) 48-50.
[777] Herbert Niehr, "In Search of Yahweh's Cult Statute in the First Temple," in ***The Image and the Book***, 93-94. See also S. Dean McBride Jr., "Divine Protocol: Genesis 1:1-2:3 as Prologue to the Pentateuch," in W.P. Brown and S.Dean McBride (edd.), ***God Who Creates: Essays in Honor of W. Sibley Towner*** (Grand Rapids, Michigan: W.B. Eerdmans Publishing, 2000) 16: Adamic beings are animate icons…The peculiar purpose for their creation is 'theophanic': to represent or mediate the sovereign presence of deity within the central nave of the cosmic temple, just as cult-images were supposed to do in conventional sanctuaries"; Andreas Schüle, "Made in the >Image of God<: The Concepts of Divine Images in Gen 1-3," ***ZAW*** 117 (2005): 1-20; Ulrich Mauser, "God in Human Form," ***Ex Auditu*** 16 (2000): 81-100 (90-93; Crispin H.T. Fletcher-Louis, "The Worship of Divine Humanity as God's Image and the Worship of Jesus," in ***Jewish Roots of Christological Monotheism***, 113-128, esp. 120-128;; John Kutsko, ***Between Heaven and Earth: Divine Presence and Absence in the Book of Ezekiel*** (Winona Lake, Indiana: Eisenbrauns, 2000), 53-60. See also idem, "Will the Real *Ṣelem 'Ĕlōhîm* Please Stand Up? The Image of God in the Book of Ezekiel," ***SBL 1998 Seminar Papers***, 55-85; idem, "Ezekiel's Anthropology and its Ethical Implications," in Odell and Strong, ***Book of Ezekiel***, 119-141; ***Theological Lexicon of the Old Testament***, eds. Ernst Jenni and Claus Westermann, trs. Mark E. Biddle (3vols.; Peabody, Massachusetts: Hendrickson Publishers, Inc, 1997; hereafter ***TLOT***) 3:1080-82 s.v. "צלם," by H. Wilderger; Garrett Green, ***Imagining God: Theology and the Religious Imagination*** (San Francisco, etc.: Harper & Row, Publishers, 1989) 91-97; Edward Mason Curtis, "Man as the Image of God in Genesis in the Light of Ancient Near Eastern Parallels" (Ph.D. diss., University of Pennsylvania, 1984); idem, "Image of God (OT)," in ***ABD*** 3:289-91.

The Mesopotamian *ṣalmu*, like the ancient Near Eastern cult-image generally, was distinguished by its ambivalent "god…not god" identity: while the idol is distinguished from the god whom it represents, it is also identified with and treated as the god itself.[778] The reason is that the ancient Near Eastern cult statue was not only a representative replica of the god; it was also the dwelling place of that god's essence/spirit.[779] "It was not considered to resemble an original reality that was present elsewhere but to contain that reality in itself."[780] It "signified…the living incarnation of the represented person,"[781] i.e. the deity. The *ṣalmu* or cult statue was the very body of the god on earth, in which his/her divine spirit/essence 'incarnated.'"[782]

> It is through an image that a god/goddess is present in the created world and executes his/her powers in history and nature…The cultic image is in fact the medium of manifest divine presence and action in the world and as such part of the divine person. It is, to put it pointedly, >god on earth<…The image was…that side of the god's person through which he entered the sphere of created

---

[778] On this 'god…not god' identity of the idol see especially T. Jacobsen, "The Graven Image," in P.D. Miller Jr., P.D. Hanson and S.D. McBride (edd.), ***Ancient Israelite Religion: Essays in Honor of Frank Moore Cross*** (Philadelphia: Fortress Press, 1987) 15-32, esp. 16-20; Michael B. Dick, "The Relationship between the Cult Image and the Deity in Mesopotamia," in Jiří Prosecký (ed.), ***Intellectual Life of the** ancient Near East: **Papers** Presented at **the** 43rd Rencontre assyriologique international, Prague, July 1-5, 1996* (Prague: Oriental Institute, 1998) 11-16. On the treatment of idols see Irene J. Winter, " 'Idols of the King': Royal Images as Recipients of Ritual Action in Ancient Mesopotamia," ***Journal of Ritual Studies*** 6 (Winter 1992):13-42; Curtis, "Man as the Image of God," 103-106. On the ANE cult of divine images see further Neal H. Walls (ed.) ***Cult Image and Divine Representation in the Ancient Near East*** (American Schools of Oriental Research Books Series 10; Boston: American Schools of Oriental Research, 2005); Zainab Bahrani, ***The Graven Image: Representation in Babylonia and Assyria*** (Philadelphia: University of Pennsylvania Press, 2003); Michael B. Dick (ed.), ***Born in Heaven, Made on Earth: The Making of the Cult Image in the Ancient Near East*** (Winona Lake, Indiana: Eisenbrauns, 1999).

[779] K.H. Bernhardt, ***Gott und Bild. Ein Beitrag zur Begründung und Deutung des Bildererbotes im Alten Testament*** (Berlin: Evangelische Verlagsanstalt, 1956) 17-68; David Lorton, "The Theology of Cult Statues in Ancient Egypt," in ***Born in Heaven***, 123-210, esp. 179-184; Curtis, "Man as the Image of God," 97-102.

[780] Bahrani, ***Graven Image***, 127.

[781] Johannes Hehn, "Zum Terminus 'Bild Gottes'," in G. Weil (ed.), ***Festschrift Eduard Sachau*** (Berlin: G. Reimer, 1915) 36.

[782] See Stendebach (***TDOT*** 12:389 sv. צלם): "The cult statue of a god is the actual body in which that deity dwells." According to Thorkild Jacobs, the statue was the deities "outer form, the external habitation." ***The Treasures of Darkness*** (New Haven: Yake University Press, 1967) 14. See also Hornung, ***Conceptions of God in Ancient Egypt***, 135: "These images may be the 'bodies' of the gods into which they 'enter' and Assmann (***The Search for God***, 46) who notes that the "basic Egyptian concept" is "*The statue is not the image of the body, but the body itself* (emphasis original)."

> life...the bodily appearance of a god, the very medium...through which he can be addressed by prayer, worship and sacrifice.[783]

In the ancient Near Eastern cult of images the idol was incarnated by the essence or spirit of the deity after the successful completion of a series of rituals performed on/with the cult image. These are the so-called *pit pî* ("Opening-of-the-mouth") and *mīs pî* ("Washing-of-the-mouth") rituals whose objective was to transform the lifeless statue into the living god.[784] It is now widely recognized that the idea behind these rituals underlie the imagery of Gen. 2:7b: "then the LORD GOD formed man of dust from the ground, and breathed into his nostrils the breath of life; and man became a living being (New Oxford Annotated Bible)."[785]

> In Gen. 2^{7} the process of animating the body of Adam is described by the words: 'And the Lord...breathed into his nostrils the breath of life; and man became a living soul.' This passage is in every detail in expression and substance typically Egyptian. To begin with, the expression 'breath of life' is the same as the Egyptian *tau en ankh.* The idea of giving a 'breath of life into the nostrils' is very common in Egyptian. The whole phrase, both in Egyptian and Hebrew, is literally and grammatically identical...Thus for instance it is said of

---

[783] Schüle, "Made in the >Image of God<," 5-6, 12.

[784] See Victor Avigdor Hurowitz, "The Mesopotamian God Image, From Womb to Tomb," ***JAOS*** 123 (2003): 147-157; Christopher Walker and Michael B. Dick, "The Induction of the Cult Image in Ancient Mesopotamia: The Mesopotamian *mīs pî* Ritual," in ***Born in Heaven***, 55-121. On the Egyptian ritual *v.* Lorton, "The Theology of Cult Statues in Ancient Egypt,"153-158.

[785] Schüle, "Made in the >Image of God<," 11-14; Edward L. Greenstein, "God's Golem: The Creation of the Human in Genesis 2," in Henning Graf Reventlow and Yair Hoffman (edd.), ***Creation in Jewish and Christian Tradition*** (JSOT Supplement Series 319; Sheffield: Sheffield Academic Press, 2002) 219-239 (224-229); James K. Hoffmeier, "Some Thoughts on Genesis 1 & 2 and Egyptian Cosmogony," ***JANES*** 15 (1983): 46-48; ***ABD*** 3:390 s.v. "Image of God (OT)" by Curtis; Walter Wifall, "The Breath of His Nostrils: Gen 2:7b," ***CBQ*** 36 (1974): 237-240; Cyrus Gordon, "Khnum and El," in Sarah Israelit-Groll (ed.), ***Egyptological Studies*** (Jerusalem: The Magnes Press, 1982): 202-214 (204-5); Abraham Shalom Yahuda, ***The Accuracy of the Bible*** (London: William Heineman Ltd., 1934) 152. S.G.F. Brandon, " 'In the beginning': The Hebrew Story of the Creation in its Contemporary Setting," ***History Today*** 11 (1961): 380-387 (384). According to R.J. Williams, "Some Egyptianisms in the Old Testament," ***Studies in Honor of John A. Wilson's 70th Birthday*** (Studies in Ancient Oriental Civilization 35; Chicago, University of Chicago Press, 1969) 93-4, the concept of a god placing breath into the nostrils of man is an 'Egyptianism.' See also Gregory Yuri Glazov, ***The Bridling of the Tongue and the Opening of the Mouth in Biblical Prophecy*** (JSOT Supplemental Series 311; Sheffield: JSOT Press, 2001).

the god Ptah that he it is 'who gives the breath of life to every nose'."[786]

Though the creation narrative of Genesis 2 dose not use the term *ṣelem*, there can be no doubt that the *imago* concept is present.[787] It is important to point out that, according to the Hebrew of Genesis 1:26, Adam was not made *in* or *according to* the *ṣelem* of God, but *as* the *ṣelem.*[788] This *ṣelem* was made 'according to the likeness (דמות *dĕmūt*)' of God's own luminous form (*kāḇôd*). This form we saw is the luminous anthropomorphic form that emerged from darkness on Day One.[789] This means that the *ṣelem* had the shape of God's own form. The Hebrew 'opening of the mouth' ritual described in Gen. 2:7 indicates that the luminous form incarnated in the *ṣelem*, *viz*., Adam. In Egypt the deity Amon, who represented the pre-cosmic 'breath' inhabiting the primordial darkness (=*rûᵃḥ 'ĕlōhîm*, Gen. 1:2c), is said to be "that breath which stays in all things and through which one lives."[790] In the Luxor Temple Amon is depicted holding the sign of life (*ankh*) toward the pharaoh Amen-hotep saying, "My beloved son, receive my likeness in thy nose."[791] This indicates that the blowing of the breath of life into the nostrils signifies the incarnation of that deity's 'breath,' also called his 'likeness.' And as Walter Wifall noted: "The Egyptian portrait appears to be an obvious parallel to the…description of God and 'the man' in Gen. 2."[792] Thus, the composite narrative (Gen. 1-2)[793] presents us with a picture strikingly reminiscent of ancient Near Eastern cult tradition: a *ṣelem* (cult-statue) is made for/by the deity[794] from mundane materials[795] into which that deity (his breath/likeness, i.e. his luminous form) subsequently enters and

---

786 Yahuda, ***The Accuracy of the Bible***, 152.

787 Schüle, "Made in the >Image of God<"; Iain Provan, "To Highlight All Our Idols: Worshipping God in Nietzche's World," ***Ex Auditu*** 15 (1999): 25-26; Greenstein, "God's Golem," 228-9; Sawyer, "The Image of God," 64-66.

788 See above.

789 See above.

790 H. Frankfort, ***Kingship and the Gods*** (Chicago: University of Chicago Press, 1965) 161.

791 Ibid.

792 "The Breath of His Nostrils: Gen. 2:7b," ***CBQ*** 36 (1974): 239 [art.=237-24].

793 As arranged by the final redactor. On reading Genesis I and 2 as parts of a (redacted) whole *v*. Sawyer, "Image of God," 64-5.

794 On the ritual attribution of the creation of the cult statute to the deity *v*. Walker and Dick, "Induction"; Dick, "Relationship," 113-116.

795 See Victor Hurowitz, "What Goes In Is What Comes Out – Materials for Creating Cult Statues" in G. Beckman and T.J. Lewish (edd.), ***Text and Artifact – Proceedings of the Colloquium of the Center for Judaic Studies, University of Pennsylvania, April 27-29, 1998***, Brown Judaic Series, 2006 (in press). My thanks to professor Hurowitz for providing a manuscript copy of this work.

dwells.[796] This indwelling enlivens the *ṣelem*, making it god and king.[797] Adam, as the *ṣelem* of God, is himself the very body of God in which the spirit (luminous form) of God incarnated.[798]

> It cannot be stressed enough that Israel…by a daring adaptation of the image theology of the surrounding world, proclaims that a human being is the form in which God himself is present.[799]

We thus have here the biblical justification for the later tradition of Adam's heavenly enthronement and worship by the angels.[800] In the Latin Life of Adam and Eve (*Vita Adae et Evae*) God commands the angels in heaven regarding Adam: "Worship the Image of Yahweh (14:3)!" As the very *Imago* of God, Adam is here the object of *cultic* veneration, as the temple language and imagery used in this text makes clear.[801] We find the same tradition in the Qur'ān (see below).

Crispin Fletcher-Louis describes Genesis 1 as an 'incarnational' cosmology,[802] and this characterization is justified.[803] Important here also is that Adam, as *ṣelem* of God, *is the abode of God as well*: "the image of a god was to be looked upon…as a temple, where this god could be both encountered and truly worshipped."[804] Adam/Aaron is

---

[796] On the divine "entering the form" of the statue *v.* Winter, " 'Idols of the King'," 23; Dick, "Relationship," 113-114; Curtis, "Man as Image of God," 97-99.

[797] On "made from dust" in Gen. 2 as a biblical metaphor for enthronement *v.* Walter Brueggemann, "From Dust to Kingship," ***ZAW*** 84 (1972): 1-18. I. Engell already read Gen 1:26-8 as a description of a divine, enthroned Adam: see "Knowledge and Life in the Creation Story," in M. Noth and D. Winton Thomas (edd.), ***Wisdom in Israel and In The Ancient Near East Presented to Harold Henry Rowley*** (Leiden: E.J. Brill, 1955) 112.

[798] As McBride puts it ("Divine Protocol," 18) Adam is "God's own incarnated image".

[799] H. Wildberger, "Das Abbild Gottes, Gen 1:26-30," ***ThZ*** 21 (1965): 245-59.

[800] D. Steenburg, "The Worship of Adam and Christ as the Image of God," ***JSNT*** 39 (1990): 95-109; *Pace* Jarl Fossum, "The Adorable Adam of the Mystics and the Rebuttals of the Rabbis," in Peter Schäfer (ed.), ***Geschichte, Tradition, Reflexion: Festschrift für Martin Hengel zum 70. Geburtstag* Band I: *Judentum*** (Tübingen : J C B Mohr, 1996) 529-539 (533) and Alexander Altman, "The Gnostic Background of the Rabbinic Adam Legends," *JQR* 35 (1945): 382.

[801] As persuasively argued by Corrine L. Patton, "Adam as the Image of God: An Exploration of the Fall of Satan in the *Life of Adam and Eve*," ***SBL 1994 Seminar Papers***: 296-98.

[802] "Image of God," 84, 99.

[803] We thus need to amend Norbert Lohfink's statement that "P's conception of God's nearness in cult must be supplemented by the New Testament's conviction of God's nearness in the *person* of Christ." "Creation and salvation in Priestly theology," ***Theological Digest*** 30 (Spring, 1982): 5. P combines God's nearness in cult and person, the person of the high priest.

[804] Frederick G. McLeod, "The Antiochene Tradition Regarding the Role of the Body within the 'Image of God'," in ***Broken and Whole; Essays on Religion and the Body*** (Lanham, Md: University Press of America, 1993) 24-25. See also ***ABD*** 3:390-91 s.v. "Image of God (OT)" by Curtis. Gebhard Selz remarks as well: "Late texts provide

therefore the first divine sanctuary, the body of God on Earth "where this god could be both encountered and truly worshipped."[805]

As *ṣelem*, Adam is not only the earthly body of God, but the *black body of God.* The Akkadian *ṣalmu* means both "image/statue" and "black," the latter meaning deriving from its verbal form *ṣalāmu*, "to become dark, to turn black."[806] This semantic duality is found also in the Hebrew root *ṣlm* (*ṣlm* I: "image/statue"; *ṣlm* II: "dark, darkness," from *ṣālam* II: "to be dark").[807] In an exhaustive philological study in 1972 I.H. Eybers suggested taking the Hebrew *ṣelem* as *ṣel* ('shadow,' 'dark image') expanded by the enclitic *mēm* (the final 'm').[808] Marshalling an impressive amount of comparative material Eybers concluded: "Taking all the data into consideration the meaning of *ṣèlèm* in Gen. 1:26-27 could be that man is a 'shadowy (and therefore weak) replica and creation' of God."[809] Earlier, Pierre Bordreuil, also noting the etymological relationship between the Hebrew *ṣelem* and Akkadian *ṣalmu*,[810] pointed out the conceptual link between Gen. 1:26-27 and the ancient Near Eastern characterization of the king as both image of a god and as residing in that god's (protective) shadow.[811] The philological data is now sufficient for Israeli biblical scholar Avivah Gottlieb Zornberg to note simply: "Image-*tselem* in Hebrew…At the heart of that word is the word 'shadow'."[812]

---

evidence that the statue of Šamaš was considered to be *a place of 'epiphany'* of the sun-god"[804]: the parallel with the Israelite Tabernacle/Tent of Meeting cannot be missed. "The Holy Drum, the Spear, and the Harp. Towards an Understanding of the Propblem of Deification in Third Millennium Mesopotamia," in I. Finkel and M. Gellers (edd.), ***Sumerian Gods and Their Representations*** (Grönigen: Styx Publications, 1997) 183 remarks as well

[805] This may support Michael M. Homan's suggestion that Aaron's name, אהרן, be taken as an Egyptianized form of Semitic אהל, *tent*, with an adjectival or diminutive suffix *–ōn*; hence Aaron is the 'tent-man.' See his discussion in ***To Your Tents, O Israel! The Terminology, Function, Form, and Symbolism of Tents in the Hebrew Bible and the Ancient Near East*** (Leiden: Brill, 2002) 120-23.

[806] ***CAD*** 16:70,77-85.

[807] ***HALOT***, 3:1028-1029 s.v צלם ; ***TDOT*** 12:396 s.v. "צלמות" by Niehr.

[808] I.H. Eybers, "The Root *Ṣ-L* in Hebrew Words," ***JNSL*** 2 (1972): 23-36 (29-32). See also ***International Standard Bible Encyclopedia*** 4vols. (Grand Rapids, MI: W. B. Eerdmans, 1979-; hereafter ***ISBE***) 4:440 s.v. "Shade; Shadow," by G. Chamberlain.

[809] Eybers, "The Root *Ṣ-L*," 32 n. 2.

[810] The first to propose such as relation seems to have been the Assyrologist Friedrich Delitzsch who described *ẓelem* as a Babylonian loanword: ***Prolegomena eines neuen hebräisch-aramäischen Wörterbuchs*** (Leipzig: J. C. Hinrichs, 1886) 141. On denials of such a relation *v.* below n. 154.

[811] Pierre Bordreuil, " 'A L'Ombre D'Elohim:' Le theme de l'ombre protectrice dans l'Ancien Orient et ses rapports avec 'L'Imago Dei,' " ***RHPhR*** 46 (1996): 368-391.

[812] In Bill Moyers, ***Genesis: A Living Conversation*** (New York: Doubleday, 1996) 19. The relation of *ẓlm* II and *ẓel* to each other and to Gen.1:26-27 has been disputed. Two relevant issues were actually debated: (1) whether *ẓlm* II "to be/become dark" ever

Adam is therefore both the image and shadow of Yahweh-El's luminous form (*kābôd*), his "shadow picture," as N.W. Porteous said

---

existed in Hebrew or Northwest Semitic (NWS) at all and: (2) if so, whether it was in any way related to *ẓelem*. This discussion often focused on the much disputed term צלמות (Jer. 2:6; Pss. 44:20; 23:4; Job 16:16; 38:17; see discussion in D. Winton Thomas, "צלמות in the Old Testament," ***JSS*** 7 [1962]: 191-200). After Friedrich Delitzsch's initial suggestion in 1886 of a *ẓelem/ṣalmu* (black) relation, he was disputed by his father, OT scholar Franz Delitzsch (***New Commentary on Genesis*** [Edinburgh, T. & T. Clark, 1888-89] 1:91. The longest lasting rebuttal came from Theodor Nöldeke, first in a review of Friedrich Delitzsch's ***Wörterbuchs*** (***ZDMG*** 40 (1886): 733-34) and latter in an article devoted to the subject ("צלמות und צלם," ***ZAW*** 17 [1897]: 183-187). Nöldeke doubted the existence of a Hebrew *ṣlm* II "to be/become dark" and derived *ṣelem* from an Arabic *ẓlm* meaning "to cut off" (on the denial of a NWS *ẓlm* II *v.* also J.F.A. Sawyer, Review of W.L. Holladay, ***A Concise Hebrew and Aramaic Lexicon of the Old Testament*** in ***JSS*** 17 [1972] 257; D.J.A. Clines, "The Etymology of Hebrew *Ṣelem*," ***JNSL*** 3 (1973):23-25; Walter L. Michel, "ṢLMWT, 'Deep Darkness' or 'Shadow of Death'?" ***BR*** 29 [1984]: 5-13). But the weakness of this Arabic derivation has now been adequately demonstrated (Bordreuil, "'A L'Ombre D'Elohim," 368-372; James Barr, "The Image of God in the Book of Genesis-A Study of Terminology," ***BJRL*** 51 (1968): 18-22; idem, ***Comparative Philology and the Text of the Old Testament*** [1st ed.; Oxford, 1968; repr. With additions and corrections: Winona Lake, Indiana: Eisenbrauns, 1987] 375-380; Eybers, "The Root *Ṣ-L*," 31-32; Clines, "Etymology," 19-21) and the existence of a NWS *ẓlm* II "to be/become dark" has been affirmed and accepted (Paul Humbert, ***Etudes sur le recit du paradis et de la chute dans la Genesis*** (Mémoires de l'Université de Neuchatel 14, 1940) 156; Baruch Margalit, ***A Matter of "Life" and "Death": A Study of the Baal-Mot Epic (CTA 4-5-6)*** [Kevelaer: Butzon & Bercker; Neukirchen-Vluyn: Neukirchener Verlag, 1980] 72 n. 1; ***HALOT*** 3:1028 s.v. צלם; ***TDOT*** 12: 396 s.v. צלמות by Niehr; Chaim Cohen, "The Meaning of צלמות 'Darkness': A Study in Philological Method," in Michael V. Fox et al (edd.), ***Texts, Temples, and Traditions: A Tribute to Menahem Haran*** [Winona Lake, Indiana: Eisenbrauns, 1996] 287-309). James Barr (***Comparative Philology***, 375) noted in 1987 that by that time the derivation of צלמות from a Hebrew root *ṣlm* "to be/become dark" had become "so completely accepted that some works have ceased to mention that the older tradition of meaning (*viz.* 'shadow of death') ever existed." Cf. Michel, "ṢLMWT," 5.

A connection between *ṣlm* II and *ṣel* is probable (*Pace* Nöldeke, "צלמות und צלם," 185 and Clines, "Etymology," 21-22) *Ṣel* is thought to derive from the basic form צלל "to be/become dark"; cf. Ar. *ẓll* IV, Eth. *salala* II, Akk. *ṣillānû*. See ***TDOT*** 12:372-73 s.v.צל; B. Halper, "The Participial Formations of the Geminate Verbs," ***ZAW*** 30 (1910): 216. On צלל *v.* further: ***The Brown-Driver-Briggs*** *Hebrew* ***and English Lexicon*** (1906; Peabody, Mass.: Hendrickson Publishers, 1996; hereafter ***BDB***) 853 s.v. III צלל; ***HALOT*** 3:1027 s.v. III צלל; ***Lexicon in Veteris Testamenti Libros***, ed. Ludwig Koehler and Walter Baumgartner (Leiden: E.J. Brill, 1985) 804b s.v. III צלל. On the Ar. *ẓll* IV *v.* E.W. Lane, ***Arabic-English Lexicon*** (2 vols.; Cambridge, England : Islamic Texts Society, 1984) 2: 1914 s.v. ظل . On the Akk. *ṣillānû v.* ***CAD*** 16: 188 s.v. *ṣillānû*.

Comparative philological evidence supports the connection between *ṣelem* and *ṣel*: See e.g.: Akk. *ṣalmu* "black::image/statue" and *ṣillu* "shadow::likeness (in a transferred sense; *v.* ***CAD*** 16:190 s.v. *ṣillu*); Old South Arabic *ẓlm/ṣlm* "darkness/black::image/statue" (see A.F.L. Beeston et al, ***Sabaic Dictionary*** (Louvain-la-Neuve: Editions Peeters; Beyrouth: Librairie du Liban, 1982) 143, 172. Thus Sawyer, "The Image of God, The Wisdom of Serpents and the Knowledge of God and Evil," 66; Eybers, "The Root *Ṣ-L*," 29-32; Barr, "The Image of God," 21. *Pace* most recently Wildberger, ***TLOT*** 3:1080, s.v. "צלם"; Stendebach, ***TDOT*** 12:388, s.v. "צלם."

it.[813] This description of Adam as the 'dark image (shadow)' of God is surely related to the biblical designation for the material from which Adam's body was made, *'adāmāh* ('earth': Gen. 2:7). This term suggests a dark reddish-brown inclining towards black.[814] Jewish, Christian and Islamic tradition describes the material of Adam's body as a dark or black substance.[815] A connection between *'adāmāh*, *'ādām* 'human,' and the hue of the first man's skin has been suggested.[816] Adam, as *ṣelem*, is thus God's black body on earth in which God's Spirit/Glory (*kābôd*) incarnates, the sanctuary in which he resides, and the place where he is encountered. The luminous form of God incarnating in a black material body is the equivalent of God's wrapping his luminous form in a bodily 'veil' made from the dark primordial matter (cf. Ps 18:11). These are two descriptions of the same event: God concealing his luminous form in a black material body.

---

[813] ***IDB*** II:683 s.v. "Image of God." In his discussion of *Poimandres* in 1935 C. H. Dodd (***The Bible and the Greeks*** [London: Hodder & Stoughton, 1935] 157-8, n. 1), observing that the Greek terms σκια and ειδος used with regard to the divine Anthropos corresponded with the biblical צלם and דמות used in the creation account of Adam (Gen. 1:26-7), noted: "...certainly there is an old exegetical tradition according to which דמות and צלם in *Genesis* mean 'likeness' and 'shadow' respectively, corresponding fairly well with the *ειδος* and *σκια* of *Poimandres*. Unfortunately, I cannot trace this tradition farther back than the Jesuit Cornelius a Lapide, who died in 1637. Is there any evidence that it was known at a date which would make it possible that the Hermetist was acquainted with this interpretation...?" We can now answer Dobb's question in the affirmative.

[814]Cf. the Akkadian cognates *adamātu*, "dark red earth" and *adamatu* B "black blood." ***CAD*** 1.94; ***TDOT*** 1:75-77 s.v. אדם *'ādhām* by Maass; ibid, 1:88-90 s.v. אדמה*'ᵃdhāmāh* by J.G. Plöger; ***ABD*** 1.62 s.v. Adam by Howard N. Wallace.

[815] Jewish: see e.g. the haggadic tradition according to which Adam was made from dust taken from all four corners of the earth, and this dust was respectively red, black, white and green-"red for the blood, black for the bowls, white for the bones and veins, and green for the pale skin." Ginzberg, ***Legends of the Jews***, 1:55; cf. *PRE* 11 (Frielander trns., 77). The green here at times substitutes for *tekhelet*, the dark blue of the high priestly robe. See Gershom Scholem, "Colours and Their Symbolism in Jewish Tradition and Mysticism: Part I," ***Diogenes*** 108 (1979): 94; Rabbi Alfred Cohen, "Introduction," in idem (ed.) ***Tekhelet: The Renaissance of a Mitzvah*** (New York: Yeshiva University Press, 1996), 3. See also Maimonides who describes the "substance of dust and darkness" from which Adam's body was made. ***The Guide of the Perplexed***, trns. M. Friedlander (New York: E.P. Dutton & Co., 1947) 3.8. Christian: cf. St. Ephrem the Syrian's description of the "dark mass [of dust] *šḥymwt*"; see discussion by Tryggve Kronholm, ***Motifs from Genesis 1-11 in the Genuine Hymns of Ephrem the Syrian*** (Sweden: CWK Gleerup Lund ,1978) 53, 57; Edmund Beck, "Iblis und Mensch, Satan und Adam," ***Mus*** 89 (1976): 214. Islam: Qur'ān 15:28 and parallels: "I am going to create man from sounding clay (*ṣalṣāl*), from fetid black mud (*ḥama' maṣnūn*)."

[816]***ABD*** 1:62; Greenstin, "God's Golem," 221. The latter's statement that Adam's "pinkish complexion and blood share their hue with the reddish clay of earth" must be modified in the light of the Akkadian "dark red earth" and "black blood." See also Josephus, *Antiquities* I, 1.2: "He was called Adam...which signifies one who is red (אדם), because he was formed out of red earth".

7.3.2. *Adam, the Qur'ān, and the Black Body of God*

Through the use of vocabulary and concepts deriving from the ancient Near Eastern cult of images, Gen 1:26-27 (and 2:7) presents Adam as the black body of God on earth. The cult statue *ṣelem/ṣalmu* is usually worshipped as the god. This latter point is not explicitly made in Genesis. It is, however, in the Qur'ān. The creation of Adam is retold in some detail in only slightly varying (though non-contradictory) ways in five surahs in the Qur'ān (*Al-Baqara* 2:28-39; *Al-A'rāf* 7:10-25; *Al-Ḥijr* 15:26-48; *Al-Kahf* 18:51-59; *Ṭāhā* 20:115-123). As Marcia K. Hermansen underlined, each version presents the story of Adam's creation in order to convey a distinct point (thus the slight differences in the retelling).[817] We will begin with *Al-Ḥijr* 15:26-34:

> 26. Surely We created man of dry ringing clay (*ṣalṣāl*),
> Of black mud (*ḥama'*) wrought into shape (*masnūn*)
> 27. And the Jinn We created previously of flaming fire.
> 28. And when your Lord said to the angels, 'See I am creating a man of dry ringing clay, of black mud wrought into shape.
> 29. When I have shaped him, and breathed My spirit into him, then fall down in prostration before him (*fa-qa'ū lahu sajidīn*)
> 30. So the angels prostrated (*sajada*), all of them
> 31. Save Iblīs; he refused to be among the prostrate.
> 32. (God) said: 'O Iblīs! What ails thee, that you art not among the prostrate?'
> 33. He answered: 'I will not bow down (*lā sujud*) before a man whom You have created of dry ringing clay, of black mud wrought into shape.'
> 34. (God) said, 'Then get out hence, for, surely thou art rejected.'

Adam is here described as being made from *ṣalṣāl*, that is "dried clay that produces a sound like pottery (cf. 55:14-15)" and *ḥama'*, fermented black mud (see *ḥamma* 'to blacken, become black'). From these materials Adam's body was wrought into shape (*masnūn*). According to the Islamic commentaries, this black body remained inert and lifeless,

[817] "Pattern and meaning in the qur'ānic Adam narratives," ***Studies in Religion*** 17 (1988): 45 [art.=40-52]. On Adam's creation in the Qur'ān se also: Angelika Neuwirth, "Qur'ān, Crisis and Memory: The Qur'ānic path towards canonization as reflected in the anthropogonic accounts," in Angelika Neuwirth and Andreas Pflitsch (edd.), ***Crisis and Memory in Islamic Societies. Proceedings of the third Summer Academy of Working Group Modernity and Islam held at the Orient Institute of the German Oriental Society in Beirut*** (Beirut, 2001)113-52; Kenneth E. Nolin, "The Story of Adam," ***MW*** 65 (1964): 4-13;

hollow like a statue for forty days (or forty years) before Allah (God) blew his spirit into it, enlivening it.[818] Behind this imagery is surely the ancient Near Eastern cult statute enlivened through the *mīs pî* and *pit pî* rituals.[819] This background is confirmed by the fact that after this 'enlivening' the angels are ordered to make prostration before Adam. *Sajada* is what Muslims do when praying to God. It is worship of God: "And to Allah makes prostration every living creature that is in the heavens and the earth, and the angels too (16:49)"; "Whoever is in the heavens and the earth bows before Allah only, willingly or unwilling." But here Adam is worshipped by the angels, on God's own orders. Iblīs, which name derives from the Greek *diabolus* "Devil," refused to worship this black Adam. Why? "I (Iblīs) am better than he; You (God) have created me from fire, him You have created of clay (7:12)." For Iblīs's pride and disobedience he was cast out of heaven to become *Shayṭān* or Satan.[820]

In surah 2:30, this black Adam whom the angels of God are ordered to worship is described as God's *khalīfa*.[821] The basic meaning of the root *kh-l-f*, as Wadād al-Qāḍī has demonstrated,[822] is "to succeed and replace or substitute for another." As the cult statue substituted for the god on earth; as the Hebrew Adam as *ṣelem* substituted for God on earth; so too does the qur'ānic Adam as *khalīfa* substitute for God on earth ('I am going to place a *khalīfa* in the earth [*fi 'l-arḍi*]' 2:30). The

---

[818] Al-Ṭabarī reports in his commentary (*ad* Surah 2:30) from Ibn ʿAbbās: "He (Adam) remained forty nights as an inert body, and Iblīs used to come to him and kick him, and he (Adam) gave a hollow ring like a clay pot...Then he (Iblīs) used to go in (Adam) through his mouth and come out through his rear, and go in through his rear and come out through his mouth; then (Iblīs) said: 'You are nothing'-to the hollow ring...When God breathed into (Adam) of His spirit, breath came from the front of his head, and everything which came to flow from it became flesh and blood. And when the breathing had reached his navel, he looked and marveled at how beautiful was what he saw." Translation from J. Cooper in ***The Commentary of the Qur'ān by Abū Jaʿfar Muḥammad b. Jarīr al-Ṭabarī*** (Oxford: Oxford University Press, 1987) 1:212-13.

[819] On the Qur'ān and ancient Near Eastern mythic tradition see: Aaron Hughes, "The stranger at the sea: Mythopoesis in the Qur'ân and early tafsîr," ***Studies in Religion*** 32 (2003): 261-279; Jonathan P. Berkey, ***The Formation of Islam: Religion and Society in the Near East, 600-1800*** (Cambridge: Cambridge University Press, 2003) Chapter Six; Mondher Sfar, ***Le Coran, la Bible et l'Orient ancien*** (Paris: Cassini, 1997).

[820] On Iblīs in Muslim tradition see Peter J. Awn, ***Satan's Tragedy and Redemption: Iblīs in Sufi Psychology*** (SHR 44; Leiden: E.J. Brill, 1983)

[821] "While some commentators have speculated whether man was made a successor to another species which held the title of *khalīfah* before him, we can safely accept the majority opinion that man was made the caliph of God." Mustanir Mir, "Adam in the Qur'ān," ***Islamic Culture*** 62 (1988): 4 [art.=1-11].

[822] "The Term 'Khalīfa' in Early Exegetical Literature," ***Die Welt des Islams*** 28 (1988): 392-411. See also Lane, ***Lexicon***, 1:792-98 s.v. خلف .

Hebrew *ṣelem* and Arabic *khalīfa* are cognate concepts.[823] Similar to the Hebrew Adam-as-*ṣelem*, the Qur'ānic Adam-as-*khalīfa* is the likeness (*mithl*) or form (*ṣūra*) of God.[824] As noted above, surat *Al-Shūrā* 42:11 *Laysa kamithlihi shay'*, "There is nothing like Him," means literally "There is nothing like His likeness (*mithlihi*)." His likeness, some taught, is Adam, the Perfect Man (*al-Insān al-Kāmil*).[825] According to the *hadith* of Prophet Muhammad, "God created Adam according to His form (*ṣūratihi*)."[826] Adam therefore has the form, the appearance, of God, as does the Hebrew Adam as *ṣelem*.

The interconnection between the concepts 'Adam-as-statue,' 'Adam-as-*khalīfa*,' and 'Adam-as-likeness' is made in a tradition recorded by the great Qur'ān commentator al-Ṭabarī, which he narrates as part of his explication of sura 2:30.[827] After molding the human body of Adam, his *khalīfa*, from the *ḥama'*, black mud,[828] the body was left standing as a hollow, lifeless statue for forty years; Allah did not blow his breath into Adam. During this time, the angels saw Adam and were terrified at the sight, none more than Iblīs. Iblīs would strike Adam's body, making a hollow ring. He then went into Adam's body through his mouth, exiting through his rear. Iblīs then said to the frightened angels: "Do not be afraid of this: your Lord is solid (*ṣamad*), but this is hollow. Indeed, if I am given power over it, I shall utterly destroy it."[829] This last statement gives us the reason the angels were terrified: they thought the Adam statue was God. As observed above, this idea has a Jewish precedent. In ***Genesis Rabbah***, we read: "Said R. Hoshaiah:

---

[823] Glaser, "Qur'ānic Challenges," 11 in her comparative look at the biblical *ṣelem 'ĕlōhîm* and qur'ānic *khalīfatu llāh* concepts demonstrated a real comprehension of neither. This is unfortunate, for Glaser's study is otherwise insightful. On the relatedness of the two concepts see Abraham I. Katsh, ***Judaism in Islām: Biblical and Talmudic Backgrounds of the Koran and its Commentaries*** (New York: Bloch Publishing Company, 1954) 26 n. 2.

[824] *Contra* Glaser, "Qur'ānic Challenges," 14. Though this idea of "likeness" is not necessarily implied by the lexical connotations of the word, the qur'ānic and traditional (i.e. *ḥadīth*) presentation of Adam invests the concept of *khalīfatu llāh* when applied to Adam with the sense of 'likeness."

[825] See discussion above.

[826] See discussion above.

[827] Cooper, ***Commentary***, 214-15.

[828] As Al-Ṭabarī reports it, God first gathers red, white and black earth, moistens it so that it becomes 'clinging clay,' which, after a while, became *ḥama'*. From this *ḥama'* the body of Adam was made. See Cooper, ***Commentary***, 215.

[829] Translated by Cooper, ***Commentary***, 214-15. On the creation of Adam in Muslim tradition see further Leigh N.B. Chipman, "Mythic Aspects of the Process of Adam's Creation in Judaism and Islam," ***Studia Islamica*** 93 (2001) 5-25; ; M.J. Kister, "Ādam: A Study of Some Legends in *Tafsīr* and *Ḥadīṯ* Literature" ; J.-C Vadet, "La creation et l'investiture de l'homme dans le sunnisme ou la légende d'Adam chez al-Kisā'ī," ***Studia Islamica*** 42 (1975): 5-37.

When the Holy One, blessed be He, came to create the first man, the ministering angels mistook him (viz. Adam) [for God, since man was in God's image,] and wanted to say before him, 'Holy, [holy, holy is the Lord of hosts].'"[830] In the Islamic version, the angels are disabused of this belief once it was learned that Adam's body was hollow; Allah, the angels well knew, has a compact and solid (*samad*), black body.[831] However, once Allah blew his breath into Adam's body, he lived, and the angels made prostration before him. That this is a picture of Allah's incarnation in the body of Adam was explicitly stated by some Muslims whom al-Baghdādi (d. 1037 AD) labeled *ḥulūlīya*, "incarnationists." He reports from ʿAbd al-Qāhir:

> I found one (of them) citing, in proof of the possibility of God's incarnation in bodies, God's word to the angels regarding Adam: "So that when I have made him complete and breathed into him of my spirit, fall down making obeisance to him". (The incarnationist) held that God commanded the angels to bow down before Adam only because he embodied himself in Adam and really abode in him because he created him in the most beautiful form. Therefore, (God) said: "We have created man in the finest form (95:4)."[832]

Al-Baghdādi's polemical tone notwithstanding, these so-called *ḥulūlīya* correctly perceived the implications of the qur'ānic narrative. In both Sunnī and Shīʿī tradition we learn that before the creation of the world God brought forth an anthropomorphic light, usually identified with *Nūr Muḥammadī* (the Light of Muḥammad), from whose body the celestial world is sometimes said to be derived. When Allah (God) breathed of his spirit into Adam, the *Nūr Muḥammadī* 'incarnated' in the molded body of Adam.[833]

---

[830]Jacob Neusner, ***The Incarnation of God: The Character of Divinity in Formative Judaism*** (Philadelphia: Fortress Press, 1988) 3.

[831] On this tradition see especially Josef van Ess, ***The Youthful God: Anthropomorphism in Early Islam*** (Tempe, AZ: Department of Religious Studies, Arizona State University, 1988) 1-2.

[832] Abu Manṣūr ʿAbd al-Qāhir b. Ṭāhir al-Baghdādi, ***al-Farq Bayn al-Firaq***, translated by Abraham S. Halkin, ***Moselm Schisms and Sects (Al-Farḳ Bain al-Firaḳ), Veing the History of the Various Philosophical Systems Developed in Islam*** (Tel Aviv, 1935) 79.

[833] U. Rubin, "Pre-existence and Light: Aspects of the concept of *Nūr Muḥammadī*, ***Israel Oriental Studies*** 5 (1975):62-119; John MacDonald, "Islamic Eschatology-1: The Creation of Man and the Angels in the Eschatological Literature," ***Islamic Studies*** 3 (1964): 285-308.

In this regard, Ida J. Glaser's work is significant. Glaser has well argued that the qur'ānic account of Adam's creation should be read as a comment on and complement to the Bible's account.[834] When the Hebrew and Arabic accounts are read together, it becomes apparent that the qur'ānic account (1) fills in gaps in the biblical account (e.g. who was God talking to in Gen. 1:26 ["Let *US* make man"]; the Qur'ān answers: the Exalted Assembly or council of angels) (2) offers explanations to aspects of the biblical account (e.g. the reason the serpent tempted Adam and Eve: because on Adam's account he (Iblīs) was cast out of Paradise) and (3) offers corrections to aspects of the biblical account (e.g. while the Genesis account has Adam and Eve prevaricating after being discovered in the wrong, the qur'ānic account has them repenting immediately). When the qur'ānic account is read as such commentary on the biblical account,[835] an unmistakable observation jumps out at us: the Qur'ān does not deny or correct the Genesis Adam-as-*ṣelem* theology, but confirms it in a most blatant way: where the Genesis account lacks only a description of the cult-statue (Adam-as-*ṣelem*) receiving the worship that cult-statues normally receive, THE QUR'ĀNIC ACCOUNT PROVIDES IT.

The History-of-Religions background to this qur'ānic tradition sheds important light on it and demonstrates that indeed the qur'ānic 'Adam-as-*khalīfa*' theology is cognate to the Biblical 'Adam-as-*ṣelem*' theology. Peter J. Awn, in his study on Iblīs in Muslim (mainly Sufi) tradition, underlined the importance of this background:

> Any summary sketch of the figure of Iblīs/Ash-Shayṭān based on the Qur'ānic text should not be attempted in intellectual isolation from the broader religious milieu in which Islam developed. For the Qur'ān is understood by Muslims to be the culmination of God's revelation of His Word, supplanting and correcting both the Torah of the Jews and the Gospel of the Christians. The sacred books of these two communities, Muslims believe, have been corrupted by the adherents of these traditions. Consequently, it is only by studying the Qur'ān that one comes to a true knowledge of the meaning of God's revelation.
>
> Because of the continuity professed by the Muslim Community among Torah, Gospel, and Qur'ān, it is not at all

---

834 "Qur'ānic Challenges for Genesis," ***JSOT*** 75 (1997): 3-19.

835 Mir's suggestion ("Adam in the Qur'ān," 1) that "the Qur'ānic version of the story (of Adam's creation) differs from the Biblical not only in respect of factual detail, but, more importantly, in respect of notional framework as well," is therefore much overstated.

strange to find resonances between the Qur'ānic Iblīs passages and particular pre-Islamic Jewish and Christian sources.[836]

One of these pre-Islamic sources that parallels and can surely shed some light on the qur'ānic account is the non-canonical Jewish work *Vita Adae et Evae* (Life of Adam and Eve) mentioned above. This work dates no later than the fourth CE.[837] In this text we find the Devil, *diabolus* (=Iblīs), explaining to Adam why he tempted him and Eve, getting them cast out of Paradise:

> (*diabolus*) replied…"It is on account of you (Adam) that I was cast down from there. When you were formed, I was cast out of God's presence and I was excluded from the company of angels. When God breathed into you the spirit of life, and your face and likeness were made in the image of God, Michael led you forth and made us worship you in the sight of God.
>
> "The Lord said: 'Behold Adam! I made you in Our image and likeness.' And Michael went out and summoned all the angels, saying, 'Worship the image of the Lord God as the Lord God prescribed!' Michael himself worshipped first, then he summoned me and said, 'Worship the image of Jehova.' I answered, "I am not obliged to worship Adam…I will not worship my inferior and junior. In creation I am his senior; before he was made, I already had been made. He ought to worship me…
>
> "And the Lord God was angry with me and he banished me together with my angels from our glory. It is on account of you we were expelled from our habitation and cast down to earth…And through deceit I cheated your wife and caused you to be expelled through her…[838]

In another version of this same tradition the Devil specifies that he refused to bow to Adam because: "I am from fire; I was the first angel formed. Am I about to bow down before clay and matter?"[839] The parallels with the qur'ānic account are remarkable. *Diabolus*, the Greek devil who became in Arabic Iblīs refuses to worship Adam because he is older in creation and made of fire, while Adam is younger and made of clay and matter. For this arrogance and disobedience *diabolus* is cast

836 Awn, ***Satan's Tragedy***, 20.
837 See above.
838 Awn's translation, ***Satan's Tragedy***, 20-21 n. 14.
839 From the *Gospel of St. Bartholomew*, fourth-fifth century AD. See Awn, ***Satan's Tragedy***, 21 n. 17.

to the earth, and for this reason temps Adam and Eve out of vengeance. The important detail here is that it is specifically stated that Adam is to be worshipped *because he is the Image of God.* This pre-Islamic tradition therefore mediates (in time and content) between the Genesis 'Adam-as-*ṣelem*' theology and qur'ānic 'Adam-as-*khalīfa*' theology, in fact capturing the essence of both.

7.4. *The High Priest and the Blue-Black Body of God*

In the ancient Near East the temple was the stage on which the cosmogonic activities of the gods were ritually reenacted by priest-actors.[840] In ancient Babylon, for example, portions of the *Enūma eliš*, the Babylonian creation myth, were theatrically presented in the temple during the *akītu* (New Year's) festival. The victory of the creator-god Marduk over Tiamat, the personified chaos waters, was reenacted in the temple by priests impersonating the divine combatants. In the cosmogonic liturgies* of ancient Israel the role of creator-god, Yahweh-El, was played by the high priest Aaron (and his sons). According to Crispin H.P. Fletcher-Louis, "*within the liturgy* of the* (Israelite) *cult the high priest plays the role of creator of the universe* (emphasis original)."[841] Thus, "As God brought *'ôr* (light) to darkness

---

[840]On the ritual re-enactment of cosmogonic myth in the ANE and elsewhere *v.* Benjamin D. Sommer, "The Babylonian Akitu Festival: rectifying the king or renewing the cosmos?," ***JANES*** 27 (2000): 81-95; Stephen D. Ricks, "Liturgy and Cosmogony: The Ritual Use of Creation Accounts in the Ancient Near East," and Brian M. Hauglid, "Sacred Time and Temple" in Donald W. Parry (ed.), ***Temples of the Ancient world: Ritual and Symbolism*** (Salt Lake City, Utah: Deseret Book Company; Provo, Utah: FARMS, 1994) 118-125, 636-645; Mircea Eliade, ***The Myth of the Eternal Return, or, Cosmos and History***, translated from the French by Willard R. Trask (Princeton: Princeton University Press, 1954).

[841]***All The Glory of Adam: Liturgical Anthropology in the Dead Sea Scrolls*** (Leiden: Brill, 2002) 74; idem, "The Cosmology of P and the Theological Anthropology in the Wisdom of Jesus ben Sira" in C.A. Evans (ed.), ***Of Scribes and Sages: Studies in Early Jewish Interpretation and Transmission of Scripture*** (2 vols.; SSEJC 8; Sheffield; Sheffield Academic Press, 2004) 69-113 (77). See also Margaret Barker, "The High Priest and the Worship of Jesus," in Carey C. Newman, James R. Davila and Gladys S. Lewis (edd.), ***Jewish Roots of Christological Monotheism. Papers from the St. Andrews Conference on the Historical Origins of the Worship of Jesus*** (Leiden: Brill, 1999) 93-111. Fletcher-Louis has without doubt most clearly and convincingly elucidated the high priestly theological anthropology implied by this intratextuality. See also his "The image of God and the biblical roots of Christian sacramentality," in Geoffrey Rowell and Christine Hall (edd.), ***the Gestures of God: explorations in sacramentality*** (London and New York: Continuum, 2004) 73-89; idem, "God's Image, His Cosmic Temple and the High Priest: Towards an Historical and Theological Account of the Incarnation," in Alexander and Cathercole, ***Heaven on Earth***, 81-99; idem, "Wisdom Christology and the Parting of the Ways Between Judaism and Christianity," in Stanely E. Porter and Brook W.R. Pearson (edd.), ***Christian-Jewish Relations through the Centuries*** (JSNTS 192; Sheffield; Sheffield Academic Press, 2000) 52-68; idem, "The High Priest as Divine

(Gen 1 $_{2-3}$), so Aaron caused *ma'ôr* (light) to shine throughout the night,"[842] i.e. during the morning and evening sacrifice performed in the Temple. The Aaronic high priest bore the ineffable name 'Yahweh' inscribed on the front of his turban;[843] he was enveloped in Yahweh's own fragrance (the 'etheric robe of divinity'[844]); and he consumed Yahweh's own portion of *leḥem pānîm* ('Bread of the Presence') during the sacrifices.[845] He was, in short, Yahweh in the Temple. Margaret Barker observes: "There is an abundance of evidence…that the high priest was the Lord (i.e. Yahweh) and that the beliefs of the first temple were still known at the end of the second temple period."[846] Crispin H.T. Fletcher-Louis has now assembled that "abundance of evidence" in a fascinating article, in which he demonstrates that during the Second Temple period (515 BC-70 AD) the high priest was treated as the very presence of Yahweh and indeed worshipped.[847]
In the ancient Near Eastern temple cult the chief priest wore the garment of his god and represented that god's visible presence in the temple, as the cult statue otherwise did.[848] The high-priestly garments (Figure 25) prescribed in Exodus 28[849] are Israel's version of the ancient Near Eastern 'garments of the gods,' which adorned the cult

---

Mediator in the Hebrew Bible: Dan 7:13 as a Test Case," ***SBL 1997 Seminar Papers*** 36 (1997): 161-193, esp. 186-193.
[842] Kearney, "Creation and Liturgy," 375.
[843] According to the normal reading of the MT (Ex. 28:36) the *ṣîṣ* fastened to the mitre bears the words קדש ליהוה, usually rendered "Holy to Yahweh." In 1924 James Edward Hogg ("A Note on Two Points in Aaron's Headdress," ***JTS*** 26 [1924-25]: 72-75) argued that the proper reading of Ex. 28:36 is simply "and engrave on it (i.e. the *ṣîṣ*) the holy name 'YHWH'." He later supported this reading with evidence from late Second Temple texts: "The Inscription on Aaron's Head-Dress." ***JTS*** 28 (1926-27): 287-88.
[844] Words quoted by P.A.H. De Boer, "An Aspect of Sacrifice. II. God's Fragrance," in ***Studies in the Religion of Ancient Israel*** (Leiden: Brill, 1972) 27-47 (39). See also C. Houtman, "On the Function of the Holy Incense (Exodus XXX 34-8) and the Sacred Anointing Oil (Exodus XXX 22-33)," ***VT*** 42 (1992): 458-465.
[845] See Roy Gane " 'Bread of the Presence' and Creator-In-Residence," ***VT*** 42 (1992): 179-203.
[846] Margaret Barker, "The High Priest and the Worship of Jesus," in Carey C. Newman, James R. Davila and Gladys S. Lewis (edd.), ***Jewish Roots of Christological Monotheism. Papers from the St. Andrews Conference on the Historical Origins of the Worship of Jesus*** (Leiden: Brill, 1999) 107 [art.=93-111]
[847] "Alexander the Great's Worship of the High Priest," in Loren T. Stuckenbruck and Wendy E.S. North (edd.), ***Early Jewish and Christian Monotheism*** (London: T&T Clark International, 2004) 71-102
[848] Sauren, "Kleidung," 96-7.
[849] (1) a long dark blue robe (*me'îl*), the hem of which was lined with cloth pomegranates and flowers and gold bells; (2) an apron-like ephod (Heb. *'êphôd*), made of "gold, of blue, purple, and crimson yarns, and of fine twisted linen (Exod. 28:6);" upon the ephod was fastened (3) a breastplate (*hōšen*) consisting of twelve precious stones; (4) a golden frontlet or diadem (*sîs zâhâb*) engraved with "Glory to the Lord"; but cf, below n. 36.

statues representing the god to whom the temple was dedicated.[850] The high priest wore a long robe (*me'îl*) made of the color *tĕkēlet*. This is a dark blue, which, in rabbinic tradition, is specifically identified as sapphiric blue.[851] Over this sapphiric blue robe the high priest wore an אפוד *'êphôd*, which was a girdle-like over-garment embroidered in gold and encrusted with precious stones and jewels (Exod. 28:6-30). This ephod is analogous to the splendid jewel-studded, golden garments that adorned the idols of the ancient Near Eastern cult of images.[852] Thus, "The high priest wears the golden and jewel studded garments which in non-Israelite religion are worn by the idols of the gods."[853] This is because, as the cult-statue represented the physical presence of the god in the temple, so too did the Israelite high-priest represent the physical presence of Yahweh-El in the Jerusalem Temple.

Together the sapphiric-blue robe and gold-embroidered ephod of the Israelite high priest corresponded to the 'sky-garment' of the ancient Near Eastern deities.[854] This sky-garment, as we saw above,

---

[850] As pointed out by Fletcher-Louis, "The High Priest as Divine Mediator," 188. See further below. On the 'garments of the gods' *v.* also Parpola, ***Sky-Garment***; Herbert Sauren, "Die Kleidung Der Götter," ***Visible Religion*** 2 (1984): 95-117; A. Leo Oppenheim, "The Golden Garments of the Gods," ***Journal of Near Eastern Society of Columbia University*** 8 (1949): 172-193; David Freedman, "Ṣubāt Bāšti: A Robe of Splendor," ***JANES*** 4 (1972): 91-5. See also Alan Miller, "The Garments of the Gods in Japanese Ritual," ***Journal of Ritual Studies*** 5 (Summer 1991): 33-55.

[851] Ben Zion Bokser, "The Thread of Blue," ***Proceedings of the American Academy for Jewish Research*** 31 (1963): 13-13 [art.=1-31]

[852] Fletcher-Louis, "The High Priest as Divine Mediator," 188; ***CTA*** 5.I.I-5; ***The Anchor Bible Dictionary*** (6 vols.; New York, NY: Doubleday, 1992-; hereafter ***ABD***) 2: 550, s.v. "Ephod" by Carol Meyers. On the ephod *v.* also Menahem Haran, ***Temples and Temple-Service in Ancient Israel*** (Oxford: The Clarendon Press, 1978) 166-68.

[853] Fletcher-Louis, "Worship of Divine Humanity," 127; "The High Priest as Divine Mediator," 188.

[854] In some later representations of Aaron the robe and ephod are depicted in such a way as to recall the association with sapphiric heavens. In the mosaic from the synagogue in Sepphoris (ca. fifth century) Aaron's robe is depicted dark blue with golden dots and in a wall-painting at Dura Europos (3 cent. AD.) Aaron dons a wine-colored, jewel-studded cape, which some scholars take to be a representation of the robe or ephod (See Ze'ev Weiss and Ehud Netzer, ***Promise and Redemption: A Synagogue Mosaic from Sepphoris*** (Jerusalem: The Israel Museum, 1996), 20ff; Swartz, "The Semiotics of the Priestly Vestments," 63 n. 16; C.H. Kraeling, ***The Excavations at Dura Europos: The Synagogue*** (Final Report vol. 8 Part 1) (New Haven: Yale University Press, 1956; repr. New York: Ktav, 1979) 127; Erwin R. Goodenough, "Cosmic Judaism: The Temple of Aaron," in his ***Jewish Symbols,*** 9:16). The yellow jewels are similar to the gold dots on the priestly robe in the Sepphoris mosaic and both suggests the stars on the divine 'sky-garment.' See Swartz, "The Semiotics of the Priestly Vestments," 63 n. 16; Weiss and Netzer, ***Promise and Redemption***, 45 n. 31. The parallel between lapis lazuli, the ANE 'sky-garment,' and these depictions of the high-priestly vestments is unmistakable.

Figure 25

Jewish High Priest in special garments

represented the sapphiric body of the creator-god. The same was true in ancient Israel's cultic tradition. "Garment" is a common metaphor for body in biblical, Jewish, Samaratain, Christian, and Gnostic literature.[855] That this was true with regard to the high priestly garments is demonstrated by a wide range of Second and Post-Temple texts associated with priestly tradition:[856] the Apocalyptic literature,[857] Philo of Alexandria (ca. 15 BC-50 AD),[858] and rabbinic tradition[859] are

---

[855] Jung Hoon Kim, ***The Significance of Clothing Imagery in the Pauline Corpus*** (London and New York: T&T Clark International, 2004); Nils Alstrup Dahl and David Hellholm, "Garment-Metaphors: the Old and the New Human Being," Adela Yarbro Collins and Margaret M. Mitchell (edd.), ***Antiquity and Humanity. Essays on Ancient Religion and Philosophy Presented to Hans Dieter Betz on His 70th Birthday*** (Tübingen: Mohr Siebeck, 2001) 139-158; April D. De Conick and Jarl Fossum, "Stripped before God: A New Interpretation of Logion 37 in the Gospel of Thomas," ***VC*** 45 (1991): 123-150; April D. De Conick, "The *Dialogue of the Savior* and the Mystical Sayings of Jesus," ***VC*** 50 (1996): 190-2; Sebastion Brock, "Clothing Metaphors as a Means of Theological Expression in Syriac Tradition," in ***Typus, Symbol, Allegorie bei den östlichen Vätern und ihren Parallelen im Mittelalter*** (Eichstätter Beiträge 4; Regensburg 1982): 11-37; S. David Garber, "Symbolism of Heavenly Robes in the New Testament in Comparison with Gnostic Thought" (Ph.D diss., Princeton University, 1974); Geo Widengren, ***The Great Vohu Manah and the Apostle of God: Studies in Iranian and Manichaean Religion*** (Uppsala: A.-B. Lundequistska Bokhandeln, 1945) 50-55, 76-83. On the Platonic use of this metaphor *v.* J.M. Rist, "A Common Metaphor," in idem, ***Plotinus: The Road to Reality*** (London: Cambridge University Press, 1967) 188-198; Dennis Ronald MacDonald, ***There is no Male and Female: The Fate of a Dominical Saying in Paul and Gnosticism*** (Philadelphia: Fortress Press, 1987), 23-25.

[856] Stephen N. Lambden, "From Fig Leaves to Fingernails: Some Notes on the Garments of Adam and Eve in the Hebrew Bible and Select Early Postbiblical Jewish Writings," in Paul Morris and Deborah Sawyer (edd.), ***A Walk in the Garden: Biblical, Iconographical and Literary Images of Eden*** (Sheffeild: JSOT Press, 1992) 79ff; Hugh Nibley, "Sacred Vestments," in idem, ***Temple and Cosmos: Beyond This Ignorant Present***, The Collected Works of Hugh Nibley: Volume 12 Ancient History, edited by Dan E. Norton (Salt Lake City, Utah: Deseret Book Company; Provo, Utah: FARMS, 1992) 91-138; John A. Tvedtnes, "Priestly Clothing in Biblical Times," in Donald w. Parry (ed.), ***Temples of the Ancient world: Ritual and Symbolism*** (Salt Lake City, Utah: Deseret Book Company; Provo, Utah: FARMS, 1994) 649-704. On Jewish interpretation of the vestments in general *v.* Michael D. Swartz, "The Semiotics of the Priestly Vestments in Ancient Judaism," in ***Sacrifice in Religious Experience***, Albert I. Baumgarten, ed. (Leiden: Brill, 2002) 57-80; Robert Hayward, "St Jerome and the Meaning of the High-Priestly Vestments," in ***Hebrew Study From Ezra to Ben-Yehuda***, William Horbury, ed. (Edinburgh: T&T Clark, 1999) 90-105.

[857] In *2 Enoch* 22:8-10 and *3 Enoch* 12:1-3; 15:1 the high priestly vestments with which Enoch was clothed are identified with a body of divine glory. See ...Barker, ***On Earth***; See further Tvedtnes, "Priestly Clothing." On the Enoch books and priestly tradition see Margaret Barker, ***The Older Testament: The Survival of Themes from the Ancient Royal Cult in Sectarian Judaism and Early Christianity*** (London: SPCK, 1987).

[858] Philo, *Leg.* 2:55-56; Kim, ***Significance***, 44-52; Conick and Fossum, "Stripped before God," 128f. Dennis Ronald MacDonald, ***There is no Male and Female***, 25. For Philo, the white tunic worn by the high priest on the Day of Atonement was the 'heavenly garment of light (*Fuga.* 110) and represented the purified soul, that 'fair and lovely form (ειδος, *eidos*; *De Ebrietate* [hereafter *Ebr.*] 157; 85-6; *Mut.* 45-6),' 'most radiant light

examples. Clothed in his splendid garments, the high priest represented Yahweh's physical, bodily presence in the Temple. His sapphiric garment represented Yahweh-El's sapphiric body. This 'sapphiric' body of Yahweh-El is related to the black, cloud-like body (ערפל *'ărāpel*) in the same way the black body of the ANE deities is related to their sapphiric blue body: the luminous *kābôd* passing through the pores of the black skin produces a 'sapphiric' glow.

7.5. *Gnosticism and the Jewish Secret of the Black God*

According to the esoteric theology of the Jerusalem priesthood God was a divine man with a black body, called in the Hebrew Bible *'ărāpel* which means literally "thick blackness." According to this priestly theology, God at creation was originally a divine man of pure light, with a body of pure light called his *kābôd* or 'Glory'. Because the intensity of this light threatened to burn the material world, Yahweh-Elohim, the Creator-God of Israel/the Bible, cloaked his luminous body, *kābôd*, with an external black body, *'ărāpel*. This black body served as a 'veil' to his luminous body, refracting the intense light so as to not burn up creation. This was the esoteric theology of the Jerusalem

---

(*Somn.* I.202, 216-17). See also Margaret Barker, ***On Earth***, Chapt. V; idem, "Temple Imagery in Philo," 91; idem, ***Gate of Heaven***, 113-115; idem, ***Great Angel***, 125; Harald Riesenfeld, ***Jésus Transfiguré. L'Arrière-plan du Récit Évangélique de la Transfiguration de Notre-Seigneur*** (København, 1947) Chapitre VIII; W. Schwarz, 'A Study in Pre-Christian Symbolism: Philo, De Somniis I.216-218, and Plutarch, De Iside et Osiride 4 and 77,' ***Bulletin of the Institute of Classical Studies*** 20 (1973): 104-117; Haran, ***Temples and Temple-Service***, 174. The blue robe symbolized the outward, visible 'soul-body.' See *Ebr.* 85-6; *Mut.* 45. On Philo's allegorization of the vestments see further C.T.R. Hayward, ***The Jewish Temple: A non-biblical sourcebook*** (London and New York: Routledge, 1996) 108-118; Coulon, "The Logos High Priest," 19ff; Margaret Barker, ***The Gate of Heaven: The History and Symbolism of the Temple in Jerusalem*** (London: SPCK, 1991) 111ff.

[859] Ginzberg, ***Legends***, 1:177, 332, 5:93; Stephen D. Ricks, "The Garment of Adam in Jewish, Muslim, and Christian Tradition," in Benjamin H. Hary, John L. Hayes and Fred Astren (edd.), ***Judaism and Islam: Boundaries, Communications and Interactions*** (Leiden: Brill, 2000) 209; M.E. Vogelzang and W.J. van Bekkum, "Meaning and Symbolism of Clothing in Ancient Near Eastern Texts," in ***Scripta signa vocis: studies about scripts. Scriptures, scribes, and languages in the Near East, presented to J.H. Hospers by his pupils, colleagues, and friends*** (Groningen: E. Forsten, 1986) 275; Gary Anderson, ***Genesis of Perfection: Adam and Eve in Jewish and Christian Imagination*** (Louisville: Westminster John Knox Press, 2001) 117-134; idem, "The Garments of Skin in Apocryphal Narrative and Biblical Commentary," in James L. Kugel (ed.), ***Studies in Ancient Midrash***, (Cambridge: Harvard University Center for Jewish Studies, 2001) 110-125; De Conick and Fossum, "Stripped Before God," 124-25; Wayne A. Meeks, "The Image of the Androgyne: Some Uses of A Symbol in Earliest Christianity," ***HR*** 13 (1974): 187-88; Smith, "Garments of Shame," 231; Lambden, "From Fig Leaves to Fingernails," 86f.

priesthood who were responsible for the Hebrew Bible as we know it. Around the 1st century AD, a particular circle of priests left the temple (certainly spiritually, maybe physically as well if the Temple in Jerusalem still stood at the time) and revolted against the faith of their ancestors. These renegade priests would become the earliest developers of the 'Gnostic myth' as classically defined.[860]

Gnosticism was a religious/philosophical movement of the 1st - 4th centuries AD. Though this movement was made up of various groups,[861] the earliest formed around this group of Jewish priests

---

[860] On Jewish traditions in (Sethian) Gnosticism see P.S. Alexander, "Jewish Elements in Gnosticsim and Magic *c.* CE 70-*c.* 270," in William Horbury, W.D. Davies and John Sturdy (edd.), ***The Cambridge History of Judaism***, III: ***The Early Roman Period*** (Cambridge: Cambridge University Press, 1999) 1052-1059; Kurt Rudolph, "Ein Grundtyp gnostischer Urmensch-Adam-Speculation," in idem, ***Gnosis und spätantike Religionsgeschichte: gesammelte Aufsätze*** (NHMS 42; Leiden: E.J. Brill, 1996) 123-43; Gilles Quispel ,"Anthropos and Sophia," ***Religion im Erbe Agyptens: Beitrage zur spatantiken Religionsgeschichte zu Ehren von Alexander Bohlig*** (Wiesbaden: In Kommission bei O. Harrass, 1988) 168-85; idem, "Der gnostische Anthropos und die jüdische Tradition," ***Eranos Jahrbuch*** 22 (1953): 195-234; idem, "Ezekiel 1:26 in Jewish Mysticism and Gnosis," ***VC*** 34 (1980): 1-13; Gedaliahu Stroumsa, ***Another Seed: Studies in Gnostic Mythology*** (Leiden: E. J. Brill, 1984); Birger A. Pearson, "Jewish Sources in Gnostic Literature," in ***Jewish Writings of the Second Temple Period: Apocrypha, Pseudepigrapha, Qumran Sectarian Writings, Philo, Josephus***, ed. Michael E. Stone (Assen and Philadelphia: Van Gorcum, Fortress, 1984) 443-481; idem, ***Gnosticism, Judaism, and Egyptian Christianity*** (Minneapolis; Fortress Press, 1990); Madeleine Scopello, "The Apocalypse of Zostrianos (Nag Hammadi VIII.1) and the Book of the Secrets of Enoch," ***VC*** 34 (1980): 376-385; Francis T Fallon, ***The Enthronement of Sabaoth: Jewish Elements in Gnostic Creation Myths*** (Leiden: E J Brill, 1978); Ithamar Gruenwald, "Jewish Sources for the Gnostic Texts From Nag Hammadi?" ***Proceedings of the Sixth World Congress of Jewish Studies*** (3 vols.; Jerusalem: World Union of Jewish Studies, 1975-77) 3:49-52 (=idem, ***From Apocalyptic to Gnosticism*** [Frankfurt am Main, etc.; Peter Lang, 1988] 207-220). On Jewish tradition in Gnosticism more broadly defined see April D. De Conick, "Becoming God's Body: The KAVOD in Valentinianism," ***SBL 1995 Seminar Papers Series***, 23-36; idem, "Heavenly Temple Traditions and Valentinian Worship: A Case for First-Century Christology in the Second Century," in Carey C Newman et al (edd.), ***Jewish Roots of Christological Monotheism: papers from the St Andrew's conference on the historical origins of the worship of Jesus*** (Leiden : E J Brill, 1999) 308-341; Fossum, ***Name of God***; idem, "The Magharians: A Pre-Christian Jewish Sect and its Significance for the Study of Gnosticism and Christianity," ***Henoch*** 11 (1987): 303-343; George W MacRae, "The Jewish Background of the Gnostic Sophia Myth," ***NovTest*** 12 (1970): 86-101; John C. Reeves, "Jewish Pseudepigrapha in Manichaean Literature: The Influence of the Enochic Library," in idem (ed.) ***Tracing the Threads: Studies in the Vitality of Jewish Pseudepigrapha*** (Atlanta: Scholars Press, 1994)173-203; idem, ***Jewish Lore in Manichaean Cosmogony: Studies in the*** **Book of Giants** ***Traditions*** (Cincinnati, OH; Hebrew Union College Press, 1992).

[861] L. King, ***What is Gnosticism?*** (Cambridge, Mass. And London: The Belknap Press of Harvard University Press, 2003); ***Rethinking "Gnosticism": An Argument for Dismantling a Dubious Category*** (Princeton, New Jersey: Princeton University Press, 1996).

Figure 26

Sophia-Achamoth, Gnostic representation of the black material body of Yahweh, the God of Israel

who,[862] amazingly, developed a disgust for the God of Israel. What was it about the God of their ancestors that they found so loathsome? Gnostic texts such the "Apocraphon of John," the "Hypostasis of the Archons," and "On the Origin of the World" leave no room to doubt[863]: it was the material blackness of this God, or his body, that this group of priests revolted against. They had come under the spell of Greek philosophy. Particularly influential on their thinking was the Pythagorean Table of Opposites. According to Pythagoras, that which is characterized by light, spirit, and maleness was good, and that characterized by darkness, materiality, and femininity was bad: the two groups were antithetical. The Gnostics thus 'split' the God of Israel in two. They worshiped as the supreme God the luminous *anthropos* of Day One of Genesis with his brilliant light-body, usually called *phōs*, which name is Greek and means both 'light' and 'man.' The Gnostics separated this luminous man (*phōs*) from his black material 'veil.' The

---

[862] John D. Turner, ***Sethian Gnosticism and the Platonic Tradition*** (Québec, Paris: Les Presses de l'Université Laval and Éditions Peeters, 2001) 257ff; idem, "Sethian Gnosticism: A Literary History," in in Charles W. Hedrick and Robert Hodgson, Jr. (edd.), ***Nag Hammadi, Gnosticism, & Early Christianity*** (Peabody, MASS: Hendrickson Publishers, 1986) 55-86. On Jewish Gnosticism see also Quispel, "Der gnostische Anthropos"; idem, "Gnosticism and the New Testament," in J. Philip Hyatt (ed.), ***The Bible in Modern Scholarship. Papers read at the 100th Meeting of the Society of Biblical Literature, December 28-30, 1964*** (Nashville, TN: Abingdon Press); idem, "Judaism, Judaic Christianity and Gnosis," in A.H.B. Logan and A.J.M. Wedderburn (edd.), ***The New Testament and Gnosis*** (Edinburgh: T&T Clark Limited, 1983), 46-68; R. McL. Wilson, ***The Gnostic Problem: A Study of the Relations between Hellenistic Judaism and the Gnostic Heresy*** (London: A.R. Mowbray & Co. LTD, 1958, 1964[2]); Kurt Rudolph, ***Gnosis, the Nature and History of an Ancient Religion***, trns. Robert McLachlan Wilson (Edinburgh: T&T Clark, 1983); Birger Pearson, ***Gnosticism, Judaism, and Egyptian Christianity*** (Minneapolis: Fortress, 19990); Jarl Fossum, ***Name of God***; idem, "The Magharians: A Pre-Christian Jewish Sect and its Significance for the Study of Gnosticism and Christianity," ***Henoch*** 11 (1987): 303-343; idem, "The New *Religionsgeschichtliche Schule*: The Quest for Jewish Christology," ***SBL Seminar Papers*** 30 (1991): 638-646; Nathaniel Deutsch, ***Guardians of the Gate***, 94-5; idem, "Abathur: A New Etymology," in John J. Collins and Michael Fishbane (edd.), ***Death, Ecstasy, and Other Worldly Journeys*** (Albany, New York: State University of New York Press, 1995) 171-79. On Mandaeaism and Jewish tradition see Deutsch, ***Gnostic Imagination***; Jarl Fossum, "The New *Religionsgeschichtliche Schule*: The Quest for Jewish Christology," ***SBL Seminar Papers*** 30 (1991): 638-646; Kurt Rudolph, ***Gnosis, the Nature and History of an Ancient Religion***, trns. Robert McLachlan Wilson (Edinburgh: T&T Clark, 1983); Dan Cohn-Sherbok, "The Mandaeans and Heterodox Judaism," ***HUCA*** 54: 147-51; idem, "The Alphabet in Mandaean and Jewish Gnosticism," ***Rel*** 11 (1981): 227-234; Gilles Quispel, "Jewish Gnosis and Mandaen Gnosticism: Some Reflections on the Writing *Bronté*," in Jacques-é Ménard (ed.), ***Les Textes de Nag Hammadi. Colloque du Centre d'Histoire des Religions (Strasbourg, 23-25 octobre 1974)*** (NHS 7; Leiden: E.J. Brill, 1975) 82-122.

[863] For English translations of these texts see Willis Barnstone and Marvin Meyer, ***The Gnostic Bible*** (New Seeds, 2006).

latter was exclusively identified with the God of the Bible,[864] whom they demonized and rejected because of his creation of a material (and thus evil) world. With his black material body, the God of the Bible (Yahweh-Elohim) was seen as evil and even equated with the devil at times.[865] Because materiality was associated with femininity according to the Pythagorean Table of Opposites, these early Gnostics represented Yahweh-Elohim's black material body as a black goddess, Sophia-Achamoth (Figure 26). This is part of the history of the Black mother Goddess that you wont get from Dan Brown's ***DaVinci Code.***

This Priestly 'theology of the Black God' would resurface again with the anonymous publication in the 13th -14th centuries of a number of texts deriving from Judaism's ancient secret tradition called today *Kabbalah*. *Kabbalah* traces the evolution of God from an infinite, abstract and formless All, called *Ayn Soph*, through ten evolutionary stages culminating in *Adam Kadmon*, Primordial Man.[866] This 'primordial man'

---

[864] On the Gnostic demiurge and biblical deity see Simon Pétrement, ***A Separate God. The Christian Origins of Gnosticism*** tns. Carol Harrison (New York: HaperCollins Publishing, 1990) Chap. I; Anne Ingvild Sælid Gilhus, "The Gnostic Demiurge - an Agnostic Trickster," ***Religion***. 14 (1984): 301-11; E. Aydeet Fischer-Mueller, "Yaldaboath: The Gnostic Female Principle in its Fallenness," ***NovTes*** (1990): 79-95; Ioan P. Couliano, ***The Tree of Gnosis: Gnostic Mythology from Early Christianity to Modern Nihilism*** (New York: HarperCollins Publishing, 1992) Chapt. 4; idem, "The Angels of the Nations and the Origins of Gnostic Dualism," in R. van den Broek and M.J. Vermasseren (edd.), ***Studies in Gnosticism and Hellenistic Religions, presented to Gilled Quispel on the Occasion of his 65th Birthday*** (Leiden: E.J. Brill, 1981) 78-91; Stevan L. Davies, "The Lion-Headed Yaldabaoth," ***Journal of Religious History*** 11 (1981): 495-500; Jarl Fossum, "The Origin of the Gnostic Demiurge," ***Ephemerides Theologicae Lovanienses*** 61 (1985): 142-52; idem, ***Name of God***; Nils A. Dahl, "The Arrogant Archon and the Lewd Sophia: Jewish Traditions in Gnostic Revolt," in Bentley Layton (ed.), ***The Rediscovery of Gnosticism: Proceedings of the International Conference on Gnosticism at Yale New Haven, Connecticut, March 28-31, 1978*** 2 vols. (Leiden: E.J. Brill, 1981) 2:689-712; Foerster Werner. ***Gnosis: A Selection of Texts*** [Oxford: Clarendon Press, 1974] 1: 11; Williams, ***Rethinking "Gnosticism"***, 63-79; idem, "The demonizing of the demiurge: The innovation of Gnostic myth," in ***Innovation in Religious Traditions: Essays in the Interpretation of Religious Change*** (Religion and Society Series 31; Berlin; New York: Mouton de Gruyter, 1992) 73-107; idem, "The Old Testament God in Early Gnosticism," MA thesis, Miami University, Ohio, 1970; Howard M. Jackson, ***The Lion Becomes Man: The Gnostic Leontomorphic Creator and the Platonic Tradition*** (SBLDS 81; Atlanta: Scholars Press, 1985.

[865] *The Hypostasis of the Archons* (NHC II, *4*, 94.25-26); *The Apocryphon of John* (II 11, 17-18). See also Joseph Dan, "Samael and the Problem of Jewish Gnosticism," in ***Perspectives on Jewish Thought and Mysticism*** (Amsterdam, The Netherlands: Harwood Academic Publishers, 1998) 257-276.

[866] On the Kabbalistic doctrine of the evolution of the biblical God *v*. Arthur Green, ***A Guide to the Zohar*** (Stanford: Stanford University Press, 2004), 101-108; Isaiah Tishby, "The Account of Creation," in Fischel Lachower and Isaiah Tishby, ***The Wisdom of the Zohar, An Anthology of Texts***, trns. from the Hebrew by David Goldstein, 3 vols. (Portland, Oregon: Oxford, 2002), II: 549ff.; Gershom Scholem, ***Major Trends in Jewish Mysticism*** (New York: Schocken Books, 1995) 222ff. On *Ayn Soph v*. Tishby, ***Wisdom***

is God in his luminous form, called *Arikh Anpin*, "Macroprosopus" or the Great Countenance. In order to protect creation from the dangerous radiation of *Arikh Anpin* God cloaked this luminous form with the primordial black matter, producing from it his external, black bodily 'veil' called *Zeir Anpin* or "Microprosopus," the Small Countenance.[867] Together the two 'countenances,' the anthropomorphic God of Light (*Arikh Anpin*) and his black external body (*Zeir Anpin*; Figure 27),[868] are called Yahweh, that is to say, the God

---

of the Zohar I:229-255; Elliot K. Ginsburg, "The Image of the Divine and Person in Zoharic Kabbalah," in Larry D. Shinn (ed.), ***In Search of the Divine: Some Unexpected Consequences of Interfaith Dialogue*** (New York: Paragon House Publishers, 1987) 61-87; Daniel C. Matt, "*Ayin*: The Concept of Nothingness in Jewish Mysticism," in ***Essential Papers on Kabbalah***, ed. Lawrence Fine (New York: New York University Press, 1995), 67-108. On *Adam Kadmon v* Schwartz, ***Tree of Souls***, 15-16; Tishby, ***Wisdom of the Zohar***, I:295-298; C.J.M. Hopking, ***The Practical Kabbalah Guidebook*** (New York: Sterling Publishing, 2001), 34f.; Leo Schaya, ***The Universal Meaning of the Kabbalah***, trns from the French by Nancy Pearson (London: George Allen & Unwin Ltd, 1971), 116-119; Gershom Sholem, "Adam Kadmon," ***Encyclopedia Judaica*** 2:248-49; Green, ***Guide to the Zohar***, 46.

[867] On the Great and Small Countenances *v.* the Zoharic texts *Idra Rabba* and *Idra Zutta*, trns by Roy A. Rosenberg, ***The Anatomy of God*** (New York: KTAV Publishing House, Inc., 1973). See also Pinchas Giller, ***Reading the Zohar: The Sacred Text of the Kabbalah*** (Oxford: Oxford University Press, 2001), 105ff; Gershom Sholem, ***On the Mystical Shape of the Godhead*** (New York: Schocken Books, 1991), 46ff. On the "veiling" of the divine luminosity Tishby (***Wisdom of the Zohar***, II:455) explained: "It is as if the divine light, which spreads out and thickens during the process of emanation, clothes itself in garments from stage to stage...Were it not for the garments that conceal and limit the flow of emanation, the non-divine substances could not survive, because every area of direct radiation from the divine light belongs to the realm of the Godhead. It is only when the divine light is filtered by the various barriers that the gradation required for the building of the worlds can be effected."; Wolfson, ***Through a Speculum***, 273-74.

[868] It is often assumed that *Arikh anpin* is a disembodied head (*v.* Tishby, ***Wisdom of the Zohar*** I:297) because his head is in fact the focus of attention in *Idra Rabba*. But a full anthropomorphic body is presumed (Sholem, ***On the Mystical Shape***, 50), and his "Divine Form," (III, 134b) including the spinal column (III, 131b), shoulders (III, 129a), heart and navel (III, 130b) are explicitly mentioned. *Arikh Anpin* and *Zeir Anpin* are respectively white and dark red. *Idra Rabba* mentions "the bright whiteness of the Ancient One (i.e., *Arikh Anpin*)(*Zohar* III, 128b)," the "white visage of his face (128b)," white cheeks (131a), and hair and beard that are "white as snow (131b)." *Arikh anpin* is thus called the "White Head" (129b). *Zeir anpin* is described with black hair and beard (129b, 139a), eyes that look entirely black (136b), but with a red face (forehead, cheeks, lips, 136b, 139a, 140b). This red is a black red, as the two colors are twins (137a). The red iridescence denotes severity and wrath (cf. the red garments of Yahweh as his treads the winepress of nations in Isaiah 63:1-4), both characteristic of *Zeir anpin*, the "impatient one." On the color red *v.* Tishby, ***Wisdom of the Zohar*** I:291; Scholem, "Colours and their Symbolism (Part I)" 108-110. On *Arikh Anpin* concealed within the body of *Zeir Anpin v. Zohar* III, 141b, which notes that the two *yods* found in *wayyiṣer* of Gen. 2:7 ("YHWH Elohim formed, *wayyiṣer*, Adam") denotes the two forms of *Arikh Anpin* and *Zeir Anpin*, "a form within a form." See also Idel, *Kabbalah*, 135. *Zohar* III,

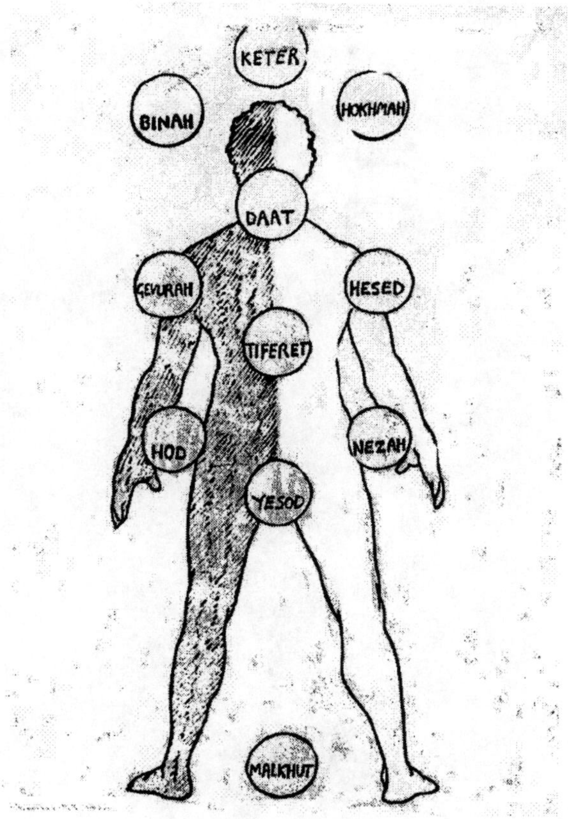

Figure 27

Adam Kadmon, with internal Body of Light (*Arikh Anpin*) and external black 'veil' (*Zeir Anpin*). From Z'ev ben Shimon Halevi, ***Kabbalah: Tradition of Hidden Knowledge*** (New York: Thames & Hudson, 1979)

128b refers to *Zeir Anpin* as the "aspect of the Divine Form that is more external." Cf. III, 133b.

of biblical tradition. Indeed, the secret of the Name (YHWH) is revealed when the Hebrew letters are arranged vertically: they produce a black human form (Figure 28), which is the black body of Yahweh (God).[869]

יהוה

The Name of Yahweh (YHWH) in Hebrew

Figure 28

The Secret of the Name YHWH. From C.J.M. Hopking, ***The Practical Kabbalah Guidebook*** (New York: Sterling Publishing Co., Inc., 2001)

---

[869] See Manley P. Hall, ***The Secret Teachings of All Ages*** (Los Angeles: Philosophical Research Society, 1988) CXXIV; Hopking, ***Practical Kabbalah Guidebook***, 99.

7.6. *Summary and Conclusions*

After examining the Hebrew of Gen. 1:1-4, 26 and 2:7 we have demonstrated the following:

(1) Genesis One does not purport to describe the 'absolute beginning' of things. Before creation actually began on Day One (v. 3: 'Let there be light') there was already some pre-existent matter whose origin is never recounted in Genesis. This matter consisted of three different forms of material darkness: [1] a dark aqueous matter called חשך *ḥōšek̲* which occupied the upper portion of all vertical 'space' (if you will) [2] a dark aqueous matter called תהום *tĕhōm* which occupied the lower portions of the pre-cosmic vertical 'space' and [3] an arid, 'mingled mass' of dark 'stuff' called הארץ*hā'āreṣ*, which somehow existed 'between' the two 'waters.' This three-fold or 'triple' darkness existed before creation began. We are nowhere told how long it was 'there' or how it got 'there.' We are simply informed that when creation began, it was already 'there.' Within this pre-existent triple-darkness there existed God's creative 'breath' or force called רוח אלהים *rûaḥ 'ĕlōhîm*, "Breath/Spirit of God."

(2) Our discussion of the Hebrew מרחפת *mĕraḥepet*, used in v.2c to describe the activity of the רוח אלהים *rûaḥ 'ĕlōhîm* within the pre-existent triple-darkness, has demonstrated that it specifically denotes the activity of a bird acting in relation to an unhatched egg or a youngling recently hatched from the egg. The 'egg,' we have shown, was the mythic image used in the ancient Near East and India to denote the primordial atom, out of which the created cosmos emerged. The term מרחפת *mĕraḥepet* therefore indicated the presence of the primordial atom with the creative breath of God within the triple-darkness, much as Elijah Muhammad claimed. Not only does the traditional Jewish and Christian interpretation of v.2c confirm this meaning of the verb - rabbinic tradition even explicitly describing the creation of the world from the egg/atom - but the recognized Egypto-Phoenician background of v. 2 also confirms the presence of the egg/atom within the pre-existent darkness. Thus, Gen.1:1-2 tells us that before creation began, there existed a material 'triple-darkness' in which was the creative breath of God and an atom. This is precisely the pre-cosmic state of the world described by Elijah Muhammad.

(3) Creation in Genesis 1 therefore does not happen *ex nihilo*, 'out of nothing.' The verbs used to describe God's creative activity (ברא *bārā',* עשה *'āśāh,* יצר *yāṣar,* בדל *bādal*) indicate that God manipulated the pre-existent matter and shaped it into the ordered cosmos. Nor does Genesis I attribute to God creation by divine *fiat* or 'creation by the word.' God did not *just* say 'let there be' and there was. God indeed began the various creations described in Genesis I with a divine command "Let/Let there be…" but then he fulfilled his own command by *making* the very object whose existence he just commanded. The important and oft repeated formula ויהי־כן *wayhî kēn* specifically emphasizes that God did some work to bring the various aspects of the cosmos into existence; he did not just say 'Let there be' and 'poof,' there they were. ויהי־כן *wayhî kēn* calls special attention to this fact.

(4) The Qur'ān likewise posits a primordial triple-darkness, understood as an aquatic, cloud-like darkness. The cosmos was created out of this triple-dark 'sea.' Most important, God existed within this dark cloud according to the Prophet.

(5) Verses 3 and 4 of Genesis describe the emergence and separation of light from the pre-existent darkness. According to Ps 104:2 this light was the luminous being/form of God himself, metaphorically described as his 'garment of majesty.' Philo of Alexandria and the Gospel of John both recognize the light of Day One (Gen. 1:3-4) as the manifest form of the creator-god himself. Psalms 104, by using the verb עטה *'ōteh,* further suggests that this emergence of light on Day One was the beginning of God's 'somatic darkening,' a process that will culminate on Day Six with God's incarnation in the black body of Adam. Because Psalm 104, Philo, and the Prologue of the Gospel of John have some relation to temple/priestly tradition and are specifically expounding on the creation account found in the priestly Genesis I, we are justified in reading the latter in the light of these sources. When we do so, we discover that the light that emerged from the pre-existent darkness of Gen. 1:2 was the luminous form of God himself. Read in the light of the Egypto-Phoenician background to this Hebrew creation account further suggests that this divine luminous form emerged directly from the egg/atom hidden in the darkness. This reading is supported by an eighth century BC Hebrew seal depicting Yahweh as an anthropomorphic sun god emerging from a lotus plant/atom.

(6) According to Jewish esoteric tradition, the Genesis creation account narrates not only the origin of the cosmos (cosmogony) but the origin of God's corporeal being (theogony) as well. The biblical accounts of the emergence of light on Day One and creation of Adam on Day Six confirm that the Genesis creation narrative also had 'theogonic' significance for the priest responsible for the final editing of the Torah, and likely for the Jerusalem priesthood as well. On Day One God's luminous form emerged from darkness; on Day six that form incarnated in a black material body called *'ādām*, Adam. P's description of Adam as the *ṣelem* of God and the description in Gen 2:7 of God blowing the breath of life into the inanimate Adam and enlivening him are both rooted in the ancient Near Eastern cult of images tradition and must be understood in that context. Accordingly, Adam is implicitly presented in Genesis as the cult statue of God, in which God's person dwells and through which creation encounters God. The Qur'ān confirms this reading. Adam, created from black mud, is incarnated by Allah's spirit as well. As *khalīfatu ḻḻāh* the black Adam is worshipped by the angels, as God is so worshiped. This is consistent with the ancient Near Eastern practice of worshipping a god through his cult statue. It is the presence of the luminous form of God from Day One within the black body from Day Six that produced the blue glow characteristic of the blue-black creator gods of the ancient Near East. We have seen that Yahweh was such a blue-black creator-god for the Israelite cult in Jerusalem.

(7) The Temple cult of ancient Israel centered round the activities of the high priest who represented the physical presence of God. The high priest's blue and gold garment was an Israelite variant of the 'sky-garment' belonging to ancient Near Eastern deities. In both the ancient Near East and in Israel this 'sky-garment' represented the sapphiric body of the creator-deity. The Israelite high priest, while draped in his 'sky-garment,' was even accorded worship by devout Jews. This is because he represented the physical presence of the creator-god Yahweh-El in the cult.

(8) This Priestly 'Myth of the Black God' was articulated in Gnosticsim and became the central secret of Jewish estoteric tradition, *Kabbalah*.

The Hebrew of Genesis I therefore presents a picture of the creation of the world that differs radically from what one gets from the

Kings James translation, and one that agrees in a remarkable way with the creation account described by Elijah Muhammad. According to Nicolas Wyatt the beginning of Genesis I describes the initial stages of a theophany, a self-manifestation of God from the pre-existent darkness.[870] Elijah Muhammad too spoke of a self-manifestation of God from the pre-existent darkness. Both Genesis I (Hebrew) and Elijah Muhammad speak of a primordial triple-darkness, a primordial atom, the creative force of God within the darkness, and the emergence of God's luminous anthropomorphic form from the atom in this triple-darkness. Elijah Muhammad said the black man was God. Genesis I says Adam, the first man, was the black body of God, in which God dwelled and through which creation encounters him. The Qur'ān adds that this black Adam was (originally) to be worshipped as God.

[870] See above.

Conclusion Part Two

> How came the Black God, Mr. Muhammad? This is the way he was born - in total darkness. There was no light no where. And out of the orbit of the universe of darkness there sparkled an Atom of Life. Long before there was a where and a when, He (the Black God) was God. A little small Atom of Life rolling around in darkness...building up itself...just turning in darkness, making it's own self...How came the Black God, Mr. Muhammad? He is Self-Created.
>
> - Excerpts from Muhammad's 1969 Saviors Day Address.

The Honorable Elijah Muhammad had a very interesting explanation of the Origin of Things and Allah's (God's) Self–Creation. What is most interesting about his History of Origins is that it is surprisingly consistent with the history of origins as recorded in the various ANE traditions discussed above. Mr. Muhammad teaches that in the beginning there was nothing but "Triple-Stage Darkness." Not just darkness but *Triple-Stage* darkness. This would imply that there was some measure of light hidden in the darkness in order for three degrees of darkness to be differentiated.

> If we see that One emerged from out of all this darkness, what force or power in the darkness brought it out? One could not have come out of darkness unless force was in the darkness to bring it out.[871]

God, as a force, was already in the darkness. For an unknown period of time this God-force laid dormant, hidden in the triple dark womb. At some point a primordial atom was produced. This atom, Mr. Muhammad taught, is the physical beginning of God.

> The beginning was when God was making Himself from an Atom of Life…The One was already in the darkness but could

[871]Muhammad , ***Theology of Time***, 92, 97.

> not be given to us until Time brought it about. It emerged in our view into a revolving Life that was hidden in darkness. We don't know how many trillions of years it was there, but It was there.[872]

God emerged out of this atom as a divine *anthropos*.

> The Atom out of which Man (God) was created came from space. It was out in space where He originated. An Atom of Life was in the darkness of the space and He came out of that Atom...What came out of space was a Human Being.[873]

God is thus called 'self-created,' not because his absolute beginning is with the atom, but because he alone created his own form or body from the atom:

> our First Father formed and designed Himself. Think over a Man being able to design His own form and He had never seen another Man before He saw Himself. This is a powerful thing.[874]

This means God used the atoms (collectively) to build up his body. This is all in agreement with what we learn from ancient Egyptian, Indic, and Israelite sources, which state :

- In the beginning there was nothing but darkness, an aquatic, material, *triple-darkness*. Within this triple-darkness God existed as a luminous force.
- From this divine luminous force developed the primordial atom (mundane egg): the first distinct piece of matter in existence.
- God resided within that primordial atom for an undetermined, though quite lengthy, period of time, developing his physical body. This means that he used the subsequent atoms that developed from the first atom to build up his body over time,
- God finally emerged out of that primordial atom in the form of a divine *anthropos* – a man of light. His self-creation of his own human body was a marvel among the ancient mystics.

---

[872] Ibid., 95, 97.
[873] Ibid., 105.
[874] Ibid., 119.

- God finally wrapped his luminous body in the black matter from which he initially emerged: thus was born the Black God.

The God of Biblical and Islamic tradition, like the gods of the ANE, is this same Black God: a divine *anthropos* with a holy, black body. The theology of the ancient Temple of Solomon in Jerusalem centered on this Black God. One (or several) of the Temple priests would later be responsible for producing the Torah, which they structured around this Temple theology of the Black God of Israel. The God of the Qur'ān and Sunnah of Prophet Muḥammad is the same Black God of antiquity.

To reject the basic contours of Elijah Muhammad's teaching on God is to reject the collective testimony of the ancients and their scriptures – our ancestors and our scriptures. The consistency of this tradition of the Self-Created Black God among the sacred texts of ancient Black civilizations suggests that 21rst century Black folk attempting to free their perspective on God from white supremacy and "the chains and images of psychological enslavement" may start by taking seriously this ancient testimony. How can a 'Black Theology' be formulated that does not take into consideration these concepts articulated almost universally by ancient black theologians? Accept your own and be yourself, so admonished the Hon. Elijah Muhammad.

Epilogue:

The Bible, the Qur'ān and Point Number 12: The Coming of God in Person

In his ***Jesus and the Kingdom of God***, G.R. Beasley-Murray notes:

> The decisive element in the theophany descriptions of the Old Testament…is the concept of the coming of God; the descriptions of the accompanying phenomena in the natural order are to be viewed as parabolic…but the supremely important matter is that God 'comes' into the world…in the future.[875]

Georges Pidoux, in his treatment of the coming of God in the Old Testament, commences with a similar observation:

> "The faith of the Old Testament rests on two certainties, equally profound and indissolubly bound together. The first is that God has come in the past, and that he has intervened in favor of his people. The other…is the hope that God will come anew in the future.[876]

Prophecies of the immanent coming of the Lord to judge man and raise the dead characterize both Old and New Testament theology.[877] Though we hear less of them today, descriptions of God's personal appearance on earth in the Last Days were widespread and numerous during the first centuries of Islam as well and were of marked importance for those scholars attempting to define Islamic theology. Like similar notions in Judaism, Muslim ideas of God's coming derived from scripture.

---

[875] G.R. Beasley-Murray, ***Jesus and the Kingdom of God*** (Grand Rapids, Mich.: W.B. Eerdmans Pub. Co., 1986) 7

[876] Ibid.

[877] On the NT cf. II Thessa. 2:9: "And then shall the wicked be revealed, whom the Lord shall consume with the spirit of his mouth, and shall destroy with the brightness of his coming: Even him, whose coming is after the workings of Satan with all power and signs and lying wonder…"

> Wait they for naught else than that Allah should come to them in the shadows of the clouds with the angels? (2:210)

> Your Lord shall come with the angels, rank on ranks. (89:22)

While current interpretations of these passages render the coming (*ityān*) of God metaphorically as the coming of God's 'order (*amr*)' to the earth, not God himself,[878] the early orthodox understood differently. Al-Dhahak, for example, read 89:22 as saying: "the angels ascend in ranks of separate lines, then the Exalted descends with Jahannam (Hell) next to him, on his left." Muḥammad b. al-Ḥasan al-Shaybānī reported from Ḥammād b. Abū Ḥanīfa:

> We said to (the heretics who deny Allah's coming): Do you consider the saying of Allah – the Mighty and Majestic: "And your Lord comes accompanied by the angels, ranks upon ranks" (89:22). They said: "As for the angels then they come, ranks upon ranks. But as for the Lord – the Most High – then we do not know what is meant by that and we don't know how he comes." So I said to them: We do not oblige you to know how he comes but we oblige you to have faith in his coming. Do you not consider that the one who rejects that the angels come, ranks upon ranks, what is he to you? They said: "A *kāfr* (disbeliever), a *mukadhdhib* (rejecter)." I said: "Then likewise, the one who denies that Allah – theMost Perfect – comes is a *kāfr,* a *mukadhdhib.* [879]

The affirmation of God's *coming* to and visible presence on earth was a part of the orthodox ' *aqīda* (creed). Al Ash'arī (d. 935) declared: "We believe that Allah will come on the Day of Resurrection, as he said, 'and thy Lord shall come and the angels, rank on rank" (*Ibāna*, 54). The famous Ḥanbalī Ibn Baṭṭa (d. 334/945) argued in his creed:

> It is necessary then to know that God, on the Day of Resurrection, will appear (*tajallī*) to those of His servants that believe. They will see Him and God will see them. God will speak to them and they will speak to Him. God will address them and salut (them). God will laugh…[880]

---

[878] See for example Ibn al-Jawzi, ***Daf' shubah al-tashbih***, 12f., 110.
[879] Quoted from Abū Uthman al Sābūnī, *'Aqīdat Salaf wa Aṣḥāb al ḥadīth*, 49.
[880] Laoust, ***Ibn Batta***, 89.

The Sunnah gives numerous accounts of God's coming. An important ḥadīth is found in Al-Bukhari, Muslim, and Ibn Hanbal in several versions narrated by Abu Said Al-Khudri:

> We said, "O Allah's Apostle! Shall we see our Lord on the Day of Resurrection?" He said, "Do you have any difficulty in seeing the sun and the moon when the sky is clear?" We said, "No." He said, "So you will have no difficulty in seeing your Lord on that Day as you have no difficulty in seeing the sun and the moon (in a clear sky)." The Prophet then said, "Somebody will then announce, 'Let every nation follow what they used to worship.' So the companions of the cross will go with their cross, and the idolators (will go) with their idols, and the companions of every god (false deities) (will go) with their god, till there remain those who used to worship Allah, both the obedient ones and the mischievous ones, and some of the people of the Scripture. Then Hell will be presented to them as if it were a mirage.
>
> Then it will be said to the Jews, 'What did you use to worship?' They will reply, 'We used to worship Ezra, the son of Allah.' It will be said to them, 'You are liars, for Allah has neither a wife nor a son. What do you want (now)?' They will reply, 'We want You to provide us with water.' Then it will be said to them 'Drink,' and they will fall down in Hell (instead). Then it will be said to the Christians, 'What did you use to worship?' They will reply, 'We used to worship Messiah, the son of Allah.' It will be said, 'You are liars, for Allah has neither a wife nor a son. What (do you want now)?' They will say, 'We want You to provide us with water.' It will be said to them, 'Drink,' and they will fall down in Hell (instead).
>
> When there remain only those who used to worship Allah (Alone), both the obedient ones and the mischievous ones, it will be said to them, 'What keeps you here when all the people have gone?' They will say, 'We parted with them (in the world) when we were in greater need of them than we are today, we heard the call of one proclaiming, 'Let every nation follow what they used to worship,' and now we are waiting for our Lord.' Then the Almighty will come to them in a form (*ṣūra*) other than the one which they saw the first time, and He will say, 'I am your Lord,' [They will say: "(God protects us from you!) We associate nothing with God!" (We will stay here

until our Lord comes to us. When our Lord comes, we will recognize Him!")[881] And none will speak to Him then but the Prophets, and then it will be said to them, 'Do you know any sign by which you can recognize Him?' ["Yes!" they will say. "***So, a leg will be uncovered*** (68:42)."] and so Allah will then uncover His Leg whereupon every believer will prostrate before Him…"

God will thus appear on the Day of Judgment in a visible form (*ṣūra*), but one that the believers don't recognize. It differs, we are told, from the form God had the 'first time' the people saw God. The commentators tell us that 'the first time' is a reference to the Primordial Covenant (*mithāq*) alluded to in *sūrat al ʿArāf* 172. The pre-incarnate souls of humanity, prior to the creation of Adam's physical body, entered into a primordial covenant with their creator to serve him alone once they are sent to earth. The first time the people saw God, then, was prior to creation; they saw then God's true form. It is this divine form the people expected to see on the Day of Judgment. Instead, however, God shows up in a new, unrecognized form. Orthodox exegesis understood the point of this test (*imtiḥān*) as a means of distinguishing the true believers from the hypocrites and others.[882] The faithful are expected to recognize their Lord, the strange form notwithstanding.

The important question is, of course, what is the nature of these two forms? In a variant of this *ḥadīth*, it reads, "Then the Lord of the worlds will come to them under a more lowly form (*fī andā ṣūratin*) than that under which they had seen Him [before]."[883] It is not clear what makes this form "lowly" or how exactly it differs from the form God had the 'first time' the people saw him prior to creation. That this first form is God's true form is indicated in two versions of this hadith reported by Ibn Ḥanbal, where we find the words, *ya'tīhim Allāhu ʿazza wa jalla fī ṣūratihi*, "God will (again) come to them in 'His form'," i.e. His true form.[884] This true form, the form that the people saw "the first time" or "before," is anthropomorphic; its sign is somehow marked on God's "Leg," his disclosure of which convinces the incredulous Muslims that this is God, however unrecognized his new form.

In other reports the form God will don in the Last days is specifically identified with that form of the Young Man (*shābb*). God will, according to certain narrations, descend on the Day of Judgment

---

881 Ibn Hanbal, ***Musnad¹***, 2:275; idem, ***Kitāb al-Sunna***, 42.
882 See Gimaret, ***Dieu à l'image***, 139.
883 Al-Bukhārī, *tawḥīd* 24/5.
884 Ibn Ḥanbal, ***Musnad²***, 13:304, #7927 and 16:527, #10906.

in this form ridding a red camel, dressed in a *jubba* (long outer garment, open in front, with wide sleeves).[885] The *jubba* will probably be green. Such an expectation eventually gave way to certain excesses that would later scandalize the Sunnis. They are cited here, however, because they demonstrate how accepted and powerful this image of God was. The Imāmī (Shī'ī) al-Ḥillī (d. 1325), in his polemic against the *ḥashwīya* (popular Sunni scholars who read the anthropomorphic descriptions of God literally) claimed that "some of them (*al-ḥashwīya*) believe that God descends every Thursday night in the form of a beardless youth, beautiful of face, on a camel, until some of them in Baghdād place fodder on the roof of their house every Thursday night (hoping) that God will descend on His camel on that roof."[886] Al-Ḥillī goes on to relate a rather scandalous narrative about a sheikh of the *ḥashwīya* in Baghdād who passes a *naffāṭ* (lowly tar thrower) "who had with him a young, beardless boy, handsome of form, with curly hair just as they describe their Lord." The narrative continues:

> The sheik stared at [the boy]. The *naffāṭ* thought of him [that night] and came to him and said: "Yā sheik! I noticed you staring at this young boy so I have come to you with him. If you have an intention with him, you are the judge. The sheik got angry at him and said: Rather, I stared at him because I believe that Allāh descends in [that form] so I thought he was God." The *naffāṭ* said: "I am in *naffāṭa* better than you in your asceticism with this talk."[887]

These excesses were likewise reported of the Ṣūfīs. Their practice of *al-naẓar ilā 'l-murd* or 'gazing at young beardless boys' no doubt originated with these *ḥadīths*.[888] Abū Tammām described in his ***Kitāb al-shajara*** a previously unknown sect called the Ḥubbīya, apparently a Ṣūfī group, who believe that God is in the form of a handsome youth. Abū Tammām reports an insider's account of a secret ceremony, obviously a *sam'*, held in Iraq. A beautiful youth, clothed in the finest

---

[885] Al-Faḍl b. Shādhān, ***Al-Īḍāḥ*** (Tihrān, 1972), 15f. See also Ibn al-Jawzī, ***Kitāb al-mawḍū'āt***, 1:180; al-Suyūtī, ***Al-La'ālī'***, 28.

[886] Al-Ḥillī, ***Minhāj al-karama***, *apud* Ibn Taymīya, ***Minhāj al-sunna***, 2:506.

[887] Al-Ḥillī, ***Minhāj al-karama***, *apud* Ibn Taymīya, ***Minhāj al-sunna***, 2: 507.

[888] Annmarie Schemmal, ***Mystical Dimensions of Isam*** (Chapel Hill: University of North Carolina Press, 1975), 290. The *ḥadīth al-shābb* was particularly in fashion among the Ṣūfīs in the 10th century according to Yemenite author 'Abd al-Raḥmān b. 'Alī b. al-Dayba', ***Tamyīz al-ṭayyib min al-khabīth fīmā yadwara 'alā alsinat al-nās min al-ḥadīth*** (Egypt: Maktabāt wa-Maṭba'at Muḥammad 'Alī Ṣubayḥ, 1963), 80. On *al-naẓar ilā 'l-murd v.* Ibn al-Jawzī ***Tablīs Iblīs*** (Cairo: Dār al-Ḥadīth, 1995), 274ff; Ritter, ***Der Meer der Seele***, 460ff.

garments, was enthroned on an elevated dais. A curtain, suspended from two hooks and raised on command by a keeper, separated the youth from the audience. The audience sung songs of desire and plaintive hymns, all the while asking permission to visit the youth. Yaḥyā b. Muʿādh al-Rāzī, our eyewitness and participant, described:

> When we implored, and begged, he (the youth) ordered the keeper of the curtain to raise it. We persisted relentlessly until the keeper raised it and when it was raised and he appeared on that throne, we fell on our faces. This continued in this fashion until dawn broke, at which time we departed and dispersed."[889]

As scandalous as these anecdotes may seem to us, they indicate clearly the powerful expectation that God will come in the form of a beardless 'youth,' black-haired and white-skinned. But this form is not the form God had at creation, and it is not the form the faithful expect to encounter upon their Lord's coming. God, at creation and at the sending of the prophets, was Black. On the Day of Judgment, we are told, he will look white. Warith Deen Mohammed, son of Elijah Muhammad, recalled looking at the famous picture of Master Fard Muhammad, white-skinned and black-haired, and wondering "why this man looking so white was supposed to be black and a black god."[890] We can answer that question. It was prophesied that the Black God will appear on the Day of Judgment in an unexpected and unrecognized form - a white form. He will not be white, he will only be white-complected. The Apostle Paul said that when the Lord comes He will come "in the likeness (*homoiōma*) of sinful flesh (Rom .8:3)," the flesh of the man of sin. The Lord's is only a 'likeness' of this white flesh, not the actual white flesh. The Hon. Elijah Muhammad said regarding Master Fard Muhammad:

> We are going to get over to you the history of this Man who is the Almighty God in Person as he gave it to me…His father was a Black Man, very much so. His mother was a white woman. He said that His father knew that his son could not be successful in coming into a solid white country being a solid black man. So He taught that His father said, "I will go and make me a Son

---

[889] Paul E. Walker, "An Isma'ili version of the heresiography of the seventy-two erring sects," in ***Mediaeval Isma'ili History and Thought***, ed. Farhad Daftary (Cambridge, New York: Cambridge University Press, 1996), 172f.

[890] Quoted from the Imam in Steven Barboza, ***American Jihad: Islam after Malcolm X*** (New York: Doubleday, 1993)100.

and I will send my Son among them looking like them…And my Son, Whom they will think is one of them, will find our lost people." So Almighty God, in the Person of Master Fard Muhammad, said to me that His father said, "I will have to make One look like them."[891]

---

[891] ***Theology of Time*** (ed. Abass Rassoull; Hampton, VA: U.B. & U.S. Communications Systems, 1992)166.

Appendix A

Yahweh, the Mighty Man of Israel

Yahweh-Elohim, the God of ancient Israel and the Bible, is not only an *'îš*, man, but a *gibbôr*, mighty man.[892] Of particular significance is Zeph. 1:14. In order to properly appreciate this verse, however, a number of text-critical issues need to be addressed.

1:14 a. קרוב יום־יהוה הגדול
b. קרוב ומהר מאד
c. קול יום יהוה מר
d. צרח שם גבור

The KJV translates this verse:

a. The great day of the Lord is near,
b. It is near, and hasteth greatly,
c. Even the voice of the day of the Lord:
d. The mighty man shall cry there bitterly.

But this is not the best translation of a verse that has given translators much trouble.[893] Verse 14 contains four versets, only one of which has provoked no scholarly controversy. [894] Versets 14c-d have probably suffered corruption by scribes[895] While all the Versions agree in their reading of the preceding line (14 a-b), they all disagree here.[896] The Hebrew presents its own difficulties. It reads literally, "The sound of

---

[892] See above.

[893] John D. W. Watts, ***The Books of Joel, Obadiah, Jonah, Nahum, Habakkuk and Zephaniah*** (London: Cambridge University Press, 1975), 162.

[894] Ehud Ben Zvi, ***A Historical-Critical Study of Zephaniah*** (Berlin: Walter de Gruyter, 1991), 116.

[895] Adele Berlin, ***Zephaniah*** [New York: Doubleday, 1964], 89.

[896] LXX reads *phōnē hēmeras kyriou pikra kai sklēra, tetaktai dynatē*, "the sound of the day of the Lord is bitter and harsh, it is set up as strong." The Vulgate reads *tribulabitur ibi fortis*, "the strong man will suffer tribulation there." The Targum reads, "the sound of the day which is about to come from before Yahweh is one in which one will be bitter and cry out, there the warriors are being killed." See J.J.M. Roberts, ***Nahum, Habakkuk, and Zephaniah*** (Louisville, Kentucky: Westminster/John Knox Press, 1991), 182; Ivan Jay Ball, Jr, ***A Rhetorical Study of Zephaniah*** (Berkeley, California: BIBAL Press, 1988), 41.

the day of Yahweh is fierce; crying there (a/the) mighty man." The adverb 'there' (*šām*, שם) is without a proper antecedent.[897] Many translators have therefore emended the verse to read הי' מרץ וחש מגבור קל יום, "the day of Yahweh is swifter than a runner and faster than a mighty man/hero"[898]; but such a large number of textual emendations is completely unwarranted and unsupported by the Ancient Versions.[899]

A major stumbling block in translating this verset is the adjective *mar* מר, translated here as "fierce." Two questions arise regarding this word: (1) what is its meaning and (2) does it belong at the end of v.14c, or the beginning of v.14d. In other words, does *mar*, whatever its meaning, modify "(the sound of) the day of Yahweh" in v. 14c or the (battle cry of) the mighty man of v. 14b. A proper reading of the text requires appropriate answers to these questions.

In regards the meaning of the word, it is clear from OT evidence that *mar* מר originates from the root מרר, meaning 'bitter.' Additionally, Laurence Kutler demonstrated in 1984, *pace* Dennis Pardee,[900] that *mar* has the double meaning in Biblical Hebrew of "strong."[901] Thus, Ball's translation as 'fierce', connoting both bitterness and strength, is appropriate.[902]

A right answer to question two is harder to pin down. The Hebrew is ambiguous.[903] It can be read either as, "Hark![904] (the sound of) the day of Yahweh is fierce; the mighty man cries there," or "Hark! (the sound of) the Day of Yahweh; the mighty man cries there fiercely." While J.M.P. Smith found legitimacy in neither of our two options (therefore choosing to emend the text[905]), I find both as legitimate

---

[897] ***The Interpreter's Bible*** 6:1018

[898] See also L.H. Brockington's variation, reading *g^e^d̲û̲d̲* "a band of raiders," instead of *gibbôr*, "mighty man/hero" (***The Hebrew Text of the Old Testament*** [London: Oxford University Press/Cambridge University Press, 1973], 262).

[899] Roberts, ***Nahum, Habakkuk, and Zephaniah***, 182; Berlin, ***Zephaniah***, 89; Ben Zvi, ***A Historical-Critical Study***, 118.

[900] Dennis Pardee, "The Semitic Root *mrr* and the etymology of Ugaritic *mr*(*r*) // brk," ***UF*** 10 (1978) 249-88.

[901] Laurence Kutler, "A 'Strong' Case for Hebew Mar," ***UF*** 16 (1984): 111-118.

[902] Ball, ***A Rhetorical Study***, 79; Ben Zvi, ***A Historical-Critical Study***, 119.

[903] *See* Smith et al, ***Critical And Exegetical Commentary***, 203.

[904] The Hebrew *qôl*, while generally meaning "sound" or "voice," as all the Versions read it here, when it occurs at the beginning of a clause and followed by a genitive may function as an exclamatory, 'Hark!' (See Ben Zvi, ***A Historical-Critical Study***, 118; Berlin, ***Zephaniah***, 89). Ben Zvi is probably correct in reading it as a *double entendre* here, conveying both meanings (Ben Zvi, ***A Historical-Critical Study***, 119).

[905] Smith *et al*, ***A Critical And Exegetical Commentary***, 203f. Smith argued, "If bitter be taken with the first half of the line, it forms an unsuitable predicate to 'sound,' and when treated as predicate to 'day,' the resulting sentence 'the day of Yahweh is bitter' furnishes an inappropriate continuation of the particle 'Hark'; if 'bitter' be connected with the second half of the line, the rhythmical balance of the line is disturbed." He

possible readings.[906] The overall meaning of the text is not much affected by one's choice here; in other words, whether it is the (sound of) the Day of Yahweh that is fierce, or the cry of a/the mighty man, the sense of the imminence and 'terror' of that day, one of the main themes of this text, is preserved.

A possible key to unraveling the meaning of this text may be in the misplaced adverb שם *šām*. As an adverb of place, its usual function, שם *šām* is conspicuously out of place; there is no antecedent here.[907] It has been noted, however, that, on occasion, the adverb can have a temporal sense, meaning "then."[908] Read so here, we get, lit., "(a/the) mighty man cried then aloud," with the Day of Yahweh as the antecedent; thus, as Ben Zvi translates, "at that time (Day of Yahweh) a warrior cries out."[909] This is certainly a possible reading of the text.[910] But it doesn't quite remove all of the difficulties. The syntax is still awkward. Even with the stylistic license of Biblical Hebrew poetry, we would not expect the circumstantial adverb (in this case "then" or "at that time") to split the verb and the subject (the Hebrew reads literally, צרח שם גבור, "cries aloud then a/the mighty man). As the ***Interpreter's Bible*** noted, "the order of the words is unusual, and not to say wrong."[911] This difficulty is only increased if we read, as many do, *mar* at the beginning of v.14b, instead of the end of 14c. We thus get, "Fiercely cries aloud then a/the mighty man." שם read as the adverb *šām*, simply does not fit here.

A possible, and in our opinion quite attractive solution was offered by Ivan Jay Ball, Jr. in his doctoral thesis on Zephania in 1972. Ball took שם *šām*, not as an adverb, but as an adjective meaning "appalling" from the root שמם *šāmam*,.[912] He was encouraged in this reading by the analogy with the preceding adjective מר *mar* ("fierce") which derived

---

therefore dropped the verb of 14d, *soreah*, "to cry aloud," emending the Hebrew to read, "Near at hand is Yahweh's bitter day, hastening faster than a warrior."

906 No compelling reasons to emend the text have come forth, with the one possible exception: the reading of שם. See below.

907 ***Interpreter's Bible*** 6:1018. Smith *et al*, ***Critical And Exegetical Commentary***, 203f.

908 Prov. 8:27; Job 35:12.

909 Ben Zvi, ***A Historical-Critical Study***, 120f.

910 Smith's objection that such a meaning "is not well established" lacks all force (***Critical And Exegetical Commentary***, 203). Such a use in Biblical poetry (as this text is) is sufficiently established to justify reading so here. See Berlin, ***Zephaniah***, 89; Ben Zvi, ***A Historical-Critical Study***, 120f.

910 Ben Zvi, ***A Historical-Critical Study***, 120f.

911 ***The Interpreter's Bible*** 6:1018; Smith et al, ***A Critical And Exegetical Commentary*** 203f noted also, "the order of the words in the latter part of the line is wholly abnormal."

912 Ball, ***A Rhetorical Study***, 42.

from the root מרר. Reading this latter at the beginning of v.14d instead of the end of v.14c, Ball obtained the following bicolon:

מר צרח
שם גבור

Which can be read:

> Fierce is he who cries aloud,[913]
> Appalling is the mighty man.

This suggestion sufficiently removes the syntactical difficulties of the verset and is perfectly consistent with the (con)text. Additionally, we have the most important rhetorical feature of Biblical poetry: parallelism. Thus, the (near) best translation of Zephaniah 1:14 is surely to be:

1:14a: The great Day of Yahweh is near,
b Hastening most quickly.[914]
c Hark! (The sound of) the Day of Yahweh.
d Fierce is he who shouts a battle cry.
Appalling is a/the mighty man.

We now come to the most important question regarding this text: who is the unidentified *gibbôr* or "mighty man" spoken of here? Is it "*a* mighty man," i.e. men in general at that time, or "*the* mighty man," a particular mighty man? The Hebrew is ambiguous because *gibbôr* is non-determined (lacks the definite article) here. But in poetic biblical Hebrew the definite article is frequently absent from definite nouns.[915] Most translators therefore render *gibbôr* here as "the mighty man" or "the warrior."[916] Who then is "the mighty man"? Ball reads *gibbôr* as a

---

[913] Ball takes צרח, a qal participle meaning "crying aloud" or, as we will see later, "roaring a battle cry," as a substantive meaning "he who shouts a battle cry." Ball, ***A Rhetorical Study***, 79.

[914] We are taking *qārôb* as an infinitive absolute of קרב in the qal pattern, and *mahēr* as an infinitive absolute of מהר in the piel pattern used adverbially. See Ben Zvi, ***A Historical-Critical Study*** 117f. Roberts, ***Nahum, Habakkuk, and Zephaniah***, 182. We see no justification for taking *haggādôl* in 14a as a divine title with Ball, ***A Rhetorical Study*** 78 or *mahēr* in 14b as "(Divine) Soldier" with Watts (***The Books of***, 162). See Hubert Irsigler, ***Gottesgericht und Jahwetag*** (Eos Verlag, 1977), 49ff.

[915] Judg 5:4, Ps 2:2; See C. L. Seow, ***A Grammar For Biblical Hebrew*** (Nashville: Abingdon Press, 1995), 157.

[916] Paul R. House, ***Zephaniah, A Prophetic Drama*** (Sheffeld: The Almond Press, 1988), 120; Watts, ***The Books of***, 161; Smith *et al*, 203; ***Interpreter's Bible***, 6:1018;

divine title, thus his translation, "Fierce is He who shouts a battle cry; appalling is the Mighty One."[917] The "mighty man" would then be God. Ball is not alone in this reading. John D. W. Watts translated the text:

> The great day of the Lord is near.
> The great Soldier[918] himself is near.
> The noise of the day of the Lord is overpowering
> Shouting: See the Warrior!

He explains: "The Day is one of battle and the Lord's appearance on the field will decide the outcome."[919] Ball and Watts are among a long list of commentators who see in this *gibbôr* a reference to God.[920] Textual evidence confirms this reading. The prophet Zephaniah explicitly refers to God as a *gibbôr* later in 3:17 in a passage linked to 1:14 by its description of the Day of Yahweh[921]:

> 3:16:On that day it shall be said to Jerusalem
> Do not fear, O Zion; do not let your hands grow weak.
> 3:17:Yahweh, your God, is in your midst
> A Mighty Man (*gibbôr*) who saves (*yôšîᵃʿ*, יושיע).[922]

It is appropriate to read 1:14 in the light of 3:17.[923] The divine identity of the *gibbôr* is further supported by the verb used in 1:14d, צרח ("to cry aloud"). This rare word occurs only one other time in the OT. It appears in *hiphil* form in Isa. 42:13, where Yahweh as the subject is again called *gibbôr*.

Both the ***KJV*** and the ***NOAB*** translate the term as a definite noun. On the other hand, Berlin (***Zephaniah***, 85) and Roberts (***Nahum, Habakkuk, and Zephaniah***, 181) read an indefinite noun.

917 Ball, ***A Rhetorical Study***, 42.

918 Watts understood *mahēr* in v. 14b as 'soldier,' a meaning clearly attested in other Semitic languages. Watts, ***The Books of***, 162.

919 Ibid.

920 Gillis Gerleman, ***Zephanja, Textkritisch und Literarisch Untersucht*** (Lund: C. W. K. Gleerup, 1942), 19f; D. Deden, ***De Kleine Profeten*** (Roermond-Maaseil: J. J. Romen & Zonen, 1953/56), 283; Augustine George, ***Michee, Sophonie, Nahum***, in ***La Sainte Bible*** (Paris: Les Editions du Cerf, 1958), 64; Rolf Freiherr Ungern-Sternberg and Helmut Lamparter, ***Der Tag des Gerichtes Gottes: Die Propheten Habakuk, Zephanja, Jona, Nahum*** (Stuttgart: Calwer Verlag, 1960), 83.96.98; Ben Zvi, ***A Historical-Critical Study***, 121. See also Irsigler's discussion, ***Gottesgericht und Jahwetag,*** 52ff. s

921 Ball, ***A Rhetorical Study***, 267.

922 For discussion of this verse see below.

923 As does Ball (***A Rhetorical Study***, 79); Ben Zvi, ***A Historical-Critical Study***, 120.

Yahweh as a mighty man (*gibbôr*) goes forth,
As a man of wars (*'îš milḥāmôt*) he stirs up His fury
With zeal He shouts a war cry
With anger He roars a battle cry (*yaṣrî^a h*, יצריח)
Against His enemies He shows Himself a mighty
man (*yithgabbar*, יתגבר).[924]

The joint occurrence of צרח *ṣāraḥ* and גבור *gibbôr*, found only here and in Zephaniah 1:14, confirms that the two passages are to be read in light of each other[925]; he who "utters a battle cry" in Zephaniah 1:14 is He Who utters a battle cry in Isa. 42:13. J.J.M. Roberts notes: "The use of the verb *ṣrḥ* in Isa. 42:13 suggests that it designates the scream or battle cry of the warrior who has worked himself up in a killing rage."[926] Ehud Ben Zvi concludes, "By the end of the poetic line (Zeph. 1:14) it is clear that YHWH is the warrior whose shouting is the source of the fierce sound of the [Day of Yahweh], and that YHWH is the one who brings distress in such a day."[927] The most accurate reading of our passage is thus:

1:14a: The great Day of Yahweh is near,
b Hastening most quickly
c Hark! (The sound of) the Day of Yahweh.
d Fierce is He who shouts a battle cry.
e. Appalling is The Mighty Man.

God will thus appear on that Day as a mighty man, shouting a war cry, about to unleash a ravaging fury on His enemies, that is, the enemies of Jerusalem. As for Jerusalem, God will on that Day be a "mighty man who saves גבור יושיע *gibbôr yôšî^a'*," Zeph. 3:17. This latter passage is construed as a response to the plea of Jeremiah (14:7-9):

7. Though our iniquities testify against us
Yahweh, act for the sake of your name
For our backslidings are many

---

924 On this passage *see* Julian Morgenstern, "Isaiah 42:10-13," in ***To Do & To Teach, Essays in Honor of Charles Lynn Pyatt*** (Lexington: The College of the Bible, 1953), 27-38; David Noel Freedman, "Isaiah 42, 13" ***CBQ*** 30 (1968): 225-6; Katheryn Pfister Darr, "Like Warrior, Like Woman: Destruction and Deliverance in Isaiah 42:10-17," ***CBQ*** 49 (1987): 560-571.
925 Gerleman, ***Zephanja***, 19; James Mullenburg, ***The Book of Isaiah: Chapters 40-66*** (Nashville: Abingdon Press, 1956), 472; Ball, ***A Rhetorical Study***, 79f; Ben Zvi, ***A Historical-Critical Study***, 120. Cf. Irsigler, ***Gottesgericht und Jahwetag,*** 52f.
926 Roberts, ***Nahum, Habakkuk, and Zephaniah***, 183.
927 Ben Zvi, ***A Historical-Critical Study***, 121.

Against you we have sinned
8. The Hope of Israel
Its savior in the time of trouble
Why will you become like a sojourner in the land
And like a traveler turned aside to lodge?
9. Why will you become like a helpless man (*'îš nidhām*)
like a mighty man unable to save (*gibbôr lō' yûkal lᵉhôšîᵃ'*)?
But you are in our midst, Yahweh
And your name upon us is called
Do not leave us!

Here Israel, through Jeremiah, confesses their sins and apostasy and pleas for deliverance and Yahweh's continued presence. Their appeal is that Yahweh should save Israel for His own name's sake, in spite of Israel's backsliding, because He has staked His honor on the election of Israel.[928] Zion is His land, chosen to be His dwelling-place. Yet it is devastated by drought and Israel is in a desperate condition of want and distress.[929] The prophet asks rhetorically, Why does Yahweh act like a sojourner passing through a foreign land, lodging for only a night then proceeding? This is Your land! Then the prophet asks: "Why behave like a helpless man (*'îš nidhām*)?" *'îš nidhām* is a contradiction in terms, as is a "mighty man who cannot save (*gibbôr lō' yûkal lᵉhôšîᵃ'*)". An *'îš / gibbôr* by definition can save.[930] Yahweh is an acknowledged *'îš* and *gibbôr* (Jer. 20:11). Why then behave thus, acting helpless and unable to save His land/people, all while "in our midst (v.9)"? This is the context in which Zeph. 3:17 should be read.[931] The prophet Zephaniah responds, "Yahweh, your God, *is* in your midst a mighty man who saves *gibbôr yôšîᵃ'*."

[928] Jack. R. Lundbom, ***Jeremiah 1-20***. The Anchor Bible (New York: Doubleday, 702.
[929] William McKane, ***A Critical and Exegetical Commentary on Jeremiah*** 2 vols. (Edinburgh: T. & T. Clark Limited, 1975) 1:320.
[930] William L. Holladay, ***Jeremiah 1*** (Philadelphia: Fortress Press, 1986), 433.
[931] Ben Zvi, ***A Historical-Critical Study***, 249.

Appendix B

The Truth of God: An Introductory Bibliography

Over the years, many people have requested from me a list of relevant books on various subjects dealing with the Truth of God. I have now complied a short (200+ titles) 'introductory' bibliography to the study of the Reality of God. This is in no way a comprehensive bibliography: 200+ titles is truly just the 'tip of the iceberg' of relevant and helpful works out there. Because this short list is 'introductory,' I have excluded works in foreign languages (i.e. German, French and Arabic), though some of the most relevant materials can be found in non-English works. I have also excluded more technical works. Nonetheless, this short list includes English works which I have found to be particularly insightful. Anyone who studies and grasps the various subjects treated in these will have a firm foundation upon which to build a more comprehensive understanding of the Reality of God.

Aaron, David H. "Imagery of the Divine and the Human: On the Mythology of Genesis Rabba 8 § 1," ***JJTP*** 5 (1995): 1-62

Altmann, Alexander. "A Note on the Rabbinic Doctrine of Creation," ***JJS*** 7 (1956): 195-206

Anawati, Georges C. "Attributes of God: Islamic Concepts." In ***ER*** 1:513-519

Armstrong, K. ***A History of God***. Ballantine Books, New York. 1993

Assmann, Jan. ***Egyptian Solar Religion in the New Kingdom. Re, Amun and the Crisis of Polytheism***, translated from the German by Anthony Alcock. London and New York: Kegan Paul International, 1995.

_______***The Search for God in Ancient Egypt***, translated from the German by David Lorton. Ithaca and New York: Cornell University Press, 2001.

_______***Death and Salvation in Ancient Egypt***, translated from the German by David Lorton. Ithaca and London: Cornell University Press, 2005.

Bailey, A. ***The Consciousness Of The Atom***. Lucis Publishing, New York. 1961.

Baldick, J. ***Black God. The Afroasiatic Roots of the Jewish, Christian and Muslim Religions***. Syracuse University Press, New York. 1997.

Barashango, I. ***God, The Bible, and the Black Man's Destiny***. IVth Dynasty Publishing, Silver Spring. 1982

Barker, Margaret ***the Great High Priest: The Temple Roots of Christian Liturgy***. London: T&T Clark, 2003.

_______***Great Angel: A Study of Israel's Second God*** .Louisville, Kentucky: Westminster/John Knox Press, 1992.

_______***The Older Testament: The Survival of Themes from the Ancient Royal Cult in Sectarian Judaism and Early Christianity***. London: SPCK, 1987.

_______ "The High Priest and the Worship of Jesus," in Carey C. Newman, James R. Davila and Gladys S. Lewis (edd.), ***Jewish Roots of Christological Monotheism. Papers from the St. Andrews Conference on the Historical Origins of the Worship of Jesus***. Leiden: Brill, 1999: 93-111

_______***Temple Theology***. Society for Promoting Christian Knowledge, 2004

Barr, James. "Theophany and Anthropomorphism in the OT," ***VTSup*** 7 (1960): 31-38.

Beck, Brenda E.F. "The symbolic merger of Body, space and cosmos in Hindu Tamil Nadu," ***Contributions to Indian Sociology***, n.s. 10 (1976): 213-243

Bell, Richard. "Muhammad's Visions," ***MW*** 24 (1934): 145-154.

Bokser, Ben Zion. "The Thread of Blue," ***Proceedings of the American Academy for Jewish Research*** 31 (1963): 1-31

Borsch, F.H. ***The Son of Man in Myth and History***, S.C.M. Press, London. 1967.

Bosch, P. van. "Yama-The God on the Black Buffalo," in ***Commemorative Figures***. Leiden: E.J. Brill, 1982: 21-64

Boyarin, Daniel "Two Powers in Heaven; or, the Making of a Heresy," in ***The Idea of Biblial Interpretation: Essays for James Kugel***. Lieden: Brill, 2004: 331-370

_______ "The Gospel of the *Memra*: Jewish Binitarianism and the Prologue to John," ***HTR*** 94:3 (2001) 243-84

van den Broek, R. "The Creation of Adam's Psychic Body in the Apocryphon of John," in ***Studies in Gnosticism and Hellenistic Religions, presented to Gilles Quispel on the Occasion of his 65th Birthday***, eds. R. van den Broek and M.J. Vermaseren. Leiden: E.J. Brill, 1981: 38-57

Budge, E.W. ***The Gods of The Egyptians***. New York, Dover Publications, 1969.

Capra, F. ***The TAO of Physics***. Boston, Shambhala, 1991.

Callender, Jr., Dexter E., ***Adam in Myth and History: Ancient Israelite Perspective on the Primal Human***. Harvard Semitic Studies 48; Winona Lake, Indiana: Eisenbrauns, 2002.
Charlesworth, James H. "The Portrayal of the Righteous as an Angel," in ***Ideal Figures in Ancient Judaism: profiles and paradigms***. Chico, CA: Scholars Press, 1980: 137-139
Cherbonnier, E.L. "The Logic of Biblical Anthropomorphism," ***Harvard Theological Review***, 551 (962): 187-208.
Churchward, A. ***The Origin and Evolution of Religion***. E.C.A. Association, New York. 1924, 1990.
_______***Signs and Symbols of Primordial Man***. George Allen & Company, LTD, London. 1913.
Collins, John J. "Powers in Heaven: God, Gods, and Angels in the Dead Sea Scrolls," in John J. Collins and Robert A. Kugler (edd.), ***Religion in the Dead Sea Scrolls*** Grand Rapids, Michigan/Cambridge, U.K.: William B. Eerdmans Publishing Company, 2000: 9-28.
Conger, George P. "Cosmic Persons and Human Universes in Indian Philosophy," ***Journal and Proceedings of the Asiatic Society of Bengel*** n.s. 29 (1933): 255-270.
Coogan, Michael David. "Canaanite Origins and Lineage: Reflections on the Religion of Ancient Israel," in P.D. Miller et al (edd.), ***Ancient Israelite Religion. Essays in Honor of Frank Moore Cross***. Philadelphia, 1987: 115-124
Couliano, Ioan P. ***The Tree of Gnosis: Gnostic Mythology from Early Christianity to Modern Nihilism***. New York: HarperCollins Publishing, 1992
_______ "The Angels of the Nations and the Origins of Gnostic Dualism," in R. van den Broek and M.J. Vermasseren (edd.), ***Studies in Gnosticism and Hellenistic Religions, presented to Gilled Quispel on the Occasion of his 65th Birthday***. Leiden: E.J. Brill, 1981: 78-91
Cross, F.M. ***Canaanite Myth and Hebrew Epic***. Harvard University Press, Cambridge. 1973.
_______"The 'Olden Gods' in Ancient Near Eastern Creation Myths," in Frank Moore Cross, Werner E. Lemke, and Patrick D. Miller, Jr. (edd.), ***Magnalia Dei,*** *the* ***mighty acts of God: essays on the Bible and archaeology in memory of G. Ernest Wright***. Garden City, N.Y.: Doubleday, 1976: 335-36.

Daum, Werner, "A Pre-Islamic Rite in South Arabia," ***JRAS*** 1 (1987): 5-14.
Dandekar, R. N. ***Vedic Mythological Texts***. Delhi, 1979.

Daniélou, Alain. ***The Myths and Gods of India***. 1964; Rochester, Vermont: Inner Traditions International, 1985: 118-121
De Conick, April D. "Becoming God's Body: The KAVOD in Valentinianism," ***SBL 1995 Seminar Papers Series***: 23-36
Deutsch, Nathaniel. ***Guardians of the Gate: Angelic Vice Regency in Late Antiquity***. Leiden: Brill, 1999.
_______ ***The Gnostic Imagination. Gnosticism, Mandaeism and Merkabah Mysticism***. Leiden: E.J. Brill, 1995.
Dick, Michael B. (ed.), ***Born in Heaven, Made on Earth: The Making of the Cult Image in the Ancient Near East*** Winona Lake, Indiana: Eisenbrauns, 1999.
Dillon, John "*ASÔMATOS*: Nuances of Incorporeality in Philo," in ***Philon d'Alexandrie et le langage de la philosophie. Actes du colloque international organize par le Centre d'etudes sur la philosophie hellenistiqu*** Brepols, 1998 : 99-110.
DuQuesne, Terence. ***Black and Gold God: colour symbolism of the god Anubis with observations on the phenomenology of colour in Egyptian and comparative religion*** London: Da'th Scholarly Services, Darengo Publications, 1996.

Eliade, Mircea ***Patterns in Comparative Religion***, trns. Rosemary Sheed. 1958; Lincoln and London: University of Nebraska Press, 1996.
_______ "Spirit, Light, and Seed," ***HR*** 11 (1971): 1-30
Elior, Rachel "The Concept of God in Hekhalot Literature," in ***Binah: Studies in Jewish Thought***, ed. Joseph Dan. New York: Praeger, 1989: 97-120
van Ess, J.***The Youthful God: Anthropomorphism in Early Islam***: ***Ninth Annual University Lecture in Religion***, Arizona State University March 3, 1988,
_______ "'Abd al-Malik and the Dome of the Rock. An Analysis of Some Texts," in Julian Raby and Jeremy Johns (edd.). ***Bayt al-Maqdis, 'Abd al-Malik's Jerusalem***. Oxford: Oxford University Press, 1992.

Farrahkan, L. ***Study Guide 19: The Knowledge of God***. United States, 1997.
_______"Who Is God" Saviors Day Lecture at Christ Universal Temple, Chicago, Illinois. February 24, 1991.
_______"A Savior Is Born For the Black Man And Woman of America," Saviors Day Lecture. Gary, Indiana. February 27, 1983.
Finnestad, Ragnhild Bjerre. ***Image of the World and Symbol of the Creator: On the Cosmological and Iconological Values of the Temple of Edfu*** Wiesbaden: Harrassowitz, 1985.

Fishbane, Michael. "The 'Measures' of God's Glory in the Ancient Midrash," in Ithamar Gruenwald, Shaul Shaked and Gedaliahu G. Stroumsa (edd.), ***Messiah and Christos: Studies in the Jewish Origin of Christianity*** Tübingen: Mohr, 1992: 53-74;

_______"The Measure and Glory of God in Ancient Midrash," in idem, ***The Exegetical Imagination: On Jewish Thought and Theology*** Cambridge, Mass.: Harvard University Press, 1998: 56-72

_______"Some Forms of Divine Appearance in Ancient Jewish Thought," in ***From Ancient Israel to Modern Judaism: Intellect in Quest of Understanding***, eds. Joshua Bell et al. Atlanta: Scholars Press, 1989: 261-270

Fletcher-Louis, Crispin H.T. "God's Image, His Cosmic Temple, and the High Priest: Towards an Historical and Theological Account of the Incarnation." In T. Desmond Alexander & Simon Gathercole (edd.), ***Heaven on Earth: The Temple in Biblical Theology***. Carlise: Paternoster, 2004. 81-99.

_______***All The Glory of Adam: Liturgical Anthropology in the Dead Sea Scrolls*** Leiden: Brill, 2002.

_______ "The image of God and the biblical roots of Christian sacramentality," in Geoffrey Rowell and Christine Hall (edd.), ***the Gestures of God: explorations in sacramentality*** London and New York: Continuum, 2004: 73-89.

_______ "The Worship of Divine Humanity as God's Image and the Worship of Jesus," in Carey C. Newman, James R. Davila and Gladys S. Lewis (edd.), ***Jewish Roots of Christological Monotheism. Papers from the St. Andrews Conference on the Historical Origins of the Worship of Jesus*** Leiden: Brill, 1999: 113-128

Foerster Werner. ***Gnosis: A Selection of Texts*** Oxford: Clarendon Press, 1974.

Fossum, Jarl. ***The Name of God and the Angel of the Lord: Samaritan and Jewish Concepts of Intermediation and the Origins of Gnosticism***. Tübingen: J.C.B. Mohr (Paul Siebeck), 1985.

_______ "Jewish-Christian Christology and Jewish Mysticism," ***VC*** 37 (1983): 26-287.

_______ "The Adorable Adam of the Mystics and the Rebuttals of the Rabbis," in ***Geschichte, Tradition, Reflexion: Festschrift für Martin Hengel zum 70. Geburtstag*** Tubingen: J C B Mohr, 1996: 529-539

_______ "The Image of the Invisible God: Colossians 1.15-18a in the Light of Jewish Mysticism and Gnosticism," in idem, ***The Image of the Invisible God. Essays on the Influence of Jewish***

Mysticism on Early Christology GöttingenVandenhoeck & Ruprecht, 1995: 13-39
Fox, Robin Lane. "Seeing the Gods" in idem, ***Pagans and Christians*** New York: Alfred A. Knopf, Inc., 1987
Frank, Richard M. "The Neoplatonism of Ǧahm Ibn Ṣafwān." ***Le Muséon*** 78 (1965): 395-424

Gaba, Octavius A. "Symbols of Revelation: The Darkness of the Hebrew Yahweh and the Light of the Greek Logos," in ***The Recovery of the Black Presence: An Interdisciplinary Exploration. Essays in Honor of Dr. Charles B. Copher***, eds. Randal C. Bailey and Jacquelyn Grant. Nashville: Abingdon Press, 1995: 143-158.
Gieschen, Charles A. ***Angelomorphic Christology: Antecedents and Early Evidence*** Leiden ; Boston : Brill, 1998.
Gonda, J. "Vedic Gods and the Sacrifice," ***Numen*** 30 (1983): 1-34
Green, Anthony. ***Gods, Demons and Symbols of Ancient Mesopotamia: An Illustrated Dictionary*** London: British Museum Press, 1992.
Green, Arthur ***A Guide to the Zohar*** Stanford: Stanford University Press, 2004.
_______ "The Children in Egypt and the Theophany at the Sea," ***Judaism*** 24 (1975): 446-456.
Griffin, Carl W. and David L. Paulsen. "Augustine and the Corporeality of God." ***HTR*** 95 (2002): 97-118.

Haddad, Robert M "Iconoclasts and *Mu'tazila*: The Politics of Anthropomorphism." ***The Greek Orthodox Theological Review*** 27 (Summer – Fall 1982): 287-305
Hall, M.P. ***Melchizedek and the Mystery of Fire.*** Philosophical Research Society, Los Angeles. 1996.
_______***The Hermetic Marriage***. Philosophical Research Society, Los Angeles. 1996.
_______***The Secret Teachings of All Ages***. Philosophical Research Society, Los Angeles. 1988.
_______***Old Testament Wisdom***. The Philosophical Society, Los Angeles. 1987.
_______***Man: Grand Symbol of The Mysteries.*** Philosophical Research Society, Los Angeles. 1972.
Hamori, Esther J. " 'When Gods Were Men': Biblical Theophany and Anthropomorphic Realism," Ph.D. dissertation. New York University, 2004.

Heiser, Michael S. "The Divine Council in Late Canonical and Non-Canonical Second Temple Jewish Literature," Ph.D. diss., unpublished, University of Wisconsin-Madison, 2004
Hendel, Ronald S. "Aniconism and Anthropomorphism in Ancient Israel," in ***The Image and the Book: Iconic Cults, Aniconism, and the Rise of Book Religion in Israel and the Ancient Near East***, ed. Karel van der Toorn. CBET 21; Leuven: Peeters, 1997: 205-228
Higgins, G. ***Anacalypsis***. Brooklyn. A&B Book Publishers, 1836, 1992.
Hiltebeitel, Alf. "The Indus Valley 'Proto-Śiva', Reexamined through Reflections on the Goddess, the Buffalo, and the Symbolism of *vāhanas*," ***Anthropos*** 73 (1978): 767-797
Hurowitz, Victor. "From Storm God to Abstract Being," ***Bible Review*** 14:5 (October 1998): 40-47
Humbach, Helmut. "Yama/Yima/Jamšēd, King of Paradise of the Iranians," ***Jerusalem Studies of Arabic and Islam*** 26 (2002): 68-77

Idel, Moshe. ***Absorbing Perfections: Kabbalah and Interpretation*** New Haven: Yale University Press, 2001.
_______ "Torah: Between Presence and Representation of the Divine in Jewish Mysticism," in Jan Assmann and Albert I. Baumgarten (edd.), ***Representation in Religion: Studies in Honor of Moshe Barasch*** Leiden: Brill, 2001: 202-206

Jacobsen, T. "The Graven Image," in P.D. Miller Jr., P.D. Hanson and S.D. McBride (edd.), ***Ancient Israelite Religion: Essays in Honor of Frank Moore Cross***. Philadelphia: Fortress Press, 1987: 15-32
Jaeger, Werner. ***The Theology of the Early Greek Philosophers. The Gifford Lectures, 1936*** Oxford: The Clarendon Press, 1947.
Janowitz, Naomi "God's Body: Theological and Ritual Roles of *Shi'ur Qomah*," in ***People of the Body: Jews and Judaism from an Embodied Perspective***, ed. Howard Eilberg-Schwartz. Albany: State University of New York Press, 1992: 183-201
Jonas, Hans ***The Gnostic Religion, the Message of the Alien God & the Beginnings of Christianity***.Boston: Beacon Press, 2001.

Kaminsky, Joel S. "Paradise Regained: Rabbinic Reflections on Israel at Sinai," in Alice Bellis and Joel Kaminsky (edd.), ***Jews, Christians, and the Theology of the Hebrew Scriptures*** Atlanta: Society of Biblical Literature, 2000: 15-43

Kasher, Rimmon. "Anthropomorphism, Holiness and Cult: A New Look at Ezekiel 40-48." ***ZAW*** 110 (1998): 192-208.

Kessler, Dieter "Bull Gods," in Redford Donald B. (ed.), ***The Ancient Gods Speak: A Guide to Egyptian Religion***. Oxford: Oxford University Press, 2002.

King, Karen L. ***What is Gnosticism?*** Cambridge, Mass. And London: The Belknap Press of Harvard University Press, 2003.

Kinsley, David R. ***The Sword and the Flute: Kali and Krishna, Dark Visions of the Terrible and the Sublime in Hindu Mythology***. Berkeley: University of California Press, 1975.

Kister, M.J. "Labbayka, Allahumma, Labbayka…" ***JSAI*** II (1980) pp. 33-49.

Korteweg, Th. "The Reality of the Invisible: Some Remarks on St. John XIV 8 and Greek Philosophic Tradition," in M.J. Vermaseren (ed.), ***Studies in Hellenistic Religions*** Leiden: E.J. Brill, 1979: 50-102.

Kugel, James L. ***The God of Old: Inside the Lost World of the Bible***. New York: The Free Press, 2003

Kuiper, F.B.J. ***Ancient Indian Cosmogony***, ed. John Irwin; New Delhi: Vikas Publishing House, 1983.

Lachower, Fischel and Isaiah Tishby, ***The Wisdom of the Zohar, An Anthology of Texts***, trns. from the Hebrew by David Goldstein, 3 vols. Portland, Oregon: Oxford, 2002.

Laine, James W. ***Visions of God: Narrative of Theophany in the Mahābhārata***. Vienna, 1989.

Lancellotti, Maria Grazia. ***The Naassenes: A Gnostic Identity Among Judaism, Christianity, Classical and Ancient Near Eastern Traditions*** Münster: Ugarit-Verlag, 2000.

Lang, Bernhard ***The Hebrew God: Portrait of an Ancient Deity*** New Haven; London: Yale University Press, 2002.

Lev Martin and Carol Ring, "Journey of the Night Sun," ***Parabola*** 8 (1983): 14-18

Little, John T. "*Al-Insān Al-Kāmil*: The Perfect Man According to Ibn al-'Arabī," ***Muslim World*** 77 (1987): 43-54.

Lubicz, R.A.S. ***The Temple In Man***. Inner Traditions International, Rochester. 1977.

Manniche, Lise. "The Body Colours of Gods and Man in Inland Jewellery and Related Objects from the Tomb of Tutankhamun," ***AcOr*** 43 (1982): 5-12

Massey, G. ***Ancient Egypt: The Light of The World***. E.C.A. Association, New York. 1907, 1990.

_______***Book of Beginnings***. William & Norgate, London. 1881.
Mauser, Ulrich. "God in Human Form." ***Ex Auditu*** 16 (2000): 81-100.
Meeks, Dimitri and Christine Favard-Meeks, ***Daily Life of the Egyptian Gods***, translated by G.M. Goshgarian. Ithaca and London: Cornell University Press, 1996.
Meltzer, Edmund S. " 'Who Knows the Color of God?'" ***Journal of Ancient Civilizations*** 11 (1996): 123-129
Miller, Patrick D. "Cosmology and World Order in the Old Testament: The Divine Council as Cosmic Political Symbol," in idem, ***Israelite Religion and Biblical Theology: Collected Essays*** JSOTSupp 267; Sheffield: JSOT Press, 2000: 422-444.
Moore, Stephen D. "Gigantic God: Yahweh's Body." ***JSOT*** 70 (1996): 87-115.
Morray-Jones, C.R.A. "The Temple Within: The Embodied Divine Image and its Worship in the Dead Sea Scrolls and Other Early Jewish and Christian Sources," ***SBL 1998 Seminar Papers***, 400-427.
_______ "Transformational Mysticism in the Apocalyptic-Merkabah Tradition," ***JJS*** 43 (1992): 9f
_______"The Body of Glory: The *Shi'ur Qomah* in Judaism, Gnosticism and the Epistle to the Ephesians," forthcoming in Christopher Rowland and C.R.A. Morray-Jones, ***The Mystery of God: Jewish Mystical Traditions in the New Testament*** CRINT 3;Assen and Minneapolis: Van Gorcum/Fortress: 147ff
_______***A Transparent Illusion: The Dangerous Vision of Water in Hekhalot Mysticism. A Source-Critical and Tradition-Historical Inquiry*** (Leiden: Brill, 2002)
Muhammad, Elijah. ***The True History of Master Fard Muhammad***, edited by Minister Nasir Makr Hakim. M.E.M.P.S. Publications, 1996.
_______***The Theology Of Time*** Lecture Series printed transcript by Abass Rassoul. U.B.U.S., Hampton. 1992.
_______***Our Savior Has Arrived***. Muhammad's Temple of Islam No. 2, Chicago. 1974.
_______***Message to the Black Man***. Muhammad's Temple of Islam No. 2, Chicago. 1965.
Mullen, E.T. ***The Assembly of The Gods***, Scholar Press, Chico, California. 1980.

Nagar, Shanti Lal. ***The Image of Brahmā in India and Abroad***, Vol. 1. Delhi: Parimal Publications, 1992.
Narby, J. ***The Cosmic Serpent: DNA and the Origins of Knowledge***. Tarcher/Putnam, New York. 1998,

Neusner, J. ***The Incarnation of God***. Fortress Press, Philadelphia. 1988.

Nobles, W. ***African Psychology***. Black Family Institutions, Oakland. 1986.

Oldenburg, Ulf "Above the Stars of El: El in Ancient South Arabic Religion," ***ZAW*** 82 (1970): 188-208

Ornan, Tallay. "The Bull and its Two Masters: Moon and Storm Deities in Relation to the Bull in Ancient Near Eastern Art," ***Israel Exploration Journal*** 51 (2001) 1-26

Pagels, Elaine H. "Exegesis of Genesis 1 in the Gospels of Thomas and John," ***JBL*** 118 (1999): 477-496

Parpola, Asko. "New correspondences between Harappan and Near Eastern glyptic art," ***South Asian Archaeology*** 1981

________***The Sky-Garment: A Study of the Harappan religion and its relation to the Mesopotamian and later Indian religion*** SO 57; Helsinki, 1985.

Paulsen, David L. "Early Christian Belief in a Corporeal Deity: Origen and Augustine as Reluctant Witnesses," ***HTR*** 83 (1990): 105-116

Pritchard, James B. "The Gods and their Symbols," in idem, ***The Ancient Near East in Pictures, Relating to the Old Testament*** (Princeton: Princeton university Press, 1954), 160-85

Quispel, Gilles. "Ezekiel 1:26 in Jewish Mysticism," ***VC*** 34 (1980): 1-13.

Rahbar, D. "Relation of Muslim Theology To The Qur'an," ***The Muslim World***, 51 (1961): 44-49.

Renehan, R. "On the Greek Origins of the Concepts Incorporeality and Immateriality." ***Greek, Roman, and Byzantine Studies*** 21 (1980): 105-138.

Ringgren, Helmer "Light and Darkness in Ancient Egyptian Religion," in ***Liber amicorum. Studies in Honour of Professor Dr. C.J. Bleeker. Published on the Occasion of his Retirement from the Chair of the History of Religions and the phenomenology of Religion at the University of Amsterdam*** Leiden: E.J. Brill, 1969: 140-150.

Rosenberg, Roy A. ***The Anatomy of God*** New York: KTAV Publishing House, Inc., 1973.

Rubin, Uri "Al-Sammad and the high God: An Interpretation of *sura* CXII," ***Islam*** LXI (1984): 187-217

Savran, George W. ***Encountering the Divine: Theophany in Biblical Narrative*** JSOTSup 420; London and New York: T&T Clark International, 2005.
Scholem, Gershom ***On the Mystical Shape of the Godhead*** (New York: Schocken Books, 1991)
_______ "Adam Kadmon," ***Encyclopedia Judaica*** 2:248f.
Schroeder, G. L. ***The Science of God***. Breadway, New York. 1997
Schüle, Andreas. "Made in the >Image of God<: The Concepts of Divine Images in Gen 1-3," ***ZAW*** 117 (2005): 1-20
Schwartz, Howard ***Tree of Souls: The Mythology of Judaism*** Oxford: Oxford University Press, 2004.
Seal, Morris S. ***Muslim Theology***. London: Luzac and Company Limited, 1964.
Segal, Alan F. "Dualism in Judaism, Christianity, and Gnosticism: A Definitive Issue," in his ***The Other Judaisms of Late Antiquity*** (Atlanta: Scholars Press, 1987): 1-40
Sertima, Ivan Van. "Among the Quetzalcoatls," in idem, ***They Came Before Columbus: The African Presence in Ancient America*** New York: Random House, 1976: 71-89
Shaked, Saul. "First Man, First King: Notes on Semitic-Iranian Syncretism and Iranian Mythological Transformation," in S. Shaked, D. Shulman and G.G. Stroumsa, ***Gilgul: Essays on Transformation, Revolution and Permanence in the History of Religions, Dedicated to R.J. Zwi Werblowsky*** Leiden: E.J. Brill, 1987: 238-256
Smelik, Willem F. "On the Mystical Transformation of the Righteous into Light in Judaism," ***JSJ*** 26 (1995): 122-144
Smith, Mark S. ***The Early History of God. Yahweh and the Other Deities in Ancient Israel***, 2nd Edition. Grand Rapids, Mi.: William B. Eerdmans Pub. Co., 2002.
_______***The Origin of Biblical Monotheism*** Oxford: Oxford University Press, 2001.
Steenburg, D. "The Worship of Adam and Christ as the Image of God," ***JSNT*** 39 (1990): 95-109.
Stoyanov, Yuri. ***The Other God: Dualist Religions from Antiquity to the Cathar Heresy*** New Haven: Yale University Press, 2000.
Stroumsa, G. "The Incorporeality of God," ***Religion***, ***13 (***1983): 345-358.
_______ "Form(s) of God: Some Notes on Metatron and Christ" ***Harvard Theological Review***, 76:3, 1983. Pp. 269-88.

Taylor, Jules "The Black Image in Egyptian Art," ***Journal of African Civilization*** 1 (April, 1979) 29-38.
van der Toorn, Karel. "God (1) אלהים," in Karel van der Toorn, Bob Becking, Pieter W. van der Horst (edd.), ***Dictionary of Deities and Demons in the Bible*** 2nd ed.; Leiden; Boston: Brill; Grand Rapids, Mich.: Eerdmans, 1999: 361-365

Vernant, Jean-Pierre "Dim Body, Dazzling Body," in Michel Feher, Ramona Naddaff and Nadia Tazi (edd.), ***Fragments for a History of the Human Body: Part One*** New York: Zone, 1989: 19-47.
Versnel, H.S. "What Did Ancient Man See when He saw a God? Some Reflections on Greco-Roman Epiphany," in Dirk van der Plas (ed.), ***Effigies Dei: Essays on the History of Religions*** Leiden: E.J. Brill, 1987: 43-55
Vos, René L. "Varius Coloribus Apis: Some Remarks of the Colours of Apis and Other Sacred Animals," in Willy Clarysse, Antoon Schoors and Harco Willems (edd.), ***Egyptian Religion: The Last Thousand Years, Part 1. Studies Dedicated to the Memory of Jan Quaegebeur*** Leuven: Uitgeverij Peeters en Departement Oosterse Studies, 1998.

Wainwright, A. "Some Aspects of Amūn," ***Journal of Egyptian Archaeology*** 20 (1934): 139-53
Walls, Neal H. (ed.) ***Cult Image and Divine Representation in the Ancient Near East*** American Schools of Oriental Research Books Series 10; Boston: American Schools of Oriental Research, 2005.
Watt, Montgomery "Some Muslim Discussions of Anthropomorphism" and "Created in His Image: A Study in Islamic Theology," in his ***Early Islam*** Edinburgh: Edinburgh University Press, 1990: 86-93, 94-100
Welch, A.T. "Allah and Other Supernatural Beings: The Emergence Of The Qur'anic Doctrine Of TAWHID," ***Journal of the American Academy of Religion. 47:4S***, (December 1979): 733-758.
Wensinck, A.J. ***The Muslim Creed***. New Delhi: Oriental Reprint, 1932, 1979.
_______ "The Ideas of Western Semites Concerning the Navel of the Earth." ***Verhandelingen der Koninklijke Akademie van Wetenshapen te Amsterdam***. Afdeeling Letterkunde, n.s. 17.1. (1916).
_______"The Ocean in the Literature of Western Semites." ***Verhandelingen der Koninklijke Akademie van Wetenshapen te Amsterdam***. Afdeeling Letterkunde, n.s. 19.2. (1918).

_______"Tree and Bird as Cosmological Symbols in Western Asia." ***Verhandelingen der Koninklijke Akademie van Wetenshapen te Amsterdam***. Afdeeling Letterkunde, n.s. 22 (1921).
Williams, Michael Allen. ***Rethinking "Gnosticism": An Argument for Dismantling a Dubious Category*** Princeton, New Jersey: Princeton University Press, 1996.
Williams, Wesley. "Aspects of the Creed of Ahmad Ibn Hanbal: A Study of Anthropomorphism is Early Islamic Discourse." ***IJMES*** 34 (2002): 441-463.
Winnet, F."Allah Before Islam," ***MW*** 28 (1938):239-259.
Wohlstein, Herman. ***The Sky-God An-Anu*** Jericho, New York: Paul A. Stroock, 1976.
Wolfson, Elliot R. ***Through a Speculum that Shines. Vision and Imagination in Medieval Jewish Mysticism***. Princeton, New Jersey: Princeton University Press, 1994.
_______ "Judaism and Incarnation: The Imaginal Body of God," in Tikva Frymer-Kensky et al (edd.), ***Christianity in Jewish Terms***. Boulder, CO.: Westview, 2000: 239-254.
_______ "Iconic Visualization and the Imaginal Body of God: The Role of Intention in the Rabbinic Conception of Prayer," ***Modern Theology*** 12 (1996): 137-62

Young, Frances M. "The God of the Greeks and the Nature of Religious Language," in William R. Schoedel and Robert L. Wilekn (eds.), ***Early Christian literature and the classical intellectual tradition. In Honorem Robert M. Grant*** Theologie historique 53; Paris: Editions Beauchesne, 1979: 45-74.

Zandee, J. "The Birth-Giving Creator-God in Ancient Egypt," in Alan B. Lloyd (ed.), ***Studies in Pharaonic Religion and Society, in Honour of J. Gwyn Griffiths*** London: The Egypt Exploration Society, 1992: 168-185

Abbreviations

ABD	*Anchor Bible Dictionary*
ANE	*Ancient Near East(ern)*
ANRW	*Aufstieg und Niedergang Der Römischen Welt*
ARW	*Archiv für Religionswissenschaft*
BA	*Biblical Archaeologist*
BR	*Biblical Review*
BSOAS	*Bulletin for the School of Oriental and African Studies*
CBQ	*Catholic Biblical Quarterly*
DDD	*Dictionary of Deities and Demons in the Bible*
EI[1]	*Encyclopedia of Islam. First Edition*
EI[2]	*Encyclopedia of Islam. New Edition*
EQ	*Encyclopedia of the Qur'ān*
ER	*Encyclopedia of Religion*
ERE	*Encyclopedia of Religion and ethics*
HB	*Hebrew Bible*
HTR	*Harvard Theological Review*
HUCA	*Hebrew Union College Annual*
IDB	*Interpreter's Dictionary of the Bible*
IDBSup	*Interpreter's Dictionary of the Bible Supplement*
IJMES	*International Journal of Middle East Studies*
IOS	*Israel Oriental Studies*
IS	*Islamic Studies*
ISBE	*International Standard Bible Encyclopedia*
JANES	*Journal of the Ancient Near Eastern Society*
JAOS	*Journal of the American Oriental Society*
JBL	*Journal of Biblical Literature*
JNES	*Journal of Near Eastern Studies*
JQR	*Jewish Quarterly Review*
JQS	*Journal of Qur'ānic Studies*
JRAS	*Journal of the Royal Asiatic Society*
JSAI	*Jerusalem Studies in Arabic and Islam*
JSJ	*Journal for the Study of Judaism*
JSNT	*Journal for the Study of the New Testament*
JSOT	*Journal for the Study of the Old Testament*
JSS	*Journal of Semitic Studies*
JTS	*Journal of Theological Studies*
MTSR	*Method and Theory in the Study of Religion*

MW	*The Muslim World*
NTS	*New Testament Studies*
Rel. Stud.	*Religious Studies*
SJOT	*Scandinavian Journal of the Old Testament*
TDNT	*Theological Dictionary of the New Testament*
TDOT	*Theological Dictionary of the Old Testament*
VC	*Vigiliae Christianae*
VT	*Vetus Testamentum*
VTSup	*Vetus Testamentum Supplement*
ZA	*Zeitschrift für Assyriologie und Verwandte Gebiete*
ZAW	*Zeitschrift für alttestamentliche Wissenschaft*

SELECTED GLOSSARY

Ashad Al-Hadith – Early Muslims who believed in and transmitted the Sayings of Prophet Muhammad of Arabia (P.B.U.H.).

Anathema – one that is cursed by religious authority.

Anthropomorphic – God possessing a human.

Anthropomorphism – God's possessing of a human or, man's belief that God possesses a human form.

Anthropomorphist – one who believes that God possesses a human form.

Anthropopathic – Ascribing human feelings to God.

Ancient Near East(ern) (ANE) - The terms 'ancient Near East' encompass the early civilizations predating classical antiquity in the region roughly corresponding to that described by the modern term Middle East (Egypt, Iraq, Turkey), during the time roughly spanning the Bronze Age from the rise of Sumer and Gerzeh in the 4th millennium BC to the expansion of the Persian Empire in the 6th century BC.

Bovine - of or relating to any of 24 species of hoofed and horned animals, such as cattle (bull, buffalo, etc.)

Canon – fixed collection of sacred texts.

Corporeal – Possessing a material form or substance.

Cosmogony – The origin or creation of the universe or world (*cosmos*).

Deity – a 'god'.

Exegesis – Contextual interpretation of scripture.

Hadith – The recorded Sayings and Traditions of Prophet Muhammad of Arabia (P.B.U.H.).

Hellenistic – Referring to the culture of Greece after Alexander the Great, particularly Greek Philosophy.

Heterodox – Beliefs of a sect which go against the authorized doctrines of faith (orthodox).

Heresy – 'wrong belief,' the opposite of 'orthodoxy'.

Incarnation – The embodiment of God in an earthly form.

Incorporeal – Immaterial, having no form of substance.

Indic – of or relating to the ancient texts and civilizations of India.

Literalism, Literalist – belief that the anthropomorphic descriptions of God in the scriptures (Bible and Qur'an) must be interpreted literally. The literalist is one who interprets these descriptions literally.

Liturgy – religious ceremonies or rituals carried out within a temple or church.

Luminous – to shine with brilliant light.

Metaphor, Metaphorical – when a description appropriate to one subject is used figuratively to describe an unrelated subject (i.e. using descriptions appropriate to animals to figuratively described human: "he is a lion among men').

Monotheism – belief in only one God.

Motif – A dominant idea or central theme.

Myth – A narrative about God or the gods. If history is a story about mortal humans, myth is a story about God/the gods. Here the term implies neither truth nor falsehood.

Neoplatonic – of or relating to those who followed the thinking of Plato after his death.

Orthodox – The authorized doctrines of faith.

Polemic – An aggressive attack or refutation of the religious beliefs of others.

Primeval – Of or relating to the earliest stage.

Primordial – First developed or created; earliest form.

Sahih – a classification of hadith meaning 'authenic'.

Semitic – of or relating to a language family and their human speakers of largely Middle Eastern origin, now called the *Semitic languages*. This family includes the ancient and modern forms of Amharic, Arabic, Aramaic, Akkadian, Ge'ez, Hebrew, Maltese, Tigrinya, among others. Semites include ancient Hebrews, Arabs, Akkadians, Canaanites, etc., among others. Semitic Religion includes Judaism, Christianity and Islam.

Sunnah – the way of the Prophet Muhammad; his sayings, doings, and tacit approvals.

Theogony – the birth of God/a god

Theophany The self-manifestation of God.

Theriomorphic – Ascribing an animal form to God.

Transcendence (Divine) - In religion, transcendence is often thought of as a condition or state of divine being that surpasses and is free from the limitiations of physical existence. More radical theories of divine transcendence, such as those of (some) Greek philosophic and Gnostic paradigms, completely disassociated God from all physicality/materiality. For these, divine transcendence necessarily means that God is immaterial and formless. In contrast, ***Transcendent Anthropomorphism***, which charaterizes the gods/God of the ancient Near Eastern and Semitic traditions, affirmed that God possesses a human form, but one that transcended the limitations of physicality because it was made of a holy, spiritual matter (versus gross, fleshy matter). Biblical notions of transcendent anthropomorphism also involves God's moral and ethical transcendence.

Versions – the 'versions' or ancient translations of the Hebrew Bible (Old Testament). These include the Greek translation of the Hebrew Bible called the Septuagint (LXX), the Aramaic translations called Targums (Targum Onqelos, Targum Ps.-Jonathan, Targum Neofiti), the Samaritan translation (Sam), and the Latin translation called the Vulgate.

Now Available

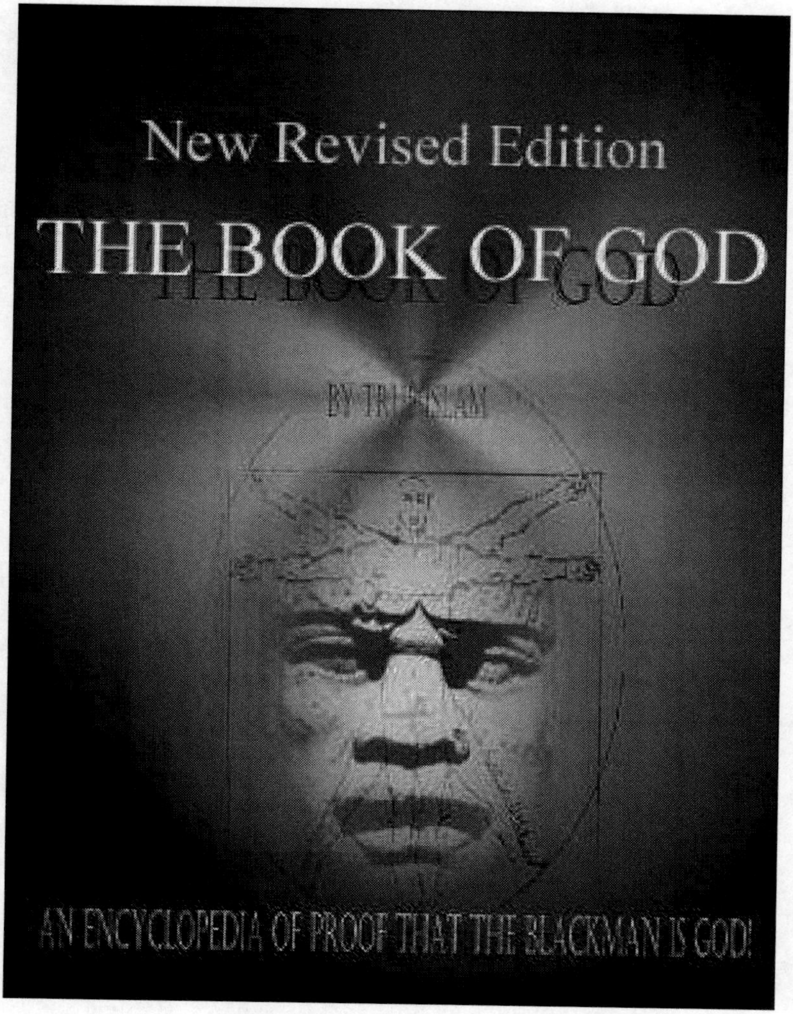

True Islam's 1997 cult classic is back in print in a new, revised edition. ***The Book of God*** has been called 'the bible of the Black God,' as it presents a wide range of scientific, historical, and scriptural evidence demonstrating that the Original Black Man is the God of the world's religious traditions, from the religious traditions of the Ancient Near and Far East such as Kemet (Egypt) and India to the Biblical religions and Islam. ***The Book of God*** answers such questions as:

- How is the Black Man God and what does this mean?
- What is God's relationship to spirit and matter?
- What does Albert Einstein's mathematical revelation "$E=mc^2$" have to do with the Reality of God?
- If the Original Black Man is God, Who is the Original Black Woman?
- Is there evidence of the reality of the Twenty Four Scientists?
- Who is Master Fard Muhammad? Was he actually an ex-con named Wallie Ford who served time in San Quentin on a drug charge?

And more. ***The Book of God*** also demonstrates that:

- The God of the ancient religious traditions around the world was a self-created Black God.
- The Six Days of Creation in the book of Genesis chronicles the Black God's Six Trillion year evolution.
- The ancient sacred texts of the Original Man and Woman from around the world agree with the Hon. Elijah Muhammad's Teaching on God.
- The fields of Genetics and Hebrew Sacred Tradition converge to reveal that the Essence of the Creator inhabits the very genetic makeup of the Original Man and Woman.
- The Secret of the ancient Mysteries, the Masonic Lodge and Shrine, and the Church of Rome is the Reality of the Black God.
- Astrophysics and ancient tradition converge to provide strong support to the hon. Elijah Muhammad's teaching on the Deportation of the Moon

And much more. To order your copy go to www.theblackgod.com

BlackGod.Com